God of Holy Love

Essays of Peter Taylor Forsyth

God of Holy Love

Essays of Peter Taylor Forsyth

Edited and Introduced by
Paul K. Moser and Benjamin Nasmith

☙PICKWICK *Publications* · Eugene, Oregon

GOD OF HOLY LOVE
Essays of Peter Taylor Forsyth

Copyright © 2019 Paul K. Moser and Benjamin Nasmith. All rights reserved. Except for brief quotations in critical publications or reviews, no part of this book may be reproduced in any manner without prior written permission from the publisher. Write: Permissions, Wipf and Stock Publishers, 199 W. 8th Ave., Suite 3, Eugene, OR 97401.

Pickwick Publications
An Imprint of Wipf and Stock Publishers
199 W. 8th Ave., Suite 3
Eugene, OR 97401

www.wipfandstock.com

PAPERBACK ISBN: 978-1-5326-5632-3
HARDCOVER ISBN: 978-1-5326-5633-0
EBOOK ISBN: 978-1-5326-5634-7

Cataloging-in-Publication data:

Names: Forsyth, Peter Taylor, 1848–1921. | Moser, Paul K., 1957–, editor | Nasmith, Benjamin, editor
Title: God of holy love : essays of Peter Taylor Forsyth / edited by Paul K. Moser and Benjamin Nasmith.
Description: Eugene, OR : Pickwick Publications, 2019 | Includes bibliographical references and index.
Identifiers: ISBN 978-1-5326-5632-3 (paperback) | ISBN 978-1-5326-5633-0 (hardcover) | ISBN 978-1-5326-5634-7 (ebook)
Subjects: LCSH: Forsyth, Peter Taylor, 1848–1921. | Theology. | Atonement. | Jesus Christ—Person and offices. | Revelation—Christianity—History of doctrines. | Conversion—Religious aspects—Christianity
Classification: LCC BX7260 F583 2019 (print) | LCC BX7260 (ebook)

Manufactured in the U.S.A.

Contents

Preface vi

Introduction: P.T. Forsyth in Focus 1

Part 1: Atonement and Revelation

1   The Atonement in Modern Religious Thought 28

2   Immanence and Incarnation 41

3   The Inner Life of Christ 49

4   Forgiveness through Atonement the Essential of Evangelical Christianity 60

5   Faith, Metaphysic, and Incarnation 98

Part 2: Christ and Christology

6   Revelation and the Person of Christ 120

7   The Disappointment of the Cross 151

8   Christ and the Christian Principle 161

9   Christ's Person and His Cross 189

10 The Christianity of Christ and Christ our Christianity . 209

Part 3: New Life in Christ

11	Regeneration, Creation, and Miracle I	223
12	Regeneration, Creation, and Miracle II	240
13	Veracity, Reality, and Regeneration	255
14	The Conversion of the "Good"	275
15	The Cross of Christ as the Moral Principle of Society	289

Part 4: Faith, Theology, and Religion

16	Faith and Mind	301
17	Intellectualism and Faith	318
18	The Moralization of Religion	333
19	Unity and Theology: A Liberal Evangelicalism the True Catholicism	345
20	Religion Private and Public	364
	Bibliography	376
	Name Index	380
	Subject Index	382

Preface

Peter Taylor Forsyth (1848–1921) is among the most insightful and challenging of modern theologians, unsurpassed as a preacher and expositor of the Pauline gospel of the righteous grace (or "holy love") of God in Jesus Christ. There is an important collection of his sermons in print, *Descending on Humanity and Intervening in History: Notes from the Pulpit Ministry of P. T. Forsyth*, edited by Jason Goroncy (Pickwick Publications, 2016), a small collection of sermons and addresses, *Revelation: Old and New: Sermons and Addresses* (Independent Press, 1962), and an out of print collection, *The Gospel and Authority*, edited by M.W. Anderson (Augsburg, 1971). Even so, many of Forsyth's first-rate essays had not been collected as a supplement to his many fine books.

This book collects twenty of Forsyth's theological essays, without overlap with prior collections, chosen to cover the main areas of his rich theology. These essays describe a faith governed by what God has done in Christ crucified, thus offering a clear portrait of Forsyth's theology of the cross. They are organized by theme into four parts: (1) Atonement and Revelation, (2) Christ and Christology, (3) New Life in Christ, and (4) Faith, Theology, and Religion. These essays also address the relation of faith in God to historical knowledge, the nature and role of divine forgiveness, and the place of moral experience in knowledge of God.

Whenever possible, we have completed any references by Forsyth that originally were incomplete and use square brackets to indicate editorial comments. We thank the editorial staff at Wipf and Stock for supporting this book. In particular, we thank our editor, Robin Parry, for his helpful guidance.

P.K.M., Chicago, IL
B.N., Kingston, ON

Introduction: P.T. Forsyth in Focus

Paul K. Moser and Benjamin Nasmith

Background

P.T. Forsyth was born in 1848 in Aberdeen, Scotland. Having studied classics at Aberdeen University, he was a student of Albrecht Ritschl (1822–89) for a semester at Göttingen in 1872. Ordained to the ministry in 1876, he served as a pastor in London, Manchester, and Cambridge, before taking an appointment as Principal of Hackney College, London, in 1901. Forsyth's facility in German enabled him to appropriate in German translation some important writings of Kierkegaard before their translation into English.

Forsyth's theological influence has been considerable, and it evidently includes Karl Barth, Emil Brunner, Reinhold Niebuhr, Oswald Chambers, J.K. Mozley, Daniel Jenkins, A.M. Hunter, and I. Howard Marshall. Robert McAfee Brown subtitles his 1952 book on Forsyth "Prophet for Today," thus indicating the distinctive character of his theological contribution. It typically has the passion of preaching God's holy grace, on the following ground: "The moral universe is not a windless vacuum. . . . It is too full of holy passion to leave room for absolutely impartial (and impossible) judgments, whether in man or God."[1] The "holy passion" of God is reflected in much of Forsyth's theological writing, and it contributes a kerygmatic component that distinguishes his writing from typical academic writing on theology.

Forsyth's early theological perspective, before 1893, was characterized by a kind of theological liberalism. He explains:

---

1. Forsyth, *The Principle of Authority*, 408.

> Liberalism had its work to do. I felt its force. I took part in it. And it has won—I might say all along the line. . . . But the result of the general victory of religious liberalism has been disappointing on the whole. . . . The movement was too sentimental. It interpreted the heavenly Fatherhood by the earthly, instead of the earthly by the heavenly. . . . Its ethic was more altruistic than evangelical, more of effort than of faith. . . . Its general tendency was to canonize freedom instead of an authority that makes free. . . It is a spent movement.[2]

By 1893 Forsyth had departed from such liberalism, as shown in his seminal essay "Revelation and the Person of Christ" (Chapter 6, this volume; he gives credit to Wilhelm Herrmann of Marburg for the general theological and religious perspective of that essay). He came to see that the biblical good news, or gospel, of God's grace is at odds with the human-centered liberalism of his early ministry.

Gospel of Grace

The mature Forsyth's signature emphasis on the grace of God's holy love accounts for his disappointment with his earlier liberalism. He remarks on the place of divine grace in Christian faith and life:

> The ultimate idea of Christianity is neither faith, works, truth, nor love, but grace. Our Christian life is our due response to that. Our faith is simply its human echo; it is God's redeeming grace returning *through* man upon itself—the Holy Spirit returning to Him who gave it. According to the freedom of the grace revealed must be the freedom of the answering faith. If grace be absolutely free, so must faith be.[3]

---

2. Forsyth, "Our Need of a Positive Gospel," 462–3. Cited in Brown, *PT Forsyth: Prophet for Today*, 19.

3. Forsyth, *The Charter of the Church*, iv–v.

Introduction: P.T. Forsyth in Focus

In this perspective, the center of the Christian message is the gracious God's free intervention in human life to elicit a free response of faith from humans. The divine coercion of a particular response to God would have no place in grace as an interpersonal reality that preserves responsible agency in humans.

Forsyth elaborates on the role of divine action in grace:

> By grace is not here meant either God's general benignity, or His particular kindness to our failure or pity for our pain. I mean His undeserved and unbought pardon and redemption of us in the face of our sin, in the face of the world-sin, under such moral conditions as are prescribed by His revelation of His holy love in Jesus Christ and Him crucified. And by the Gospel of this grace I would especially urge that there is meant not a statement, nor a doctrine, nor a scheme, on man's side; nor an offer, a promise, or a book, on God's side. It is an act and a power: it is God's act of redemption before it is man's message of it. It is an eternal, perennial act of God in Christ, repeating itself within each declaration of it.[4]

The powerful act of divine grace, then, includes God's "undeserved and unbought pardon and redemption" of humans on the basis of the divine holy love found in Jesus Christ. Such grace is thus a candidate for experience by humans, beyond any talk about it.

The human experience of the divine grace of holy love includes moral severity. Forsyth remarks:

> I venture to think John Newton's [hymn] "I asked the Lord that I might grow" one of the greatest and most realistic utterances of Christian experience. And it represents the course our sunny liberalism must take as it passes from a trout stream of the morning to the river of God which is full of deep water. Our young lions suffer hunger.[5]

---

4. Forsyth, *Positive Preaching and Modern Mind*, 3.
5. Forsyth, *Positive Preaching and Modern Mind*, 106.

Forsyth suggests, in accordance with the hymn, that humans need, and get, a serious moral challenge from the God of holy love, even if they expect divine approval of their goodness.

Newton's hymn identifies the following kind of moral severity from the hand of God:

> He [God] made me feel
> The hidden evils of my heart,
> And let the angry powers of hell
> Assault my soul in every part.
> Yea, more, with His own hand He seem'd
> Intent to aggravate my woe;
> Cross'd all the fair designs I schemed,
> Blasted my gourd, and laid me low.
> Lord, why is this?: I trembling cried,
> Wilt Thou pursue Thy worm to death?
> "Tis in this way," the Lord replied,
> "I answer prayer for grace and faith.
> These inward trials I employ
> From self and pride to set thee free;
> And break thy schemes of earthly joy
> That thou may'st seek thy all in Me."

The divine severity in moral experience is an aspect of divine judgment, but it seeks the redemption rather than the condemnation of humans. Specifically, it seeks the reconciliation of humans to God in holy love.

The grace of God is not just the grace of love; it is the grace of *holy* love as perfectly *righteous* love. Forsyth follows the apostle Paul in linking divine grace to divine righteousness, in particular, to a divine "gift of righteousness" and of reconciliation in Christ (Rom 5:10–17). In this Pauline perspective, God aims that "grace might reign *through righteousness* to eternal life through Jesus Christ our Lord" (Rom 5:21, RSV, italics added). This is not righteousness earned by humans from God, but righteousness offered to humans as an unearned gift from God, to be received by "the obedience of faith" in God (Rom 1:5). Such righteousness is central to the gift of grace as reconciliation with a perfectly righteous, holy God.

Introduction: P.T. Forsyth in Focus

Forsyth describes his experience of grace in relation to ordinary love: "It also pleased God by the revelation of His holiness and grace, which the great theologians taught me to find in the Bible, to bring home to me my sin in a way that submerged all the [academic] school questions [about theology] in weight, urgency, and poignancy. I was turned from a Christian to a believer, from a lover of love to an object of grace."[6] In neglecting divine holy love, one easily can neglect the human need of divine grace by the standard of God's perfect righteousness. In that case, one also can miss the heart of the Pauline gospel of God's gracious redemption in Christ, and thus fail to become a self-conscious "object of grace." That would be to miss the point of the gospel of God in Christ.

The Pauline gospel, according to Forsyth, is a powerful fact of divine "redemptive action," and no matter of mere talk. He remarks:

> What [the earliest Christians] had was what they called the *kerygma*, with all its foolishness (1 Cor. 1:21, where we hear of the scandal of the cross, the absurdity of what was preached, not of preaching as an institution). *The gospel was an experienced fact, a free and living word long before it was a fixed and written word.* This is the manner of revelation. . . . The most precious thing in Christ for the church is not his life story but his deed of gospel. It is not his teaching, not his personal influence, but his redemption. *It is a theological gospel, but it is not authoritative as dogma, but as revelation, as redemptive action.* It is the gospel, not in an exact theology, but in a theology of glow, and power, and range. It is this gospel that has made the New Testament. What inspired the apostles was not Christ's legacy of teaching about God or grace; it was grace itself, as the large burden of his life.[7]

God in Christ does something powerful on behalf of humans for their reconciliation to God, and this redemptive action forms the center of the gospel. Forsyth speaks of the gospel as an "experi-

---

6. Forsyth, *Positive Preaching and Modern Mind*, 193.

7. Forsyth, "The Evangelical Churches and the Higher Criticism," 30, 32.

enced fact" among humans. A key issue concerns *how* it is experienced.

Forsyth elaborates on the experienced gospel of grace:

> The gift to men in Christianity is the Gospel deed of God's grace in the shape of forgiveness, redemption, regeneration. *Im Anfang war die Tat.* But I should perhaps define terms. By "grace" is not here meant either God's general benignity, or His particular kindness to our failure or pity for our pain. I mean His undeserved and unbought pardon and redemption of us in the face of our sin, in the face of the world-sin, under such moral conditions as are prescribed by His revelation of His holy love in Jesus Christ and Him crucified. And by "the Gospel of this grace" I would especially urge that there is meant not a statement, nor a doctrine, nor a scheme, on man's side; nor an offer, a promise, or a book, on God's side. It is an act and a power: it is God's act of redemption before it is man's message of it. It is an eternal, perennial act of God in Christ, repeating itself within each declaration of it.[8]

The experience of the gospel, according to Forsyth, is in the experience of what it offers: forgiveness, redemption, and regeneration from God in Christ. Such experience is not mere talk, because it makes a powerful life-changing difference in and among humans who freely and obediently receive it in faith. Forsyth develops his position in connection with the role of Christ in conscience.

Christ, Conscience, and Authority

Forsyth portrays Christ as a living Savior, and no mere historical figure:

> We need a living Redeemer to plead for us in God, not against God, but against our accusing conscience, to be our Advocate with the Father against our self-condemnation. We need Him as the human conscience

---

8. Forsyth, *Positive Preaching and Modern Mind*, 3.

Introduction: P.T. Forsyth in Focus

> of God to come to our rescue against our conscience—and the more so as our conscience is quickened, socialised, exalted, and aggravated by solidarity with all the damnation of the world. Conscience makes us men and heroes. Yes, but it is conscience, too, that mocks our manhood with the memory of our sin, our neighbour's, and our kind's. If we were left alone with our conscience it would do more, on the whole, to overwhelm us than to redeem us or support us. We need some surety more sure and merciful and universal than our conscience. We need something more worthy than our natural moral manhood. We need to be made "more sure that we are Christ's than that we are men," more the servants of Christ's conscience than the heroes of our own, more penitents than stalwarts, more saints than ironsides. That is our need of a Redeemer, of a living human Redeemer, a moral owner and King.[9]

Christ, then, has authority as the human conscience of God, and thus has authority over any human conscience apart from Christ. Human conscience alone does not give us God's authority, because it does not include Christ, as the conscience of God, on its own.

Forsyth elaborates on the role of divine authority in human conscience:

> [Ultimate authority] is the authority of an absolute, holy Person. And in religion nothing is authoritative except in so far as it shares the authority of God Himself, and holds of the holy. The degree of its authority is that of its true sanctity. But the holy [God] is the absolute conscience. So this divine authority is exerted upon a conscience. But on a conscience which, as soon as it realises the holy, realises itself in the same act as sinful and lost. "Depart from me, for I am a sinful man." It is therefore, farther, the authority of a Saviour (for nothing damns like what saves). It is the authority of a Saviour Who effects a new creature, with

---

9. Forsyth, *God the Holy Father*, 93.

> the absolute right over it that creation always must give. It is the new creative action of the perfectly holy conscience of God on the helplessly guilty conscience of man. It is life from the dead.[10]

Forsyth thus emphasizes the contrast between God's perfectly holy moral character and the morally deficient character typical among humans. God's presence in human conscience can enable this contrast to prompt guilt in human conscience, thereby leading to repentance before God and a new human relationship with God.

Forsyth explains how an inquirer should proceed in relation to Christ. He discovered that his congregation could not simply "accept my verdict on points that came so near to their souls," but rather that "there were Christian matters which [people] must decide for themselves, trained or not"[11] He adds: "Religion without an experimental foundation in grace readily feels panic in the presence of criticism, and is apt to do wild and unjust things in its terror. The Churches are not, in the main, in the spiritual condition of [moral] certainty which enables them to be composed and fair to critical methods."[12] Forsyth links a certain kind of antireligious scholarship to a spiritual condition, and he suggests a spiritual condition for facing such scholarship without shame.

Forsyth contends that "it is the wills of [humans], and not their views, that are the great obstacle to the Gospel, and the things most intractable."[13] He does not preach the Christian faith as an elaborate worldview or philosophy. Instead, he challenges people to place their faith in Christ crucified as central to their Christian experience. He thus seeks "to restore some sense not only of love's severity, but of the unsparing moral mordancy in the Cross and its judgment, which means salvation to the uttermost; to recreate an experience of redemption, both profound and poignant, which should enable [Christians] to deal reasonably, without extravagance and without panic, with the scholars' results as these

---

10. Forsyth, *The Principle of Authority*, 58.
11. Forsyth, *Positive Preaching and Modern Mind*, 282.
12. Forsyth, *Positive Preaching and Modern Mind*, 283.
13. Forsyth, *Positive Preaching and Modern Mind*, 288.

came in."[14] One important consideration is that the Christian gospel preceded the New Testament and does not depend on the inerrancy of the New Testament.

Forsyth affirms the value of theology for Christian life. "Well do I know," he writes, "how little a theology in itself can do, and how the mighty doer is the living faith. But I know well also that that faith is not the real thing unless it compels and loves an adequate theology; and if it cannot produce it, it dies."[15] Christian theology, in his perspective, requires articulating an individual or corporate Christian experience. Christ crucified inspires articulation, as a historical and moral fact that confronts us in our Christian experience. "The theologian," then, "is not a syllogist but an experient, an observer. He gives an account of faith, and especially of his own, as a creation by a historic fact and not the dialectic of a fertile idea."[16] Theology is not the ultimate Christian authority.

Christ crucified serves as Forsyth's ultimate authority in theology and ethics. He writes: "It is in the Forgiver and Redeemer of the Cross that the seat of moral, and so of all, authority for the renovated race must be found."[17] Rather than appealing to theology or religious tradition, Forsyth acknowledges the authority that confronts him in Christ crucified. He holds that we can experience this authority that both judges and welcomes. The experience of Christ crucified has fixed features, because we "cannot conceive a Christianity to hold the future without words like *grace, sin, judgment, repentance, incarnation, atonement, redemption, justification, sacrifice, faith,* and *eternal life*. No words of less volume than these can do justice to the meaning of God."[18] Philosophy, Forsyth contends, is no preamble to or prerequisite for Christian experience. Christian theology makes no "appeal to a prior and surer philosophy; but a philosophy comes later, and it must take due account of the facts, and especially of the revelatory and experienced fact

---

14. Forsyth, *Positive Preaching and Modern Mind*, 283–84.
15. Forsyth, *Positive Preaching and Modern Mind*, 287–88.
16. Forsyth, *The Principle of Authority*, 93.
17. Forsyth, *The Principle of Authority*, 404–5.
18. Forsyth, *Positive Preaching and Modern Mind*, 288.

which theology expounds."[19] Divine revelation, then, takes priority over philosophy and even theology.

Forsyth puts Christ crucified first in Christian experience, leaving Christian theology and philosophy to articulate an experienced gospel of divine power. He adds: "Neither philosophy nor psychology is there in order to determine what we may know, but to find and set out the conditions of what we do know."[20] A Christian theology and philosophy, then, should explain Christ crucified in experience, rather than seeking perpetually to prepare the way for (knowledge of) him. The historic fact of Christ, Forsyth submits, is there prior to our interpretation of it—and interpret it we must.

One might ask whether Forsyth's approach is overly subjective, because it apparently invokes experience as our authority. Forsyth replies: "A real authority is indeed *within* experience, but it is not the authority *of* experience; it is an authority *for* experience, it is an authority experienced."[21] The fact of Christ intrudes in Christian moral experience, but this experience is not itself the source of the divine authority in Christ. Christ crucified, Forsyth remarks, is "a public, social, natural fact and history, with a claim and a truth independent of the soul's experience. Such experience is the medium but not the canon of religious truth."[22] Conscience is not itself our authority but is rather the context where we encounter authority. "The authority is nothing in us, but something in history. It is something given us. What is in us only recognises it."[23] An appeal to Christ crucified, then, is no subjective appeal, but is an appeal to a historic and moral fact that calls for our attention and interpretation.

As a *personal* authority, Christ crucified differs from a presupposition, axiom, community standard, or worldview. Unlike the latter phenomena, Christ crucified is a powerful *intentional* source of distinctive evidence and life. Forsyth describes the difference:

19. Forsyth, *The Principle of Authority*, 106.
20. Forsyth, *The Principle of Authority*, 101.
21. Forsyth, *The Principle of Authority*, 83.
22. Forsyth, *The Principle of Authority*, 66.
23. Forsyth, *The Principle of Authority*, 454.

> We are not merely inserted into our foundation. It is more than a ground that will not give way; it is a source that will not fail or dry. We draw life from it, and it is a medium in which we live. It does not simply uphold us—it carries us, feeds us, slakes us. It is not only true for us, but mighty for us. It supports us as food does, and not simply as a floor does. It is better, of course, to be on rock than sand, but to be in soil is better still. We are rooted, and not only grounded, on our God.[24]

Forsyth thus offers advice that moves Christian inquiry beyond talk of presuppositions, community standards, and worldviews to a uniquely powerful *agent* in Christian moral experience. This agent is intentional in Christian conscience, and thus is purposive and capable of leading cooperative humans in communion with God. We should expect divine *lordship* in Christ to offer such moral *leading* in the experience of Christian conscience.[25]

The key experience in conscience differs from an experience of an ordinary fact. Forsyth explains:

> It is an event which is a divine act uttering and effecting the divine will. And as divine it is an act interpreted by itself, an act inseparable from its own account of itself through men it raised up for the purpose. We can have no faith in a mere fact, but only in a personal power working and reaching us through the fact. When we ask if a historic fact can become a present experience, so that the history do not starve the experience, nor the experience ignore the history, the first step to an answer is to become quite clear that the fact is not a mere occurrence but a salvation.[26]

Forsyth holds that God is at work not only in the historical cross of Christ, but also, on that historical basis, in the kerygmatic message stemming from it. God thus continues the redemptive work via personal intervention in human moral experience, courtesy of

---

24. Forsyth, *The Principle of Authority*, 41.

25. See Romans 8:14; for elaboration of such a view, see Moser, *The God Relationship*.

26. Forsyth, *The Principle of Authority*, 61.

God's Spirit, the Spirit of the risen Christ. Such intervention makes the kerygmatic message morally powerful in a way that mere talk or theory is not.

Purpose, Evil, and Judgment

Forsyth offers a broad perspective on human history, complete with a practical theodicy of divine self-justification. God has a definite purpose in human history and the cross of Christ figures at its center. Forsyth remarks:

> For the Bible as a whole, whether rising to the Cross or spreading from it, history is viewed under the category of judgment (though saving judgment) and not under that of progress. . . . The eschatologies are here in the true style of the Hebrew teleology of history. Its atmosphere was that of catastrophe and crisis rather than development. It thought of conversion, or regeneration, or restitution rather than of growth. The course of historic events is that of a series of judgments, each like an automatic release when the cup of iniquity was filled. But it was an ascending series, rising from purification to redemption, through good men to prophets and through prophets to God's Son (Matt. 21:37). It was a long crescendo of judgment, ending in a crisis of all the crises, a harvest of all the harvests which had closed one age and begun a new.[27]

The "crisis of all the crises" is the crucifixion of the Son of God, the execution of the blameless one sent from God for human redemption. The human motive in this crisis was to remove Jesus from human history, but God had, and has, a deeper purpose: to redeem humans from their alienation from God, that is, to reconcile them to God.

We cannot read God's purpose off of empirical history on our own. God must play a role even in our interpretation of redemptive history. Forsyth explains:

---

27. Forsyth, *The Justification of God*, 178.

Introduction: P.T. Forsyth in Focus

> We cannot frame some teleology of life, and then rise from it to a living God who is serviceable to it; but we must descend upon it from that God, from a God otherwise given, self-given, given, therefore, with absolute certainty, and not with a high probability. For He is the end, He does not simply cherish it, and He does not simply declare it, and He does not simply produce it. He *is* our peace. We began in Him in whom we end. We die in our nest. The light of our first sight came from Him who is the object of our last faith. Our great destiny is as certain as He is absolute and holy.[28]

Forsyth holds that we start with God as divinely self-given, or self-presented, to us in conscience, and not with some presupposition or theory about God. God *shows* divine holy love to us in conscience (see Romans 5:5), and this serves as a benchmark for our understanding of human history, including its crises of divine judgment.

Forsyth has in mind what he calls "moral certainty," and not the kind of logical certainty found in mathematics and logic. He remarks:

> That moral certainty of God's conquering holiness is the only foundation of any faith in man's unity, when the last pinch comes. It is not in himself but in his God as his Saviour. It is his unity in a Redeemer and a Redemption, a unity not natural but supernatural, not by evolutionary career but by mortal crisis, not in the first creation but the second, not in generation but regeneration.[29]

Forsyth thinks of moral certainty as grounded in divine holy love that leads to the regeneration of humans for the sake of communion with God. Such certainty does not depend on an argument for God's existence; instead, it depends on receiving God by faith in response to divine intervention in human experience. God thus becomes the ultimate guarantor for humans of divine reality and goodness.

28. Forsyth, *The Justification of God*, 57.
29. Forsyth, *The Justification of God*, 21.

We should not expect to have a full explanation of God's purposes in allowing evil in human history. As Forsyth remarks, much of the detail of God's working in history is "hidden from us."[30] Even so, we can find God "self-given" to us in the holy love of Christ in conscience. Forsyth adds:

> With this security we can sit loosely to many anomalies which seem to role God out of the course of thugs. Our faith did not arise from the order of the world; the world's convulsion, therefore, need not destroy it. Rather it rose from the sharpest crisis, the greatest war, the deadliest death, and the deepest grave the world ever knew—Christ's Cross. We see not yet all things brought under salvation but we see Jesus the Saviour of all. We taste Him. The Church is not there to exhibit progress and its optimism, but to reveal Christ and His regenerating power.[31]

Having Christ self-given to us does not entail having a complete explanation of God's purposes given to us. We have no reason to expect such an explanation from God. Even so, we can have a basis for the moral certainty of God's reality and goodness in the self-giving of Christ to us in our moral experience.

Forsyth has in mind the crucified grace in Christ which he takes to be God's purpose for the world, and not just for the Christian church. As he says, "the grace of God, with its method, is the ground plan of the universe."[32] This grace includes communion with God as an end, and not just a means. Forsyth thus offers prayer as an end, and not just a means, in God's purpose: "Prayer is often represented as the great means of the Christian life. But it is no mere means, it is the great end of that life."[33] He portrays it as bringing us into contact "with reality," the reality of God, analogous to the way that original research in science can bring one

---

30. Forsyth, *The Justification of God*, 58.
31. Forsyth, *The Justification of God*, 57.
32. Forsyth, *The Justification of God*, 58.
33. Forsyth, *The Soul of Prayer*, 16.

into contact with reality.[34] Forsyth's approach to prayer confirms the inherently interpersonal approach to theology he offers.

The church has a special role in witnessing to the redemptive purpose in grace, but the church is not the sole object of this purpose. God seeks a larger audience for the divine kingdom. The overarching aim of divine revelation, in Forsyth's language, is "the regeneration of the whole of Humanity."[35] The crucified Christ is thus the moral crisis of the human race, and not a tool just for the benefit of a subgroup of humans. Forsyth thus promotes a Christian view of humanity as "a family of nations to be loved, gospelled, and saved." On this basis, he contends that "the Word of the world's moral redemption by holy love must seize the conscience in the world's great heart."[36] Forsyth's passionate theology of the God of holy love aims at this passionate, and holy, end. This aim is part of the distinctive power of Forsyth's contribution to theology.

Chapter Summaries

In "The Atonement in Modern Religious Thought," Forsyth assumes that Christian interpretation of the cross must mature and progress from generation to generation. The *action* of Christ on the cross is final for religion in a way that *interpretations* cannot be, and Forsyth corrects a number of interpretations. These include: God as needing to be reconciled to humans, rather than the reverse; God's being beyond suffering, rather than the cross as costing God dearly; the cross as an equivalent substitutionary punishment rather than God's judgment upon collective human sin. God is not mollified by the cross of Christ, according to Forsyth, but graciously accepts the obedience—not the suffering—of Christ as due recognition of God's holiness in judgment upon the world.

Forsyth distinguishes the cross of Christ from both the parable of the prodigal son and the Sermon on the Mount. He contends that revelation is redemptive and not mere communication. The revelation of God in Christ is hidden in the act of redemption,

---

34. Forsyth, *The Soul of Prayer*, 78.
35. Forsyth, *The Church and the Sacraments*, 102.
36. Forsyth, *The Church and the Sacraments*, 102–3.

in Christ crucified, not in the teaching or parables of Christ. This revelation as redemption involves God's judgment upon a sinful world, made manifest in Christ crucified, and recognized as such by the crucified Christ, and by us through him.

In "Immanence and Incarnation," Forsyth contrasts religion as evolutionary human progress and religion as historic decisive redemption. He regards this distinction as central to the greatest theological dispute (about the cross of Christ) facing the Christian church since the gnostic controversies of the second century. The dispute manifests the importance of Christ crucified in Forsyth's account of Christianity. The critical element for Christology is not the incarnation of Christ in the flesh but the incarnation of Christ crucified as Christ made sin for redemption. The key to the person of Christ, then, is his cross, not his birth. The revelation of God in Christ is a divine moral intervention in human history, not a high point in human moral progress, and our access to this revelation is moral. We experience the historic cross of Christ as the source and basis of our experienced forgiveness and peace with God. Forsyth thereby joins the subjective experience of redemption to an objective historic atonement in Christ crucified.

In "The Inner Life of Christ," Forsyth criticizes two approaches to history and Christian faith: faith as assent to knowledge (however meager that knowledge may be given the results of historical criticism) and Christian history as a myth that carries forward an ahistorical truth or impression. Forsyth acknowledges the cruciality of history for Christian faith, but he denies that history alone is a sure foundation. The results of historical inquiry are always in flux, subject to revision. Forsyth also resists reducing religion to an impression of the cross upon us, a third approach. It must be a real power to regenerate and recreate. Forsyth's proposed fourth way—meant to avoid orthodoxy, impressionism, and rationalism—involves treating faith's object as a living fact that acts upon us, with continuity between history and our present experience.

Forsyth describes the inner life of the historical Jesus using his actions, more than his words, as evidence. Jesus set his face toward his death in Jerusalem, for the sake of obeying his God and Father. We understand the inner life of Christ only as we grasp his march toward the cross, his motives and self-commitment to that end. This march toward the cross involved a growing realization of what God would require of him. The historical obedience of Christ even to death is a creative power for us. We ought not to obscure it by the teaching of Christ alone or his impression upon us. Not all historic facts about Christ are equally available to us in our present moral experience. The cross and resurrection of Christ identify who Christ is for us. The key to his cross is his focus on God and God's demand of his life, not his nation or people. This perspective on the historical Jesus fits with Albert Schweitzer's portrait of Jesus as one who gradually comes to understand that God would require his life.

In "Forgiveness through Atonement the Essential of Evangelical Christianity," Forsyth articulates a basis for Christian faith in communion with Jesus Christ. Jesus is understood as a historic personality whose crucifixion changed the moral relation between God and the world in a final way. Rather than making the teaching of Jesus foundational, Forsyth holds that his atoning death must take priority in our interpretation. Forsyth refuses to let the Gospels overshadow the Pauline epistles, arguing that through Paul the risen Christ interprets his own life and death. To understand Christ today, we must experience the same forgiveness through atonement that Paul did—grounded in Christ's historic obedience even to death. Christ's death is not a martyr's death but rather one that reaches us today in our moral experience, prior to our understanding of it. Forsyth identifies a basis for belief in the deity of Christ. Such belief is an attempt to best explain an experienced redemption, not an intellectual prelude to redemption.

Forsyth exhorts his readers to interpret the cross of Christ, since Christ is for us what we interpret his cross to be. Forsyth laments a tendency to make the parable of the prodigal son the chief image of God in Christ, rather than the costly atonement of Christ's historic act. The holiness of God in judgment upon human sin is made manifest in Christ's obedience even to his death. To neglect the cross in our theology is to miss the holiness of God and replace it with a less demanding form of love of our own making. The cross reveals both the human moral predicament and the God of holy love who would solve it. To grasp these realities, we must turn our attention from what Christ suffered passively and toward Christ's active obedience—Christ with his face set toward his death in Jerusalem. He thus acts toward Jerusalem, as he saw God's holy judgment upon the world, even as it fell upon himself. His passion ought to evoke our terror, not our sympathy. We should attend to God's holiness to understand God's love. Forsyth stakes the health and future of the Christian church at the point of interpreting an experienced yet objective atonement by God in Christ.

In "Faith, Metaphysics, and Incarnation," Forsyth explains how experienced redemption precedes belief in Christian doctrines that some might call "metaphysical." He notes that many in the churches either doubt or fear the collapse of orthodox doctrines about God, Christ, and the incarnation. In their traditional form, such doctrines reflect the metaphysic of a different age, and Forsyth holds that they are subject to re-articulation in modern language, namely moral language. Doctrines about the deity of Christ or the Trinity, for instance, are not products of speculation for its own sake. They are fallible attempts to articulate a collective and historic experience of salvation. The individual Christian need not understand or believe these doctrines, at least not beyond that which their own experience of grace warrants. Collective experience is anemic, however, if it cannot inspire a collective articulation of such doctrines.

Forsyth describes a process that we might call *experience seeking understanding*. Doctrines about Christ or the Trinity may seem incoherent or paradoxical because they are attempts to articulate a moral experience of redemption. Naturally, such attempts will vary in their clarity. Forsyth describes a kenotic christology of pre-existence along these lines, appealing to an experience of redemption as the basis for belief in Christ as divine. He denies that such beliefs are required for redemption, or that they are always warranted at the beginning of Christian life. Rather, they follow in due course as one reflects upon one's own redemptive experience and that of the collective church. Likewise, belief in miracles is not preliminary to faith. Miracles can only be received by faith. The same is true of knowledge of the incarnation of God in Christ. The doctrine of justification is first in the order of Christian experience, with incarnation subsequent, even though incarnation is conceptually prior as an explanation of an experienced justification. Christology follows an experienced redemption, rather than preceding it.

In "Revelation and the Person of Christ," Forsyth construes the revelation upon which Christianity depends as a matter of the will, rather than of just thought or truths. Such revelation comes by way of a historic person and his will as revealed by his actions. Specifically, revelation is redemption, and it cannot be suitably received apart from the experience of being redeemed. Revelation is not crystalized into a book or church, nor is it the evolving progress of human moral intuition. It is something final yet elusive, hidden in Christ crucified. Forsyth distinguishes Christ from other people in his relation to God. With his face set toward his death in Jerusalem, Jesus reveals the will of God in a final way in virtue of his unique obedience to that will.

Forsyth explores the topic of the deity of Christ. He holds that high Christology ought to be a religious conclusion, based on an experienced redemption, and not a premise. Those who receive the revelation of God in Christ as redemption will exalt Christ in their thinking. The historic Christ becomes present in the experience of the redeemed, as the will of God in action. Faith is not just assent to information but rather the obedient response of the redeemed to what God reveals in Christ. Forsyth elaborates upon Melanchthon's "To know Christ is the know his benefits." The key to the person of Christ is the action of Christ, specifically his cross, as the site of final revelation and the source of confidence for all future ages. It is a revelation that we encounter as an experience of God's holy love by sinful people, a revelation that both condemns sin and restores us to fellowship with a holy God.

In "The Disappointment of the Cross," Forsyth explores the process in which it dawned upon Jesus, and then upon his disciples, that God required of him his own life. Forsyth sketches the early optimism of the disciples as they realize that Jesus is their Messiah. Deep gloom follows, however, when Jesus insists upon the cross. Forsyth invites his readers to imagine themselves in a similar position, prosperous or at least hopeful, with every reason to expect a bright and blessed future. He then describes a process whereby a divine imperative emerges, perhaps gradually over time, and threatens to undermine everything. He narrows the image to that of a preacher, whose former success and popularity face shipwreck if he obeys a costly conviction emerging in conscience.

Forsyth adds to his image some details about the inconvenient conviction. The preacher must preach judgment where before he preached only mercy. He must speak of the weight of sin, the holiness of God, and the cross of Christ as central. The preacher begins to preach along these lines, grasping the severity of holy love but leaving the congregation bewildered. His deacons and friends try to restore him to his former optimism, warning him about squandering his pulpit career and influence for the kingdom. Forsyth's imagined case may be autobiographical, describing his own theological conversion and its personal cost. In any case, this essay explores the costly burden of divine conviction from the perspective of those who, like the crucified Christ, find themselves driven by the Spirit of God.

In "Christ and the Christian Principle," Forsyth contrasts a religion dependent upon the historical person of Jesus with one dependent upon his enduring insights as encapsulated in a Christian principle. Forsyth addresses Lessing's famous gap between history and eternal religious truth, responding that the fact of Christ is a source of power, and not mere knowledge or belief. History is not accidental but sacramental: it is the means to encounter the eternal. Christ does not bring us the Christian principle in a way that permits us to receive the principle and finally dispense with Christ. It is the enduring authority of Christ as a historical personality that concerns Forsyth, and not simply Christ as a messenger surpassed by his message.

Christians commune with a living Christ rather than an eternal idea. What God offers in Christ is moral communion with the holy one, not absorption into the divine ideal. Moral reality is fundamental reality, according to Forsyth, and this is made manifest through persons in history rather than in abstract. Forsyth connects preoccupation with a principle above a person to a rationalism that misunderstands revelation as a statement of truth. Forsyth's chief concern is that we not lose the finality of Christ by distilling his person to a principle, capable of further evolution or clearer manifestation through some future individual. Rather, the person of Jesus Christ manifests, with finality, that God is holy love. This revelation is inextricable from the person who brings it, Jesus Christ.

In "Christ's Person and His Cross," Forsyth addresses the priority of personality for religion. Personality is manifest in moral action, and the person of Christ is expressed through the cross of Christ. Forsyth traces the meaning of the atonement from Anselm to Ritschl, commenting on the turn from Christ's objective action upon God to his subjective impression upon humans. Forsyth makes his own argument for atonement grounded in God's nature as holy love, neither ignoring judgment as with liberalism nor dividing judgment and love as with some versions of orthodoxy.

Forsyth describes action as that which manifests personality, arguing that Christ the person is known by his actions, and most of all his climactic action leading to the cross. The action of Christ is key to Forsyth's understanding of the cross as a revelation of God's power to redeem and not just of divine sympathy. The cross of Christ is the sacrament of his person, the true site of his real presence being an act. Forsyth interprets the life of Christ in terms of his death, so that the cross was the vocation of Jesus, and not the defeat of his true ministry.

In "The Christianity of Christ and Christ our Christianity," Forsyth addresses those who put the Gospels ahead of the epistles in their interpretation of Christ, who emphasize his teaching and character ahead of his cross. Against this tendency, Forsyth contrasts Jesus with Socrates, observing that his actions dwarf his words and that our written Gospels of his career are secondary effects of the gospel he wrought in deed and power. The person of Jesus is unique in a way that his teaching is not. His finality lies in God, and not in his teachings. The God who is *our* Father was uniquely *his* Father. He died for his place as God's appointed king, the unique Son of Israel's God, not for his Sermon on the Mount or his teaching about the kingdom of God.

Forsyth draws upon the apocalyptic self-understanding of Jesus, stressing his position as rightful judge, who sometimes teaches to harden hearers for purposes other than education and enlightenment. Jesus flung himself upon the wheel of history, to use Schweitzer's phrase, to become God's appointed king forever. He founded his kingdom through the cross. Forsyth makes his case with biblical criticism in view, arguing that the records retain this Christ in action even if various phrases invite dispute. He appeals to the immediate impact of Jesus on his followers and the early church, who sometimes exalted him beyond the limits of their monotheism.

In "Regeneration, Creation, and Miracle I," the first half of a two-part essay, Forsyth discusses new creation through Christ crucified. He calls for theology to return to the saving facts that yielded other alleged authorities, like the Bible and the church. Theology articulates a power hidden in Christ crucified, not directly manifest in various records or traditions about him. This power is the moral power of Christ's historic obedience unto death, not his passive suffering. It is the power of an irreducibly moral new creation, a new humanity with Christ for its conscience that does justice to the holiness of God. The moral must guide the metaphysical in such a theology. Forsyth interprets God's freedom to create in terms of new creation, with creation being an action morally necessary to a God of holy love acting in moral freedom. Love moves God to create, and holy love moves God to create the new creation. The free soul is the true object of God's creative work, with nature the workshop.

In "Regeneration, Creation, and Miracle II," Forsyth defends a theology of the freedom of God, guided by a moral necessity intrinsic to God's own nature. God does not grow in holiness through creating and creation. Rather, God creates as a result of God's holy love. God is redeemer first and creator second, creator because redeemer. The holy love that we encounter in redemption is a love that creates. Forsyth compares creation from chaos to new creation from crisis. New creation makes prior creation inevitable, yet creation does not yield new creation via historical evolution or progress. *God* creates the redeemed conscience, with the cosmos as its arena.

Forsyth identifies the human will, rather than human nature, as the object of new creation. God's action on the human will is a gift of divine power. Unlike natural birth, new birth is an experience of an imperative. It is not a transfusion of substance or some other transformation external to the conscience of the reborn. We encounter God as a will to forgive, a holy love that empowers and transforms. This will seeks and requires our cooperation and trust. Revelation is not progressive growth in knowledge but a crisis of the will that provokes human decision. The Spirit of God is a spirit of conversion, not human evolution. Miracle finds ultimate expression in conversion. Forsyth describes how the historic risen Jesus is present today, not merely via posthumous influence but in power. We relate to Christ via our response to his act of world-redeeming obedience, as a fellowship of wills. We relate to Christ not just as one individual to another but in an act of faith toward the climactic act that founded a new humanity.

In "Veracity, Reality, and Regeneration," Forsyth writes about preaching and the formation of preachers. Preachers must strive to find a message, and the positive gospel is the pearl of great price for them. This pearl is hidden in God's action in history through Christ crucified. Preachers must grasp and preach new creation in power rather than human evolutionary progress. They must strive to think their gospel through to a finish and test for themselves whether their message is reality or mere symbol. The final reality is moral divine action, and preachers must build from God's action in Christ. This final reality guides Christian understanding of all other reality, as we interpret creation in the light of new creation. The power manifest in Christ and his people is the Spirit of new creation, the Holy Spirit. Christ makes no mere impression upon us, but instead is the soul's new creator and the creator of a redeemed humanity.

In "The Conversion of the Good," Forsyth describes how Jesus and John strove to address their nation, beyond individual Israelites. They called upon Israel's best to repent, including its leaders and representatives. Theirs was a call for national repentance, from the least to the greatest, and the collective fate of Israel hung upon a collective response. God's counterpart in Israel was the nation, not the individual soul. The religious leaders would respond for the people, and their response would count as Israel's response, for better or for worse. Jesus called for repentance as deep as the zeal of the zealous, daring his nation to scorn its prior hopes and embrace his kingdom of righteousness. Jesus preached repentance and not inheritance, Israel at God's disposal and not God at Israel's disposal. Jesus judged the good in their goodness and was most harsh with those closest to his own cause. He was no partisan, and thus he spoke without partiality. The collective life of Israel was at stake, and he strove to sway his nation.

In a controversial passage, Forsyth attributes the first century destruction of Jerusalem to the providence of the risen Christ. He interprets it as the direct consequence of Christ's crucifixion by Israel's leaders. While the historical Jesus and biblical authors might have interpreted this subsequent disaster that way—prophetic warnings and the pre-exilic destruction of Jerusalem are closely related in scripture—it is debatable whether we should form the same conclusions today. Forsyth seeks to interpret world crises theologically, both ancient and current, using a notion of national perdition. He writes during the First World War and seeks to interpret it as a war between Christian nations. He specifically interprets Germany as a nation facing international judgment on account of international sins.

In "The Cross of Christ as the Moral Principle of Society," Forsyth writes, again in the context of the First World War, that the Christian church must offer society its moral knowledge of the human predicament: guilt before a holy God and redemption by God's historic action in Christ. Forsyth magnifies the cross as humanity's "moral Armageddon," dwarfing all war before and since. For the church to speak during a present historic calamity, it must grasp and weigh the calamity of the cross and the power at work through it. The genius of the church, when grasped, is the moral knowledge of the cross. Society needs this knowledge, especially in times of crisis.

Forsyth discusses society as a quasi-personality, more than the pooling of individual wills but rather as a collective will formed by moral factors and pressures. The state is a fundamentally moral entity that exists, like the individual, in the presence of a holy God. The cross provokes the collective will of the state, and not just the individual, and it ought to shape the state through the collective witness of the church. The cross does not provide an idea, ideal, or hero upon which to form a society. It rather provides Jesus Christ in action, a moral personality unveiling of the will of a God as holy love.

In "Faith and Mind," Forsyth distinguishes primary or positive theology from secondary or scientific theology. Primary theology is the attempt to articulate an experienced revelation. Secondary theology is the detailed study and elaboration of Christian doctrines to an extent that often exceeds experience. Forsyth warns against both a pietism that finds primary theology burdensome and a rationalism that leaves it behind. The church must state its gospel, and primary theology is a corporate necessity even though some individuals cannot articulate it. Primary theology is a moral theology, since it articulates the moral revelation of the cross. It is inseparable from the religion it describes.

Forsyth discusses creeds as crucial articulations of the church's faith in the context of the intellectual disputes that provoked them. Creeds are never final because the faith they describe eludes final description and the language of a creed is shaped by the language of the controversies that provoke it. New times and places, with new controversies, call forth new creeds to describe the same living faith. Creeds carry moral power, not intellectual power, and strive in the arena of competing wills rather than competing ideas.

In "Intellectualism and Faith," Forsyth describes the sharp dialectic of Jesus and of Paul, on display in the New Testament, and he dispenses with the impulse to treat Christian writing as necessarily dull, simple, or straightforward. Even so, Forsyth suggests that the Christian intellect weighs moral reality more than general truths or concepts. Christians should then study to prepare for moral action in the world rather than merely intellectual debate. The Christian intellect should strive to interpret the human moral situation before a holy God, for the sake of obedient action. Theology strives to weigh the human tragedy and to know the power of God amidst it.

Forsyth depicts the move to return to the simple teaching of Jesus as a form of intellectualism and orthodoxy. Christ brings God in action, his face set toward his death in Jerusalem, and not a teaching or message alone. Christ brings power rather than mere information. Any theology that exalts Jesus for the sake of information is intellectualist, whether that information be straightforward aphorisms or sophisticated theological systems. An intellectualism of the Sermon on the Mount is no different from an intellectualism of the Athanasian Creed. The antidote to both is attention to the cross, the historic Christ in action. The Christian mind weighs the finality of the cross, and not just the eternity of certain truths, teachings, or systems.

In "The Moralization of Religion," Forsyth describes Christianity as a response to an irreducibly moral revelation of holy love.

It is fundamentally moral and best understood in moral terms. Writing during the First World War, Forsyth criticizes the notion that sacrifice is the true measure of moral power. Both sides sacrifice, yet German sacrifice, Forsyth proposes, serves a great international evil. Sacrifice, then, is no sound basis for religion. To obey, Forsyth reiterates, is better than to sacrifice. Christ died for holy love, for the sake of righteousness, and not for love alone. We cannot understand Christ's sacrifice apart from his obedience for the sake of God's holy name.

Forsyth questions whether the spirit of sacrifice manifest by many during the war was sufficient to face the problems of the subsequent peace. Christ died for the kingdom of God, a kingdom of righteousness. Forsyth argues that religion today must grasp anew the kingdom of God as collective and international righteousness manifest in the present. We return to the cross as the climactic revelation of the power of God at work in history, up to the present.

In "Unity and Theology: A Liberal Evangelicalism the True Catholicism," Forsyth proposes that Christian unity comes by way of a shared positive theology (the primary theology discussed above), and not by casting creeds aside for the sake of unity. Forsyth qualifies appeals to religious experience (in a significant passage given his regular appeal to experience elsewhere). That which unites is the *object* of Christian experience, not the religious experience itself. The spirit of Christian unity is the shared spirit of the cross, not a shared spirit of Pentecost. New creation emerges in experience, but it is the new creation and not the experience itself that unifies those who share in it. There can be no meaningful unity apart from a shared new creation that demands shared description.

Forsyth looks to the power behind a primary theology as the source of unity. He holds that such a power must be one that addresses the actual moral evil in the present world. Unity involves a collective theology of a shared salvation, not merely the uniformity of the theologies of individuals. Different churches hold different truths in trust. They must not abandon their convictions for the sake of unity. Rather, ecumenism requires the theological work of weighing and adjusting the convictions that each party brings by the standard of the moral revelation of the cross.

In "Religion Public and Private," Forsyth struggles with the First World War as a war within Protestant Christendom. Why, he wonders, has the Christian revelation entrusted to both combatants failed to prevent this calamity? What accounts for the futility of the Protestant gospel in international affairs? Forsyth suggests that Christian worship must extend to great public actions and works, not merely to individual religion. The Christ of Christianity is the Christ of the cross, Christ in action. Jesus was driven by concern for the kingdom of God, a kingdom of righteousness, and Christians should likewise strive for the same in the public realm. Where Christianity remains private, the public state need not act for the sake of righteousness. A nation of individual Christian piety will then become a force for evil on the world stage.

The God of the cross has power to heal the nations. The Christian gospel is a revelation of the righteousness of God, and this includes a public and international righteousness. There are many who preach to local congregations, but few who preach with prophetic power to ruling state authorities, provoking the national conscience. Christ provoked his nation through its leaders, rather than through the crowd alone. The gospel speaks to public affairs and must not be limited to private piety.

1

The Atonement in Modern Religious Thought

I—Negative

"Back to Christ" is a most necessary movement in every unsettled age; but the Reformers' version of it is the true one. If the word is taken in spiritual earnest it means "back to the Cross," and back to the Cross means not only back to the moral principle of sacrifice, but back to the religious principle of expiation. Moreover, to go back to a principle which is really the act of a person is to go back to a power. And the one power the Church needs to have revived is that power of personal faith which gathers about the reality—and the experience—of justification. There is no real revival of the Church which does not revive that.

It is impossible in this region to separate religion from theology. A religion of sympathy may be so separated, but then it is not, strictly speaking, a religion. It might be Positivism, or some other fraternity. But a religion of forgiveness must be a religion of theology. It is our answer, not to a human need, but to a Divine revelation.

If the faith of the Church is to take a new departure it must proceed from a new and practical grasp of revelation; and of the revelation which deals with the central human situation—the situation of sin and guilt. It is a faith and revelation which are concentrated in an Atonement.

The mind and soul of the Church returns to this perennial interest. The Church must always adjust its compass at the Cross. But in so returning it does not simply retrace the steps or tread the round of those that have gone before. There is a deepening evolution of human thought in this regard. The efforts to pluck the heart from its mystery are not a series of assaults renewed with blind and dogged courage on an impregnable hold. They form the stages of a long spiritual movement of slow battle, of arduous illumination and severe conquest. We have gone, *e.g.*, through the "moral theory," and come out at the other side, not where we went in. To this movement little or nothing is contributed by the inferior branches of human thought or knowledge. The revelation of God in the Cross of Christ is its own reforming principle and its own cleansing light. Nothing gained in anthropology, psychology, or philosophy can really do more than remove the misconceptions which they themselves created in their first blundering stages. The Cross is its own interpreter, and its own reformer, and its own sanctifier. It is its own principle, its own corrective, its own deliverer from misconstruction rational or irrational. It is its own evidence to our moral need. No conclusions of anthropology, for instance, about a historic fall, or the connection of sin and physical death, affect the matter. The need of Atonement does not rest on an historic fall, but on the reality of present and corporate guilt. And the fact of it rests on an experience as real as any which forms the basis of science. The Christian mind, moved and lightened by the Holy Ghost, does not rotate but march. And the progress is no less sure because it is neither continuous nor direct. We have much to drop on the route as a condition of getting home. We have to save truth by losing it, though it seem part of our soul. We shed the husk to grow the tree. And in this matter of Atonement some things are clearly learnt to be wrong, some are as clearly found to be true as we move from faith to faith.

1. We have outgrown the idea that God has to be reconciled. We see, as we never did before, how unscriptural that is. We know that the satisfaction made by Christ, no less than the sacrifices of the old law, flowed from the grace of God, and did not go to procure it.

2. We have outgrown the idea that Redemption cost the Father nothing, that He had only to receive the payment, or even the sacrifice, which the Son made. We realise more clearly that the Son could not suffer without the Father suffering. We realise that forgiveness did cost, that it was not a matter of course to paternal indulgence, that it involved conditions of sorrow which were not

confined either to Christ or to man, that a forgiveness which cost the forgiver nothing would lack too much in moral value or dignity to be worthy of holy love or rich in spiritual effect.

3. We have outgrown the idea that Christ took our punishment in the quantitative sense of the word. What He offered was not an *equivalent*. So also there can be no imputation as transfer of quantitative merit. We are agreeing to see that what fell upon Him was not the equivalent punishment of sin, but the due judgment of it, its condemnation. But we are also returning to see that what He bore was sin's condemnation, and not a mere sympathetic suffering. He did not indeed bear our guilt in the sense of a vicarious repentance. That for His holiness was impossible. He who was made sin for us could never be made sinful, nor, being made a curse for us, was He accursed. But yet what He bore was much more than the *Weltschmerz*,[1] the human travail; it was the condemnation of sin in the flesh.

4. We are only just escaping from the modern and sentimental idea of love which found no difficulty placed by the holy law of God's nature in His way of forgiveness. It is an immoral love which has no moral hesitation about mercy. There are conditions to be met which reside, not in man, but in the very nature of God Himself, and so of human dignity. The key to the whole situation on this question lies in some words I have already quoted in public.

> The dignity of man would be better assured if he were shattered on the inviolability of this holy law than if for his mere happy existence it were ignored.

I hope that we are beyond the idea that punishment is an arbitrary ordinance of God, that the conjunction of sin and suffering is the result of a mere decree, and that the same will which decreed it can dissolve it at His kind pleasure. We realise, in our moral progress under the Christian revelation, that the law which ruins the sinner is as eternal and holy in the nature of God as the passion to make him a saint. And we have in the whole New Testament a standard of Divine love which is truer than those domestic analogues so dear to a theology popularised among great classes

---

1. ["World-pain."]

with no interest in life higher than the affections. There are some to whose experience the parable of the prodigal means more than the death of Christ.

5. We have outgrown also the other extreme—that forgiveness cost so much that it was impossible to God till justice was appeased and mercy set free by the blood of Christ.

6. We have further left the idea behind that the satisfaction of Christ was made either to God's wounded honour or to His punitive justice. And we see with growing and united clearness that it was made by obedience rather than by suffering. There is a vast difference between suffering as a condition of Atonement and suffering as the thing of positive worth in it, what gives it its value. We are beyond the idea that there was any saving value in the mere act of dying, apart from the spiritual manner of it. It is not a mere fact, but the person in it, that can mediate between soul and soul. It is true the effect would not have been won if Christianity had been complete in the Sermon on the Mount and Christ had passed to heaven from the Mount of Transfiguration; but not because He would not have paid the death penalty, but only because a vital and terminal portion of human experience would have been excluded from acknowledging in Him the righteousness of God. The saving value both of His sorrow and death came from a holy obedience, owning, in His most intense and extreme actuality of life—viz., agony and death—the righteousness of the broken law. The law was a law of hungering holiness, and the submission and sacrifice were not to mere clamant justice or Divine wrath.

The wrath of God, we all must agree, could not fall in this form of displeasure on His beloved Son. There can be no talk of placation or mollifying. And by the wrath of God we mean, and see that the Bible means, the judgment of a holy God upon sin even more than the disposition of God towards the sinner.

7. We can no longer separate Christ's life of obedience from His expiatory death. He was obedient, not simply *in* death, but *unto* death. But this means not a tuning down of His death, but a tuning up of His life. It means that His whole person was expiatory in its ultimate function and supreme work. It was on this ground that He forgave sin during His life. Each miracle cost, and was preceded by, a small Passion. His sorrowful existence was an expiation. All His sufferings were death in advance, deaths man-

ifold, chastisements of sin, and in their nature expiatory. He was inwardly in deaths often before He died the outward death.

8. We are, I hope, all giving up the tendency to twist Scripture into support of our theories, orthodox or liberal. In particular, scholarship more and more unanimously compels us to give up the Roman idea that justifying in St. Paul means making just and not declaring just; or that "the righteousness of God" means the ethical attribute of God conveyed to us, rather than the gift of God as a status conferred on us. On such points the old theology and the new exegesis unite. The finality of Paul's authority, of course, is a separate question, but his meaning should not be longer in dispute.

By justification Paul at least meant something more forensic than ethical, a fiat more than a verdict of God, something more creative than appreciative, more synthetic than analytic. It was most original and wonderful, a new morality more moral than any natural ethic, and high removed from the judgment of the natural traditional conscience.

9. We are leaving behind us, to all appearance, the hazy idea that we have the fact of the Atonement and that no theory need be sought or can be found. The fact of the Crucifixion does not depend on theory, but a fact like the Atonement can be separated from theory of some kind only by a suffusion of sentiment on the brain, some ethical anæmia, or a scepticism of the spiritual intelligence.

10. We are abandoning the idea that any adequate treatment of this great and solemn theme can rest on the basis of a merely personal experience. Amateur and dilettanti theologising, however devout, is, by its very individualism, disqualified for any very valuable verdict on such a universal theme. The history of the question in the Church is as little to be despised as it is to be idolised. If we fall back on experience the question is too vast for any single experience, and what we must use is the experience of the Church. Yet even that is not final. The Bible must still save us from the Church. And I hope we have outgrown the idea that anything so subjective as the Christian consciousness can be the test of truth which, in its very nature as a saving power, must be in the first place objective. Our forgiveness has an objective ground, and is inseparable from the death of Christ, and from that death

considered as something more than the source of a new type of experience.

11. Expiation and forgiveness, it has been said, are mutually exclusive. If a sin has been expiated the account is cleared; there is then no need of forgiveness or question of Grace. This was the criticism of Socinius on Anselm. May we hope that we are beyond that, that it is seen to miss the mark as soon as the quantitative and equivalent theory of Christ's suffering is given up? Of course, an expiatory *amount* of penalty purges the offence; and, the debt being paid, the culprit is beholden to no grace for his open door. But if we say that God, who had a right to destroy each sinner, offers pardon to those who really own in the Cross the kind (not the amount) of penalty which their sin deserved, then the contradiction vanishes. Grace is still sovereign, free and unbought. It is grace in God to accept an Atonement which is not an equivalent but a practical, adequate, and superhuman acknowledgment in man of the awful debt foregone.

II—Positive

12. We must go beyond even the texts bearing on this subject. The classic texts have for the present been well-nigh exhausted. The separation of Biblical from dogmatic theology has left the Church free as it never was before to recognise where the value of texts ceases and to abstain from pressing them to their hurt. And I come now to the more positive part of my work when I say that we must start from the actual spiritual situation of our day, and begin with the ruling contemporary idea to which the Spirit has led us in His teaching and unteaching of His Church. That ruling idea is revelation. Jesus Christ makes the claim He does upon the world not as being a religious genius, but as being the Revelation of God. What, then, is involved in the way of Atonement or Expiation in the Christian revelation of the love of God; in God not simply as the Father, but as the Father *of our Lord and Saviour Jesus Christ and Him crucified?* I mean by the Christian Revelation the revelation that Christ effected, and not only what He taught. Is it a revelation of such love as includes in itself, in its own spiritual necessity, the judgment upon sin, and includes it not as a mere principle, but as an accomplished and exhibited moral fact? Have we a rev-

elation of love which not only produces repentance by its effect upon man, but also includes within itself the actual judgment and destruction of sin; and includes it not as a necessity probable in human thought, but as an active constituent of the revelation? Is it possible to have any adequate sense of the actual love of God in Christ without an equally real sense of His actual condemnation of sin?—its condemnation *in act*, note, not its mere hatred; and its condemnation, not in our experience but in Christ's. Is revelation separable from judgment, as an actual element of it and not merely as a coming corollary? Can there be any assertion of *forgiving* love without an assertion, equally actual and adequate, of the moral majesty of that love, and its difference from mere kindness? Was the revelation of holy love not equally and at once, in the same fact, a revelation of sin, a developing of sin to its utmost crisis, and to its final judgment? "God is Love" has in the New Testament no meaning apart from the equally prominent idea of righteousness, of God as the author and guardian of the moral holy law. The Christian principle of pardon is not forgiveness to repentance (no strong man forgives a real wrong on a thin repentance, a mere attrition), but to due repentance. And a due repentance means a repentance not only sincere (and certainly not equivalent), but containing some adequate sense of the evil done. And that means an adequate recognition in experience of the majesty and inviolability of the law of holiness. But such a recognition is not possible to a sinful soul or race. It could only be made by a conscience unblunted in its moral perceptions because sinless in its moral obedience, yet identified in sympathy with the sinful race. It is this practical and experienced recognition that is the Atonement or Expiation. It is ratifying by act and experience, by assent which was response and by a response which was lived and died, God's death sentence on sin. It is not repentance in Christ's case, but it is the source of repentance in us who are joined with Him. And the two polar experiences, joined in one spiritual and organic act of mystic union, form the complete type of Christian faith. The repentance is ours alone; the penalty is not, the judgment is not. The penal judgment or consequence or curse of sin did fall on Christ, the penitential did not. The sting of guilt was never His, the cry on the Cross was no wail of conscience. But the awful atmosphere of guilt *was* His. He entered it, and died of it.

Our chastisement was on Him, but God never chastised Him. The penalty was His, the repentance remains ours. His expiation does not dispense with ours, but evokes and enables it. Our saving repentance is not due to our terror of the judgment to fall on us, but to our horror of the judgment we brought on Him. The due recognition of the wounded law was His, but the sense of having inflicted the wound is ours alone. Yet not possibly ours till we are acted on by what was His. The truth of penalty is penitence. The end and intent of the judgment on Him was our judgment of ourselves in Him. The use of penalty is to rouse the true punishment in all penalty, viz., the sense of guilt and personal repentance. Repentance is never regarded in Christianity as a thing possible by itself, or a condition effectual by itself without God, but only as that part or action of the complete work of Christ which takes effect through us. It is the form assumed by the work of Christ, the judgment on Christ, as it enters our atmosphere of personal guilt.

The question really is, Where did the difficulty lie that was to be overcome by Redemption? Was it in forgiving the penitent, or in producing the penitence that could be forgiven? Was it in God or in man, in the Divine conscience or the human? Where did Christ feel that the obstacle lay with which He had to deal? Was the objective of the Cross our human impenitence or something superhuman? Did He close with something which had no right, or something which had every right, with human hostility or Divine claim? Was He dealing with a human attitude or with a Divine relation? Was He engrossed with what He was doing toward men or toward God?

If we select one of these ways of putting it and ask whether the difficulty lay in producing forgiveness or forgiveableness, we must answer that it was both. The antithesis is but on the surface. They unite below. That which really produces forgiveable penitence in man is the expiation to law which bore first on God. It was to the law that produces penitence that forgiving grace had to die. The moral effect of the Cross on man is due to a nature in man continuous with the moral nature of God.

Love's awful moving cost in satisfying the broken law and maintaining its holy and inviolable honour, is the only means of producing such a sense of guilt as God can forgive. The difficulty of true repenting is the difficulty of realising that God took the broken law of His holiness so much to heart that it entailed the obedience in agony and death of the Holy One. Without the death of Christ the sinner feels that he is pursued only by an unexhausted judgment; and the end of that may be panic, but not penitence. It is the exhaustion of judgment and not its remission that produces the penitence which is forgiveably sensible both of the goodness and the severity of God.

It is the impossibility of remitting judgment that makes possible the remission of sin. The holy law is not the creation of God but His nature, and it cannot be treated as less than inviolate and eternal, it cannot be denied or simply annulled unless He seem false to Himself. If a play on words[2] be permitted in such a connection, the self-denial of Christ was there because God could not deny Himself.

I repeat, the form in which the question presents itself to-day is whether Redemption is a constituent element of Revelation or only a consequence of it; and whether it is so, both in a theological analysis of the idea, and as an interpretation of the spiritual fact and act, Christ, in His historic totality.

We may mark these stages at which my space will only allow me to hint.

(1) Redemption is a part of Revelation. Revelation is not Revelation till it is effectual, *i.e.*, till it come home as such. A revelation merely displayed is none. It is not revelation till it strike light on the soul. The very first revelation involved the creation of a man to receive it; Revelation and Creation were one act. So the second and greater Revelation was not mere illumination or mere impression. It was Redemption. It involved the recreation of the soul to take it in. Revealing was *ipso facto* remaking, as a great and original genius has slowly to create the taste to appreciate him. The act which reveals his soul makes his world. If only we could grasp the idea of revelation as something done instead of something shown, as creation instead of exhibition, as renovation instead of innovation, as resurrection instead of communication.

(2) Atonement is a constituent of Redemption. The thing we are to be redeemed from is not chiefly ignorance or pain, but guilt. The thing to which revelation has first to address itself is guilt. The love

---

2. I take shelter under Matthew 26:25.

of God can only be revealed to sinful men as in primary relation not to lovelessness but to guilt. It can only appear as atoning love in some form of judgment.

We are to be redeemed by judgment somewhere from condemnation, from the wrath of God. There is no question of placation, but there is of expiation, of owning the holiest law by the holiest sacrifice and the humblest grief. There is a question of that law which to recognise as co-eternal with love is *the* sign of religious earnestness and virility. Salvation must be salvation not *from* judgment, but *by* judgment. Christ did not simply pronounce judgment, but effected it. And He gave it effect in His own person and experience. He bore the infinite judgment He pronounced. The prophet of woe becomes in a few chapters the victim of woe (Matt 24–26). The agent of judgment becomes the object of judgment, and so becomes the agent of salvation. As Judge of all the earth, as the Conscience of the conscience, Christ is absolute in His judgment, unsparing and final in His condemnation. But as the second Adam and Man of men He attracts, accepts and absorbs in Himself His own holy judgment; and He bears, in man and for man, the double crisis and agony of His own two-edged vision of purity and guilt. He whose purity has the sole right to judge has by the same purity the only power to feel and realise such judgment. And His love made that power for Him a duty. And so He was their Saviour.

(3) Need it be said that Atonement for us is as impossible by us as it is necessary to holiness? Amendment is not reparation; and repentance even cannot lift itself to the measure of the broken law or gauge how great the fault has been. If made, the reparation must be made by God Himself. The sacrifice flows from grace and does not produce grace. It is not a case of altering God's disposition but His relations with man, of enabling Him to treat man as He feels. It is persistently overlooked that it is an act of grace and not of debt on God's part to accept even the satisfaction and Atonement of Christ for human forgiveness. We must never use the word satisfaction, even of Christ's sacrifice, in any way which would suggest equivalence, and constitute mere claim on God, any more than mere exemption for us.

Atonement is substitutionary, else it is none. Let us not denounce or renounce such words, but interpret them. They came into existence to meet a spiritual necessity, and to sweep them away is spiritual wastefulness, to say no worse. We may replace the word substitution by representation or identification, but the thing remains. Christ not only represents God to man but man to God. Is it possible for any to represent man before Holy God without identifying himself in some guiltless way with human sin, without receiving in some way the judgment of sin? Could the second Adam be utterly untouched by the second death? Yet if the Sinless was judged it was not His own judgment He bore, but ours. It was not simply on our behalf, but in our stead—yet not quantitatively, but centrally. Representation apart from substitution implies a foregone consent and election by the represented, which is not Christ's relation to humanity at all. Let us only be careful that we do not so construe the idea as to treat the sufferings of Christ as in real parity with ours. That is a moral impossibility, and lands us, as has been said, in all the anomalies of an equivalent theology which it is the merit of Socinus to have destroyed. The principle of a vicarious Atonement is bound up with the very idea of Revelation, of love emerging into guilt. There is an atoning substitution and a penal; but a penitential there is not.

(4) I can only here say a closing word on this last distinction. I do not see why we should avoid describing the suffering of Christ as penal. Nor do I see how we can. Sin is punished by suffering. And it was because of the world's sin that Christ suffered. It was the punishment of sin that fell on Him. He came deliberately under that part of the moral order which we may call the Divine and universal Nemesis. Christ loved holiness at least as much as He loved man; and the willing penalty of the Holy One was the only form in which wounded holiness could be honoured, and love be revealed as in earnest with sin. It was, moreover, the only way in which penalty or law could produce its fruit of repentance, and so of reconciliation. Expiation is the condition of reconciliation. Penalty, if not vicarious, if its source do not also suffer, only hardens and alienates. The suffering was penal in that it was due in the moral order to sin. It was penal to Christ's personality, to His consciousness, but not to His conscience. It was not penitential. There was no self-accusation in it. He never felt that God was punishing Him, though it was penalty, sin's Nemesis that He bore. It was the consequence of sin, though not of His sin. And it was the con-

sequence attached *by God* to sin—sin's penalty; and He so recognised it. It was judgment, and therefore penalty, and not mere pain or trial. Suffering does not repair sin; only penalty does, working to repentance. But it was not substitutionary *punishment*. There is no such thing in the moral world. The worst punishment is to see the penalty we brought on Christ—whether we see it with faith in a saving way, or without faith to our deeper condemnation.

To the question what the worth was which God saw in the work of Christ, and what the delectation which gave it saving value to His eye of grace, the answer can here be but in useless brevity. First, the practical and adequate recognition of a broken law in a holy and universal life is an end in itself, and therefore a Divine satisfaction. Second, the effect of that vicarious and loving sacrifice on men must bring them to a repentance and reconciliation which was the one thing that God's gracious love required for restored communion and complete forgiveness. He could now deal with them as He had felt from before the foundation of the world. It satisfied the claim and harmony of His holy nature, and it satisfied the redemptive passion of His gracious heart. Thirdly, that effect on men is due to the satisfaction of God's moral nature in the constitution of man. God was in Christ reconciling the world by the sacrifice and satisfaction of Himself.

Human illustrations are more useful for impression than for explanation in a case so original and unique as Christ's, yet I may close with one less common than some.

Schamyl was the great religious and military leader of the Caucasus who for thirty years baffled the advance of Russia in that region, and, after the most adventurous of lives, died in 1871. At one time bribery and corruption had become so prevalent about him, that he was driven to severe measures, and he announced that in every case discovered the punishment would be one hundred lashes. Before long a culprit was discovered. It was his own mother. He shut himself up in his tent for two days without food or water, sunk in prayer. On the third day he gathered the people, and pale as a corpse, commanded the executioner to inflict the punishment, which was done. But at the fifth stroke he called "Halt!" had his mother removed, bared his own back, and ordered the official to lay on him the other ninety-five, with the severest threats if he did not give him the full weight of each blow.

This is a case where his penalty sanctified her punishment both to herself and to the awestruck people.

Every remission imperils the sanctity of law unless he who remits suffers something in the penalty foregone; and such atoning suffering is essential to the revelation of love which is to remain great, high and holy.

Finally, if the Cross be penal we have not only to *admit* that it is so, but to *urge* it; for it is of the essence of its value for the soul, and the real secret of the Church's action on the world.

2

Immanence and Incarnation

In the remarks I here venture on I should like it to be understood that I am dealing with a school, or rather a tendency, developed mainly in Germany, whose representatives differ considerably among themselves on certain points. I mention this because I do not wish to act as the critic of individuals. There are few individuals in whom all the features of the movement are embodied. And any individual may readily and truly say that such and such a feature does not mark him.

The idea of the divine immanence affects the preacher's mental world rather than his moral message. It belongs to his study and not to his pulpit. It pertains to his scheme of the world rather than to his gospel of its destiny, to his culture and not his vocation. It is not even a theologoumenon, but rather a philosopheme, whose influence for thought has been great, for theology, but indirect, and for saving faith nothing. We certainly do owe it something that it would be unfair to ignore. We owe something to a theory of the divine immanence which, more than a century ago, rescued us from a distant deism, confirmed our faith in the rationality of the world, and went on to deepen our cosmic emotion to be almost an order of religion. It is a theory which has thus had its effect on some moods and expressions of religion. But with evangelical faith it has little to do. It preoccupies us with the physical notion of monistic process, instead of the moral notion of personality and freedom of action and crisis, sin and sanctity. It does not go to the depths. It speculates about a Christ made flesh, but it never gauges the true seat of Incarnation—a Christ made sin. It is not a theology of Incarnation. You do not surmount by it the Unitarian position, but only the deistic. Plenty of Unitarians would hold it, and do. The whole New England school of transcendentalists did, with their opalescent creed. Its classic head is Spinoza, who came to his own a century ago. Without a positive Christianity it becomes pantheist, and not theist, because it destroys the fundamental relation of God to the world as Creator to creature. It promotes a theosophic mysticism detached from positive faith. It makes God at best more of a near presence than a moral historic power. And faith is above mere piety in that it does not think of God's presence so much as of His saving power. Christianity did not come to teach us God's presence, nor merely to convey it. And, above all, the notion, dear as it is to the modern mind, is defective in this, that it discourages the sense of guilt and the miracle of grace. It antiquates the Reformation. Every modern tendency has to be discarded which does that. It loses redemption in evolution. And if a modern idea so great as that of God's immanence in the world be pressed to the denial of God as a self-complete moral person, complete and holy, and not at the mercy of nature and evolution, then the doctrine must be left to the philosophers entirely and the iridescent religionists. It is of no value for morals. It has not the note of redemption. It is even of mischief. And for moral purposes we must turn to a doctrine which the young readily confuse with immanence—the doctrine of Incarnation. Immanence is only philosophic, Incarnation alone is ethical; not because it is human, but because it is seriously human, human in the large and thorough style, *i.e.*, historic. We turn from a doctrine of God's immanence in nature, and especially in human nature, to the doctrine of His Incarnation in a Redeemer from nature and from the moral enmity of its egotism against God. Monism is quite irrelevant to the Christian life, which is not concerned as to how we construe God but how we face Him. For moral life we must have a dualism and a reconciliation, not a monism with a mere identity and continuity. And with monism the preacher has nothing to do, unless he is a philosopher in the wrong place, and a guesser where we want a revealer.

Such at least is the line the Protestant preacher must take, who is more concerned with a gospel than a theosophy, and more engaged with sin than sentiment. His theosophy of immanence will give him but a relative sin, not an absolute—a lapse and not a sin; and therefore it yields but a relative Saviour and not an eternal,

Immanence and Incarnation

who brings an amnesty and not a salvation, who claims from us but a partial devotion and not an entire, and who asserts a kingship more figurative than real. The immanence of God in human nature gives you but the development of the divine in man in unbroken unity—which is a mere philosopheme, absolutely fatal to a gospel, and welcome chiefly either to the half-taught, or to moral minors. I say moral minors, because it is a doctrine which when translated into ethics means determinism, and the extinction of that freedom of will which gives morality any existence.

The doctrine of immanence, taken alone, means, further, that in this process of spiritual evolution every religion has its place, and Christ's place is but on the summit, and on the summit only up till now. As we progress His place may be, probably will be, taken by another. For, whereas the theology of the Gospel teaches that the whole Trinity was involved in revelation and redemption, this theory teaches that the whole and final Godhead was not acting in Christ. You cannot expect the finality of what is merely an evolving series in its middle, but only at its close, which is still far away. God, it believes, has yet more light and truth to break out of our holy race than was contained in Christ. We may yet have what Tyndall used to desiderate—a figure yet to come who should add to the sainthood of Jesus the genius of a Helmholtz and of a Milton. So in Christ we have neither final revelation, absolute guilt, human dignity, nor eternal salvation. All is flattened, diluted, and dispowered. And the cross is but in the nature of things. It is somewhere in the suburbs of Godhead, and not at its centre. Sin, therefore, does not go to God's heart. It does not sting Him mortally. It is not death to God, but a negative factor in His scheme. It does not challenge and kill what makes God God. It does not raise the last issue of humanity, and it does not elicit the last resource of God. It lives in the region of idyll and high-class melodrama. Guilt is not the tragedy of the universe. And indeed wise men do not take things tragically at all. And so they lived happy ever after.

You may lecture about all this with great charm and interest. It is the nemesis of our godless cult of simplicity, due to mental casualness and want of intellectual will in Christian people. But it will not preach. Effective preachers hold it, but it destroys a preaching church. There is not enough moral passion left for preaching. It makes an optimistic, congenial, ethereal, limpid religion:

> O fons *Bland*usiæ, spendidior vitro,
>   Non sine floribus
>   Unde loquaces
> Lymphæ desiliunt tuæ, [1]

but it makes no Gospel, for it demands no grace.

And I will confess that I am more concerned about the effect of this doctrine in erasing the miracle of grace from God's relation with the soul than I am about its discrediting of miracle in God's relations with nature. For the idea of God as immanent love may turn Him into no more than the upper Nature, Nature on a higher plane. He is a striving Nature, which at last experienced the immense relief of complete self-expression in Christ. And that is all that some mean by the satisfaction offered to God in Christ. A pent-up God at last got relief in Christ, and His joy lies in that relief. I need hardly point out that that is a deification of Christ beyond what is claimed by any doctrine of Incarnation known to the Church. The practical result is that our religion, in becoming part of the action of this immanent love, becomes a quite natural thing, and easily drops to a matter of course. Christianity becomes but natural religion highly spiritualized. Its goal is nature refined and not redeemed, saved not from itself but only from its lower self. And our faith loses the sense of wonder.

It has been pointed out that a distinguishing feature of the literature of last century was the revival of the sense of wonder at the world. It seems to me that if it be so in literature, it has been at the cost of religion. The sense of wonder in poetry has been stolen away from faith. The only sense of wonder left in modern religion is a poetic, æsthetic thing; it is not moral. There has passed away from faith that moral amazement and awe which are inseparable from the mystery of grace. It has ceased to be to us a most strange thing that God should love, forgive, and save us. And to-day there is only a minority of Christians whose piety takes the form of standing and overwhelming wonder that God should touch or save *"me."* We wonder at prodigies, and sensations, and a thousand things supplied to us by the news of the day. We wonder at cosmic discoveries and physical imaginations. Our

---

1. ["O fountain of Bandusia, more brilliant than glass, worthy of sweet wine, not without flowers, . . . from where your babbling waters tumble down."]

wonder is plied till it is almost benumbed and we lose the power to wonder. But whether or no it be from a like cause—stupidity from over-feeding, or from the trivializing of grace—we have lost the power to wonder at grace. And we do not marvel, as Christ did, at the hardness of the human heart. It was the one thing unintelligible to Him. We dispute hotly about miracles, and all the time we lose the sense of marvel, because we have lost the sense of grace.

And yet how shall an evangelical faith or pulpit endure, how can it, if in wonder at the universe of God, it lose its wonder at the grace of God—wonder that God should think, and think to such loving, saving purpose, of small and evil me; should have sought me sorrowing, and snatched me to His joy; should have faced for wicked me His own holiness and judgment; should have conquered for good and all the evil power that held me; that He should have borne my judgment, cancelled my guilt, and taken away the sin of the world? It was no theology of immanence that uttered the bold, old cry, *O felix culpa!* O blessed sin, that brought thrice blessed God for its radical damnation.

That is not the work of the immanence of God, the immanence of His world salvation, and His evolving Atonement. Rather is it from His eternal eminence, and His descent on a created world. The mere doctrine of immanence reduces God's action from a historic *moral act* of universal effect to a *cosmic process* extending into the moral world, and, in so far as it is process, destroying ethic. To our moral consciousness grace is not God's emergence from nature to find Himself, and to draw His full eternal breath in Christ It is His invasion of our nature to find us. The faithful Creator, as Redeemer, finds the creature that the mighty Creator has made. And grace alone turns to a Son the Child that love had framed.

It is very curious to note how the critics of an Atonement, as something offered to God (who, they say, needs no such thing), continue in principle that old fallacy. It only shows how little they work principles out. They translate Atonement simply as something offered for saving purposes by man to man. But it is still offered by man. What they do not seem to know is that in a theology of grace, *i.e.*, in Christianity, Atonement has meaning and value only as offered by God to Himself.

In the discussions which abound at present there are two features that may be noted.

1. A cosmological interest is being substituted for a teleological. That is to say, preachers (of all men) are more concerned to read Christianity in the light of theories about the universe than to read it in the light of God's moral purpose with the world, which is redemption in Christ's cross. It is singular to learn that the great need is for ethical restatement of doctrine, when the whole thought moves in semi-physical categories that have no ethical quality. You cannot ethicize religion (certainly not theology) except by starting from the requirements of the supreme ethical category known to us—the holiness of God as Jesus Christ revealed Him.

2. The present conflict in the Church is more critical for Christianity than any that has arisen since the second century. The issue in the Reformation was small beside this. What is at stake is the whole historical character of Christianity. And what is substituted is an ideal Christianity. The position of many (and of some of our ministers) is that the Christ in the unseen to-day is not identical, or not necessarily identical, or continuous, as a personality, with the historic Jesus. The eternal ideal Christ is a divine principle quite separable from its classic instance—the personality of the historic Jesus. The reproduction to-day of the second-century Gnosticism is extremely close, and often startling. There are the same vague speculations, often able, but often also of a pseudo-philosophic and dilettantist kind, welcome to connoisseurs of religion and amateurs of thought[2] rather than to men of faith and due knowledge. There is the same etherealized conception of matter, the same amalgam of physics and dreams, the same animus against historic Christianity. There is not one of the positions or negations, which are ignorantly described as the New Theology, which did not in some form or another burn in the Gnostic age and was not discussed by the first minds of that time and dismissed. It was then that the Church had the first and the greatest fight for its life. If Gnosis had prevailed, the Church and the Gospel would have gone under. And Gnosis means the rationalist, speculative theosophic Doppelgänger of Christianity which works with some

2. I mean among the laity.

of its ideas, plays with its facts, and is indifferent or hostile to its historic finality.

We have really, and often exactly, the same issue to-day as then. And it is equally to-day a question of life and death. Far more is involved than a theology. The worst peril of the time is the number of people who have no power to see that situation, either from geniality of heart, poverty of nature, or lack of training. The whole of the Christian Gospel is involved, the whole future of religion indeed. Let there be no mistake. This is no case of selecting certain views from many which may be held without affecting the prospects of the human soul. It is a case of choosing, I do not say for the choosing individual, but for the Church, for its Gospel, and for society, life or death. If those who think with me are right, the tendencies I allude to mean death. If we are wrong and yet succeed, we mean death to Church and Christianity. If, on the other hand, *they* are wrong, their success means that death. For in its thorough results it is another religion. It is two religions we have at bottom. It is not variants of the same. Before we decide let us clearly and sharply grasp the issue without bland clouds and rosy mists.

There are modifications of the old theology which are demanded by the nature of evangelical faith itself, and there are criticisms of it which do not arise from faith, but from the demand that faith's experience shall submit to be trimmed and even licensed by the pattern of a natural reason organized into a philosophy of the world. It is this latter claim that constitutes a new religion, with which when it comes to the last pinch there can be no terms made by the Church. Christian experience can never consent to be licensed by any philosophy, science, or criticism (however some of its statements may be modified) without adopting another religion in the act. If I am sure that my Redeemer Christ is Jesus, that Jesus is my forgiving Christ, it is a conviction deeper than any other possible; and the conviction which denies that must rest on another religious foundation than Christianity. For Christian faith there is nothing so certain as that. There is no certainty, possessing a certitude which has the right to challenge that. Because our Redeemer is more central than the conscience He saves.

Jesus is the Christ of God. God exalted Jesus to be both Christ and Lord, King to be obeyed, and God to be worshipped. He so saves us that we must worship Him, by that moral necessity in experience which alone gave rise to worship by the whole Church. If He be not such a Christ, but only Christ in such a sense that we are potential Christs; if we have an equal right with Him in the principle which made Him Christ in such a successful degree; if our only right in that principle of divine Sonship is not conferred by Him; then the worship of Him which differentiates Christianity from an enlightened Judaism is idolatry. The historic prophet of our religion becomes one of its great obstacles, not to say corruptions. Jesus becomes the rival and not the revelation of God. And the godly rationalist, who has outlived (I will not say outgrown) his first faith is bound in his prayers to apply to Jesus with a most pathetic poignancy and trembling voice the familiar words:

> The dearest idol I have known,
>   Whatever that idol be,
> Help me to tear it from Thy throne
>   And worship only Thee.[3]

---

3. Cowper, "Walking with God," lines 17–20.

3

The Inner Life of Christ

There are several attitudes taken at the present time to the facts and principles of the Gospel history. To give age its precedence, there are people who still cling to the old style which was after this recipe. First, you procure the raw material. This may be had from any dealer. He will find you the historical fact. He will tell you what you must believe. He will bring it to your *knowledge*. There is of course no religion in that. This some take home and pass it slowly through a sieve, coarse or fine. They give it an attention more or less critical. And then give to what remains, all or part, your assent. There is still no religion. Then you set the material in full or in part to simmer in your mind till you feel a gentle warmth from it. Some let it boil. You receive a certain tonic from its essence of meaning. But as the material is not God but something about God, the religion is defective, however passionate, and it is apt to become a zeal for truth instead of reality. If I may change the metaphor, by the time you have fully examined the fact or truth you may have chilled it down pretty well, and there is a crust of ice on its surface, not without certain forms or designs. As you go on with the treatment which is to crystallize your assent the ice thickens. And one day you decide that it will bear, and you trust yourself to walk on it with great confidence, or, if you are a scholastic theologian, to skate in figures. It is the old sequence of *notitia*, *assensus*, and *fiducia*, whether with orthodox fulness or rationalist reduction. You understand, believe, trust certain things about God. This sequence makes a poor and mechanical account of the psychology of belief; and such a description of the process suffers no wrong in being described as I have done. It is a scheme which is intellectualist, scholastic, and catholicist in its nature, though it was taken over by early Protestantism and still survives in many quarters.

Secondly, there are those who start from the opposite extreme. They are indifferent to historic facts and their burthen of grace. They are content with the impressions that flow from personalities or ideas. Never mind if the personality did not really exist. The story carries an ideal fact if not a historic. It need not seriously matter if behind the idea no reality can be proved to work. We have the value. The aesthetic effect on us, the impressiveness, is all. A myth is held to be as valuable as a fact if it produce the same impression on the soul. The story can serve as a parable, if its historicity be dissolved. Never mind if we lose a historic Jesus so long as we have a living church inspired with the ideas that crystallized in that myth.

Now that is all very well with certain stories, which in their nature are more impressive than creative, and exist more for edification than for regeneration. It may be quite well with some of the early parts of the Old Testament. But it is not well for the redemptive facts to which faith owes its existence, and from which the new life is born. The atonement is not the piece of imagination that the story of the prodigal was. It was not a lesson but a deed. To treat the saving facts as mere symbols is to reduce deeds to words and action to picture. It is to treat impression as if it were faith, and to reduce the Church to masses of moved auditors in the hands of the preaching temperament. But we have to go on and ask if the vivid impression wears. Does it last as long as does creative regeneration working from historic fact? Will it carry a Church? The idea cannot be separated from history when we are dealing with the salvation of history, nor can personality from moral reality. You cannot continue to create moral personality from legends and ideas. If love could live on mythology, faith could not. Love will keep poets going but not apostles, and it will kindle circles but it will not carry a church. The capital of the Church is a faith that works out into love because it is faith in love; and faith as a moral power can only rise from revealed fact, from love in action, not from fictitious persons nor from imposing ideas.

Thirdly, there are those who take a middle course. They pursue a criticism not merely critical but constructive. They are not critical only but historical. They recognize the central and creative value of fact. And what they do is to prune and not to fell. They work by reduction. They trim down the record to a nucleus of fact like Schmiedel's nine pillars of Christian belief. To such residuum they refer faith. There is but the ground-floor left of the Gospel record after the bombardment, and they occupy it—believing they thus keep close to the street and the man in it.

Their procedure keeps a reminiscence of the first group. Let us become convinced of a body of fact, or its biographical truth, even if it is but a minimum, and then let us devote ourselves to it. They do not all do this on the same scale as Orthodoxy but the course is not very different. The first thing is historical substantiation; and faith must wait till that is done by us or for us. They ignore the psychological fact that religious faith does not wait on logical process, that belief rests on much more than evidence as its authority, that its intellectual assent is wrapped up in emotional thought and floats suspended in the act of faith itself. They also ignore the fact that the original Christ was not so much an object of men's knowledge as a power that first knew them; that He was not simply an object of attention but from the first was inseparable from the power that made them attend and gave to their attention vision; that He was more the Creator than the recipient of the faith of His apostles; that the real Christ was first the Christ in action and then the Christ preached, and not the Christ remaining at the end of an analysis. He began as the Christ of faith and not of knowledge. And so He still begins. Our knowledge of Him is not an antecedent of our faith but a factor in it, not a mere cause but an ingredient. Christian thought is emotional thought, moral thought, thought suspended in an experience of something else than thinking. It is implicit in the religious response, in the moral committal, in the experience of the conscience. It is not the parent of faith—although neither is it its handmaid; it is its twin sister at least. That is the difference between committal to a scheme we must first examine and committal to a Person to whom we leap or move by a great surmise in the act of committal, whom we know as we trust Him and to whom we give our love before we realize how worthy He is of it. We must love Him ere He seem worthy of our love. No foundation which is merely historic will carry a faith certain, absolute, and eternal, a faith in which the soul is committed for its eternity, because the results of historic investigation can at no stage be called quite final. They are always revisable. And the Person of Christ which is to be the foundation of living faith must be something else than the residuary legacy of historic research. He must come to us in a more living and sacramental way, as the Christ of the creative Cross comes. And this can never be done by Christ as a calm, sane, noble but statuesque personality or presence, however attractive, fine, or ideal. We must found anything so real as eternity on a historic fact; but on one too creative of history to be given by history alone. We cannot found on the mere impressiveness of such a fact, on its value to us apart from questions of its reality. Such impression is not the chief work of the Spirit. It must have in it a more regenerative and creative power. Is the Cross but an affecting expression of Christ's person; or is it the nature, genius, ground plan, the constitutive principle and formative purpose of it? Is it the last action of reality on reality? It is one of the banes of religion that it becomes more impressive than real.

The fourth way is more religious and less academic than the other three. It treats the object of faith as more of a living thing. It does not begin with our critical action on inert fact at arm's length as it were, but with the action of the living fact on us. It does not begin with Him as a mere object of common knowledge, nor as a residue of critical science. It does not wait to feel Christ till it has proved Christ. Its fact is the inner life of Christ, which does not emerge from critical methods, is not at their mercy, and leaves faith immune from their results. This, it is said, is the reality on which faith stands. This is what elicits faith, creates it. The figure pictured in the Gospels steps from its frame, and lays hold of us, winds its way into us, and makes abode with us. It convinces us of its reality, not prior to our faith, but in the act of creating it.

Now, we have here something that seems to deliver faith from a rationalist license to exist. The object of faith proves itself in making the faith. We have a worthy psychology of belief, a religious one. We are on right lines.

But is it certain that even here we have really escaped from the ban of impressionism? It is doubtful if we have really got a faith which is more than aesthetic, which is ethical enough to overcome the world. Have we more than a profound impression of Christ's

The Inner Life of Christ

personality, an impression so ethical, so intimate that it seems final religion? Have we here created a real evangelical trust in Him as Redeemer? And by real I mean a trust which disposes of our whole personality to Him, and masters, redeems and renews the whole world forever. I mean a faith which is a self-committal forever and not a mere venture. Is our faith faith in a redemption which can be treated as at bottom a new creation? We have delightful books which aim at a sympathetic or a romantic psychology of Christ; they teem with happy stories with the conjectural freshness of a vivid mind, reading between the lines of the record, but missing the roar of the buried stream and the force of its pressure at the Cross which altered the configuration of the world. Indeed some disfigure their work, otherwise able and engaging, by letting themselves gird at those theologians who work at such fundamental constructions below the garden beds and *aperçus*. Does the whole person of Christ run up into the Cross and its crucial effect? Is it there for redemption's sake?

Of all the German theologians on the liberal side, Herrmann, whose view I have been describing, is the one whose theology is most bound up with personal religion; but does Herrmann get to the core of evangelical faith as a revolutionary power, the world-power and the last power? What does he mean by the inner life of Christ? The very inmost life of Christ we cannot get at. For it was lived in the closest communion of the Son with His Father alone. None can tell what passed in those nights of prayer. None could hear. Could we understand if we were told the communion of the eternal Father and Son? But leaving that as inaccessible, and keeping to what would usually be understood as Christ's inner life, what was it? We get glimpses of the contour of His thought. All His teaching was more or less autobiographical. What was its paradigm? What was its note? What was it that filled His consciousness? It was not a mere sense of His personality—that were too egoist. Nor of the presence and blessing of the Father—that were but saintly. It was more than a piety, it was a purpose, and one mystically moral, national, and historic. You should not speak of the Jesus of history unless you treat His problem as first national. Seek first the Kingdom of God, He said. And His precepts, as I say, are autobiography. He did not prescribe what he did not do. The Kingdom of God engrossed Him. It was His first concern always in life and death. It was the keynote of His theology as it must become of ours. Round it gathered His profoundest piety, but also much more. The effect it produced in Him was more than devoutness of the first water. Allowing that He gave His inner self to us, that was not as man gives himself to man, and friend dominates friend. It was *for* us, more than *to* us. It was as the King gives Himself for the Kingdom, the Redeemer for His people. The Person that comes to us is not simply a spiritual splendour, a divine benediction, a moral boon, in the highest degree sympathetic, impressive or revelationary, but He is redemptive, He is creative. He is regenerative. He does the royal thing and not just the kindly thing. He forgives. He does not simply get the revelation home to a native religiosity, but He redeems us into the power of taking it home. There is a new creation. And all in virtue of what the Gospels show to have been Christ's first charge. His prime concern was with the Holy Father King, with the delighting, the satisfying, of Him. He it was that filled the Saviour's thought at the end—He rather than man, He and what was owed to Him. All benefit to man was in virtue of an atoning death to God. The Kingdom was not simply righteousness, joy, or peace as subjective frames, but as social relations between the members of the community rising out of the kingship of God (See the exegesis of Romans 14:17). It was a moral standing with God, and a moral relation to each other, no less than a subjective and personal piety. It was also the destruction of the Prince of this World no less than it was the power of our eternal life. The Kingdom was something which was set up for good and all in the Cross, by a finished work corresponding to the complete holiness and energy of His person. The holy kingship of sovereignty was met by an equally holy kingship of subordination. It was such a Cross that came to fill and make the inner mind of Christ—the Cross not just as the principle of sacrifice but as the power of the Kingdom of God and its redemption,

Herrmann, it has been pointed out, has put us on the right question—what is the inner mind of Christ as a fact and a power, and not only as a consciousness—as a power to be owned and not simply as a character to be sympathetically met? What was His purpose, His lifework, His goal? What did He come to do with all that it was in Him to be? What was the act on which His whole mind constantly and growingly crystallized? Was it a case simply of coming in, and sitting down, and supping with us severally to our great refreshment and cheer? The gift from God is Christ of course. Also it is Christ's gift of Himself. But of Himself as what? As the chief of saints? The prince of sages? The heavenliest of friends? The divinest of benedictions? The holiest of influences? Did He do anything decisive for us, or did He just infuse us with His personality in the way of intercourse? Did He act chiefly in a redemptive or only in a sacramental way? Does He just walk with us always unharmed amid the world's flames? Does He but hold our hand as we die unto the world? What was the active mind, the purposed consciousness of Christ, the deed into which the whole personality went? There is something in Herrmann to suggest in Christ a fixed quantity, if we may so say, a vivid, vital, but closed personality, with a place for us—the Father's house with many mansions—or a power in us. And there is too little to suggest His atoning work and His new creative power. There is not enough to suggest, as part of His work and conquest, the growth of His personality in realizing and facing the necessity not of sacrifice merely but of an atoning Cross as the end closed in on Him. Herrmann is anxious to meet the crux of the hour and to deliver faith from a dependence on the critics—so anxious that he thinks the inner life of Christ lays hold of us in a way which secures our soul though the recorded facts may crumble like the sacramental bread. Indeed the whole value of Christ for him seems more sacramental than creative. Christ as a personality seizes us so mightily that this capture may be called the redemptive thing, and we become immune from any trouble from the questions raised about the outer detail in the tradition of Him. Herrmann says the redemptive value is in the whole inner life, and not in any particular in the story of it. If he had said not in every particular, one could but agree. But, as Hunziger notes, it is another matter to say not in *any* particular of the story. That gives away too much to the mystics, who are only too ready to detach revelation from history and from a crucial redemption. Of course the vital thing is the Person of Christ in His action. There we found. But we do not found in a Person independent of every fact in His story; not in a Person that could survive their dissolution; not in a Person whose efficacy (like a parable) quite transcended His actuality, and whose power sat loose to soluble events associated with it. For if we press an independence like that we must be prepared to say that the *cross* just falls into line with the other facts; that, like any one of these, it too might be otiose; that there could be a revelation of God which was mere exhibition, or mere impression, without definite and decisive action on the moral universe; that the Cross, as the consummation of such action, especially on God (as in prayer), did not run implicit through the whole inner life of Christ, and swiftly grow upon it, and grow more deeply engaged in it; that the element of action upon the last reality of things was to that extent lacking, and was not supplied, as moral redemption requires it, by those beneficent activities of Christ's which survive criticism, like the miracles of healing.

So we have a fifth attitude to the historic fact, in which, while it is not only not inert for our observation but active for our impression, it is active in the way not of mere impression but of regeneration, of new creation.

There are historic facts which can be verified in our own experience, and there are those that cannot. The latter would be represented by the Virgin Birth, the former by the Cross and the Resurrection. We can say we have met with the risen Christ, or that in the Cross so crowned God has spoken and dealt with us in a way more certain than all else. And these facts, so verifiable in the religious experience, differ very widely indeed from the other facts in history, even in Christ's history, as man differs vitally from all the career of Nature before him. They come from the last interior of His life, and they go to the centre of ours. They unload on us the grand burthen and purpose of His soul. He poured out His soul unto that death. All the current of His being came to a head and issued there as in no other act of His whatever, and certainly as in no word of His. His soul had a history and not only a being, not only a vitality. His inmost self was ever more deeply elicited by events. It had a drama, a conflict mounting to a real close. It was acted on by circumstances, and it reacted on them; and in the double process it found itself. In a real sense He proved and found His soul and with it the whole moral world. He discovered what was in Him. He was born to die, and constituted by His very holiness to atone. And this came home to Him, always infallibly, but always more and more perfectly, as He passed deeper into the tragedy of the conflict. And it was action that was drawn forth from His last depths. Cross and Resurrection did not just happen to Him, they were done by Him as the consummation of all else. They make Christ Christ for us. They make Him God for us. They are what faith seizes as the creative source and power of the new life. They give us our certainty. And remember, the question is as to that certainty. Therefore it is not a scientific question but a moral. It is not a question of psychology but of conscience. Religion needs less to be psychologized than moralized. It is not a question of the way faith rises in time, but of what gives faith final and eternal foundation. And the real foundations of the universe are in the moral region. There we touch the last reality. And chiefly we do so in the greatest and most universal of all the moral acts known to us—in the atonement of an unholy world by a perfectly holy God in His perfectly holy Son. It is in the meeting of God's holiness by a holiness equal to His own. That is the foundation of all ethic as of all religion. Whatever in the tradition shakes this must not. It could not, without bringing to the ground at last the whole fabric of Christian faith. The detachment of religion from its centre in a real atonement is what most impairs the note of Christian ethic. That atonement makes Christianity a religion apart, and not only the superlative of all religion. Lighted by the Resurrection it was what gave all the rest of Christ's life meaning to the disciples, whom it translated into Apostles. The Gospels are not biographies, not *memorabilia*; they are *Leidensgeschichten*.[1] They preach the gospel of Redemption. They crystallize on the Cross. They make all Christ's inner life full of such crucial meaning to the Church and to the world as no other man's nor indeed the whole of history can be. He would of course have been eminent without Cross and Resurrection, but not divine, not saving, not of equal and final value for all men. He would have been a splendid figure but not an eternal Saviour, a glorious example but not inimitably creative—the prince of saints but not the King of the Kingdom of God, the Lord of a New Humanity He called into being. He would not have lifted the world out of its impotence and its alienation from God. His life would not have been lived *for* us so much as *before* us, with an effect more aesthetical than ethical. He would have been man's spiritual jewel, our Morning Star—displayed as a glory more than

1. ["tales of woe."]

felt as a power or worshipped as Lord; but He would not have been our atonement. He would not have been Redeemer, however priceless a gift and possession. His mere inner life, however it impressed or exalted us, could never by itself have redeemed us. He would have idealized all sacrifice, and put on it a divine seal, but He would not have made His sacrifice the very act of God as our Saviour. And that is what we need really—not simply redemption *to* God but *by* God. It is in His death that God Himself with certainty speaks to us, redeems us, and works on us the new life. Christ's inner life impresses us so much only because His death makes it do more. It makes it all converge to redeem and regenerate us. And it does that because it did justice to the God we had wronged. That inner life becomes the slow emergence and rising action of the Cross of our atonement. The whole history of Christ's soul if it is studied historically, *i.e.*, nationally, without the importations of our too modern idealisms, or our too subjective piety, shows a growing detachment from action on men and a growing concentration on action on God. It shows a retreating consideration for men's claims behind a preoccupation with God's. Till at the close it was God, and what was due to God, that engrossed Him. God's need of His death threw into the shade even man's need. And the moral necessity to atone became the first condition of His power to recreate.

We should realize that the inner life of Jesus was not a thing stationary in its intense movement, like a teeming or a revolving globe. It was nothing which descends on us in a finished form as a closed personality from the very first. Personality is not mere individuality. It is a thing that does not come with us but grows in us; and it had a growth in Him as He deepened and rose to the fulness of His true vocation, and from prophet became priest. There He came to His real self. The inmost life of Jesus was, through His growing experience, always coming to the top, finding its final self, and ripening to a goal of action. I have said that we could not reach the inmost life of Jesus in His midnight communion with God. I should not however stop there. We have indeed no express information about it. He was not of the kind to proclaim such hours, and make them common. To preach a full and free salvation is not to unload our secret soul to the man in the street or in the stye. But we do get a hint as to the nature of some such seasons in the story of the Transfiguration. There He spoke of the theme of His most interior and uplifted mind in contact with heaven; and it was of the decease He should accomplish at Jerusalem. And on Calvary, and there only, we do reach His last spiritual reserves. That sacrifice, that atonement, was what was always the dominant in His soul, even if in the early stages its full significance may have been below the level of His explicit experience and consciousness. His inner life was not stationary. It was not intense only in its rotation or its fertility. But it was the gradual growth in clearness, depth, and power, of the conviction that the Cross would not only be His fate but was the requirement of God, was above all an offering to God, and needed by God more than by man. It was giving to God His own. He did not meet it till He accepted it; and He did not accept it till He was sure of that, sure of the divine δεῖ in it. And He was not perfectly sure till the very end. He was not without hope His Father might find another way. "If it be possible." Martyrdom He may have expected early in His public life but to die as the atonement God required for the hardened people, and so for the world—that was not early. The murder of John impressed Him with the conviction that death would be His fate, and sent Him to Jerusalem to force the issue and, with little hope, to force the nation to its last choice. As He lost hope in the people, as He failed as prophet, He poured out His Soul to God as priest. He gained power with God. That His death was needed by God as atonement was the conviction of the passion; and its offering was His consummation, the consummation of His person as well as of His vocation, the effectuation of His inner life, of all He was. He did not start with the Cross in a clear programme. How could His appeal to the nation have been *bona fide* if He was sure from the first it was all to be in vain. He had in Him not the programme of the Cross but the principle, which matured in the way great principles do, as the pressure of events and experience forced it out. The inner life of Christ was not so much a living forth of the Cross as a living *on* to the Cross, and to the Cross not as the sacrificial principle of life and being for great souls everywhere, but as the crucial atonement to God by His Son for a nation and a world that inflicted it as a doom and refused it as a redemption.

4

Forgiveness through Atonement the Essential of Evangelical Christianity

One of the acutest problems of the church at this moment is that raised by the pressure of the critical method upon the New Testament. It is not only to apply to the New Testament the criticism which has been so fruitful with the Old Testament. That is intricate enough, and much more intricate for the New Testament than for the Old Testament. But the problem is more than intricate. It is profound and spiritual. It comes nearer than Old Testament problems do to the centre of the soul, the word of conscience, the essence of faith, and our eternal hope. It is to apply criticism to the New Testament, regardful of the fact that we have there what we do not have in the Old Testament. We have everything clustering round a historic personality, with whom the soul is in direct and living communion to-day, and a final and eternal act of God as the consummation of that personality—an act which fundamentally altered the whole moral relation of the race to Him. We have to do in the New Testament with the person of Christ and with the cross of Christ. And in the last issue with the cross of Christ because it is the one key to his person.

In approaching this subject let us be clear about our starting point. In our modern psychology we start from the primacy of the will, and we bring everything to the test of man's practical and ethical life. And so, here also we start ethically from the holiness of God as the supreme interest in the Christian revelation. The standpoint taken throughout is that which I believe to be the position of the New Testament. That book represents a grand holiness movement; but it is one which is more concerned with God's holiness than ours, and lets ours grow of itself by dwelling on his. Christianity is concerned with God's holiness before all else; which issues to man as love, acts upon sin as grace, and exercises grace through judgment. The idea of God's holiness is inseparable from the idea of judgment as the mode by which grace goes into action. And by judgment is meant not merely the self-judgment which holy grace and love stir in man, but the acceptance by Christ of God's judgment on man's behalf and its conversion in him to our blessing by faith.

By the atonement, therefore, is meant that action of Christ's death which has a prime regard to God's holiness, has it for its first charge and finds man's reconciliation impossible except as that holiness is divinely satisfied once for all on the cross. Such an atonement is the key to the incarnation. We must take that view of Christ which does most justice to the holiness of God.

So viewed the atonement is central:—

I. To the New Testament Gospel (Harnack);

II. To the leading features of modern thought;

III. To Christian experience.

I shall reserve II. for treatment elsewhere as being perhaps less suitable for an occasion like the present.

And by centrality is meant something far more than that the doctrine is the pivot of an adjusted and balanced system of thought, something much more vital and effective for moral life and the life of the soul. By centrality is meant finality for human history and destiny. It is meant that when Jesus died for our sins he died once for all, that he did not merely signalise in a classic way the expiation all must dree, and illustrate and cheer every man's atonement for his own misdeeds. It is meant beyond that, first, that in the atonement we have primarily the act of God, and the act of God's holiness; second, that it alone makes any repentance or expiation of ours satisfactory to God; and third, that as regards man it is a revolutionary act, and not merely a stage in his evolution. It is further meant that our view of what Christ was and did, must be the view that does most justice to the holiness of God and takes most profoundly and seriously the hallowing of his name.

A true grasp of the atonement, not only meets many positive features of the present age, but above all it meets the age in its need and impotence, its need of a centre, of an authority, of a creative source, a guiding line, and a final goal. It goes with our best positive tendencies and it meets our negative need, our lack of a fixed point. All around us is in a growing flux; change is everywhere; and it may or may not be development according as our fixed standard and goal may be. With no centre, either for its own action or for our estimate, it means disintegration. And especially does our religion need a moral centre. It grows on the one hand evolutionary, and therefore inevitably unearnest; and on the other hand sentimental. It harps on love till it reaches the condition of those decently demoralised people who read nothing but the literature of love, dwell on nothing else, slacken every moral fibre by the submission to this of every other interest in life, and finally gravitate to a chief interest in its morbid or immoral forms. Fraternity grows at the cost of fidelity, the democratic sympathies and pities monopolise the moral world, the moral type changes, another scale of virtues fills the ideal. "Among the working class," says Miss Loane from a long experience as district nurse, "generosity ranks before justice, sympathy before truth, love before chastity, a pliant and obliging disposition before a rigidly honest one. In brief," she continues, "the less admixture of intellect required for the practice of any virtue the higher it stands in the popular estimation." But what does that mean but the retreat of the protestant type of life before the Roman, of the evangelical virtues before the catholic, of heroic faith before humanist, of Paul before Pelagius. It means the removal of authority from a positive centre in Christ's redeeming act to what I might call a diffused centre in the church, from a new moral man once for all in the cross to the man periodically renewed in kindly sacraments. What is lacking to current and weak religion is the very element supplied in the atoning cross as the reconciling judgment of the world.

That is the general theme which I would enlarge.

I

In regard to Christ's cross, and within the New Testament, we are to-day face to face with a new situation. We are called upon, sometimes in the tones of a religious war, to set Jesus against Paul and to choose. We are bidden release him from Paul's arrest, to raise him from that tomb in which he was buried by the apostle of the resurrection, and loose him and let him go. The issue comes to a crisis in the interpretation of the death of Christ. To treat that death as more than a martyrdom, or to allow it more than a supreme degree of the moral effect upon us of all self-sacrifice, is called a gratuitous piece of theology. To treat it as anything more than the seal of Jesus's own faith in the love of God, or in his prophetic message of reconciliation is to sophisticate. To regard it as more than the closing incident in a life whose chief value lies in its history (which all the time criticism slowly dissolves), is a piece of perverse religious ingenuity much like the doctrine of Transubstantiation. To regard it as having anything to do with God's judgment on man's sin, or as being the ground of forgiveness, is a piece of grim Judaism or gloomy Paulinism. The death of Jesus had no more to do with sin than the life of Jesus; and Jesus in his life made no such fuss about sin as Christianity has done. The death of Jesus had really no more to do with the conditions of forgiveness than one of Fox's martyrs. Every man must make his own atonement; and Jesus did the same, only on a scale corresponding to the undeniable greatness of his personality, and impressive accordingly.

Such teaching removes Christ from the Godhead of grace and makes him but the chief means of grace. It is not ours. In my humble judgment it is quite foreign to Congregationalism, and incompatible with it. For a Congregational church is not a band of disciples or inquirers, but a community of believers, confessors, and regenerates in Christ's cross. Congregationalism, as an evangelical body, has stood, and stands, not only for the supreme value of Christ's death, but for its prime value as atonement to a holy God, and as the only atonement whereby man is just with God. The atonement which raises that death above the greatest martyrdom, or the greatest witness of God's love, is for us no piece of Paulinism.

Of course, we have all felt the reticence of the Gospels on that doctrine. But how can we avoid feeling its real presence in them except by coming to them with a dogmatic humanism, or a heckling criticism, or a conscience mainly æsthetic. Why one of the most advanced New Testament scholars in America is, I believe, at work on a book to prove that the main interest of St. Mark is not biographical, but dogmatic on such matters as baptism and atonement. The Gospels stand at least on the atoning deed, they were written for a church created by it, and they give singular space to it. Even in John, Jesus is not a disguised God urging people to pierce his veil; he is there to do a work that only his death could do, as a corn of wheat must die to bear. And the Epistles are full of the meaning of that deed.

And where did their interpretation of its meaning come from? From Paul's rabbinism? From the Judaism of his upbringing? From the fanciful speculations of his environment? Was it an interpretation or an importation? Well, where does Paul himself say he got the atoning conception of Christ's death? He received it from the Lord? What does that mean? Was it really but some flash of insight peculiar to his own genius or his idiosyncrasy. Was it a feat of ingenious interpretation? No doubt it took, in certain lights, the colour of his rabbinic mind, but was it in essence just an original and daring application of Judaic theology to the crucifixion? Was it a brilliant construction whose flash he mistook for a special revelation? No, in its substance it was a part of the Christian instruction which completed his conversion at Damascus. It was from his teachers that he had the atoning interpretation of Christ's death. He delivered to his churches what he received among the fundamentals (ἐν πρώτοις) from earlier Christians, that Christ died for our sins, that his blood was shed for their remission, that his death set up a new relation or covenant between God and man, and that all Israel's history and Bible meant this. In the year 57, that is, he states that such was the common faith of the apostolic community when he was converted, three or four years after Christ's death. It was nothing he developed or edited, but it was something which came from Jesus himself. Paul received it from the Lord because it came to him from those who had so received it at first.

And how came the apostolic circle to have this view of Christ's death? Could *they* have foisted on the cross an interpretation so audacious? Must they not have been taught by Christ so to view it, in such words as are echoed in the ransom passage and at the Last Supper? We have the same idea, with natural enough variants, in Peter, in John, and in Hebrews. No; the first teacher of the

Forgiveness through Atonement

atonement was the Christ who made it. It is no Paulinism, except in certain side lights. Had the apostles held the humanist view that what mattered was but the life, character and teaching of Christ, would they have given the hand of fellowship to Paul when he came to them with the view that these mattered little compared with Christ's death? Would Paul have taken their hand, with that gulf between them. And what a gulf! It is at bottom all the gulf between the Judaism which killed Christ as Beelzebub and the Christianity which found in his death his deity. The whole history of the church shows that there can be no standing unity of faith or spirit between those to whom Christ's death is but a great martyrdom and those to whom it is the one atonement of the world and God, the one final treatment of sin, and the one compendious work of grace.

We have been warned against the idea that Christ taught about himself or his work as an essential element of his own Gospel. We are told that he is detachable from his Gospel, if not in history yet in principle. We received it through him, to be sure, but we do not necessarily have it in him. But let us leave the question whether he taught himself, and go back to the prior question. Is the Gospel, is Christianity, primarily what Jesus taught? Is that the whole Gospel? Is it the focus of it? Or the standard? Is the Gospel confined to the Galilean ministry? Are we to test every teaching of an apostle by what is left us of the teaching of the Master—either by that alone or by that in chief? Where in the New Testament do we find the authority for that limitation. Where does Jesus impose it? It is surely clear that those he taught never understood him so. If they had, could they have done anything else than go about retailing that teaching, with a lament at its premature arrest? But is that what they did? The prime thing, and the earliest thing, we know about their teaching (I have just said) is that Christ crowned Israel by dying for our sins. It has not the note of regret, nor the note of transmitted precept. When precepts were wanted they made new ones for the occasion, on the free evangelical principle, and not on the canonist. They applied the redemption to particular junctures freely, in the spirit; they did not make a casuistic application of Christ's maxims. They did not attack Jew or Gentile even with the parables. James himself, who might have been expected to abjure the Pauline method, and take the strictly ethical line, does not draw his precepts from the armoury of synoptic injunction, or treat Christ as the Chief Rabbi of Israel. Nay, they did not even work with the mere personal impression made on them by Jesus, with the magnetism of a personality whose acts or whose words another Rabbi might criticise. They worked with his person as itself the message, and the final message, with a faith which was not a piece of impressionism but the worship of their new creator, which therefore did not fade as an impression does, but grew as a new life. Whether Christ taught himself or not, what he gave, what he left behind, was himself above all; and himself as no mere impressionist but as the Saviour, the New Creator. His legacy was neither a truth nor a collection of them, nor a character and its imaginative memory, but a faith that could not stop short of giving him the worship reserved by all the past for God alone. And what did this? It was the cross, when it came home by the resurrection through the Spirit. It was then that Jesus became the matter and not merely the master of gospel preaching, then that he became Christ indeed, then when he became perfected! Perfected! He became the finished Saviour only in the finished salvation. And, for those who worshipped him first, all he was to them centred in the cross and radiated from there. It was he who was made sin for them in the cross that became for them God reconciling the world to himself. He was all to them in the cross, where he died for their sin, and took away the guilt of the world, according to their Scriptures. It was then that he finished the universal task latent in their national religion, and dealt once for all before God with the sin of the world. That was the starting point of the Gospel; that made it missionary, made the church; and it is the content of the Gospel. And it is always to there that the church must come back, to take its bearings, and be given its course.

The very silence of Christ makes his atonement the holiest place of Christian faith. But it was not absolute silence. It was reserve. And he broke it in Paul. The exposition in the Epistles is the Saviour's own work upon his work. He becomes his own divine scholiast. If he lived in Paul submerging Paul (Gal 2:20) then Paul's word here was a continuation of Christ's work. It is Christ giving that account of himself which in the Gospels was restrained, partly for want of an audience that could understand or a disciple that could apprehend. His silence is not so surprising.

Forgiveness through Atonement

If he showed himself after his resurrection only to the disciples, if he refused to make it a miraculous appeal to the sceptical world, so, in the still holier matter of his cross, he may well have been reserved, even to his own. The great doers are greatly dumb. And Christ was straitened in the doing of the mighty work. But his church—it is no wonder that his church has been prompt to praise it, keen to pierce, and eager to construe it. For the church is the organ which cannot but speak and praise when the Master's silent touch on the keys sets free its soul.

It is sometimes said that the great question of the hour for the church's belief is Christological; it is the question of Christ's person. That is true. But it is the question of the cross all the same. For the question of the Christ is the question of the Saviour. It is not a metaphysical question, but a religious. It is not philosophical, but experimental. It is theological chiefly as being ethical—as turning on sinful man's practical relation to the ethic of eternity, which is the conscience of a Holy God. The question of Christ is not the question of a divine hypostasis, but of a divine Saviour. Technically spoken, the Christology turns on a soteriology.

But the question of a Saviour is the question of a salvation. It turns not only on an experience, and the experience of a historic person, but upon what is for us a *revolutionary* experience and not a mere impression, however deep. The sot*erology* turns on a soter*iology*. The centre of Christ is where the centre of our salvation is. He is Christ, he is God, to us in that he saves us. And he is Christ by that in him which saves us. He is Christ and Lord by his cross. Christian faith is our life-experience of complete and final forgiveness in Christ. It does not *include* forgiveness; It *is* forgiveness. Its centre is the centre of forgiveness. Only the redeemed church, the church that knows the forgiveness, has the key to the Saviour. His blessings are the key to his nature; they do not wait till the nature is first defined. No philosopher, as such, has the key, no theologian, no scholar, no critic; only the believer, only the true church. And we have it where the evangelical experience has always found its forgiveness—in the cross. Our faith begins with the historic Christ. But not with the biography of Christ (except for propædeutic purposes). We begin, in principle if not in method, with Christ the crucified. Not with a writer's picture of Christ the prophet but with the work of Christ the Saviour, continuous in the church it made, and made the mother of our own soul. Mere historic knowledge can create no salvation; which is not given by certainty about a historic fact, nor by any intelligent grasp of it, but by faith in it, in that within it which is superhistoric. And faith finds in this fact of the cross worlds more than a prophet's martyrdom. It finds the depth of God, and not merely the depth of the martyr's convictions. The Christ that we trust all to is not one who died to witness for God, but one in whom God died for his own witness, and his own work on us. God was in Christ reconciling. The prime doer in Christ's cross was God. Christ was God reconciling. He was God doing the very best for man, and not man doing his very best before God. The former is evangelical Christianity, the latter is humanist Christianity. Christ's history, his person, can only be understood by his work, and by a work we apprehend in our moral experience even when we cannot comprehend it by our intelligence. We believe with the unity of our person much that we cannot yet reduce to logical unity. And our soul, our self, finds itself in him long before our mind does—just as, in the case of his own life, he but gradually appropriated and realised by experience the content of his own personality. The Christ we worship is Christ as forgiver, as redeemer, new creator, and judge of all. His relation to the God of thought is something we can wait for; it is a question of the metaphysic, or the theosophy, of Christian faith and ethic. But the church's belief in the divinity of Christ is the result of her experience of justifying faith, of being restored and raised into the communion of God by union with His Christ in faith. To be united with Christ is, in our experience, to be united with God. Therefore, Christ is God. I am redeemed in Christ, and only God can redeem.

Our chief legacy from the past is distance and alienation from God. The chief problem of the present (and of every present) is to reduce and destroy that. It is reconciliation. But reconciliation is no æsthetic, or educational, or impressionist affair. It is not a revival. It is not a question of moving a certain number of individuals, and gathering them for salvation out of a lost mankind. It cannot be done by a magnetic temperament, a noble character, or a lofty sage. It means changing a race's relation to God. We have to be redeemed into that reconciliation, and redeemed as a race. It is a work that has to be done, and not merely a personal influence that has to be conveyed. Christ did not die simply to affect men but to effect salvation, not simply to move man's heart but to accomplish God's will. It is all the following up of a great and final deed—the cross.

It is the cross, then, that is the key to Christ. None but a Christ essentially divine could do what the church beyond all other knowledge knows the cross to have done for its soul. The divinity of Christ is what the church was driven to to explain the effect on it of the cross, the new creation, so much deeper than any impression on us, and calling for an author so much more than prophetic in soul. The atonement of the cross is the key that opens the door, but the house we enter is not made with hands. It is the very heart of God. We are not landed in a vestibule but straight in the sanctuary of the place. This Son of God is God the Son.

II

In the life of Dr. Dale it is mentioned that in his closing years he was much impressed with the remark of a friend that it was high time the word grace returned to our preaching. He felt that it had been ousted by the word love, in our vehement reaction from theological orthodoxy. And he knew that any gospel of love which was not dominated by the idea of grace had but a short and feckless life before it.

Now, though the idea of grace has returned to our preaching, it has not returned to an extent that would have satisfied Dr. Dale. And one reason for that is that the attention of the Christian public in the interval has been deflected. It has been deflected towards social sympathies, at the cost of personal experimental and I will say ethical religion. At the cost of ethical religion, I will say. For we have lost the sense of sin, which is the relation of the conscience to the conscience of God. And apart from sin grace has little meaning. The decay of the sense of sin measures our loss of that central Christian idea; and it is a loss which has only to go on to extinguish Christianity.

It is reported from most quarters in England that there is a serious decline in church membership. For this several explanations are given. But it is well to face the situation, and to avoid extenuation. And if we do, we should admit to ourselves frankly that the real cause is the decay, not in religious interests or sympathies, but in personal religion of a positive and experienced kind, and often in the pulpit. Religious sympathies or energies are not Christian faith. Faith is Christian certainty. We have become familiar with the statement (so welcome to easy religion) that there is as good Christianity outside the churches as in. This is not quite false, but it is more false than true. It would be true enough if Christianity meant decent living, nice ways, precious kindness, business honour, ardent philanthropy, and public righteousness. But all these fine and worthy things are quite compatible with the absence of personal faith as Christ claims it, in the sense of personal experience of God in Jesus Christ, personal repentance, and personal peace in Christ as our eternal life. Yet that is God's first charge on us. And it is the kind of Christianity which alone makes for a church and its membership. A Christianity merely ethical, refined, or sympathetic certainly makes for the social state, if you can keep it up; but the Christianity that makes for the church is of a much more intimate, personal, and positive kind. And its absence must not only diminish the roll of membership but reduce interest in the great religious issue between church and state. The reports that come in are as clear about the cooling of that interest as they are about the drop in the membership of the churches. My diagnosis is that both are due to a decay of membership in Christ. Our social preoccupation has entailed real damage to personal and family religion. For even among those who remain in active membership of our churches the type of religion has changed. The sense of sin can hardly be appealed to by the preacher now, and to preach grace is in many even orthodox quarters regarded as theological obsession, and the wrong language for the hour, while justification by faith is practically obsolete. Well, it may be wise not to preach about grace, but it is fatal if that is because we do not have it, instead of because we reserve it, if the reason be of truth and not of its economy.

I know what is said in reply, and it is said with much force. It is said that the sense of sin has not departed but has only changed its form. We are more dull to individual sin because we are more alive to social sin. We have public compunction instead of personal repentance.

To that remark I would answer two things.

First. Public compunction does not move to seek forgiveness, which is the prime righteousness of the kingdom of God, but to pursue redress and reform. And redress and reform is not what makes Christianity. Christianity is a religion of redemption, but that is a religion of amelioration or assuagement. It is engrossed with the wrong done to our brother and not to our God, and it is therefore to that extent the less religious.

But second. The tendency is welcome in so far as this, that we cannot stop there. The more public it makes the sin, the more social and racial, so much the more does it drive us upon a treatment of sin which is ethical and not temperamental, racial as well as personal, and not only racial but divine. Now there is no treatment of it which satisfies these demands of the soul, the conscience, society, and God, but the atonement in Christ's cross. In the old juridical theories the social, or racial, aspect of the atonement, its connexion with the moral order, is one of the great truths. And the more these theories become unsatisfactory on other grounds the more should their social sense of sin be developed in terms of modern society. But then the more sin is socialised so much the more imperative becomes the necessity of an atonement. As man grows the sin grows, our sin becomes unified, organised, and must therefore be dealt with at a centre. The social organism has a common and organic sin. And a collective sin must have a central treatment. The more I lament and amend social wrongs the more I must realise before God the responsibility for them of me and mine. It is not only the Plutocrats. If it is man that is wronged it is man that has wronged him, it is man that has sinned, man that is condemned. You cannot split up the race. You insist, indeed, on its solidarity. Its unity and solidarity is one of the commonplaces of modern thought. So, if sin there be, man is the sinner. Surely, therefore, the wrong inflicted on man sets up a corresponding responsibility on man at his centre; and it makes any atonement a matter of judgment, and not mere repentance or reparation. That seems inevitable if we believe in responsibility, and also believe in the unity of the human race. It seems logical.

But there is much more than logic in it. It comes home far more mightily and solemnly from the belief in another unity, the belief in the absolute moral unity of God, in a word, a real belief and a real sense of his holiness.

To bring sin home, and to bring grace home, we need that something else should come home which alone gives meaning to both—the holy. The grace of God cannot return to our preaching, or to our faith till we recover what has almost clean gone from our general, familiar, and current religion—I mean a due sense of the holiness of God. It has much gone from our public worship, with its frequent irreverence; from our sentimental piety, to which an ethical piety with its implicates is simply obscure; from our public morals, to which the invasion of property is more dreadful than the damnation of men. If our Gospel be obscure it is obscure to them in whom the slack God of the period has blinded their minds, and hidden the Holy One who inhabits eternity. This holiness of God is the real foundation of religion—it is certainly the ruling interest of the Christian religion. In front of all our prayer or work stands "Hallowed be Thy name." If we take the Lord's Prayer alone, God's holiness is the interest which all the rest of it serves. Neither love, grace, faith, nor sin have any but a passing meaning except as they rest on the holiness of God, except as they arise from it, and return to it, except as they satisfy it, show it forth, set it up, and secure it everywhere and for ever. Love is but its outgoing; sin is but its defiance; grace is but its action on sin; the cross is but its victory; faith is but its worship. The preacher preaches to the divinest purpose only when his lips are touched with the red coal from the altar of the thrice holy in the innermost place. We must rise beyond social righteousness and universal justice to the holiness of an infinite God. What we on earth call righteousness among men, the saints in heaven call holiness in the eternal God.

Have our churches lost that seal? Are we producing reform, social or theological, faster than we are producing faith? Then we are putting all our religious capital into the extension of our business, and carrying nothing to reserve or insurance. We are mortgaging and starving the future. We are not seeking first the Kingdom of God and his holiness, but only carrying on, with very expensive and noisy machinery, a "kingdom-of-God-industry." We are merely running the kingdom, and we are running it without the cross—with the cross perhaps on our sign, but not in our centre. We have the old trade mark, but what does that matter in a dry and thirsty land where no water is, if the artesian well on our premises is going dry?

Forgiveness through Atonement

To bring *sin* home, and *grace* home, then, the *Holy* must be brought home. But that again can be done, on the scale of the church and the world, only by replacing the *cross* at the centre of Christian faith and life, as an atonement to this holy love. The centrality of the cross belongs to it only as an atoning cross. Only if Christ atoned for the world did he culminate in the cross, and do the great thing there. And it is as an atonement that the church has kept the cross at its spiritual centre. This is still the moral problem of the church in relation to society. The form, indeed, of the church's moral problem will always depend on the social conditions of the hour; but the substance of it is always the same. It is practical. It is to place the moral centre of society upon the moral centre of the soul, upon the centre of the moral universe. And what is that but to place the conscience of society on Calvary. What is our problem to-day? It is to take the mass of men (and not only the masses)—inert and hopeless some, others indifferent, others hostile to God—and to reconcile them with God's holy will and righteous kingdom, to reconcile them not with the *ideal* of a kingdom of God, but with his way of it. It is to destroy our national and social dislike of that new enthusiasm, to supplant lust by a higher ardour, to bend the strongest wills to the obedience of the holiest, and by moral regeneration, to restore men both physically and socially. This is a tremendous task. It is the grand object of history. It is far beyond socialism. And no laws can do it, and no change of circumstances, but only Jesus Christ. It is the fruit of his work, of his holy love, his Holy Spirit, and his holy church, all flowing from his holy cross. And the more we are preoccupied with social righteousness so much the more we are driven to that centre where the whole righteousness of God and man found consummation, and adjustment, and a principle and a career, in the saving judgment of Christ's cross. The cross alone gives moral freedom, and moral independence to the mass of men, who were left to slavery by the heroic moral aristocracy of stoicism. It is the cross that makes moral worth an infectious power, and keeps character from being self-contained, and gives a moral guarantee of a social future. The cross is the spring, not of self-possessed and individualist righteousness, but of that creative and contagious goodness which makes possible the social state. Only at the centre of the cross does the man find himself in his kind, and both in God. A creative, missionary, and social ethic springs only from religion: and it springs most from the religion which is able to clothe us with the power of the creative, loving, outgoing God.

III

When we speak of the centrality of the atonement, I have said, we mean much more, worlds more, than its place in a religious system. This is no congress of scientific theologians, but an assembly of faith and a communion of saints. And we are speaking of that which is the centre, not of thought, but of life, conscience, history and destiny. We speak of what is the life-power of the moral world and its historic crisis, the ground of the church's existence, and the sole meaning of Christ himself. Christ is to us just what his cross is. All that Christ was in heaven or on earth was put into what he did there. And all that man's moral soul needs doing for it was done centrally there. Neither cross nor Christ is simply a historic fact by which we order our mental calendar; they make the sun in our heaven, the force in our world. They make our vital centre, not as mere facts, but as sacraments, not for their occurrence, but for their significance; not because we reckon from them, but because we live from them.

It is sometimes said, "There are several theories of the atonement, but we have to do with the fact, and not with our understanding of it." This frame of mind is the root of all that is most feeble and ominous in our churches to-day. The one thing we need is to understand the atonement, with a life's understanding, with a vital conscience. There it is that Christ comes to himself for good. There, as it were, he finds his tongue, and takes command of the deep eloquence of moral things. Christ, I repeat, is to us just what his cross is. You do not understand Christ till you understand his cross. Nor have you measured the moral world. Such a fact as Christ or his atonement only exists as it is intelligible, as it comes home to us with a moral meaning and a moral nature. It is only by understanding it that it becomes anything else than a martyrdom, that it becomes the saving act of God. It is only by understanding it that we escape from religion with no mind and religion which is all mind, from pietism with its lack of judgment, and from rationalism with its lack of everything else.

If I may be pardoned for another reference to Dr. Dale, he said that one of our great needs was more preaching about Christian ethics. Well, since his time that need has been largely met, especially in the region of social ethics. Perhaps, indeed, it has been overdone, considering the amount of insight into ethical principle which we mostly have at command. We have been made to attend to the Christian life, in the sense of Christian conduct, at the expanse of the Christian life in the inner sense of justifying faith. Ethic has been externalized. The effect of faith in conduct has been ethicized, but the nature of faith in experience has not; it has been sentimentalized. The centre of gravity has been transferred from the cross to the parable of the prodigal. So that what we need is the ethicizing of religion itself, and not simply of the fruits of religion. We want a religion ethical in itself, in its nature, genius and effect; we want more than a manner of life which is morality suffused with piety. And to ethicize religion we must restore to it, from its centre, that note of judgment which it has lost, that note of supreme reference to a holy God. The moralizing of Christian conduct is not the moralizing of Christian faith. But it is the faith that needs moralizing most. If conduct is wrong, it is the religion that needs reforming; the life will follow the faith. And to reform our religion we must be driven, not only *to* its centre but *into* its centre. You seek the ethicizing of religion, its rescue from theology and sentiment? Well, you can only get it by theology. The prime need of religion to-day is a theology. No religion can survive which does not know where it is. And current religion does not know where it is, and it hates to be made to ask.

The ethicizing principle of religion must be the creative element in its source. Has it a moral source? To answer that question is theology; and it is a theology of judgment. Ours is an eternal faith, and it can only be moralized by the eternal righteousness, *i.e.*, by its source in a holy God. The source of an eternal faith can only moralize that faith if there be established at its centre with might what reigns in the universe by right—the moral majesty, the holiness of God. That is theology; but it is also essential Christianity.

Yet so far have we got from this supreme concern of Christ, that when the effort is made to give it its true place for his work on earth, some minds, demoralized by their very religion, cry out against theology, and metaphysics, and academics. It is a cry charged with the ruin of the Christian future. There is nothing that need surprise us in the failure, the ebb, of any church which treats the holiness of God as a piece of theology, and its centrality to the conscience as a piece of metaphysic. What is the worth to the Christian gospel of a piety which calls the theology of holiness academic. Protest as you like against the language of pure thought, and the inaccessibility to relative man of the unconditioned absolute in the ethic of pure thought. Protest strongly against making salvation depend on assent to the metaphysics of Trinity. But when we have come to be so saturated with the religious impressionism of the hour that an ultimate concern of heart, soul and mind with the holiness of God is a strange tongue to us, and its satisfaction a mere piece of theology, then the kid is seethed in its mother's milk, and the soul sodden with the very religion that should be its food. Of course most men, even religious men, are unfamiliar with the holiness of God, but the unfamiliar is not the academic.

We are paying bitterly now, and we shall pay more bitterly yet, in the bewilderment of our youth, for that neglect by the church to educate its ministry in its own subject at the plastic time, which makes such talk possible. When preachers denounce theology, or a church despises it for literary or social charm, that is to sell the cross to be a pendant at the neck of the handsome world. It is spiritual poverty and baldness, it is not the simplicity in Christ, to be sick of grace, judgment, atonement, and redemption. The holiness of God has become a spent force if a gospel which turns entirely upon it is called metaphysical or academic.

IV

Be not ashamed of the cross of Christ, for there alone the final and public righteousness of God is revealed to our growing faith. A moral order of the world is our one modern certainty, among those who are certain of anything. And if, as we Christians believe, this moral order reflects the nature of a holy God (without exhausting his being) then the supreme interest of the world lies there. That interest is the first charge on an ethical religion. All the bearings of a faith like Christianity therefore must be taken from there, and from wherever that is supremely revealed. Christianity is only true if it deal with this, and it is only final if it come to final terms with it. The cross of Christ has more than a passing place only if it give final effect to this holy thing, and is understood in relation to it. It has no meaning as an incident, none except as it is understood; none as a piece of history, only as it is superhistoric. It is presented to out conscience, and not to our sympathies or tastes. It is not an impressive spectacle, but a decisive act, with the moral order of God's holiness for its central issue and first charge. The understanding of this is the one thing needful for the internal troubles of our religion to-day. An enlightened Judaism can preach a gospel of forgiveness, but our Christian religion has primarily to do with the terms of forgiveness; not with God's readiness to forgive, but with his way of redemption; not with his willingness, but with his will; and with his will not merely as his aim, but as his deed; not as intended, but as achieved. The feeble gospel preaches "God is ready to forgive"; the mighty gospel preaches "God has redeemed." It works not with forgiveness alone, which would be mere futile amnesty, but with forgiveness in a moral way, with holy forgiveness, a forgiveness which not only restores the soul, but restores it in the only final and eternal way, by restoring in the same act the infinite moral order, and reconstructing mankind from the foundation of a moral revolution. God reconciles by making Christ to be sin, and not imputing it (2 Cor 5:21). The Christian act of forgiveness at once regards the whole wide moral order of things, and goes deep to the springs of the human will for repentance and a new order of obedience. This it does by the consummation of God's *judgment* in the central act of mercy. Do not think of God's judgment as an arbitrary infliction, but as the necessary reaction in a holy God. There alone do you have the *divine* necessity of the cross in a sinful world—the moral necessity of judgment. A judgment upon man alone would have destroyed him. And a judgment borne by God alone would be *manqué*, it would be wide of the mark, as being irrelevant to man's experience and regeneration. But borne by God in man, in such a racial, nay cosmic, experience as the cross of Christ, it is the creation of a new conscience, and of the new ethic of the race. When Christ died, all died. Dying with Christ is not a mere ethical idea, complete only as we succeed in doing it. It is a religious or mystic idea, which is ethical, as taking effect in a holy act, where it is already complete in principle. It is not applying the principle of salvation to life, it is the foregone salvation which becomes our life; and practical Christianity is living it out, and not merely squaring life to it. The judgment involved is one that fell on Christ once for all. It is not a judgment in individual men, but in man in Christ. It is not the sum total of our self-judgments under Christ's light; rather say, all our self-judgment is but inspired by the complete judgment on Christ once for all. It is on us as we are in him, yet not as judgment but as grace; not as punishment, but as salvation; not as a scourge, but as a cross.

Without such a cross and its atonement we come to a religion of much point and no atmosphere, much sympathy and no imagination, much kindness and no greatness, much charm and no force—a religion for the well-disposed and not for the rebel, which loves our neighbour, but not our enemy, and not our Judge; a religion for the sensitive, but not for the world. When the world-cross goes out of the centre of religion, religion in due time goes out of the centre of man's moral and public energy. The public goes past the preacher because he is not strong enough to arrest and compel them. He has too much to say and too little to tell. He hangs to his age by its weakness, and not by its strength. He does not reach its soul with such gospel as he has. The pathos of Christ takes the place of his power. We canonize the weak things of our Christian world in our haste for rapid success with the many. Religion becomes too æsthetic, too exclusively sympathetic, too bland, too naturalist. Our very Christmas becomes the festival of babyhood, Good Friday the worship of grief, and Easter of spring. To use the old theological language, under an obsession by culture and its pensive delicacies, we become dominated by the passive obedience of Christ instead of his active. We treat the cross as a passion only, instead of a principle, or as a principle instead of a deed. Christ becomes a pathetic, tender, helpful and gracious figure rather than a mighty. We prefer the flavour of the evening service to that of the morning. The religion that is driven out of business and our energetic hours takes refuge in our tired hours and our evening time. And it takes on that hue. It acquires that type—even in the preachers too often, whose active business it should be. We tend to overprize the subdued, composed, and vespertinal type of religion, whose patron saints are outside the evangelical succession with Francis and Fra Angelico; or we are engrossed with the genial, brotherly, and bustling type. And all the time the church is dropping into a vague Arianism: it is losing faith in the incarnation, faith in the real presence of the redeeming God, and therefore faith in a strenuous and historic ethic. Is it wonderful that it should be deploring a decline which it cannot stay by all its religious galvanism and its forced enterprises? The idea we are offered is a kingdom of man, with God to serve it, rather than a kingdom of God, with man to serve it. It is a consecration of the natural man *by* God instead of his redemption *to* God. It trusts to man's Christian culture instead of his conversion. The God within exploits the God without. The historic facts of our faith become not so much unique organs of God's self-revelation, as they are means of making us aware of the God within us, and living up to him. We do not so much owe our soul to the fact of Christ, we impose on that fact the soul within us, the human soul, crude, but still very capable; dim, but unlost; and so we really receive but what we give. Revelation is then not an objective authority, given at a point once for all; it is but a subjective way of treating history. The course of history is the real revelation. The deification of a point in it, of a person in it, is only a passing mythology, forced on us by a psychological necessity, though it may be very valuable when properly guarded. But Jesus cannot be regarded as an objective revelation. He lives while we believe.

The tendency to dwell upon the passive obedience of Christ is but the theological way of expressing the tendency to dwell on God's sympathy and to ignore his salvation. There is little doubt that the sympathetic tendency is the more popular to-day, and to press salvation in a real sense is to be accused of a reactionary bias to theology. But a God who is merely or mainly sympathetic is not the Christian God. The Father of an infinite benediction is not the Father of an infinite grace. We are often warned of the dangers of anthropomorphism, especially by those who are preoccupied with the superpersonal element in God (though it is better described as intrapersonal). But what we need much more to-day is a caution against anthropopathism, or a conception of God which thinks of him chiefly as the divine consummation of all our human pity and tenderness to man's mischance, bewilderment, sorrow and sin. A being of infinite sympathy would not rise to the height of the Christian God. And a religion of far more sympathy than we have yet felt would not be the Christian religion. It is needless to dwell on the preciousness of sympathy. The man who needs none is something less than human; and the man who receives none remains so. But a sympathy which has no help mocks us with an enlargement of our own sensitive impotence, which means so much better than it can. And a sympathy which could only help would not secure us against the fear that all its help might be at last in vain. It might not reach me, or not my worst need; or it might be arrested by a power more mighty to foil than to help. We must have a sympathy that can not only help but save, save to the uttermost, and not only bless but redeem. Nay, far more, we must have, for the entire confidence of faith, a sympathy that *has* redeemed, and already triumphs in a conclusive salvation. If God, indeed, could not sympathise, he would be less than God. There would be a region, large or small, into which he could not pass. There would be an insuperable obstacle set to Almighty God by a something which by so far reduced his power and resisted his access. He would be a limited being, tied up, as impersonal things are, by their own nature, and incapable of passing beyond it. But all the same, if God were all sympathy, if his divine power lay chiefly in his ability to infuse himself with superhuman intimacy of feeling into the most unspeakable tangles and crises of human life, then also he would be less than God, and we should have no more than what might be called a monism of heart. Even a loving God is really God not because he loves, but because he has power to subdue all things to the holiness of his love, and even sin itself to his love as redeeming grace. A sympathetic God is really God because he is a holy, saving, redeeming God; because in him already the great world-transaction is done, and the kingdom of his holy love already set up on his foregone conquest of all evil. The great and crucial thing is done in God and not *before* him, in his will and not in his presence, *by* him and not *for* him by any servants, not even by a son. It is an act of his own being, a victory in his own immutable and invincible being. And to be saved, in any non-egoistical sense of the word, means that God gains his own victory over again in me, and that I have lost in life's great issue unless he do. God's participation in man's affairs is much more than that of a fellow-sufferer on a divine scale, whose love can rise to a painless sympathy with pain. He not only perfectly understands our case and our problem, but he has solved it. The solution is for ever present with him. Already he sees, and for ever sees, the travail of his soul and is *satisfied*. All the jars, collisions, contradictions, crises, pities, tragedies and terrors of life are in him for ever adjusted in a peace which is not resigned and quietist, but triumphant and exultant; and nothing can pluck us from his hands. All history, through his great act at its moral centre, is, in God, resolved into the harmonies of a foregone and final conquest. And our faith is not merely that God is with us, nor that one day he will clear all things up and triumph; but that for him all things are already triumphant, clear and sure. All things are working together for good, as good is in the cross of Christ and its saving effect. Our faith is not that one day we shall solve the riddles of providence, and see all things put under us, but that now we see Jesus; and that we commit ourselves to one who has both the solution of every tragic thing and the glory of every dark thing clear and sure in a kingdom that cannot be moved and, therefore alone, moves for ever on.

Our current religion of sympathy is but a section, and not the central or effectual section, of a religion which is a religion of redemption; and of achieved redemption, else it must at last cease to be a religion at all. That, and only that, is the fulness of the evangelical gospel.

But in all the subjectivism I have named are we not slowly passing to another religion, a religion which starts with man's spiritual nature and not with God's self-revelation, with humanity and not with history, where man becomes "his own Holy Ghost." We are bidden to study human nature, not the Bible, not Jesus Christ except to look for classic cases of spiritual humanity and high prophetism. The Bible becomes then but a valuable deposit of that irrepressible spiritual energy in man which in every age takes its own form, and finds no kind of finality in any age. That, of course, reduces Jesus to a mere historic link instead of a perennial presence, and his cross to one of the crises we have surmounted, or are in process of doing so. The greatest personality is but a node in the great evolution. Man needs but evolution and not revolution. He only needs that his face be cleared, and not turned steadfastly to Jerusalem.

Let us see exactly where the point is, and let us be quite fair to the kind of liberal religion in view. It does not, of course, exclude God. It does not say that the religious development of man is a smooth or an automatic thing. Progress still needs the help of God, or whatever stands for God. It needs even the act of God. The origin of faith within man is an act of God. But the point is that this act is not a revolution in man, not a new creation, not a regeneration, not an absolute redemption but only a release, an impulse from God, the elimination of our best, a delivery of the innate spirituality and goodness of man with which history is in travail until now. It is not a salvation from death but only from scanty life. There is no real critical life and death catastrophe in the moral history of the race, but what we have is a deep consistent progress, harmonious on the whole, each step attaching to the step before. We have the happy perfecting of those decent, just, or tender instincts which are the original righteousness of human nature, the gradual surmounting by moral culture of sense and self. God is our helper and no more. He is not in a real sense, but only a figurative sense, our Redeemer. He helps us to realise our latent spiritual resources and ends. There is no break with self and the world, only a disengagement from an embarrassing situation.

It should be clear that this is another religion from that of redemption, and it has no room or need for atonement. And if it be true, then Christianity is not so necessary as we were led to think. Its whole complexion is changed. Nothing so very serious has taken place. Things can be bad enough, but not so bad as all that. Human nature is very mysterious but there is nothing marvellous, miraculous, in God's relation to it, nothing that needs much penetration or agony of holy thought. Incarnation becomes a metaphor. These greatest words are so great and useful because they can be made to mean anything. Well, faith in the incarnation is bound to become a metaphor, and to sink, if we count it mere theology to take it seriously that God was in Christ reconciling the world, and to press on to understand the mighty God hallowed in the atoning cross. It is bound to sink so as to become the incarnation of man instead of God, if in the cross we see but the extreme suffering of the most loving man instead of the supreme act and victory of the most holy God. If Christianity do not make a revolution in human nature we make a revolution in Christianity. A religion centring wholly in the graciousness of Christ, or his submission, or his spiritual insight can be no foundation for a commanding ethic or a triumphant faith. He lacks the virile note. It did not come as a grand spiritual personality, but as the Redeemer. It was not to spiritualise us but to save us. Moral verve is bound to relax if the religion of the cross become but a hallowed addition to life's spiritual interests or touching moods, if it do not carry the stamp of moral crisis and personal decision for death or life. Ethic is bound to grow less strenuous, even while we bustle about ethical conduct, if the sublime ethical issue of the universe is not the marrow of our personal divinity and the principle of our personal religion. We can find a strong foundation only in that centre where the holy God both bears our load and performs his new creative act. If in the cross we have but the greatest of love's renunciations instead of the one establishment of God's holy will, then the sense of God's presence in the cross, and in the church, and in the world's moral war, is bound to fade. The eternal ruling God cannot be God in a passive or touching cross merely. A religion of mere service is no religion to rule; such a world as this. We shall come to feel that in the cross there is no God, but only a victory of God's foes, another and a tremendous case of the world crushing the good and just, another case of the soul's defeat by fate. Then, of course, Christianity must die. "The cross is either the life of our religion, or it is the death of all religion. Either it is the supreme atonement and so the final guarantee of God's Fatherhood and its victory, or else it is a mere martyr death, and so an eclipse of that fatherhood, its greatest historic eclipse, which would mean its extinction." Christ trusted a God who did not give him the victory. A pathetic, mystic, and martyred Messiah could stir the sympathy of many, but could not win the worship of the world. He could impress but not forgive; he could move men but not redeem them; he could criticise society but not judge the world. A king the world could just crucify is no king the world could fear; it needs a king who in his cross judged the world, and did not simply find his fate there. There is nothing central, nothing creative for life in such a fate. There may be much in it to appeal to our sympathetic and religious side, but nothing to establish faith, nothing to ethicise it from a creative centre, nothing to fortify us against the unholy, nothing to set conscience and holiness on the throne of the world. If Christ died to saving and central purpose, then he died by the act of God. His death was God's act in the sense that it was the moral activity of God. God was in Christ and his death, acting there, setting up an everlasting kingdom, and not simply inflicting, nor simply suffering, a racial penalty.

Moreover, a pathetic cross sends our active sympathies mainly to Christ's teaching and his miracles. If we see in Christ and his cross chiefly the passive and the affecting side, and not the active and creative side, if we see Christ's love enduring judgment more than God's holiness triumphant in judgment and doing there the grand, nay, the one, moral act of the world, if we see but that, no wonder the vigorous world turns away from the cross to the teaching of Christ and his beneficence. For these *are* acts of will, positive deeds with active effect. It is no wonder a cross of pathetic and appealing suffering, a cross of mere sacrifice, should become decentralised in favour of these. And yet these have no permanent value for us in themselves, but only as expressions of Christ's person. The great thing is not that they were said or done, but said or done by *him*. And the person of Christ would be dumb and inert for us in our last crisis, apart from its active assertion and cosmic triumph on the cross. The cross, therefore, was no martyr passivity of the finest prophet, led like a lamb to the slaughter; it was the work of a Messiah king with power over himself. Christ never merely accepted his fate; he willed it. He went to death as a king. It was the supreme exercise of his royal self-disposal. The same great picture which presents the sheep before the shearers dumb deepens before its close to one who poured out his soul unto death. And when we obscure that, when we pity where we should worship, melt where we should kneel, or kneel where we should rise to newness of life, it is no wonder if faith become a mere affection, or a mere ethical ritual, and cease to be the absolute committal of ourselves to him for ever. It is no wonder, then, if it cease to be the practical and eternal consignment of our spirit into his hands who has redeemed us as our Lord God of Truth. Faith is really self-disposal. But currently it is not. It is any of a multitude of things but not that, except in some feeble or breezy sense which does not save the moral asthenia of the church. The church has lost much moral tone even in its occupation with ethical subjects. It has lost power to guide the instinct of self-sacrifice by reducing the cross to nothing else. It has lost religious weight in the weightiest matters. And the deep cause is its modern failure to understand the cross, to see in the judgment of the cross God's righteousness, God's holiness, coming to its own, and to realise this as the one object for which man exists or the world. This failure is bound to tell acting on the scale of a church, however secure many fine souls may feel, living in a coterie and painting angels in their solitary cells.

It is only as God's act then that Christ's death can retain or regain a central place in faith. Second it is only as an act revolutionary for man. And farther, it is only as an act in which his holiness gives the law to his love, and judgment make grace precious. Holiness must be the first charge on the Saviour. If we spoke less about God's love, and more about his holiness, more about his judgment, we should say much more when we did speak of his love. And we should keep that supreme in our faith which was supreme in Christ's, in that saving hour when the sense of love was dimmed, when communion failed, and nothing was left but faith by which to save the world.

And it is round this sanctuary that the great camp is set and the great battle really waged. Questions about immanence may concern philosophers. And questions about miracles may agitate physicists. But the great dividing issue for the soul is neither the Bethlehem cradle nor the empty grave, nor the Bible, nor the social question. For the church at least (however it be with individuals) it is the question of a redeeming atonement. It is here that the evangelical issue lies. It is here, and not upon the nativity, that we part company with the Unitarians. It is here that the unsure may test their crypto-unitarianism. I would unchurch none. I would but clear the issue for the honest conscience. It is this that determines whether a man is Unitarian or Evangelical, and it is this that should guide his conscience as to his ecclesiastical associations. Only if he hold that in the atoning cross of Christ the world was redeemed by holy God once for all, that there, and only there, sin was judged and broken, that there and only there the race was reconciled and has its access to the face and grace of God—only then has he the genius and the plerophory of the Gospel. If he hold to Christ as this head, then, whatever views he may hold on other heads, he is of the Gospel company and the Evangelical pale. Only thus has he a real final message for the age. Only thus is he more than one that has a lovely voice and can play well on an instrument for the ages' pleasure—and its final neglect.

V

There are two sets of admissions that should be made here. One concerns the history of the doctrine, the other concerns its place in individual experience.

(1)

As to the doctrine in history, we ought to admit the value of much of the socinian and rationalist criticism of it. The value is negative and corrective, but it is value. The ecclesiastical form of the doctrine is the source of most of the prejudice against it. And I mean particularly the forms it took among the Protestant scholastics of the 17th century. Many of these forms will not bear the light of Scripture any more than of reason. They are more aristotelian than apostolic. I do not say they depart from the New Testament doctrine, because it would be hard in the present position of New Testament knowledge to say the New Testament had a complete doctrine. But it has a principle and a norm which is positive enough to enable us to rule out many notions which misrepresent God's grace. For instance, we can no longer treat the atonement as a deflection of God's anger, as if the flash fell on Christ and was conducted by him to the ground, while we stood in passive safety, with no part or lot in the incomprehensible process. We can no longer speak of a strife of attributes in God the Father, justice set against mercy, and judgment against grace, till an adjustment was effected by the Son. There can be no talk of any mollification of God, or any inducement whatever, offered by either man or some third party, to procure grace. Procured grace is a contradiction in terms. The atonement did not procure grace, it flowed from grace. What was offered, was offered by God, within the Godhead's unity. The Redeemer was God's gift. Farther we must not think that the value of the atonement lies in any equivalent suffering. Indeed, it does not lie in the suffering at all, but in the obedience, the holiness.[1]

And it is both a moral and a psychological impossibility that an amount of suffering equivalent to what we deserved should ever have been undergone by Christ or any personality in our stead. Again, we must speak very differently about the transfer of guilt, and never as if it were a ledger amount which could be shifted about by divine finance, or a ponderable load lifted to another back. We have to be cautious in using the word penalty in connection with what fell on Christ. We must renounce the idea that he was punished by the God who was ever well pleased with his beloved Son. The chastisement of our peace was upon him indeed; but if we think there is no chastisement left for us in him, we have against that idea the whole classic Christian experience, which finds the truest, deepest, and bitterest repentance at the end of the Christian life rather than at the beginning. But it is one of our present misfortunes that so much criticism of the popular doctrine, with its abuse of repentance, is conducted by people who seem not to know what bitter repentance, spiritual brokenness and total humiliation mean. I would rather repent truly with a Salvationist theology than criticise that theology with a judicial superiority which needs no repentance.

(2)

But in respect of personal experience, do we deny all true faith which does not grasp the atoning cross? Surely not; so long as it is not denied or denounced; and so long as the experience of particular individuals is not made the measure of the message of the church.

I hope I take due account of the effect of Christ's person, word, and deed before the cross. I have often recalled Zaccheus, the Magdalen, Peter, and, I may add, Judas. And to-day still the life, the words, the acts, the death of Christ have a precious power to rouse men, to break, heal, and restore them to him, without direct reference to his atoning work. The saving action of Christ for many

---

1. I have developed this in Forsyth, "What is Meant by the Blood of Christ?". [Also published as Forsyth, *The Cruciality of the Cross*, chap. 4.]

individuals begins there—in his life especially to-day, and it only attains late unto the from the dead. We do ill to force the ripe experience of the cross on those who can as yet feel but its dawn. Any theology of atonement must be adjusted to the indubitable fact that Christ's forgiveness may and does reach personal cases apart from conscious reliance on his atoning work or grasp of its theology. To do otherwise would be to show ourselves the victims of a pedantic dogmatism or a theological papacy. To preach Christ is indeed fundamentally to preach his atonement, but it is not incessantly to preach about it. We must always preach it, but we need not always preach about it. Only it must not be denied or denounced, never ignored or levelled down to the category of man's efforts to atone his own sins. It is true there are stages and junctures when to preach Christ in the more theological form is the only preaching relevant to the mental and moral situation. It was so at the Reformation. But to-day it may be more needful in certain positions to preach the Christ of the cross than the cross of Christ. There is a strategy in the holy war. It is the crisis that calls the reserves to the front. But whether we preach the Christ who atoned or the atonement of Christ it is still an atoning Christ and an atoning cross we preach. To preach only the atonement, the death apart from the life, or only the person of Christ, the life apart from the death, or only the teaching of Christ, his words apart from his life, may be all equally one-sided, and extreme to falsity. I will only stop to remark here that the more the conscience is affected by Christ's words or behaviour, the more is that standard generated within us which demands the atonement in the cross. It was the Christ of the cross that said these words, and did these things. It was the Christ who himself was driven by his experience to recognise that the crowning thing he came for was to die. And another remark must be made. What we are chiefly concerned with is the great message and experience of the church; and that cannot be whittled down to the experience of individuals and their early stages. It is a minimal gospel that is paralysing the cross. Preach the total Christ therefore in the perspective of evangelical faith, but with immediate stress on that aspect most required by the conscience of the hour. For the Reformation age the ethical concern may have been satisfaction and its true form; for our age, with another public ethic, it may be judgment as the demand of a social righteousness. For that age the interest was far more directly theological and juristic, now it is more psychological and ethical. Then it was the Christ of the two natures cohering in one person that gave value to the cross, now the stress is the Christ of the one, holy, obedient personality. The unity we prize in the Saviour is not one realized previous to the cross metaphysically, so much as a unity by and in the cross as the crowning moral act both of God and of humanity in Christ. But a point of unity we must seek if our faith is to be unified, if life is to be unified out of its present distraction, if religion is to have a vital core and cease to be a frame of pious moods or morals. Our relation to God must be a real one and not subjective. It must turn on a positive fact and act, which gives it both reality and unity; and on a fact of history. It is not enough to say this fact is the person of Christ. If his be not a mere loose-hung personality with a religious casualism it must itself have a principle of unity. This principle cannot, with our data, be psychological; even with more data perhaps it would still be beyond our comprehension psychologically. "Du gleichst dem Geist den du begreifst, nicht mir."[2] But it is a theological unity converging on his death and the consummation there of all that made his person what it was, took him out of the category of other men, and made the ground of our salvation. He saved us by his difference from us. He did not redeem us because he represented us; rather he represents us because he redeemed. Had he redeemed man by representing him, man would be self-redeemed. It is the atoning death of Christ as the representative of God that makes Jesus a complete and closed personality with a final action on the world. He died once for all, the just for the unjust, that he might bring us to his finality of God.

VI

But after these admissions let me lay the more stress on the necessity of this atonement for that maturer Christian experience which gives us the true type of faith.

The conscience has many functions, and the atonement of Christ satisfies or stirs them all. It strikes light from many angles,

---

2. ["You are like the spirit you understand, not me."]

and it is presented in the New Testament in various complementary ways. But its chief action on the conscience is to pacify its accusations with the love and grace of God. Faith is above all the life of a conscience. It is the life of a conscience which is stilled and established by the forgiveness of God. True enough, as I have said, this may take a true, though an incipient form, in the deep impression made by the tender mercy of the kindly Christ. But many never rise above this level. It is enough for them to respond to Christ's gracious way with the sinners he met. They place themselves among the sinners he forgave and healed during his life. And they may question the need of any atonement. The assurance from Christ of God's forgiveness is enough. But that is a very naïve and all too simple faith for such a conscience as ours, and such a world. Let its value for certain individuals not be denied. Who would be exacting with the simple souls? But surely it condemns them to be perpetual moral minors. And it keeps faith at the lay level. Ours is a lay faith, but the Christian could not live on it at lay level. If such people go on to think and ask, as they should for their soul's life, in passing from disciples to regenerates, must they not begin to have certain misgivings? Must they not, for instance, say to themselves at some time: "Those cases that Jesus forgave were but single cases; is mine quite parallel? If he forgave them must he forgive me? Is God's forgiveness just a series of acts, one for each soul? If so how do I know where they may stop, whether they will reach to me? Or is his forgiveness one great act into which I am built, so that when one died all died?" Moreover, the soul goes on to think thus: "As I grow in Christ my sin grows on me, and the tremendous thing in my pardon grows on me. The damnability of sin grows on me and with it the incredibility of grace. How do I know not merely that God is willing to forgive but that he has forgiven, that what is so incredible is equally unalterable?" Still farther. The believer sins after he has been forgiven. "Am I fit," he says in his repentance, "to stand with those that Jesus forgave. They did not betray him. I have sinned against a light and an experience they never had. I am a chief of sinners. I have sinned my mercy." Moreover, there rises on his soul a deepened sense of Christ's demand. His forgiving words to special cases lose force compared with the exigence of his general demand and the holiness of his standard. His judgment grows more serious than it seemed in our first forgiveness. How shall we stand? Better people than we he left outside his kingdom. And so we oscillate between the goodness and the severity of God. We are tossed from the one to the other. They alternate as it were according to our mood, they are not entwined and fused. They thwart each other, and get in each other's way; they do not sustain each other. And the conscience gets no rest till it find in the cross the one final fact in which both are reconciled and inwoven, with the grace uppermost. I meet the atonement where the sin of the whole world is taken away, which carries in it the foregone forgiveness of sins I dread and yet am sure I shall do. There are various ways in which a man finds it hard to take home the forgiveness he craves by a general declaration of God's love. Some may not feel so much the greatness of their sin as the incredibility of anything so vast as God's love. There may not be grievous blots on their life, yet they feel that the state of the world's conscience must call out God's judgment on the race, including them. On the other hand if there be such blots in life, and especially if a man sins after his forgiveness in a grievous way, he gets such a shock in the revelation of sin's tough and subtle power that it needs something very final and decisive to assure him of its destruction. He must then have a grace which is not simple and self-evident—for "lightly come, lightly go." He must have a finished work, and a God who has made a full end. A conscience in his state, as soon as it thinks on a world scale, must have a grace and salvation which is not benignant only, but gathers up the total moral situation in one act, which settles the great strife for good and all. He must have more than a full forgiveness, he must have a complete redemption. And that means one which pursues, captures, and subdues to God's holy purpose those consequences of our sin which have long gone beyond our control or knowledge, and are out on the world doing evil work at compound interest on their own account. He needs something to make him confident that his past sin, and the sin he is yet sure to commit, are all taken up into God's redemption, and the great transaction of his moral life is done. The real complete forgiveness is the appropriation of the world's atonement.

It is not easy. For a man to make Christ's atonement the sole centre of his moral life, or of his hope for the race, is not easy.

Nothing is so resented by the natural self as the hearty admission of man's native lostness and helplessness, especially when he thinks of all the heroisms, integrities and charities which ennoble the race. It is not always pride, it is a mere natural self-affirmation. It is a native self-respect, which makes him shrink from submitting himself absolutely to the judgment of another. Even in his repentance he does not want to lose all self-respect. He feels he cannot amend the life of conscience, and repair the old faults, without some remnant of self-respect to work from. His new shoots must come from the old stump, which must not be rooted out. He is fighting for the one remnant of a moral nature which if he lost he fears he would be less than a man. He does not easily realise what a poor thing his self-justification must be compared with his justification by God. He does not feel how sterile the stump is, how poorly his moral remnant would serve him for his moral need, how recuperative vitality is the one thing he lacks, how absolute God's grace is, and how complete is the moral re-creation in Christ. He palters with a synergism which is always trying to do the best for human nature in a bargain with God. And he does not realize how this starves and pinches the conscience itself, compared with the moral fulness of a total gift of grace and a new man in Jesus Christ. There are thus a thousand influences of no ignoble kind which may arrest a man's total committal of himself and his kind to the new creation in Christ's cross. And it seems a reasonable self-respect which solicits him to reserve a plot of land in his interior where his house is his castle and he can call his soul his own, even at the challenge of the holy and all-searching Judge. He does not, perhaps, venture to say that God and the soul are coequal foci in the moral ellipse, but he struggles, sometimes pathetically, to set up what is as impossible morally as mathematically—a subsidiary centre; which is a contradiction in terms. There is but one centre, one Lord, one cross, one faith, and one spirit of a new life in Christ Jesus.

VII

It has been asked concerning Christ, Was his will to die one with his will to save? Is there any doubt about the answer the church has given to that question from first to last? The forgiveness, the redemption has always been attached to Christ's death, from New Testament days downward. Not indeed without challenge, especially in recent times, but the challenge has not affected the catholicity and continuity of the church's witness as a whole to that truth of its foundation. And the salvation is attached not to Christ's death as an incident of history or even as an object lesson of grace, but as the effectuation of grace, not indeed its procuring but its putting in action. It is not the fact of Christ's crucifixion that saves but the inner nature of that fact as understood, and not simply swallowed, by faith, understood as the atonement which makes reconciliation possible (2 Cor 5:19–21). Such is the witness of you may say the whole church about its central relation to its creator, its living tenant, and perpetual Lord.

But this suggests a serious question. It is declared that, if we be true to the true Christ of the Gospels we shall relegate a final atonement in the cross to the region of apostolic theologoumena. That means that Jesus did not understand his will to save to be one with his will to die. So that his death would be either an arrest of his saving work, or an indifferent sequel to it. It would be a mere anecdote of his life, not its denouement. And the serious question that then results is this, How came such a teacher, such a prophet, to be so deeply, so long, and so continuously misunderstood? If Christ's atoning death is not the central effect of his person, and the central thing to our faith, if that notion of atonement has overlaid Christ's real gospel, how has the whole church come totally to misread its creator, and to miss what for him *was* central. There has surely been some gigantic bungling on the church's part, some almost fatuous misconception of its Lord, a blunder whose long life and immense moral effect is unintelligible. An error of that kind is no misprint but a flaw. It is not mistake but heresy. And, as it concerns the centre and nature of faith, it must destroy any belief in the guidance of the church by the Holy Spirit—which, however, is not a very lively faith among those whose challenge concerns us.

But leaving that, I will keep the question upon lines which represent a less doctrinal interest. What a poor thing human nature must be to have been affected so mightily, nay in great measure revolutionised, by a mistake so complete. What a poor and untrustworthy thing human nature must be, to have found in such a moral blunder the charter of a new ethic, the foundation of a new humanity, and the secret of eternal life. The church has done its Lord many a wrong, but none so grave as this, to have determinedly perverted his legacy, and grieved his spirit in regard to the central object of his mission on earth. It has often travestied his methods, misconstrued points of his teaching, and even compromised his principles; but these things have been done against its best conscience and its holiest spirits. They have passed, and been reformed, and renounced. But this perversion I speak of is greater than these, less culpable possibly, but even greater as a perversion. For it has been the misrepresentation of Christ's central gospel by the church's best and wisest. It has been a more total and venerable perversion than even the papacy. For even had all such passing ills been cured this travesty of Christ's central intent would still have gone on, and gone on with all the force lent by a purified church, and all the spell of saintliness to wing the central lie. If the cross was but little to Christ in comparison with his real work, if it was a mere by-product of his mission, a mere appendix and not a purpose, and if his church has yet made it central and submersive of all else, then the enemies who swore Christ's life away did him no such bad turn as the disciples whose stupidity has belied him over the whole world for all time. And those browbeaters who would let him say nothing did his cause less harm than those apostles who made him say what he did not mean.[3]

3. I would here anticipate a remark that may occur to some to the effect that I am allowing too much to the authority of the church, and that it the arguments I apply in respect of the nature of redemption were applied to polity we should be delivered into the hands ot Rome and an episcopal succession. In reply I would point out that the church stands to the nature of its generative redemption in a relation quite different from that which it has to every other doctrine. It was the one thing that created the church, and therefore the church's verdict upon it has an authority quite interior to her views on all besides. We may take the constitution of the church, the ritual of the church, or its theological system at any stage; and not one of these has the same creative relation to the church as Christ's atoning death. We may even select from the system of the Catholic dogma the doctrine of the Incarnation; that truth, central as many find it, has no such centrality as the principle of atoning forgiveness. The doctrine of the Incarnation did not create the church; and the doctrine of the cross did—in so far as that can be said of any doctrine, and not rather of the act and power which the doctrine tries to state. The doctrine of the incarnation grew upon the church out of the experience of atonement. The church was forced on the deity of Christ to account for its saved existence in Christ. We can experience the redemption as we cannot the incarnation. I have already said that the sot*er*ology sprang from the sot*eri*logy—the creed

But we cannot stop here. There is worse to follow. What was Jesus about to leave such a blunder possible? What a *gauche* Saviour! What a clumsy teacher! How awkward a prophet! How unfinished with the work given him to do. Regard it. Suppose the central thing committed by the Father to Christ's charge was not the atoning task; suppose he himself was not central to his own Gospel, yet he departs and leaves a body of disciples who do believe his atonement to be the great work, and his person their God. And these have grown and spread into a Catholic church, which, amid many distractions and divisions, still founds upon this evangelical rock, and is the greatest product of humanity. Well, I say, if there be this central perversion of him by the body of his disciples and apostles, first and last, then and now, what are we to think of him? If he so discharged his real mission from God, and so gave his message during three years of public and responsible life, that a central misunderstanding swamped that message as he really meant it, and smothered his word in his cross, what kind of testimony was that he bore, and with what face would he return to

of the person grew up in a church which had been created by the experience of his salvation. The authority of the church, therefore, in respect of the manner of its salvation is primary compared with its authority in regard to the constitution of its Saviour, far more in respect of its polity or its practice. Its testimony as to the cross is its witness to its own life. Here Loisy is right enough. There is a *continuum* in the church which takes precedence of every specific view the church may hold. It is the continuous, supernatural, eternal life. Only that life is not an indefinite vitality, without feature or content, and capable of almost any. But it is life as the new creation, carrying in its very heart its mark of origin, and having the seal of proceeding from the cross as the action of God's holy love on sinful man. My point then would be this. As the witness of an illiterate saint to God's grace in the redemption which has made him what he is has a value for the objective nature of that redemption that belongs to no other piece of his theology, so with the large testimony of the household of faith. Its witness to the divine act which called it into being and made it what it is, is on another footing from any matter of its polity or speculation. The church might have gone widely wrong on grave points like these without wrecking its own existence; but to have gone so widely wrong on the point I am treating would be for the church to commit suicide, to cease to be the thing that God once made, and practically to deny the Lord that bought it. For that there would be no repentance. The church of the papacy and the mass was reformable; but a church that renounced universally its atoning redemption would not be reformable. It would be extinct, however long it kept the name to live. All turns on the cross (*i.e.*, the total person of Christ put into the cross) being the power creative of the church, and on the church's relation and witness to this source and secret of its life.

him that sent him? If his cross cost him not only his life but his true message, and if his apostles of the cross have been among the most active obscurantists of his real kingdom, surely when he consented to death he signed away his commission, he consented too soon to die, and he accepted the one thing that foiled his true intent. The hour was not ripe when he thought it was that he should return to the Father. Never did he think his death would be captured, exaggerated, and exploited like that to obscure the Father and the kingdom. I say, if he left his disciples convinced that what was to him a side interest was his supreme bequest, and if the net result of his act all these ages has been to deepen and spread the mistake, then was he any fit trustee for the purpose of God? Observe this, too. The mistake is most deeply held and hallowed by those most near his own saintliness; its effect has been to generate that sanctity as nothing else has; it is only discovered to be a mistake late in history, by men who, however good, have more sense of what is rational than of what is holy. Well, noting this, can you suppress the question whether sainthood to Christ is good service to God? If, I say, the saints nearest to him have done most to decentralise in favour of the cross what was really dearest to him; if his greatest cloud of witness becloud his real word, and help but as the crowd helps at a fire; if those who know they are saved only in his blood are in effect one with those who were guilty of his blood in silencing his real testimony—what are we to think of him who so mismanaged things as to allow the blunder to be possible, who left his work in a condition that permanently spoiled it, and bequeathed to his best believers the doom of perverting the counsel of God?

Nay farther, if the effect of Christ has been that the church has worshipped a Redeemer on the cross when it should but have hearkened to God's prophet in his words, if it gave him worship where it owed him but attention, what must be the frame of mind in which he now lives and sees the misbirth that has come of the travail of his soul? If the church was left by him in such a state that it has gone on living on another centre than what was really his and God's, how shall we conceive the bitter regret with which he now views his old effort in the light of experience and of heaven. He who, we thought, had redeemed Israel botched the work, and left it to harden into a mere theology. And he who, we thought, ever lived to make intercession for us, must ever live in petition for himself, that God would graciously forgive the well-meant failure he must sadly own. If the effect of the church's evangelical faith upon Christ in heaven is to surprise and disappoint him by its central note, then, before the Father, he has to apologise for this diminution of *his* glory, he has to lament that the work was not put into better hands, and given to one without the genius of being misunderstood most by those who loved him best. And what before God he would have to confess for us, and deplore for himself, would be not only the diminution of God's glory but its unhappy eclipse by his own. He has been taken and made a king in spite of himself; and a king whose effect has been, not to hallow the Father's sole and suzerain name, but to obscure it by his own, to divide the worship and deflect the work of God.

I trust these thoughts will not be deemed extravagant. They are efforts to think to the end and to think with the foundation of faith, the intelligence of conscience, and the experience of life. They are not the exercises of an ideologue. They are efforts to recall our minds to the need for concentration, decision, finality, and footing; to call them in from dawdling and dabbling in eternal things; to protect them from the current susceptibility, discursiveness, and distraction; to guard them from a too mobile sympathy, which answers every novelty, joins every society, reads the latest thing, and sows itself on every wind; to secure them from a morbid vivacity which has a brisk interest in everything, and may even reach a curiosity about the Eternal; to shelter our minds from the humane optimisms in which the devil whispers that the devil is dead and the perfection of manly culture is at hand. I would force our concern on one vast world issue in which time is won or lost for eternity, and the whole human soul for the all holy God. We handle matters where to be right is to be right upon a final, sublime, and eternal scale. But to be wrong there is to fly from orbits of celestial range, and do damage at last to the inhabitants of heaven as well as the dwellers on earth. To be right here is to secure the church's future, to be wrong here is to doom it. But for the church to be right here is for the church continually to cry "Holy, Holy, Holy, O Lamb of God, that takest away the sin of the world, have mercy upon us and grant us thy salvation."

5

Faith, Metaphysic, and Incarnation

Much must be said, in religious thought about the absolute, and it may raise in some a protest against the introduction there of metaphysic—though for faith the absolute is the holy. Stated in the language of religion the absolute is the holy; and the holy is in religion the first interest. Let us, however, examine this protest.

A reaction has long been promoted against the metaphysic involved in the Christology of the church. And since the Anglo-Saxons, like the Jews, are not a metaphysical people, as the Greeks were and the Teutons are, and since it is not comfortably thought among us that God should be more in any land than meets the middle register of thought, where alone we are at home, so, we consider, while he may perhaps "geometrize" he does not philosophize. The philosophers do not think his thoughts after him, they only guess. The positive sciences, in which we are so strong, represent for us the main lines on which any God must move. The middle register marks the limits which we must not pass if we are to think judiciously about him—one wonders how the soul could live if God thought as soberly about his Son or his sinners as we strive to think of him—and the result has been the specifically English philosophy of Agnosticism—now happily asphyxiated as we rise to higher thought and breathe a rarer air. The further result is that, in a crisis of thought which involves the whole mentality of the world, culture is not equal to the spiritual situation of the world, though it was so in the Catholic age or when the Puritans had touch and commerce with the great Reformers. A long isolation within our seas, now ended with results none can forecast, has secluded our religion from some leading movements of the world's thought and has cast some minds upon obsolete patristics and others upon poor pietisms, so we are unready for the modern crisis of faith and vulnerable to rather shallow challenge. Many plod along in a provinciality of thought and an inadequacy of faith which is much more prone to pick up the thin questions of the dilettantist than to grasp the thorough answers of the master.

> We yet do taste
> Some subtleties of the isle that will not let us
> Believe things certain.[1]

The two chief mental movements which to-day tend to monopolize the interest of cultural religion and to impair a positive faith in Christianity may be described as Historicism and Psychologism. Historicism tends to dissolve the objective of faith into a handful of facts that will not carry it down the course of time, and psychologism tends to resolve religion into subjective processes or symbols which do not guarantee objective reality, but are, at most, the emergence into conscious action of man's own subliminal resource. Neither the one nor the other can give us a religion, and the tendency of their correction of religion is to correct it out of life. For a religion the first requisite is an objective reality, a reality which is objective to the whole race and which we either reach or receive. According as we receive it we have it as revelation and by way of living faith; according as we reach it we have it by way of discovery, of thought, of metaphysic. But then metaphysic is the movement of thought which historicism and psychologism unite with sentimentalism to reject, and in cases even to despise. Hence, if metaphysics be disallowed in aid, and if religion or faith (which has been described as popular metaphysics) fail, the sense of a real and objective God fails; the note of reality goes out of such religion as we have left, and with that in due course all fails. We become subjective illusionists, surer of mood than of reality. We have more religion than God. We are more occupied with religion than with God, and more influenced by it. We have no stay. We rotate on our own axis, and having no sun we stagger along without an orbit. We are driven to and fro with the hour and its events, with the world and its fashion. Religion itself becomes but another of

---

1. Shakespeare, *The Tempest*, 5.1.124–27.

our vivid interests instead of our vital center. We become unfit, and then palpably unfit, to be leaders of life or to control it. The public, which, after all, needs a reality and an authority more than anything else, passes us by disappointed. To placate it we take up practical social enterprises, partly in despair and partly in hot fits, and we are not able to carry them, after a time, as we become disillusioned with their results.

The Anglo-Saxon mind, I say, is not metaphysical. We suspect such a pursuit on the whole. We dislike such words as "the absolute" or as "finality," we distrust people who tell us that if God is not absolute he is no God, and if faith is not final it is not faith, and yet we get up a certain toying interest in things like Monism, which cannot even be discussed without grasping the idea of an absolute, whether it is believed in or not. But mostly we are prone to think we have got on wonderfully well with God as a working hypothesis, or as a tacit assumption, or as an entailed property, when he has ceased to be an object of direct and inexplicable certainty for our living, personal trust. And so far, it is time, we have done fairly well. We do not have our feet on rock, but it is wonderful what can be done by skillful shoring and upheld by clever device. We are hung up with surprising success where we cannot stand. We are floated with almost invisible cords from the flies, so to say, and we are able to go through our part, and to seem to stand, in scenery which would not bear our real weight. Religion may lack footing, but the lack is veiled, so far, by the old traditionalism, constitutionalism, and nationalism which suspend our faith. Faith rests on churches deeply interlaced in the whole fabric of the social order or the national mind, which does not care to inquire too deeply on what the church itself rests. So that the lack of personal faith, in the evangelical sense of the word, and the lack of metaphysical interest or aptitude are veiled, and for a time to some extent made good, by these stays. But we are passing into a time when these cannot strengthen the mast. What is the state of its socket? Is its stump rotting in bilge? Questions are being rapidly raised which cannot be answered by a mere appeal to tradition, nor by a mere young optimism. The mast cannot hang from the shrouds. By the present failure of civilization in a Europe called Christian issues are being stirred which cannot be laid by a mere reference to the way in which religion has become inspissated in our social existence or the soul carried by use and wont. Many of the churches drop the apparatus of history, institution, or nationality which suspend the average soul and give it security over the abyss. They have not the historic sense. They dismiss it with claptrap about slavery to tradition. They retain tradition only in the form of the Bible, or of an orthodoxy, or, at the other end, a legacy of liberty—all ill-understood. And now that the critics are exploiting even the halfpenny press it is questionable how much longer the biblical strand of the old cable will hold. It is certain, moreover, that the daily and practical use of the Bible among Christians as a means of either grace or truth is not what it was. Orthodoxy has become a pillar of salt, and liberty, for want of a creative center, turns to mere liberalism and that to credal anarchy, and, accordingly, the sense of the abyss is coming home. Thousands now feel that they are swaying where once, though only suspended, they were safely held. The steadying cords, the guys, are cut; will the carrying cords and cables last? Not only individuals but congregations are in this state of oscillation. They grasp at one device after another to give themselves a reason for existing. They plunge into social interests or social work for that purpose, and sometimes into more work than their degree of faith carries; work which may be an expression of restless energy more than of powerful faith; work, therefore, which produces only the limited effect of mere activity and then leaves the workers disheartened because they do not get the returns that can come only from spiritual conviction and moral power. The effect of detachment from a national past was less marked so long as the old theology lasted, with its philosophic affinities and its metaphysical base. When personal faith felt weak the pious community still had a creed there, unwritten sometimes but understood, which claimed to present reality in ordered and adequate Christian thought, and so beneath them people still felt the everlasting arms and they had a tacit but real base for liberty. But these serious theologies are in popular discredit. We hear how absurd metaphysic is, and especially the metaphysic of Orthodoxy. The Chalcedonian Trinity goes, along with Hellenic thought. We learn not only of the futility of metaphysic, but of its mischief for religion; and we prize much the touch and tone of literary religion, and the religion of the minor culture and the *petit maître*. The metaphysical contact with reality therefore is rudely broken, on the one hand, and on the other the contact with it by personal faith, in the evangelical sense of the great reformers, is much weakened. So little is the Reformation understood that its principle is described, by its very friends, as the right of private judgment—even when that is no more than opinionated ignorance. This is the *reductio ad absurdum* of religious atomism. It is the necessary outcome of the substitution of religious individualism for personal religion. It is religious atomism (that is, irreligion) working itself out by an innate logic and revealing its paganism in religious chaos; for it is a pagan principle whose source is the Renaissance, the Rationalist Illumination, the Revolution. It is not the principle of the Reformation. That principle is personalism, and not individualism; it is personal faith, which has submission to authority in its very being, since it owes itself and everything to absolute grace, and which has a church lying, inevitably, in its very nature, because it means union with him whose presence dissolves egoism in a common salvation and places the believer in a church by his very act of belief in such an object as a common Redeemer. The principle is not an individual self-sufficiency in love with its own uninstructed views and more jealous for its rights than concerned about truth, which is what private judgment has but too often come to be. Between a rationalist individualism and an evangelical personalism all the churches sooner or later will have to choose. For these live together like acid and oil. It is a misuse of words as well as a failure of insight which calls it mere polemic to make this issue clear to the easygoing, and sure to the shallow optimist, who is the happier the less he knows, and the more hopeful the less imagination he has to pierce the present and gauge the future. The greater the originality the keener also may be its polemic with the actual situation. There is no such polemical power as Christianity. There is nothing that wars with the world, and with the church as it settles in and enjoys itself in the world, like God's holy love. The New Testament is the most polemical of all books. It is occupied with the most polemical figures in the world—Christ, Paul, and the church. It is polemical and dogmatic. Therefore it begins and ends in the Cross and its holy war. And it has nothing of the degenerate charity which is so easy to the sciolist who believes himself to have already appre-

Faith, Metaphysic, and Incarnation

hended, who cultivates a thin judiciousness, and thinks that sharp issues are but sharp tempers striking fire.

But, though not metaphysical, Anglo-Saxondom is in its own way deeply religious, and its faith has all along protested against its native agnostic thought. Its Christianity has at heart always protested against its philosophy, or rather, if one may coin a word, its misosophy. And the churches have, at the deep core of their practical limitations, cherished a general faith which finds the mental habit of the positive sciences too strait for it and which now seeks in Idealism or in mysticism a place where it may dwell. The metaphysical instinct so deep in faith runs wild, when its satisfaction is denied it by agnosticism, in a grandiose Idealism, on the one side, and on the other in a mystic Monism which will not bear thorough thinking and is, after all, but a spurious or belated metaphysic served often in warm milk with nutmeg. The faith of Christianity reacts against a meager Monism as much as against a dark Gnosticism—which after all Agnosticism is. It is Gnosticism with the current turned off. Certainly the faith of the Church Universal does so react, and, while protest against the Athanasian Creed grows, it is not so much protest against its metaphysics as against its freezing of metaphysic and its condemnation of those whose metaphysics advance upon its own. Not only does the metaphysic in that creed represent at bottom an element essential to Christian faith, and inevitable in its development, but historical relativism especially should remember that it was the high-water mark of the thinking of the world at that age and stage. It is not to metaphysic that we ever object but to archaic metaphysic made final and compulsory. When thus abused that Creed ignores history both backward and forward. It ignores the historic Jesus and it ignores the moving church. But whenever intelligent Christianity again reaches any philosophy parallel to that of the Athanasian age it will produce another Athanasian Creed as metaphysical—or more so, as being more adequate to the empire of thought and access to reality opened since that time. But it will not be enforced with penalties, and it will not be Greek metaphysic. It will not be so intellectualist, but far more voluntarist. Since Kant opened the new age must it not be a metaphysic of ethic? And since the discoveries of recent science about the contribution of matter must it not be a metaphysic of energy rather than of substance? And especially now, since Wundt and his peers, must it not be a metaphysic of psychology, of the moral psychology, and of the psychology of active and positive faith in particular? And it will be neither compulsory nor damnatory, because it will not be the church's faith, but the science of its faith. And it will not be without its mystic note, only it will be the mysticism of the conscience and that of imagination, investing personality rather than nature, history rather than thought, and action rather than essence. But the historic Christ, who was submerged by ancient metaphysic, suffers but little less at the hands of the modern Idealism—a fabric more fine and stately than anything outside Plato. It occupies mighty minds, but also descends to the public as theological liberalism, or a religion of general ideas which are made the criterion of all positive and historic faith and become the popular substitute for metaphysic thorough and scientific. In the critical camp the historic Christ is dissolved, under this influence, where in the orthodox he was buried. And it is a question, which they may discuss who have the data and the leisure, whether it is better to be immured in a great, elaborate, and artistic tomb or to decay under a solvent which destroys the possibility of resurrection. What we have from a despotic metaphysic, or an inadequate metaphysic, or a vague warm metaphysic, or the denunciation of all metaphysic, in a reduction of religious weight and the impoverishment of public faith. Popular belief of course cannot be a belief in metaphysic, unless it is very implicit. But a church whose ministerial belief and teaching reject it with contempt must lose weight and grasp in the long run, and must starve the religious intelligence of the public and its own effect on a world scale. As with the sacraments so with metaphysics—the deadly thing is not the omission of them but their scorn.

 Why does Christianity cherish this pertinacious gravitation to metaphysical belief? The tendency is incorrigible, especially, for instance, in connection with the person of Christ. Why is it that faith, as soon as it has served the more near and urgent uses of the soul, will not consent to be denied access to questions and convictions about the essential nature of Christ and his relation to Godhead? Why does it shrink so passionately from agnosticism about the Incarnation? Is it because the genius of the church is metaphysical and she finds "a higher gift than grace" in "God's essence all divine"?[2] Is it because she has drawn into her communion chiefly those who have philosophical interests and metaphysical tastes? Quite the other way. The great mass both of her members and ministers are nothing of the kind. Most of them, indeed, are people of the other kind, bewildered by metaphysic as such, skeptical of it chiefly, impatient and, even angry with it, as involving a kind of effort to which their energies and interests do not naturally run, even in their supernatural consecration—to say nothing of those who regard such interests as no energy at all, but a way of wasting time—while, on the other hand, the philosophers are mostly against the church, or outside. No, the church does not cling so tenaciously to profound conviction about the God of Christ because that doctrine gives popular shape to speculative principles or general ideas, but because it is a prime necessity for the collective (though not always for the individual) faith which makes a church what it is. It is the nature of Christian faith that urges the church, more, indeed, than it consciously knows, upon thought and statement, even of a metaphysical kind, about the absolute nature of the Christ it absolutely trusts. Christian faith, in those classic types which give the true normality, is the sinful soul's committal to Christ for ever and ever. It concerns the undying soul's eternal rock and rest. It is not a matter of aspiration, nor of spirituality, nor of love, nor of ideal humanity. It is the redeemed soul's absolute trust and total self-disposal to its Redeemer for eternity, so that it is a case of more than loyalty—of property. It is the peculiar, the characteristic act of an eternal soul and will. And to belittle it is to belittle the soul and to reduce religion from its place as the life total and eternal to be but one of the leading interests of life. Christian faith is such absolute faith in Christ. The soul intrusts itself to God-in-Christ for ever. But what ground or stay is there for such an unshakable faith unless we have an unshakable Christ? And how can we have an unshakable Christ for an eternal soul if we have not in him our soul's eternal God? And how can we really have God in him without some suggestion of ontological continuity, however defined? A voluntarist union of will and will is not enough, and we press for something that makes a di-

---

2. Newman, "The Dream of Gerontius," lines 802, 805.

vergence between them impossible. What is the truth in *non potuit peccare*? We have God in Christ, not simply through him. And in Christ's essential unity with God we have the only condition of that absolute trust in him which is true Christian faith, however loosely the word faith is used for lower levels of religion. A man might pray to Christ as many pray to saints. But that is not Christian faith except at an early stage, perhaps a morning twilight. It is another and a greater thing; it is the supreme Christian thing to "roll the soul on Christ," to make him responsible for it forever, to commit the soul to Christ's salvation and keeping as its committal to a saving God. The soul then finds Christ to be its universe. It finds all the world in Christ, as well as its own eternal destiny of communion with God. What is the real nature of that world?

The necessity, therefore, is not speculative but practical. It is a necessity of the personal and experimental religion of the conscience to treat Christ as God reconciling, redeeming, guaranteeing our eternity. If is a necessity which is but another expression of the finality of Christ's salvation.

I would here repeat that it is not so much the challenge of some revelation in Christ that makes the great religious crisis of the hour, now that agnosticism is dead, and materialism; but it is the challenge of his *finality* as a revelation, of his note of eternal crisis and redemption. Many own a revelation in Christ who do not admit its absolute nature. It is this note of ultimacy and of reality that favors metaphysic. You cannot hold to this finality of Christ's revelation without a faith in the Godhead of Christ which hankers for some metaphysic of it in the church's schools. Other and more sectional religions put a halo about the founder's head as a mighty saint; but faith in Christ is universal and final because the prodigal soul comes home and finds its Father and heaven in him, and invokes him not as divine but as God—which the New Testament does. It is a religious interest, a practical and not a rationalist, not a philosophic, that urges the church into the deep interior of Christ's person, even to the metaphysic of it. For religion would not be Christian if it did not rouse thought also in the stirring up of *all* within us to bless his holy name. And to think as thoroughly as we are saved is to become metaphysical in spite of ourselves. I know that the impulse of many who denounce metaphysics is religious also. They think metaphysic starves, deflects, and distorts religion. And no doubt they have some ground in history for this, but they have none in reality. The church has certainly suffered from metaphysic. It has persecuted for metaphysic. But so, and more so (it is now said much more so), the State has persecuted thought, and penalized certain political opinions, without therefore dooming political or constitutional science. It is a poor and negative campaign to fight an inadequate metaphysic with none, to meet misuse here with total abstention, or to sock in monistic meditation a stay which can come only from energetic thought. In special connection with the preexistence of Christ the interest became metaphysical only in a secondary way. It is not mere love of dogma (except as dogma means depth, footing, and clarity) that leads Christian thought to pierce the interior of Christ and to find in him not only the key but the Creator of the world. If we read the New Testament with the eye of the biblical theologian we discover that it was not an intense but doctrinaire belief in Christ as the organ of creation which led to a faith in him as Saviour. It was the other way. The faith that found in him the eternal secret and security of its soul found in his vast personality also the key and crown of all souls. It found in him, therefore, the destiny of all history, and so the consummation of the whole world. But it could not stop there. It made then an inevitable step forward by thinking backward, and by finding that the world which was made for him must have been made by him, that he could not issue supreme from the world's close unless he had been supreme when the world rose. *Nihil in eventu quod non prius in proventu.* The Christ who had become Lord to the first Christian age, and who would be Lord to all ages when history was wound up in the Kingdom, must be the Lord before all ages and before the foundation of the world. And the same thought has been forced on the church from its sense of God's love. The eternal love needs an eternal Son. Could that love find itself again in an idea of its own? Could the living God love an idea as his Son? The lover of an idea might be a philosophic God, but not the Holy Father. And if an eternal Son was a necessity for an eternal love was Jesus Christ not he? Or had the eternal Father two in whom he was perfectly well pleased—one in heaven and another upon earth? If God loved but his world it was only a cosmic emotion. Or was it humanity he loved? Was humanity the eternal Son, with Christ for its most representative and illustrious unit but a unit still? In that case humanity was increate. But if we shrink from that, if God loved a created and manifold humanity, ungathered into one person, loved it not philosophically, as an idea, but heartily, as a race of hearts and souls, then it was a love distracted and dissipated into millions of points without concentration or unity. Therefore his love was without a passion corresponding to his divine unity; it was mere discrete benevolence. It was a love infinitely vagrant, passing from individual to individual, upon some detained and brief upon some, a love merely preferential, so that Jesus was but his best beloved, but it would have nothing in the object of it corresponding to the unity, power, or eternity of God as its subject and source. Love would then not be divine enough to rise above individualism on a larger or smaller scale, and election would not be the whole action and economy of love, the providential order of love, so to say, but would come too near the caprice of favor and the volatility of taste. The eternal Son alone gives to the moral element in love the priority over the natural and the capricious. We have a divine love of humanity only in the eternal Son, only if we are loved in the Father's holy love of the Son. For it would be but a sanguine and amiable surmise of ours that human nature, in itself and as we find it, was so divine as to be the worthy object of God's love, to say nothing of his habitation. But if the eternal Son made man His "tent," on his way to making the church his body and all men the church, then humanity was such a nature still as could receive and house him (though not express him) without his being either lost in it or soiled. Its constitution remained divine enough for that, even if its moral state had become hopeless and as impotent of itself to draw him by an affinity from heaven as to rise boldly to his side.

All the metaphysic of the Trinity, therefore, is at bottom but the church's effort to express in thought the incomparable reality and absolute glory of the Saviour whom faith saw sitting by the Father as man's redeeming and eternal Lord, to engage the whole and present God directly in our salvation, and found the soul in Christ on the eternal Rock. It is a metaphysic of personality that is involved and of personal action. Also in so far as the doctrine of the Trinity is metaphysic it is not the property of individuals; nor is the belief in it the measure of individual faith. It is a belief so great that it is at home but in the range of the collective faith. It is, first, the

Faith, Metaphysic, and Incarnation

matter and property of the collective church; second, of the competent representatives of the church; but, third, it is active in its power with many who are not competent nor forward to discuss it, but are in living relation by evangelical faith with the reality of the saving God it enshrines. A doctrine of the Trinity may be, so far as the crude individual goes, a piece of theological science, but for the church it is a part of its essential faith. It could not renounce it and remain a church. Its power would decay. For the individual it can be implicit, but it must from time to time become explicit for the church in some form corresponding to the age and stage of thought, if the church's great Word is to survive and its general faith is to meet the greatness of its Word. The whole fabric of belief round such a doctrine is an indication that faith which works out in love works out, by the very kindling, subduing, and universal power of love, also in thought. It is all an effort by some of the best minds of the race to take in thinking earnest the church's faith that Christ is Lord, and that he is throned with God because he does for practical experience what God alone can do for the soul. With the experience of the first church, and its worship of Christ, there was only one choice—the choice of his displacing the Father in the church's religion, or of his becoming the Son in having whom we have the Father also, and forever must have him. And the creeds of the church have all along been in heart and intent its formal expressions of its infinite faith that when God gave his Son he gave himself, that in his Son he *came*, that he dealt with men so closely as he never did before and so finally that he can never do it again, that he gave them not a messenger but his own heart, and not an opportunity of being saved but an achieved salvation. When that faith is raised from popular language and thought out, it means a doctrine of the Trinity, finding in the historic Son the Father's real gift of himself and his achieved purpose, and not a mere intimation nor a movement of willingness toward us. In Christ God did not send a message of his love which cost the messenger his life, but himself loved us to the death, and to our eternal redemption. The revelation of God's love could only be God loving. God alone could reveal God. The Godhead of Christ is therefore much more an element of the gospel of experienced grace than a result of philosophic thought. This is shown by the fate of that modern philosophy which promised to do most by philosophical ideas for the Trinitarian truth. Hegelianism split into two streams, of which the left has carried the day and become the chief motor in those who not only deny a divine Christ but dissolve an historic. It is by no metaphysic that we come to the faith of Christ's Godhead; but, having come there, some metaphysic of it is inevitable wherever religion does not mean mental poverty, the loss of spiritual majesty, and a decayed sense of the price of the soul and the cost of its sin. It is not possible, indeed, to adjust to any category of thought faith's certainty of the absolute union of the sinner and the sinless, of man in his struggle and God in his calm. The Incarnation is a peace that passes understanding. But faith would be so far dead if it did not compel the mind to revolve the theme, explore the gift, and swell the praise.

The reasoning from faith, therefore, would be in this wise: God's love as we have it in Christ his Son must be taken with infinite, seriousness and reality. It is not a partial mood or a passing fancy of God for us; it is God's eternal nature, relation, and purpose to us. If God be there at all, that is what is there. You may of course deny that God is there, or that he does love; but, if he does, that is how he loves—altogether or not at all. The absolute God, the holy, knows nothing of half measures with the world, or half gospels. Christ may have been wrong in speaking of such a God or in believing in him, or we may be wrong in so construing what Christ did believe or say, but if Christ was not wrong, and we are not wrong about him, God's love in Christ was that absolute and eternal, love for all mankind which involved the whole and holy God forever, from which love no power can separate us. About this absolute love we need something more than assurance from a third party. When it is the last issue between the soul and God no third party can intervene. Certainty is not to be had by stationing the most luminous and piercing religious genius at some point where he can see both God and man, each being invisible to the other, and where be can report to either hand that the other part is satisfactory and trusty. What we need in Christ is not an external ground for God to trust our faith, or for us to trust God's love. We need to have in Christ God's love itself; God loving; not an effect of God's love, but that love in immediate action and contact with us. Christ's love is really God's love, not the sublimest testimony to it. Christ is not God's love-letter to the world. It is the church that is God's epistle. Christ is God writing it. That is Revelation. It is Redemption. How far we have traveled in this beyond the idea of Revelation as something emitted from God! It is God coming as something and doing something. It is not something given by God, it is God giving himself. When we truly pray we pray *for* God, for God's gift of himself, more than *from* God, more than for gifts from God. Revelation is not a word from God, it is God the Word. It is not a man from God, it is God as man. It is not man doing something for God. That is not the essence of Christianity. It is God doing something in man and for him. It is the real action of God's person—direct, yet in the Son. It is the real presence in Humanity of God's being—immediate, yet not unmediated.

Some may hesitate, perhaps, about that phrase—immediate, yet not unmediated. Well, it is much worth hesitation; it is worth lingering on it. It is a stumbling block to many. It is either nonsense or it covers something so true that nothing but a paradox can express it. The latter is our alternative. It is strange in terms but it is all the more true. It corresponds to a real process. It is even psychological. May I illustrate? Nothing, I suppose, could be more direct and immediate than your sight of me or mine of you. But in fact neither of us sees the other at all. All we see directly is an image on the retina. Indeed, I, sitting at my remote center, may not see even that directly. There may be several processes between that image and my perception of you. Before I could interpret that image as you, and realize that it was a solid weight of body with which I could collide, and a resisting power of will with which mine must deal—before I could develop the image on my retinal film into a real you—I had to go through a long but totally forgotten process of visual education by the aid of touch, by what used to be called the muscular sense, and by much other similar discipline during the first stage of life. That immediate perception we have of each other is condensed and crystallized mediation. It is a vast abbreviation. It is a portmanteau act. It is mediation become habitual, automatic, unconscious of itself. It has mediation embedded in it, subliminal to it. It is mediation become immediate. It is immediate but not unmediated. This is only meant to show that the phrase is not philosophic nonsense, but good science in the region of psychology. It is no less sound in the region of theology. We all admit that our faith in the Father is mediated by history, by Christ's presence in history. But that fact—Christ—might be quite empirical. Christ might be but the first link in a chain, the first medium instead of the standing Mediator. We are not such positivists as to stop there, with that piece of historicism. He is to us all that he was to the first century, or more. Our faith is mediated through Christ in the way of spiritual process as well as part transmission, in the region of the spiritual world no less than the historic, by the present sacramental value of tradition and of the world in the action of God himself on us thereby. The historic fact becomes a spiritual sacrament on which God glides into our soul. Indeed, in Christ we have the Word which makes all sacrament. In Christ we feel we have the action of God direct, yet mediated. The mediation does not impair the directness. It did not precede it; it is always acting in it. We have God in Christ at first hand, and seeing him we see the Father. So that the sacramental relation between God and man in Christian history and experience is but the correlate of an essential relation within the Godhead itself. The relation between God and man is not identical with that between Father and Son (as those say who promulgate the doctrine of humanity as eternal in God), but it is parallel, it is correlate. "I in you as the Father in me." And God's love to man in historic revelation has under and behind it God's love to the Eternal Son, for whose sake the Father loves man, as Christ himself loved mankind not for its own amiable sake but for the sake of God and of his miraculous grace in loving us. What we possess in Christ is so much God's love that it is the love eternally directed upon Christ. God in his grace loves us with the same love as he bestows without grace on Christ. By grace we are caught up into the Father's love of the Son. It is not a case of the natural love of offspring transferred by us to God, but it is the action of a more eternal and holy love transferred by God to us in Christ. Christ transmits it vitally, as its eternal living object and not as its mirror; not as a medium, but as a mediator; he does not even testify to it as an historic genius or a prophet with splendid insight into it might do. Now the eternal object of God's love could not be an idea unless God were an idea and no more. It must be in a parity. It must be as real as the living God. God the beloved must be as real, personal, and eternal as the loving God. The beloved Son must be a constituent of the divine nature and personality. For,

Faith, Metaphysic, and Incarnation

if not, God was determined into loving by something outside of himself, and something therefore less eternal, which would leave him not absolute and holy God. Only if the beloved Son was God was self-determined, and eternally determined, into love. By the very nature of God as love we are moved to the belief in an eternally preexistent Christ—and to his real preexistence, not merely to an ideal. Christ is the object of God's love; not as if that were an intellectual love for the intellectual beauty, not in the sense of the Son's having an ideal preexistence in God's thought or purpose, as if God were an eternal dreamer or infinite speculator enamored of his own thought, but in the sense that he had a real preexistence as personal as the love bestowed. The divine thing in Jesus was eternal in God. And what was the divine thing in Jesus? Some nucleus or core in the historic personality? Some astral entity, as it were, which could be drawn out of the deciduous man Jesus as a finer soul in soul? No; neither real history nor scientific psychology will let us think like that. The divine thing in Jesus covers, and indeed constitutes, the whole historic personality, that whole moral entity, which Peter, James, John, Judas, Caiaphas, and Pilate all knew as Jesus. The divine thing was Jesus Christ. The actual, historic, personal Jesus was no mere temporary correlate of God's love, or of its ideal object. The divine thing that came to us was not a message nor an influence, nor a spirit, but a person, and not a prophet's person but the divine presence. He, his person, *was* the divine thing. He did not contain it. He was not simply its tenement. He was not a prodigious human personality completely filled by the (less personal?) Spirit of God. That wore in the end quite docetic. It would mean that the more we developed the divine element the more thin we wore the finite receptacle to give it room. The Son of God as the Son of man was not the divine wine in a goblet of flawless crystal. The divine thing in him was that which made his person, and did not simply fill it. The same personality must be both God and man. Else which redeemed? If it was the indwelling Spirit, then was the personality of Jesus redeemed? Or shall we give up an idea so embarrassing as Redemption? Even human personality is no mere receptacle; it is a power. And God can only be in it by some mutual involution, as power interpenetrates power, or, even more intimately than that, as person lives in person, as the Father dwells in the Son of his love. Jesus, in fashion and person as he moved among us, was the eternal object, peer, and polar continuity of God's love, else we cannot cross the gulf between Christ's conviction and God's reality. If Christianity is absolute faith (and we cannot trust for eternity the merely probable), the real personal Father had the real and personal Son Who is our life for his love to rest on in the depth and mystery of eternity. All the analytic objections or impossibilities which can be raised against such a faith by the lower rational man are our old familiar friends, who disagree in the basement while worship goes on in the church above them. And this Son, as a constituent element of Godhead and not a mere phase of God, was not only sent by the Father but himself came with equal spontaneity into the world to save it. He came *ex proprio motu*, through his own free responsive obedience to his Father's saving will, and through his love to both God and man, in some form of self-emptying and self-renunciation. The Son willed our salvation as surely, as creatively, as the Father, and willed his own work for it. All the acts of Christ's self-sacrifice here were but the explication of the one compendius, renunciatory act of his person in coming here. He came to save God's holy name and purpose by saving man's forfeit soul—first to gratify and delight the Father, then to save God among men, and then (and thereby) to save men for God. God spared not his Son, and the Son spared not himself. So that we may say that, while a personal Humanity the product of God's love in creation, a personal Christ is the object of God's love in eternity. Humanity is personality in finite detail; Christ is personality in its infinite but compendious and holy power. And we are loved for Christ's sake.

We may, therefore, perhaps, sum up thus:

Christ reveals to us God's holy love. He does so not as a prophet with its message, but as the Son with its presence. His work was God's work, not in report, nor in effect merely, but in action. What, then, does Son here mean? It means that the revelation, as taken home by the faith it creates, is final. Nothing in God was dearer or higher than his Son. When the Son came there was no more to do; and no higher revelation possible. No future revelation can separate us from the love it reveals—that is, can transcend it by a greater and leave it behind. It is absolute and eternal. Christ is the real revelation of God's being, in the sense of its self-communication. He is the one supreme visitation of God.

God's being as love was eternally resting on the Christ who came to us, upon no Christ with an existence merely ideal, as if the earthly Jesus were but an historical avatar of an idea capable of various other visits. But upon this personality the personal love of the Father forever rested, well pleased, in the depth and mystery of Godhead's eternal life. It was a real preexistence—though here formal thought is soon obliged to stop, and we believe by experience what we cannot construe in scheme.

I am well aware, I have hinted, of the difficulties on either side of such an idea as Christ's preexistence. Both the man who ignores these and the man who treats the belief as nothing but fantastic theology discount their own right to a weighty opinion because they do not show that they have gone into the subject far enough to discover the difficulties of dispensing with such a thought. It is what the Germans describe, by an untranslatable but useful word, as a *Grenzbegriff*. A *Grenzbegriff* is a notion of which we can form no explicit conception, but which is forced upon our total thought as inevitable. It is an idea which contains the necessity of something transcendent without being able to describe its processes, movements, qualities, or colors. One side of it is known, the other is unknown. Such is matter, for instance, in the region of natural science. It is a notion that carries us over the limit of our sensible or scientific knowledge, but it is indispensable for the reality both of me, who know, and of anything to be known. A *Grenzbegriff* is an impenetrable but luminous reality against which all our thinking is brought up, or rather to which all our thought moves, but which, if it cannot be construed, is yet so rational that it cannot be denied without giving thought the lie and making the conceivable, the formally rational, the test of reality. To admit such an idea is much more rational than to deny it. The necessity is rational, however illogical. It was thought that forced us to it, though it be not amenable to a rational scheme, and it is inaccessible to the processes of conceptual thought. It cannot be thought, and yet it must be owned. Our thought cannot go here, but we do, our soul does. For our thought is but one function of our personality, which has a larger projection and intent. We commit ourselves, by an act in which the whole person disposes of itself in faith, to a region where, though we cannot see our way, we yet hear a call and feel an outstretched hand. It is a leap in the dark, but it is a vocal dark.

The eye fails us, but from the cloud there is a voice, which does not fail, saying, "This is My Eternal Son." So for our Christian faith the eternal preexistence of Christ is as indispensable as it is inexplicable. *How* the Eternal Son could empty himself to the historic Jesus Christ is quite inexplicable, though we may trace analogies, but religion taken seriously, thoroughly, makes the faith eternally inevitable. Our inability to conceive the "how" of a kenosis need not make us renounce the fact. And most of the difficulties about a kenosis turn upon the method rather than the principle.

The difficulty of the Antiochene view, which regards Christ as a human personality specially prepared, and then filled, at a certain time or by a certain development, with the divine Spirit, is this (and it is what drives one on some form of kenosis): In such a theory the divine is not the element which forms the personality. It fills it when formed, but it does not constitute the personality—where, however, the modern accent falls. It is not compatible with modern views of the historic personality of Jesus as the acting and effectual power. That historic personality, with which we start as a thing so real, becomes a thing less and less real as we ascribe the ruling action to a divine content which is not personal in the same sense, while, on the other hand, if we throw all the personal action on the human tenement we reduce the divine factor to a mere influence. For there could not be two persons in the one man Jesus Christ. Also, on this view we do not secure the divine initiative for the work that engrossed the personality of Jesus. The divine Spirit is reduced from the doer to the suggester, and God does not redeem so much as inspire redemption. Besides, if human nature must be redeemed to receive the Spirit how can the Spirit fill even the greatest human personality before proceeding to redeem? And could a Spirit that only fills a person, and does not act as a person, redeem human personality? It is such difficulties as these that forbid us to speak of "the Deity residing in that man in transcendent fullness, but in the same way as in the souls of other men." That sounds pious and modest, but it is inadequate to a situation so serious as to be soluble only by redemption. It is beneath the classic Christian experience, where redemption is the central need. Faith is humble, but it is not modest. It is very bold and daring. And we are therefore led on to think less of a man with a measureless gift of the Spirit than of Godhead becoming man by a kenotic and renunciatory act. This leaves possible the idea of Redemption; the former discourages it.

It cannot be too often emphasized that the chief breach with traditional dogma is partly in the method and partly in the use of it. This appears especially in connection with the doctrine of Christ's deity. In the old dogma the admission of this deity was necessary to make a man a Christian; in the new it is believed because the man is a Christian. We apply the modern principle of belief in miracles to a special and crucial case. The miracles used to be viewed as a help to faith; now it takes all our faith to believe in the miracles. So with the great miracle of the Incarnation. You must be a Christian to believe it instead of believing it to be a Christian. We need all our Christianity to believe it as it took all Godhead to effect it. The Incarnation is the ultimate doctrine of Christianity, but it is not the first in the order of individual experience, which is justification. So far the pragmatists are right. We work from results; but backward. Our theology rises out of our religion. We must pass through a certain experience of faith, in which Christ does on man the work of God, ere we can believe him to be God. Without the experimental faith of redemption that belief is impossible, but with it it is inevitable. I have already suggested that the metaphysic of the future seems to be indicated as a metaphysic of the ethic and psychology of the soul in its moral experience. The metaphysic involved is the metaphysic of personal faith as life's life, the metaphysic which that faith implies (though it can produce no faith), the metaphysic not of substance but of energy, of spiritual energy especially, and most especially of redemption, through the faith which answers redemption. It is the metaphysic not of Being but of the Holy Spirit. It is not the condition of faith but the conclusion from it. We must experience Christ in order to realize that in so doing it is God we experience; we can then go into the metaphysic of that moral fact. The traditional method constantly tends to put formulæ over faith, and to set theology in the place of religion instead of at its heart. Men may and do define Christ's deity to the practical neglect of his person, and without any communion with himself. We may come to lay more stress on the Virgin Birth or on the Christology of the Logos than upon Christ as our living God and Saviour. We may see more clearly the truths that underlie Christ than we feel and confess him to be the grand fact of God's intervention underlying our life. But it is as such an intervention that we must feel him for New Testament faith. To treat him only as the *beau ideal* of aspiring faith is to do him even more injustice than to treat him as the incarnation of certain eternal ideas. To regard his faith but as the classic case of our own faith is to be no more fair to him than when we try to reach him by metaphysical formulæ. To regard God's presence with him as but the purest nearest case of his presence with every soul is to treat him more as our superlative than as our Saviour. He is the fact and act in which God the Saviour comes to us, and not the great instance of our coming to God, His gospel is one of God visiting us; and he is the visitation of God which he declares. We can never have the same relation to God as Christ had. We can never realize his relation to God as he did. Even religious psychology here comes to a standstill. We cannot follow the spiritual process between him and the Father. He never told that love. It was his own secret. He died before his disciples knew it. He had to die that they might know it. And when they knew it they could express it only in their personal and practical faith as a church. Their theology of it was mainly allusive—as in the great kenotic passage of Philippians.

By such an experience and such a belief he is the foundation of our experienced faith and not simply its historic source. It did not simply begin with him long ago; it rests on him now. It is his gift now. What rests on him is not simply the other end of the historic chain, but the weight of our present souls in every age. His function does not cease, nor does he disappear, when he has introduced us to God, but in him God always descends on us, emerges in us, seizes us, forgives us, changes us, creates us anew. It is this experience of the new creation that has really demanded from thought the metaphysic associated with Christ's deity—but demanded it from faith's thought and not from thought's faith. For God is will with thought in it, not thought with will in it. The ontological deity of Christ is a necessary condition of the new creation, but my belief in any formula of that deity is not a necessary condition of my being created anew; it is only an inevitable corollary or expression thereof. It is one thing to feel secure before God, but the sense of security (guaranteed, say, by a church) is not the experience of salvation; and it is another thing to desire and possess God, the living God. The deity of Christ is the real means whereby this possession is possible; it is not a matter of assent for attaining the security without personal certainty. The redeemed do not see how they could be redeemed if the redeemer is not God; but no man is redeemed by simply believing that he is. Redemption is so great a miracle that we cannot be surprised that its great thinkers, the theologians, should have put in the forefront the Incarnation as the miracle of miracles. It made redemption possible. But that is not the same as to say that its admission must precede our experience of redemption as a reality. We do not infer the redemption in Christ, deducing from his deity, but we move to his deity regressively from our redemption with its quickening of all our power and insight. It is the experienced power of the Redeemer that forces on us, that has forced on the church, his deity. It is our new creation in Christ Jesus that makes us seat him on the Creator's throne. None but the Holiest could offer the Holiest that which our sin owed; and it is that sense that makes us find our God in him who is our atoning peace. It is because we are overwhelmed thus with God's visitation in him that with all our heart and soul and mind we begin to ask how it is possible. If indeed we could *fathom* that we should be looking down over the God before whom we ought to bend. But we may at least discern some vital things about Christ's relation to God which do not presume to fathom it, and when we find God actually reconciling us in him we cannot help inferring some more substantial unity between him and God than between God and ourselves. The inner life of Jesus could not really reveal to man the inner life of God if at his center he was not more God than man, and doing the redeeming thing which God alone can do. But it is in Christ's person, and not behind it that we must look for the secret; in its historic act and not in it's putative essence; in an act of his person (even though that act was begun before the world was) and not in the process or mutual behavior of two natures in that person about whose qualities we have no sure information except in the revelation in him. Through his work which the Godhead of Jesus reaches us and finds us. But it is a work which the great experience of the church finds not only to impress us but to recreate us, it is a work that it finds begun before the foundation of the world. And it it be metaphysical to venture anything about what transpired in such an eternity then metaphysical we must be.

6

Revelation and the Person of Christ

I

Amidst[1] the Churches, sects, and parties of Christendom, there is one cross division which does not correspond with any of the familiar lines. It is the mark of a spirit rather than of a doctrine, of a tendency more than a polity; and it may be described as the division between those whose chief aim is spiritual *safety* and those to whom it is spiritual *certainty*. Roughly speaking, it follows most closely the distinction between the Roman genius and the Protestant; but it separates even Protestants among themselves in a way which forbids us to regard it as the dividing line of the two communions. It expresses, however, the difference between the Roman and the Protestant spirit in whatever Church it is found. And if ever that great breach is to be healed it must be by such recasting of doctrine as shall harmonize these two principles, and discover a certainty which itself *is* the soul's saving health, and not merely leads to it, promises it, or fulfils its preliminaries.

The doctrine which is most directly affected by this distinction is the doctrine of Revelation. The varieties in our conception of what is meant by Revelation resolve themselves into two classes. There are some who view it as providing a set of conditions, to

---

1. The writer of this essay desires to express his obligations, both in thought and occasionally in phrase, to the writings of Professor Herrmann, of Marburg. These obligations, however, are religious and theological, and he would not be understood to share the philosophical position which is the negative side of that school. The stress laid upon the experiential rather than the philosophical side is due to the fact that the essay is more a tract for the times than a balanced scientific discussion—which indeed space did not permit.

comply with which secures by a divine but arbitrary connexion the future *safety* of the soul; and there are others who regard it as conveying something which is in itself the soul's *certainty*, its natural food, its health and salvation present and eternal—briefly, as a Soul coming to be the soul's life. The whole change and deepening now going on in our idea of Revelation may be said to be due to the progress of the latter view. It is the protestantizing of Protestantism itself under the influence of its own principle of salvation. This lies not *through* certainty, but *in* certainty, in certainty of a kind which itself *is* salvation. The way is the truth and the life. Revelation, that is to say, is not *through* Christ, but *in* Christ. Nay, the old inveterate error can only be erased by boldly saying, Revelation is Christ. Revelation is not a thing of truths at all. It is not scientific. It is a matter of will, not of thought. For it would then be but an adjunct of salvation, and its answer would not be religion, but assent, not choice, but knowledge. Truths dwell but in the forecourt of the soul. Freedom of thought is a far less precious thing than the freedom of the soul, and at this moment far less imperative. It is for this latter that Revelation exists. It is not for illumination, but for redemption; and as only a soul can free a soul, as only a soul can mediate between soul and soul, Revelation is therefore not a thing of truths, but of persons and personal acts. It is not truth about God, but God Himself as truth; and it is not met by any belief about the soul, but by the soul believing.

When the purpose of Revelation is viewed as the soul's certainty rather than its mere safety—its inward self-security rather than its happy situation—it follows that the Revelation must be in a fact. That fact, we have just seen, must really be a person. It must be a fact of history. A real Revelation must be historic, and its power personal.

To make Nature the site of Revelation, to seek it in the Kosmos rather than in the Ethos, is the very genius of Paganism, and it is the source of the humanist and scientific Paganism of our own day. And this is true, however refined our Kosmos may be; though it be the most rarefied system of principles or diamond network of ideas. It is a procedure which leaves the character of God too much at the mercy of any particular stage in the history of discovery, or any passing phase in the history of poetry. It ends in nature-worship and idealized atheism. All truth is from God, but it does not all lead us back to God. It does not reveal Him, though it act divinely on us. Much truth passes to us through valves, as it were, which prevent the current of thought from returning by the same channel to its source, and compel us to reach it by another circulation. If we will use words carefully, there is no Revelation in Nature. There can be none, because there is no forgiveness. We cannot be sure about her. She is only æsthetic. Her ideal is harmony, not reconciliation. She may hold to her fitful breast her tired child, soothe her fretful sons, kindle her brilliant lovers to cosmic or other emotion, and lend her imagery to magnify the passions of the heart; but for the conscience, stricken or strong, she has no word. Therefore she has no Revelation. For Revelation is not of thought, structure, or force, but of will and purpose. Nature does not contain its own teleology; and *for the moral soul* that refuses to be fancy-fed, Christ is the one luminous smile upon the dark face of the world.

Nor can we find Revelation (in the sense of religious certainty) in the movements of our own pure, pious, and genial hearts, in a natural piety, or even a Christian humanism. These are but heavenly witnesses. It is not the men who have known the heart least that have been most distrustful of its verdict on things divine. It is too unstable. What is at best but a reflection, and not a revelation, of God is oftenest a broken reflection. The polestar itself dances in that stormy sea. But, still more, the heart's voice is the voice of a sinful heart. Sin is no accident, like blindness, which leaves the faculties and the conscience clear; and it is in the hour of our most thorough and guilty confusion that we chiefly turn to seek the certainty which a Revelation exists to give. What is so often called a religion of the heart is but a mystic and sentimental piety, with a fuss about reason and a stress upon ethics, but without the ample thought, the profound passion, and the moral verve of faith. It emphasizes what starts from us rather than what starts from God. It makes light of history, and constantly tends to view Christ as indeed the chief contributor to Christianity, but as a point that we have passed. It treats Him as the discoverer and prophet of the filial principle, but still as its mere agent and subordinate. If the Revelation of God have its immediate source in a movement of our own natural soul, then not only is Pantheism inevitable, as the most refined Nature-worship, but it is inevitable that Christ should come to be viewed as only a medium or preparation for this experience; and it will be felt that He may be safely forgotten in the hour of our rapt absorption with God, as every mere instrument, vehicle, and step of the process must be in the consummation of such an end. But that isolation of the soul with God which is so impressive to minds of the austere, mystic, and individualist type, is not Christian communion. In their solitude with God these devout souls are less lonely than they think. The mediation of Christ is equally necessary to every age and every stage of our Christian intercourse with God, who is to be found not *through* Christ, but only *in* Him. And the true idea of Revelation is that which regards Christ, not merely as the historic cause of redemption, nor even as its theological *prius* but as its abiding spiritual ground and active principle for every man. If He be left behind in the progress of His own religion, both He and it are less than universal. For the universality of Christianity stands on the universality of Christ; and He would be less than universal had He been more to the first stage of the Church than He is to the last—had He been then more real and near. It is just His uniqueness that He is equally necessary to the religious reality of every age, and is a portion of it in no posthumous, but in a very present sense; that He, in His living person, is an element of our moral world and not merely its legacy, its heir and not its inheritance, the test and judge of every age, "the rock on which it stands or the stone on which it falls;" that He belongs to our personal reality as Christians, and is the ground of our religious self-certainty; in whom we not only see ourselves, but find and acquire ourselves, of whom we are surer, in the classic examples of faith, than we are of ourselves or our subjective experience.

Nor can a source for Revelation be found in philosophic idealism, or the principle of divine sonship severed from the person of Christ, any more than in the æsthetic Christ. The active contents of Revelation, it must be reiterated, are not truths, ideas, or even principles. That is the fatal error shared also by the vicious notion of an orthodoxy or saving system. The sole content of Revelation, the power and gift in it, is the love, will, presence and purpose of God for our redemption. There, and there alone, must the divinity of Christ be sought. He was equipped with those powers, and only those which were essential for that work. If He was God, it was because only in that way could the very power and life of God touch us, seize us, change us, and pass us from death to life. It was not chiefly because of a metaphysical necessity. It is incapable of any adequate metaphysical explanation. The constitution of the Godhead before the birth of Christ is no direct portion of His Revelation, however necessary as its corollary. It is possible to believe in His pre-existence as a logical necessity of redemption, while we yet deny that it forms any portion of Revelation so direct as were His historic faith and obedience unto death. The demand for Revelation which is created by the actual situation of the soul and the actual needs of the conscience is not a demand for knowledge, but for power and life; and what Revelation gives is not scientific certitude. It is not an extension of our knowledge. The more we know, the more we need Revelation. So many discussions of Revelation seem to proceed on the supposition that it is to meet our ignorance instead of our helplessness, the craving of one faculty instead of the hunger of them all, the demands of our freedom instead of the passion of our bondage, a sinless intelligence rather than a guilty conscience. They set about assuring us of a "disinterested" knowledge of God, and offering Theism as an experimental basis for religion, whereas no disinterested knowledge of God is possible. Practical Christianity does not begin with Theism. An object of disinterested knowledge can never be God for us, whatever power or reality it may have; and certainly such knowledge is not Revelation, and therefore cannot have much value for personal religion. Revelation has less to do with divine causes, than with divine motives and purposes. It is not aetiological, for it would then be science, and not religion. It is teleological because it is moral. It regards our end and destiny, not our origin. It has nothing to say about Creation; it has everything to say about Redemption. It is silent about the origin of sin; it recognizes the fact and brings the remedy. It is obscure even about the origin of the Redeemer. Its agents are not principles, but personal powers; and what it carries home to us is not so much the thoughts of God, nor even the affections of God taken alone, but what God has *done* on our behalf. We come back to the nature of Revelation as a historic personal fact, which is the object of our soul-certainty and not simply the condition of our safety; in which it is health and not prudence to believe.

And we are sustained in this view of Revelation when we realize that it is not complete till it become intercourse. It is not an act declaratory, nor an act of mere manifestation. It is much more than a theophany. God does not simply show Himself, He *gives* Himself; and a gift is not a gift (however genuine the giving) till it is received and realized as such. Revelation is of such a nature that it can only be completed in a life of converse with the Revealer, of intercourse which takes effect not in ecstasies, but in the actual duties and occasions of our calling in life. It is not a simple act, but an act if mutuality. Its sphere is the world of experience, yet of moral and concrete experience—not ecstatic. Its response is our faith, yet a faith sober, strong, and practically sure, not quietist, pietist, and elate. And while we refuse the Catholic view of the Church as the continuation of the Incarnation, we must yet regard the Kingdom of God as the necessary complement and response without which Revelation would not be Revelation, but only emanation or exhibition. It is a factor without which the Incarnation is not complete, the second pole without which Revelation would have nothing mutual in its nature, but would only move self-contained on its centre like a revolving light. So impossible is it to separate Revelation from Redemption, or the knowledge of what Christ is from the experience of what He did and does. It is not the philosophy of the two natures, but "the benefits of His work" that gives the key to understand His Revelation.

The false ideas of Revelation are due to a false emphasis laid either on the past or on the present. What they fail to realize is Jesus Christ, the same yesterday, to-day, and for ever. Undue stress upon the past leads to the apotheosis of a book or of a system. It may be called in a word *Confessionalism* (including Scripturalism). It means faith in some utterance of faith, at the cost of the active object of faith. The Bible is certainly on a different footing from the creeds in some ways and especially in normality; but in this respect they are alike. They are alike the product of the Church's faith in its Lord. It was not one act of Revelation that gave us the Son in Christ, and a second that gave us the Spirit in the Bible to supply what was wanting to the first. There is but one Revelation, and it is Christ. The Lord is the Spirit. There is but one Christ, and the Bible is His prophet. The Bible is the musical echo of the

Revelation—its reverberation at its first discharge into history in the deep caves and sonorous pillars of the soul.

Christ created the Church, and the Church answered first with the Bible, when faith was pure and positive, and then with the creeds, when it had lost in a refined secularity the glow of its first love. But Christianity is not a book religion. It has a book, but the book is not the Revelation. It does not even contain the Revelation any more than the reflecting telescope contains the heavens. It is the echo of the Revelation repeated, and, in a sense, even enhanced among the hills and valleys of the redeemed inspired soul. All question of a book as a revelation ought to cease when we recall that the Revelation Himself never wrote a word, never ordered a word to be written, and apparently never contemplated any Bible more extended than the Scripture He Himself had used. He thought of the New Testament as little as He thought of the creeds. And so far as His authority goes, there is just as much reason to believe in the infallibility of the one as of the other. If that infallibility be carried beyond Himself, if it be not confined to Himself, and to Himself in His direct equipment for Redemption, there is no lexical halting-place till we arrive at the Vatican Decrees. And yet people wonder why Rome flourishes. Rome conquers as the savages may occasionally beat our troops—with weapons our factories supply. Rome flourishes by working out to their conclusion principles on which a purblind Protestantism hazards its own life.

The other false idea of Revelation is mysticism or idealism, the apotheosis of a heart intuition or of a philosophic idea. They are at bottom one, and they both issue in mere contemplation. Here the undue stress is laid upon the present and not the past. Far be it from us to say that there is nothing mystic about the faith of Christ, or about His Revelation. But it is a mysticism fatal to Revelation when the affections of the individual, or the ideas of a school, supersede the historic Christ as the voice of the living God, and when the echo of Christ's influence is turned into the criterion of His Revelation. He is the test of our hearts; they are not the test of Him. He is no more to be judged by our conscience than His Gospel is to be measured by the Church's success with it among men. To make the heart the judge of Revelation is to raise sentiment and individualism to the control of Revelation, and so to make them the real Revelation. It is fatal not only to the place of

Christ but to the humility of the Christian, as we have evidence in much current Christianity which is generous, rational, beautiful, and sympathetic; but is sometimes irreverent, often self-conscious, and mostly too weak in objective authority to cope with the importunity of the sensible world. A Revelation whose very being is in forgiveness, and whose action is Redemption, is denied in the act of submitting it to be judged by the soul it redeems or the conscience it creates. If a test of anything purporting to be Revelation is to be found, it must lie in its necessary and organic connexion with the inner consciousness of the historic Christ. It is not our conscience that judges, not even "the Christ in every man," but the conscience of the historic Christ in His confessed disciples. It is yesterday's Christ that is the Christ of to-day. It is the Christ of that old yesterday that is the living Christ. It is not "the living Christ" that is the Christ of yesterday. Think what you will of the record of His birth, but do wake up to the irony of the situation when you bring Him to the bar of the conscience which owes itself to Him; and realize the fatuity of testing Him by a culture His Gospel has made possible, but whose sympathies are not with Him and whose terms He probably would not have understood. If such procedure be possible then it is we that have the Revelation, not He; and were He to revisit earth He would have to learn of His God from us, whom once He taught a message that we have outgrown. The Christian consciousness is an obedience, not a criticism; Faith is a response, it is not a source. It is not a judgment, it is an answer to the historic soul of Christ, and evoked by that alone.

II

In the true sense of the word Revelation it must be final. If we possess a criterion of Revelation it is the criterion that becomes the Revelation. Revelation can only be judged by Revelation. Christ's witness to Himself overbears all criticism, except that of the record. Rationalism, whether orthodox or heterodox, consists in measuring Revelation by something outside itself. But it must be borne in mind that Revelation is a religious idea, that its counterpart and response is not knowledge, nor even poetry, but faith. It is for faith, it is not for science, that Revelation is final. It is *the soul's* certainty and power that it assures. It is a religious finality that Christ claims. What He gives is peace with God. His Revelation is final, not in compass, but in kind. All is revealed but not everything. It is a qualitative and not a quantitative finality. He declares the whole counsel of God, but not every counsel. He does not give us a programme of history or a compendium of doctrine, as the Catholic and old-Protestant theory of a book-revelation is. He gives us a power of God, a certainty of faith, a quality of life, a finality of destiny, in contact with Him. Many things were unsaid, yet He said all—all that faith needs, but not all that knowledge craves; all that makes men, but not all that makes civilization— and yet all that makes civilization possible. He declares the depths of God's will, but not the details of His counsel. The Revelation of Christ is final, and was by Him meant to be final, for all that concerns God's decisive will, purpose, and act for our salvation. Christ is Himself the final expression of that. He is not final in the sense of exhausting knowledge. To be exhaustive is just not to be final. It closes one region only to set our interest free for another. He is final because He is inexhaustible, and His silence has the same mastery, depth and suggestiveness as His speech. He is final in the sense of placing us sinful men in living, loving and trustful union with the final reality of life and the world. Our ragged rocks and roaring shoals are flooded into peace by His incoming tide. No higher revelation in kind is possible or thinkable. Later ages might extend the spiritual horizon, but nothing was left for later ages to do in the way of reconciling man and his destiny, man and God. Christ is final in respect of His undying personality and work. Whatever is to be done for human redemption He and no successor does it. Whatever comes to us in the way of revelation is the appropriation of Him. He is the ultimate impulse in the spiritual, and so in the whole progress of man. He cannot be forgotten while His work grows mighty and prevails. He cannot be parted from His work like any mere discoverer. His work is just to make Himself indispensable, to renew Himself in every age and every experience, to become in every life the one power which, amid the withering of all things, neither custom nor age can stale, but which from its throne evermore makes all things new. And he is final, furthermore, in virtue not simply of His harmony, but of His solidarity with the Father. He is thus the organ to us of a certainty which is the final certainty of life, and which would be impossible were He merely harmonious, as we all may hope to be one day, with the Father's will. The finality of His Revelation and the absoluteness of our certainty are bound up with the uniqueness in kind of His person; which is to other persons what His Revelation, considered as truth, is to all truth else—not so much compendiary as central, pervasive and dynamic.

Christian faith has never found the ground of its certainty in itself, but always in Christ. It does not even believe in Christ because of the Bible, for that would be believing because of the effect of Christ, or the Spirit's work, upon others. Rather does faith believe in the Bible because it believes in Christ, and it descends upon historic facts with a trust in the personal fact, Christ, which is more certain to our experience than any mere historical evidence can be. Whatever account an individual here or there may give of his religious moments, in the great classical instances of Christian experience, and in the large witness of the Church itself, it is Christ, the historic Jesus, that is experienced. It is an experience that cannot be explained away as a vision might. It becomes the new life itself. Paul and Luther did not simply see the Lord. That might have been a projection of their exalted selves. But it was a creative, not a created experience. It created a new life, it was not created by the old. Their experience for ever after was a self-consciousness of Christ, as Christ's was of God. He became not an episode to them but their world.

> This vision, far from perish, rather grows,
> Becomes their universe which sees and knows.

Moreover it was an experience without which they would have had no saving knowledge of God.

But no human being ever did for Christ what He does for us all. There is nothing in His experience of any man analogous to our experience of Him. Revelation did not come to Him as He comes to us. He depended on none as we do on Him. There was a directness and a solidarity in the relations between Him and the Father which do not exist between the Father and us without Him. The self-consciousness of Christ in respect of God was not parallel to the God-consciousness in man. The source of religious knowledge was not the same for Him as for us. To judge from history He found His certainty in His consciousness; we find it in Him. For Him self-consciousness was the source of such knowledge; for us it is only its site. Revelation was not made to Christ, but to us in Christ. The matter of Revelation was not a principle which He and we alike apprehend by the same method only with different degrees of completeness. It is not a truth which would thrive in our perception, even if the memory of Him grew dim. To take Him away from present religious reality is to cut off our spiritual supplies, and close in ice our waterway to God. No man is indispensable to truth; but Christ is. He is the divine truth of man. What He revealed was not a conviction, but Himself. His experience of God was His experience of Himself. He was God's self-expression in humanity. He was that even more than the expression of humanity in its ideal. He creates a new humanity more than He embodies the old. His first purpose was not Shakesperian—to reveal man to man. The relief that He gives the race is not the artist's relief of self-expression, but the Saviour's relief of Redemption. He did not release the pent-up soul, but rebuilt its ruins. It was another power than man remaking man; it was not tongue-tied man made happy at last in a rapt hour of complete self-realization.

He is absolutely essential to our personal realization of the principle of His Revelation; and that not as its historic medium, but as its ever living mediator. He is not the founder of Christianity, but the living object of its faith and worship. He taught, he constrained, men to pray in such a way that their prayers turned in spite of themselves to Him. "I besought the Lord thrice." Was Paul there a saint-worshipper, an idolater? If Jesus never expressly invited worship, His Spirit led His nearest disciples to it by an irresistible necessity of faith. He hardly claimed Messiahship in so many words: but He so spoke of the Kingdom, and so embodied it, that the conviction of His Messiahship became to His closest companions irresistible before He died. And so after He rose He came home to them as an object of prayer—by His own injunction indeed, but by His injunction in the shape of a necessity of faith. He is not an instance but a portion of our highest religious consciousness. He is not our ideal; for an ideal is imitable, and we cannot imitate our Redeemer. He is not our ideal, for we transcend and leave our ideal, when we have absorbed him into ourselves. The liker we grow to him, the more we can dispense with him. He does for us what it was in him to do, what at a stage we needed done; and we pass on, to remember him with gratitude but not with worship, to find our freedom in escaping from him, and not in owning his sway. But the liker we grow to Christ the more indispensable He is to us. The closer we come to Him in character, the more He rules us. Those nearest Him have called themselves His slaves, and been their own freemen and the world's in the act. The more abundant our revelations the more of the Revelation we find Him to be; and the more we are redeemed the more we know His sole power to redeem. The higher He lifts us the loftier we find Him; and the more power He gives us the more we spend it in submitting to Him. Ideal is no name for what we find Him to be, and to be capable of being, to us. It seems as if our likeness to Him were only given us to enable us to realize our difference. It is in His difference from us, rather than in His resemblance, that the core and nerve of His Revelation lies. Our resemblance only provides the condition for appropriating it, and making it intelligible. The flesh is there for the sake of the Word. Why should we strive to reduce this difference? It brings Him nearer than any resemblance can. It is just His difference from all men that He identifies Himself with every man. The dearest and the likest us cannot come to us as He can. He is our Saviour, not because He is our brother, but because he is our Lord and our God. We are not His peers. We are not even His analogue, when it is a question of our knowledge of God. His experience is not simply a glorified version of ours. Throughout the New Testament Father has a different meaning in relation to Christ, and in relation to us, with an equal reality for both. The New Testament Father is the God and Father of our Lord Jesus Christ. He is our Father in Christ. "When *ye* pray say Our Father." Did Christ ever say *Our* Father along with His disciples, or in their name? Rather He spoke of "my Father and your Father." Part of the offence He gave was by claiming God "*His own* Father, and so making Himself equal with God." There is a gulf between the Fatherhood of the New Testament and the sentimental fatherhood of literary theology and its popular Christianity. It really concedes the whole Unitarian position to say, that God is the Father of every man in the same sense in which He is the Father of Christ except that He was His Father pre-eminently. "No man knoweth the Father but the Son, and he to whom the Son shall reveal Him."

He *knew* the Father whom He *revealed* to men. It was not by Revelation that He received what in Him is Revelation to us. These words are not among the disputable portions of the Gospels; and they are decisive as to Christ's unique solidarity with the Father, and the dependence of all men on Him, as He depended on none, for the knowledge of God. As Paul puts it, Christ is the Son of God with power, while we are sons by adoption, in all that pertains to the moral relationship as distinct from the natural in creation. Exception may be taken to the metaphor of adoption, but to except to the fact and the difference it seeks to cover is to except to the consistent teaching of the New Testament. There God is revealed as Father, not in our feeling of childship, but in our certainty of sonship in Jesus Christ. He is essential to constitute the sonship, and not merely to aid us to discover it. The intrinsic quality of our religious act is our sense not of a divine principle, but of Christ revealing Himself in us. And Revelation takes effect in us, not as an act of insight, but only as an experience of being redeemed. There are pure souls, reared in the lap of Christian culture, cloistered with thought, and unfamiliar with the deepest, darkest, and most passionate experiences either of sin, the soul, or the cross, to whom this may seem both unphilosophical and untrue. But in a long-established and hereditary Christian culture there is a new danger of a lofty and noble sort, lest the world by goodness know not God.

III

Revelation then may be defined as the free, final and effective act of God's self-communication in Jesus Christ for man's redemption. It is not simply an act of manifestation, or even of impressive representation, but it is a historic and eternal act of deliverance, prolonged in an infinite number of acts *ejusdem generis*[2] in the experience by Christian people of their redemption in Christ. It is a free act as being wholly marvellous and unbought. It is a final act because it embodies, in an aforesaid sense, the whole purpose of God with man. And it is effective because it is only completed by its return on itself in man's experience and response. A sound

2. ["The same kind."]

returns void, but not a word, not a revelation. A Christ is not a Christ without a Kingdom. It is, moreover, the self-communication of God, because it is not a witness to God by His closest intimate even in Eternity, but God Himself at work as our Redeemer. God so loved that He gave Himself in His Son; not, God was so lovely that the Son could not help giving report of it to men. That would make Christ a religious artist more than the Saviour. Nor is it thus, God was so eager to redeem that the Son's heart filled with the design to give the helpless divine passion voice and course among men. That makes the Son the prophet of God, not to say that He came to God's rescue. But God in the Son conveyed Himself, not a report, nor an expression, nor an echo, nor an engine of His will to redeem, but His own present redeeming will. It is impossible to separate Revelation from Redemption. Revelation has no real and final meaning except as the act of Redemption to the experience of being redeemed. Its response is by faith, not by scientific certitude, by faith as the certainty and experience of reconciliation. It is a religious and not a scientific act, and only by a religious act can it be met. Its express object in us is not to produce assent, nor to facilitate discovery, nor to vindicate a rational unity in things, but to establish soul-certainty. It has nothing directly to do with the identity of thought and being. It is free to discuss that and other questions because of a certainty, which cannot wait for their solution before beginning, to live and rule—the soul-certainty "if God be for us who can be against us?" This is a certainty which, as a certainty, is only to be found in Christ. "Cogito ergo sum," says Descartes, and sets modern philosophy forth on its sublime orbit. But, "alas, poor cogitator," as Carlyle says, "what then?" But the certainty which is of faith speaks on this wise: "By the grace of God I am what I am." Religion cannot wait for the certainty of speculation. It did not wait for it in the actual course of history. The certainty of faith is surer than any experience which makes a basis for the criticism of faith, and the autonomy of faith is a more self-sufficient power than the independence of science, or even the final intuition of thought. It is the foundation of our practical life and eternal committal as Christian men. The certainty of faith is a portion of our own self-certainty, because the revelation of Christ becomes a portion of our own personal reality. We acquire a self-consciousness of Christ. As He has passed beyond all dispute into the reality of the world's history, so that by our very birth to some extent we put on Christ, in like manner He passes into the reality of the individual's history. And, as He has become in one sense the conscience of civilized Europe, so, in a deeper and more thorough sense, He becomes the conscience of the redeemed soul, and its organ of intercourse with God. It is impossible for the Christian to pray to God except through Christ, and it is equally impossible on occasion not to pray to Christ or, praying to Christ, not to feel that we are worshipping God. If a disciple had never addressed to Christ on earth the words, "My Lord and my God," there can be little doubt that the sense of them has always risen from the bosom of the Church's experience of its Lord, and could as little be holden as He was of death. That only is a revelation of God for our Christian experience, which can be worshipped as God. The curtain is the picture. A revelation which cannot be worshipped is no revelation, but only the vehicle of it; it is but a communication about God. But Christ is the revelation. He did not receive it. God came *through* Christ, rather than *to* Christ; therefore we praise, we bless, we worship Him.

Indeed, God is in Christ in such a way that Christ's express statement of unity with the Father is of less moment for us than the total impression produced by His whole life and person. This experience teaches us that His presence is God's presence. His action on us God's action. His forgiveness of us God's forgiveness. To convey a living person to us in such a way is more than manifestation, and more even than inspiration. What indeed is inspiration but the glow upon the Revelation as it passes through our human atmosphere? Men were not inspired *for* the Revelation but *by* it. It is the result of Revelation, not its antecedent. The Revelation inspires, it is not the inspiration which reveals. The Christ who taught Paul to say, "I live, yet not I, but Christ liveth in me," was more than an inspirer. And in conveying to sinful men, actually and effectively, the person and will of God, Christ was much more than inspired, more even than completely and constantly filled with God. We may not think of Christ as a human receptacle, whose consecration was in the contents alone. It is quite inadequate to say that the mould of His human personality was willingly and entirely filled by the Spirit of God. Nor may we cherish the common error which understands by the will of God, not the living God who wills, but some counsel or expression of His intent Christ was more than an expression or work of God's will. He was God's will in action, not its work but its working. That is the key and the distinction of His personality. His person was absolutely one with His work. It was not, as Anselm said, a means to His saving work as an end; it was not there to give divine value to His sufferings. Nor, conversely, was His work a means to His person as an end, which is the case with breadwinners like ourselves. There was, in His own view of it, such complete identification of His person with His work as can only be expressed in the idea of Revelation, when truly understood in its connection with Redemption. But, His work was the final will and purpose of God with man. God has no end in reserve beyond Christ. He has no end to which Christ's personality could conceivably be immolated, no purpose which would justify its destruction, without bringing down the whole fabric of our moral world. His person, therefore, was the expression, the energizing of the central final will of God for our salvation, of that will in regard to man which makes God God. His whole self was identified with the sole and final act of God for us. His *whole* self one with the *sole* act of God for us! Does that not lift Him into a place which is of Godhead far more than of manhood, and of manhood only because so uniquely of God? I think it must be so if the statement is understood. But the chief difficulty, in an age so impoverished in moral imagination as the present, is to get statements on such great and deep moral subjects understood before they are denied, or appreciated even when understood.

IV

Real revelation is always Christ revealed in us, and revealed as Redeemer. In a loose and secondary sense any bright imperious perception which occurs in our higher life is so called; with the misfortune that the neophyte in his early raptures mistakes an importunate fancy for a divine call, and treats as revelation what is but a suggestion of his own raw mind under the stimulus of religious exaltation. Faith, the answer to revelation, is the sense of reconciliation with God in Christ. That is the real, direct, yea, sole object of revelation. Revelation does not tell us what to do or believe. It gives us in Christ the power, life, and certainty of reconcilement. It leaves that habitual sense to act on the character, and mould the moral judgment. It is thus that Christ reveals Himself in us and to us. He breaks forth on us from the record. His inner self comes out, seizes us, turns us from historians to Christians, from inquirers to devotees. The picture steps in awful fashion from its frame, and as we sink to the ground it lays its cheering hand on us, and we are at home in the spiritual world. The statue steps from its pedestal while we examine its lines. It steps down glowing, and speaks a comfortable wisdom which begins with fear. No imperfections or accretions in the record prevent this result. Every line and limb is not there, there may even be some restoration in a later spirit, but the idea, the figure, the character, is distinct in our minds even as historians. And from within the historic figure there issues upon us, to make us Christians, the immortal reality itself as a living power, a present Lord, a really present God. And we know then our Redeemer has found us, as surely as we knew that we found Him beautiful and great. If this be not sure nothing is sure on the basis of which we question it. He becomes His own witness in us. What we then have is no mere insight of ours into a revelation set down in the past. It is that revelation individualizing itself into our case. It is the eternal living act of the historic Christ still acting in a particular instance, as the body's life is repeated in the life of its cells. It is the same Christ carrying out in individuals the eternal act he did once at a historic point for the race, and completing revelation in response. No phenomenon in history is revelation except in so far as it comes home to individual souls, is understood and welcomed as revelation, does in experience the work of revelation, and gives man the power amid all the pressure, illusion, and blight of life to be his own freeman in Jesus Christ.

To the individual Christ is this revelation; from which our position seems to follow that He Himself cannot be a mere recipient of revelation, like the man He finds. A Christ who merely witnessed to God's revelation might be a valuable medium of religious knowledge, and a powerful religious stimulus. He might be a great aid to faith and a great benefactor of the soul. But he would not exclude the possibility of mistake, nor quench the question whether he had quite correctly apprehended and transmitted the revelation he received. Then the absolute certainty of our faith would lack historic ground, and we should be driven to seek it in the disputed region of metaphysics. We might trust Christ but we could not trust in Him. We could not feel that we owed to Him our eternal selves, or could commit to Him our eternal souls. His experience would be analogous to ours, and historically the source of ours, but not, in the nature of spiritual reality, the ground of ours. He might be central to religious history, but not to religious reality. If he only realized the principle of religion, if he was only the first to grasp it in its fulness as sonship to God, if he left this principle as his great legacy to the race, if he but succeeded as none else ever did in adjusting his person to a principle, in living up to his high sweet creed, and leaving his life as an object lesson for all men to come—then indeed he might be the greatest of our soul teachers, but not the soul that makes a soul's certainty, not our revelation of God. That would then have to be sought, as he sought it, somewhere in each soul's own area, and in our dimness and vexation seldom found. His person would then have been wholly at the service of the light, but it would not itself be the luminous thing. He would be the founder, but not the object of our faith, the creator of the Kingdom, as Heine said Moses *schuf Israel*[3] but not its life, its permanent King and Head, not its revelation equally necessary for the reality of all time and both worlds, and equally indispensable for every man's forgiveness and reconciled intercourse with God.

V

The form of religious certainty then was different in His case and ours, so far as we can trace Him in a record too scanty for an imitable ideal, but enough for the focus of spiritual force. For us that certainty is attached to a historic, and therefore an external, event, which transpired outside our experience, however it may be echoed and appropriated there; but for Him it had its source within His self-consciousness. We have to seek in Him what He found in Himself and found for the race. He is for us a source which had no analogue for Him. The more we realize Him the more we feel that we can only realize God in Him. And the more free and self-certain He makes us before God so much the more do we repudiate the idea of repeating His experience on our own ac-

3. ["Created Israel."]

count, of ever claiming for ourselves the same position to God that He did, or of finding in Him simply the great spiritual classic, the glorification of the God-consciousness or of the filial principle in Humanity. Doubtless He is the great spiritual classic, our ultimate religious fact, whose experience is worth far more for the nature of religion than all the rest of the race. But it is just the close interrogation of this fact which compels us to regard Him as so much more than the great example of faith, if we use the verdict of His own self-consciousness, and take Him at His own worth. He began with a unity—a religious and not a metaphysical unity—with God, which none created in Him, but which He alone can create in us. We need not haggle about the philosophical definitions or hypostases of this unity. These are largely (even in Scripture) efforts of devout intellect, devised to explain the fact in His consciousness that He started from a unity with God which others only hope at the last to attain, and to attain only in Him. We need not go behind His own experience, which was not metaphysical, and which religiously indeed we cannot go beyond, without claiming a greater. We are face to face with the fact that so far as the Gospel record carries us into Christ's inner life, He did not *achieve* His unity with the Father by obedience and worship, but that His worship and obedience were the continuous expression of that unity. He "learned obedience," but He did not learn to obey. The form of the Father's will changed and deepened for Him with the tragedy of His life, but His unity with that will was as real and complete in its first demand as in its last. He came to know more of the counsel of God, but He never grew more close and obedient to His will. In all His moral and spiritual energy He was not pursuing or cultivating His unity with the Father. He was exerting it. With us there comes a growing, sense of unity with God as we progress in moral obedience to His will, and especially to His incarnate will in Christ. The sense of unity with God as a standing feature and habit of our character is a product, and mostly a very slow product of our practical faith. It is the fruit of much revelation. But with Christ Himself it was otherwise. It was not the result of revelation; for that would call for another Christ between God and Him. And it is more correct to say in this case that the practical faith and obedience was a product of His original sense of unity with God. This is a statement ventured not as the corollary of any dogmatic position assumed in advance about the person of Christ, but simply as the result of an effort to read the nature of His own consciousness from the Gospels. He does not appear to rise to a sense of His unity with the Father in proportion as He overcame the world, but He overcame the world in the progressive strength and exercise of that unity. His victory was the energizing of His relation to the Father; it was that relation in action. It was His life's work not to achieve it but to set it forth and make it actual in a real, a moral, and not a dramatic way. It was not a prize, a capture,[4] for Him, but a gift in Him for us. It was His work to reveal it in the shape of a life, not to shape His life so as to attain it. He revealed it under the concrete conditions of a life which was constantly called on for moral decisions of the gravest kind, and spiritual sagacity of the most profound. Such a life was the element, as it were, in which His intercourse with His Father took effect. It is a mistake to isolate His times of retirement and prayer, and regard them as seasons of intercourse with God different in any true sense from the other activities of His spirit. His labour was not to win His own soul, as with us, but to approve it, to express it, and so to win others. And the soul He had to express was a soul in constant intercourse, even if not in specific prayer, with the Father. "His task was not an ideal which looked in to cheer Him and to light up His weakness." And His intercourse with God was not a mystic process that went on behind the distracting energies of an active life. Soul and life for Him were one, and His actions were part of His total intercourse and unity with the Father. His person, as we have said, was one with His work. In all He did He was giving effect to the spiritual ground behind it. And this ground, this *prius*, was His constant vital solidarity with God. He did not live toward God, He lived God forth toward men. He did not so much face God with us. He faced us with God. And amid all our admiration of His moral power or beauty, amid all our sympathy with His humane and lofty heart, amid the softening of our pity at His sweet soul's bitter fate, we are arrested, we are solemnized, and in a measure rebuked from sympathy into religious awe. We are smitten into faith and worship by the discovery that He is the pitiful and the pitiable are we, that here is no seeker after God, but even in His wrong and agony

---

4. οὐχ ἁρπαγμὸν ἡγήσατο, Phil 2:6.

God's Bringer, His very self and real Presence; and our Martyr is our Redeemer. We kneel down in something more than loyalty as we find in Him the constant sense that He was not visited by great ideals, or sustained by a great principle, but was in every movement of His life setting forth God in an unembarrassed, however burdened, way, and doing what in the circumstances God would do. Who could cherish that consciousness as Christ did without a vision of the circumstances which was God's in kind if not in compass, without a sense of the will of God which was much more God's sense of His own will than any other's vision or apprehension of it!

VI

It may be said that all this makes him irrelevant to life because His obedience thus becomes a different thing from ours, and an easier; for we start from no such unity with the Father. To this it must be answered that it is just the contention of these pages that His obedience was a different thing from ours. But then it was effective for salvation, and ours is not. It was the obedience which makes ours possible; it was inimitable, but reproducible. It cannot be emulated, it can but be repeated by Himself in the members whose life and whole it is. Our great act of obedience is to give up the hope of any similar and rival obedience, of any obedience so comparable or parallel to His that we could harbour the jealous complaint that He had an advantage. He who so complains is outside Christ. Our one obedience is to welcome His obedience as the gift of God, which we must accept, enter, and share as a new and saving obedience. The obedience of faith is faith as obedience. It is faith's nature, not its result. Certainly, He had one advantage; He forestalled us in the claiming of none, in the self-emptying power which so few covet or grudge Him. His advantage over us, too, is our only hope of eternal advantage for ourselves. It is all ours, unless we reduce Him to our competitor.

If the saying of it would discourage our efforts in emulation of Him, perhaps it were well to say frankly that the more they are discouraged the better; if only they are discouraged by that which puts a higher obedience at our disposal, and breaks the self-respect which is the chief inward enemy of grace, and which, in the shape of moral pride in our uprightness and respectability, is the chief obstacle to our salvation.

As for His obedience being easier than ours, the reply is really the same. The antithesis is a false one. It begins by regarding Him as one of us, and so a rival, instead of God's gift of grace to us, to save us from rivalry as our common Redeemer and our King. But the objection is not real, as may be readily tested by asking which of the murmurers would be willing to exchange lots with Him, and accept, instead of their own vocation, that of the world's Redeemer. The answer is not doubtful when we consider how many are willing to drink their own misery to the dregs rather than take the yoke of Christ—even with the aid of His fellowship and strength to bear it. Unless, indeed, this last be what they most resent. For the last enemy to be destroyed is that all but invincible pride and recalcitrancy in man, which will readily yield to an impersonal *law* but must be broken to pieces ere it give way to another *person* as absolute king. This is why social and political progress is so much more rapid and welcome than religious; and it is a fact which removes all parallel between the work of the politician and the preacher, the socialist and the saint. To return, if it is a question of comparative ease in the obedience, the account may be more than balanced when we remember that there was none to be for Him what He is to us, and that He had to seek in Himself alone the resources which He has enabled us to find in Him.

VII

With this ground under our feet we need not fear falling into the hands of the Socinians or their descendants if we feel unable to get our way about in the technical theology of the two natures in one person. If the Incarnation is to cease to be the property of the schools, and become what it is not now, an essential principle of each man's conscious faith, it must cease to be a mere palladium, and become what the Godhead of Christ is in the New Testament—a gospel. It must be stated as a truth of historical and experimental religion, where the wayfarer, however simple, shall not err, so long as Christ has in him his effectual work. And the line we have taken should not be beyond such a man if he know what Christian experience is in any real and final sense. With others it is hardly possible to deal. No one can cherish a Unitarian Christ who recognizes that Jesus not only saw God truly, or truly reflected Him, but knew that His acts were God's acts, His resolves God's resolves, and His love God's love; that His thoughts of Redemption were God thinking (and not efforts to think His thoughts after Him), His person God's real presence, and His work the immediate (though not unmediated) action of God turned on every one of us to seek and save. The things He did were not only well pleasing to God but, God's deeds. Christ was God saving, and no mere agent of God's salvation. It is a difference which seems sometimes to constitute nothing less than another religion. His knowledge of some things was limited, but there was no limit to His love, to His obedience, to His sense of God's holiness, to His knowledge of the Father's will. His solidarity with it, and with the work given Him to do. With that work He was completely one; and it was this, to make good the actual redeeming presence of God in man, first in His own personal life, and next in the slow experience of history. He was one, that is, with the Kingdom of God. His continuity with the Father is expressed, not in his perception of God, nor in deeds which God approved, but in His habitual action in God's name, in His sense of a life which in its totality set forth God the Redeemer, and, especially, in His power to work in us to this day a work like forgiveness, which is the erection of the Kingdom and the work of God alone. The Unitarian or prophetic view of Christ carries us really no further than the orthodox and Anselmic view. Each is the extreme reaction from the other—on the same line and level. They each reduce Christ to an agent of forgiveness. The one makes Him an agent before the fact, in that He met a condition which made forgiveness possible; the other makes Him an agent after the fact who made forgiveness public and credible. But He was more than either allows. He did not simply prepare forgiveness by making a satisfaction possible only to a divine nature; nor did He only declare it with all His heart and faith. By His historic personality, His actual life, death, and resurrection, He effects it in us. "He forces us to feel in His forgiving will the mind and will of God. In this act of Christ, God lays hold of us. And as the Saviour winds Himself into our life, it is God Himself that is setting up a real intercourse with us." To know the inner life of Christ is a thing possible to thousands who have no adequate idea of His biography. Indeed, it seems hidden from many who are deeply versed in the biography. But it is, in the same act and by no inference, to know the inner life of God. And though it is a bold and even extreme thing to say, yet it is a thing which the faith, and not merely the theology, of the Church has often said in prayer and hymn, it is a thing which we must always reserve the right to say, with reverent rarity and upon solemn call—in the death of Jesus it was God that died. It is wrung from us by the maturity of our experience of forgiveness, as well as by reflection on its corollaries. And it is the culmination even of a philosophy like Hegel's, who quotes, in pressing his meaning, the hymn, "Gott selbst ist todt."[5] It is a belief from which mere religious intelligence is much more likely to revolt than Christian thought.

Socinianism is a very natural concomitant of an age like the Reformation, or our own, when a new ethical departure is correcting many of the abuses and corruptions of the religious life, and joining with science to criticize the true supernatural out of the historic record or the personal experience. But it is only general when this ethical Christianity has ousted the specific type of Christian experience (especially the central experience of forgiveness), and its decisive perception of the deep meaning of God in Christ. Much of it is due to a not unamiable deficiency in historic and especially spiritual imagination. Now, as in Paul's day, it is patent enough in many quarters that the world by righteousness knows not God, that its spiritual perception is dimmed by the keenness of its ethical sense, and it stands, as Milton's Satan once stood, "stupidly good." To such a mood the law of Christ is clear, but His person is but thinly understood. It is truly intelligible only to the deepest Christian experience, the experience which chiefly inspired the Reformation, the experience of Redemption—in the Christian and not the Buddhist sense of the word—from sin, and not from grief or wrong.

VIII

But to this experience the uniqueness of the person of Christ is not only intelligible but above all certainties. It is the Revelation which

---

5. ["God himself is dead."]

is the light of all our seeing, and the source of all our day. And it is a Revelation which does its own work upon the soul. It has not to wait for our conclusions on knotty prior points, or our submission to an authority which undertakes to settle them for us. One effect of the true Revelation in Christ is to destroy the abuse of ecclesiastical authority, by removing from the conditions of salvation the scholastic truths which the Church promises the layman to warrant. The saving knowledge of Christ is religious knowledge of Him; by which is meant, not the religious department of knowledge, but a kind of knowledge which is religious, i.e., which is only possible to a genuine religious experience. To this knowledge there are no unintelligible preliminaries. He is unto us Redemption, and *then* we know He is our God. If the Deity of Christ do not stand upon our personal experience of Christ and His forgiving work on man, then it has footing and value only in the schools. Perhaps the most widespread error in Christendom, which is at the root of all its abuse, perversion, and futility, lies here—that assent is demanded from the world for mere statements about Christ as a necessary preliminary of saving, or at least sanctifying, contact with Him. These truths are beyond the intelligence or the verification of most, and so the Church comes to the rescue, with a claim to know and a demand for *implicita fides*[6] which really co-operate with the world in barring men's way to Christ. The priesthood is but the religious form of the tyrannical specialist. Certain statements must be believed, it is said, before you can get any good from Christ. But you are not in a position to believe or disbelieve, you simply do not understand. Then let *us* understand and *you* shall believe, says the ecclesiastic. So you shall come to Christ with a clean bill of theology, and a certificate that the necessary preliminaries have been complied with. How can you hope, says the Church, to be blessed by Christ, if you do not approach Him in faith? To approach Him in faith you must at least believe in the Incarnation. You ask what that means. It means, you are told, the mystery of the two natures in one person and the miraculous birth. It is all Greek to you. (Indeed the Greeks had much to do with the ecclesiastical statement of the matter.) But you are invited to a *fides implicita* on the subject, to confide in the religious specialism of the Church, and trust the

---

6. ["Implicit faith."]

experts of faith, who, to ease your difficulty, will tell you they only formulate what is in Scripture, and that in believing them you are only believing the Bible. The Bible indeed never demands any faith in itself as a preliminary of faith in Christ. It is for certain truths of Scripture that the claim is made. To ensure the apostolicity of these formal but saving truths, the figment of the apostolic succession of the episcopate had to be invented, by a process which culminated in Irenæus; and truth was based upon office where, at the outset, office had stood upon truth. So one lie leads on to another, as in childhood we were often told. An edifice of falsehood rises round a central delusion. A religion of mere position grows out of a religion of proposition. Orthodoxy demands a miraculous clergy for its vouchers. Their unbroken succession guarantees the purity of necessary but unintelligible truth. So now concurring in such truth at such hands, you may go to Christ without fear of offending Him—"Lord, I believe in Thy Church and Incarnation; have mercy on me."

The like use may be made of the doctrine of the Atonement and even the historicity of the Resurrection. The value of the latter in particular is really for faith, not for unfaith; for the Christian, not for the mere historian. It is worth little as a weapon against the sceptic compared with its worth as a seal to the believer. Its force as a converting agent is but secondary. It is not for the world, but for the Church. It is not a condition of faith, but credible only to faith. It was believers who first believed it. This is an old sneer. We can only confound the enemy by accepting it, and extract the sting by glorying in the fact.

All this procedure is not justification by faith, but by works. It is a matter of labour and difficulty to acquire a belief in the Incarnation in this sense. Many toil a life-time, and hardly gain such a conviction on the subject as would qualify them to appear before the ecclesiastical Christ. It is all a huge mistake. That is not faith at all. Faith is the response to Revelation; and what God revealed was neither the Incarnation nor the miraculous birth. It was Jesus Christ, the living God as the living man. We have been going the wrong way to work. We have been beginning to build our church at the spire. These great doctrines are most true, but they are the fruit of Christian faith, not its condition. To assent to them is no answer to the divine Revelation. Plenty assent, and assent intelligently, who never felt Revelation in their lives, and never will. That can only be felt as the soul's reconciled answer to a soul. What has first to be brought to bear upon the world is Christ, not the Incarnation, nor the Atonement, nor even the Resurrection. What is often meant by the Incarnation is the Christian explanation of Christ, rather than God's Revelation in Him. That revelation is life and power, forgiveness and peace. It is Christ as a moral force, as the Almighty spiritual force, as the will and love of God in direct action on the soul for its release. What we have to approach is Christ, the man Christ Jesus. The channel of access is no theory of substance, origin, or person. It is the true, simple manhood of Jesus which we approach, not in search of knowledge or a creed, but of help, forgiveness, strength. It is His business then to convince us of His Godhead, to reveal to us behind His human person the very inward life of God. We have not to begin by explaining Him as a phenomenon, but by responding to His influence and enjoying His benefits. And, while we may criticize His intellectual knowledge, we worship His spiritual place in words no lower than "My Lord and My God." Such we know He is, with a certainty no criticism can shake. "For He hath redeemed my soul from the lowest hell." This is a redemption whose power depends on the practical effect of Christ's person on us, and it is not destroyed by any criticism of the record. It is the first condition of critical justice to the record. It is *only* the Church that can wield criticism justly. For it is criticism of the record of One who has done thus and thus for my soul, and still more for the soul of the greatest society on earth—the Church He created, and creates. A mere scholar on the Gospels is like a pedant on a poet; a mere poet on them is like a church window against the sun, beautifying beauty's source.

It is fit here to quote the great words of Melanchthon in the introduction to the first edition of the *Loci*: "*Hoc est Christum cognoscere, beneficia ejus cognoscere non ejus naturas, modos incarnationis, contueri.*"[7] Nor should this, from among many similar passages from Luther, be passed by:

> These sophists of schoolmen have painted a Christ.
> They have set forth the way He is God and man. They

---

7. ["To know Christ is to know his benefits, not, as those people teach, to contemplate his natures and the modes of his incarnation."]

have numbered all His bones. They have blended the two natures in strange sort. And it is but sophisticating the knowledge of the Lord Christ after all. Christ is not called Christ because He has two natures. What is that to me? He has this glorious and comfortable name from the office and work He took. That He is by nature God and man, is a matter for Himself. But that He took a certain function, and poured His love out to be my Saviour and Redeemer, that is my comfort and my blessing.[8]

IX

It is not only the doctrines of Scripture and of Authority that are readjusted under the true light of Revelation, but the doctrine of Redemption itself. One conclusion we come to is, that the person of Christ can only be understood by His work. This will seem a truism to some who have always held that the Atonement is the true key to the Incarnation. But these are abstractions compared with what is here meant. We mean that the person of Christ can only be understood by His work, His action, upon the world, the Church, and the believing soul—by His effect in experience; that is to say, it can only be *religiously* understood. The authority of the Bible is the authority of Christ's person; and that authority has no other root *for us* than in our experience of His unique and divine function in forgiveness. No views as to the constitution of the Trinity can establish Christ as an authority for the conscience, however impressive they may make Him for the imagination; and in the Catholic Church and theology they have impressed the imagination deeply. But the moral authority of Christ does not experimentally turn upon His consubstantiality with the Father, or His relation to the universe of thought. These positions are efforts at explanation, inevitable but inadequate, on the part of those who had already owned His moral authority. It is in our experience of the actual redeeming effect upon our conscience of the man Jesus that our sense of His authority rests, our sense of His Godhead, and indeed the whole world's ultimate sense of a divine authority at

---

8. Quoted by Harnack as motto of Book II. in his third vol.

all. And be it noted that it is just the sense of a divine *authority* that the world, after centuries of metaphysical theology, now chiefly needs. The sense of a divine *presence* is not so hard either to attain or to own. It is attained by mysticism, poetry, religiosity, philosophy and even spiritualism; and it may be owned without much sacrifice of our darling self-will. But the divine *authority* which ere long will be the one famine in the social soul mad with the peril to its own life, *that* is to be rooted nowhere but on the evangelical foundation of a redeemed conscience. It can rest only on an authority of Christ, drawn, not merely from the fine dignity of His character, or the tradition and succession of a Church, but from that sense of Him given us in the act by which we take the germ of our new life in the shape of forgiveness from His sole hands. The authority in the history of the future is God at the only point where He is indubitable, in His self-revelation and saving action, at the point of Christ in the history of the past Real history must have an authority which is historically real. And whatever moral science may say, practical morality must, with the democracy, increasingly find its impulse and sanction, not in the apotheosis of the paternal sentiment, but in the evangelical experience of Redemption. If the Gospel do not save society, there is no social force that can; interests outgrow affections and there is no authority left. And by the Gospel is meant the historic actuality of Christ's person and its practical effect upon sinful men.

For a second conclusion about Redemption as Revelation is that in so viewing it we transfer the grievous obstacle in the way of forgiveness from God to man; and we direct the work of Christ accordingly upon man rather than upon God. What was to be overcome was less God's wrath than man's rebellion. The wrath of God is not a mode of passion, but a phase of Providence; not a temper, but a treatment on God's part as the Holy Redeemer. What was to be extorted was not punishment, but the true practical recognition of God's holiness. Without that God cannot remain God; He would be Father, but a partial not sovereign Father. But it is the very thing that sinful man cannot and will not give. It is an expiation which must be found by God, and not by man; therefore in God. Jesus Christ is the human revelation that it is so found. In Him God honoured within man the law of His own changeless holiness; He condemned sin in the flesh. He made human response to His own holiness, and a response damnatory. It is too much ignored that the revelation in Christ being a revelation of holy love, must be condemnation as earnestly as mercy. In Christ God did not simply show pity on men, but God was in man expiating sin to His own holiness. He revealed the fact that power to do even that was not sought with God in vain.

The extinction of our guilt is a pure, unbought, inexplicable act of miraculous grace. And the revelation of such extinction can only be the transfer of that act of grace into our personal experience. Its transfer, observe, not its declaration. This is a work that no mere declaration could do, no mere exhibition of pure or even devoted love. Only a person's act and experience can be a revelation to a person. Nor is it real till it be transferred within us. In this case it is God's active experience that must be brought home to us and repeated in us. Such is the work of Christ—to realize and transfer to us the experience of God's holy love in the conditions of sin. It was not to give an equivalent for sin, but to effect in man God's own sense of what sin meant for His holiness. Christ's sorrow and death were a sacrifice offered by God to His own holiness. Christ did feel His death as a divine necessity, a necessity in God, not as an earthly necessity divinely borne. And this feeling on His part, in willing, utter obedience, was God's practical recognition of His own eternal holy nature. Christ accepted sorrow and death at the hands of God's holiness, and bore sin's damnation in humble obedience. And He did so because He knew it was the divine purpose to carry home to us by the effect on Him the holiness of God's love. It was not the sorrow that saved, not even the negative sinlessness of it, but its positive and complete obedience. It was not even the death that saved, but the living act of obedience in it. It was Christ's recognition of it as a divine necessity, which was God Himself meeting the law of His nature and satisfying in man His own holiness.

In some such way may Redemption be treated as Revelation, without becoming a mere exhibition of God's pitiful desire for man, but remaining a work and act of God demanded by His own nature and calculated in its effect to bring us to true saving repentance. As the sole organ of this repentance Christ represents us before God, no less than He represents God to us; and so He is the sole condition of our repentance being saving repentance with God. Nothing here said is meant to impugn the uniqueness of Christ's work for us all. As His religion was essentially different from that of other men, so was His sacrifice. It was not simply the classic instance of the cross we have all to bear. When we have done all, something has to be done in our stead, something unique in its bearing on human sin before God.

In what sense the person of Christ is Revelation, is therefore only to be understood when we appreciate in experience the value of His work for us as sinful men. It is no final revelation for sinless intelligence. The philosophical discussion of this person is full of intense interest and all but supreme value; but for our moral need, which is *the* need of Humanity, it is comparatively sterile. Only the beneficiaries of the cross can effectually discuss the cross, and through it the Incarnation—of which the cross, and not the birth, is the key; the cross, and not the miraculous birth, because the one can be verified in our Christian experience, while the other is a question of the record alone, and cannot. It is the one and not the other that is *used* in Scripture. It is in the one, not in the other, that our certainty lies, and so our Revelation; for nothing is Revelation in the close use of words, which is not verifiable in our Christian experience.

With regard to revelation before Christ and outside Christ, that is so far from being denied here that it is only the revelation in Christ which enables *us* to call these real revelations at all, and which seals the soul of them as the prelude of that complete and saving self-donation in God which in Christ was won and assured for ever. The certainty which only *visited* the heralds of the Kingdom *abides* with us by the indwelling of Him who is the Kingdom. It is only in Christ that their certainty, their revelationary element, is verified and transferred to us.

The doctrine of the Holy Spirit, it may be added in closing, is one that needs re-examination from our point of view. But upon that we cannot enter here. We can but confess His Power, beseech His presence, and beg Him to amend the flaws that lurk in every such effort as this to search His depths and account for His mighty doings in our souls.

7

The Disappointment of the Cross

"And He began to teach them, that the Son of Man must suffer many things, and be rejected by the elders. And Peter took Him and began to rebuke Him. But He rebuked Peter, and said, Get thee behind Me, Satan" (Mark 8:31–33).

The time had come for a new departure between Jesus and His disciples. He must introduce them to the cross. They had found the Messiah in Him; but they could not have kept Him as the Messiah without going on to the crucified. They would have ceased to honour Him as Messiah had they not been carried on to Him as Redeemer. The soul's absolute king must be its priest. If the life of Christ do not lead on to the cross of Christ, it will not continue to hold the place it did as a life. If Christ the ideal do not become Christ the Saviour, He will not remain the ideal. He comes down to be the victim of more or less delusion about Himself. And certainly He will not be able to do for experience what would keep up love and honour for Him as ideal. Admiration, if just to itself, passes into worship. He will not remain the hero unless He is the king.

Jesus did not begin by teaching His disciples about the cross. I am not sure that it was much in His own thought at first. But when it was, He led them on gradually. He did not even begin about His Messiahship. He began about the kingdom, and He slipped Himself into the kingdom in such a way that they could never think of it except as gathering round Him. Was that not equivalent to thinking of Him as King? Such was the meaning of Peter's great confession. It was the sudden crystallising of a conviction, that had long been growing both in him and in the rest, that in their Master they had the Christ. For this recognition Christ had been working and waiting. It was a discovery, but it was, like the greatest discovery always, inspiration. It was the flash of a train long laid.

But the time had now come when they must be carried even beyond that if they were not to fall back. And how did Christ take this next step? He lifted them above the mere idea of a king by shattering it. He took the great step by apparently destroying everything. He broke the old pitcher to show the light of the world. He fell upon their ideas of progress and hopes of prosperity with a flash which withered them. He threw His disciples into a bewilderment they had never felt before amid all their wonder at His mysterious ways. Since the great confession they had had no conception of anything but a career of swift and boundless popularity. How could a Messiah hold back longer, and how could He be anything but popular with Israel? It was the one thing Israel waited for. He would be acclaimed by the people and fêted by the authorities as the Man of ages and of God. They would hasten to place their services, their offices, their allegiance, their religious influence at His entire disposal. This was to be the most popular hero that ever appeared in Jerusalem. The disciples were in the best of spirits—so glad they had clung to Him, so glad they had seen through His humble position, delighted with His delighted recognition of Peter's bold faith. Would the Messiah Himself not be equally bold? Already they saw Jerusalem, Israel, Rome, the world at His feet. And no words can express the shock to them when He said that He must be refused by the country and its grandees, even be persecuted by them yea, die at their hands. The royalists would be His regicides. Why, if He had gone on to say that He would be deserted by themselves, it would have made no difference to their mood. They were stunned and stupefied already. They would not have understood it. They were so benumbed at His words that their faculties would have refused to work and take it in.

You have seen all the sequel of the cross, and you are surprised at their stupidity. But put yourselves in a parallel position. You are prosperous, let us say, and going on to prosper. It is due to your industry, your knowledge of your business, your integrity, your good character, and it has all been supported and consecrated in a way by your religion. You have been a good, useful, and re-

The Disappointment of the Cross 153

spected member of some Church, and you have held the doctrines the Church generally held. Your family has grown up about you and done you no discredit. You expect to go on to the end, and die, as an honest and respectable man should, in the faith which has satisfied your fathers and fellows for long. You have always said that with honest and Christian principles a man is sure to attain to public respect and a comfortable, it not a striking, degree of business success. But suppose, now, that your fortune was embarked in something which could only be saved from ruin by an act which would not stand the finer light. Suppose it were in some concern which you came to perceive could only be kept going by widespread ruin to a great number of innocent people. Or suppose that a voice came to you, as no divine voice ever came to you before, and convinced you (rightly or wrongly) that you could not please God without selling almost all you had for the poor that that concern had made. Suppose it came to you, as it has come to some, that you could not be true to Christ without taking a certain step that would ruin your reputation; or that for Christ's sake you must be silent, though your silence cost your reputation. Suppose these demands were made on you in what claimed to be the name of Christ. I will go farther. Suppose a preacher, in the height of his popularity, had laid upon him a message which left his conscience no alternative but to give it, though it was likely to cost him half his kingdom, weaken his influence with the public, and make his friends look cold on him and distrust him henceforward. Suppose any such case where the will of God came home to a man as an utter reversal of all that he promised and was expected to be or do. The disciples were in a position like that.

I should like (as I have named it) to enlarge the illustration of the preacher, and make it fit the situation of the disciples still more closely. Christ was a preacher, and at first a popular one. I suppose again a most gifted and eloquent young preacher; and he comes newly to a town and a church. The congregation and its managers are delighted. They look for such a time of prosperity as the place has never yet seen. Strangers are swarming into sittings. Never was heard such sweet, poetic, lucid, winning discourse. It was full of charm and light. It had not a tragic note in it. It was just a little above the ordinary way of thinking—enough to interest and instruct, and not enough to bewilder. It gave the maximum of pleasure with the least demand or strain on attention. He had plenty of energy and a pleasant way with him. The children loved him, the press followed him, no meeting was complete without him. He inaugurated several forms of active work. Never had the love of God been made to seem so lovely—such an accession and extension to the love of home, of poetry, of our neighbour.

But there comes to him (it matters not at present how) a new revelation of the love of God in the cross of Christ. It comes upon him in quite a new light. His song had been of mercy, now it was of mercy and judgment. In the cross of Christ he saw the judgment of God. The desperate wickedness of his heart comes home to him, the exceeding sinfulness of sin. In the word of Christ he found quite as much about judgment as about kindness. He would go looking for a text in the Gospels to enable him to preach lovingkindness and tender mercy and gentleness and the childlike mind; and one after another the solemn utterances of the Lord would offer themselves to his eye, and the gentle gracious words would hide themselves away. He had led his people in simple green pastures, watered with much quoted poetry, as if the terror of the Lord existed no more, and the deep agonies, doubts, penitences, abysses, horrors of the soul had no existence outside the stage and problem novels; as if his decent congregation were a fair sample of the world. The *Weltsch-mertz*[1] had never drawn blood from him. The real note of sacrifice, of suffering, of sin, of blood, had never sounded either to him or from him. It had been all altruism and no tragedy, all sacrifice and no curse. The severity of the divine holiness had never come home to him, and he had never sent it home. He had never realised, as he did now, that though Christ came for love, He died for holiness. It was not His love but His holiness that made Him hated and slain. If we owe all to His death, it is to His holiness we owe it even more than to His love—if the two could be severed. But now it had come home to him, and the new tone made itself felt beyond him. People went away more puzzled than comforted, somewhat annoyed at being disturbed, disappointed to miss the quotations and find the commandments, angry to have their snug world upset and their peace troubled. He had much to say on self-scrutiny of the searching sort, of sin still mingled in a

---

1. ["World-pain."]

perilous way with sanctity, of resisting unto blood, of the righteous being scarcely saved, of the most laborious being unprofitable servants, of the gospel release being just as much a gospel demand, of comfort as a spiritual narcotic, and piety in some popular forms as blunting the edge of conscience and stifling the voice of justice. He reasoned of sin, righteousness, and judgment; of such conviction as the work of the Spirit. He asked himself and others how the cross could ever be really popular; how numbers of people in a prosperous, cultured, humane age could ever be brought to rejoice in the very judgments of God, and find comfort in them as part of the cross; how the shattering, humiliating message of the cross to human nature and human pride could ever be welcome but to a few; how its shock to the general self-complacency could be anything but resented by most; how they could stand its trituration of that conscience which told them they were honest, worthy, respectable, good and kindly people.

The love of God came home to him as a new and deeper revelation in this vein of grace. And those who heard him and hung on him were bewildered. They wondered if he had committed some secret sin which lay on his conscience, and was making his position a hypocrisy. They were not enamoured of this disquieting discourse. It took the sunshine, the happiness, the gay domesticity out of life. They complained that such Sundays were no Sundays now: that they brought concern instead of rest, that they did not return to business refreshed, but with new care. Sittings became more easy to procure on the floor of the church (the gallery did not show the effect so much). The offertory began to fall from summer heat to temperate. Some pleasant tennis families withdrew, and the golf people moved near a better links across the town, as their young people were not interested. He began to feel less than his old brisk faith in the human heart as a stay and security. "Appeal to the heart," he used to say to the lay-preachers. "Hold close to the great human affections and interests. Take hold of people where they are tender, and use the love of men as your point of attachment for the love of God. Systems will fail you and theologies leave men unmoved, but the human heart you can always rely on." Alas! he began to have misgivings about that stand-by. He had had some glimpses of his own heart that shook him, and did anything but stay him. He began to realise that Christ did more for men by breaking them than by developing them; that "What must I do to be saved?" was a more hopeful frame, as a first inquiry, than "How can I develop my character?" or even "What can I do for Christ?" He was reading one day the life of a great saint recently dead, and he came on a letter which referred to a famous preacher of the popular sort thus: "If he should waken up to the perception of a God of absolute love, his popularity will probably vanish, and he will have a terrible conflict with himself, perhaps a period of unutterable darkness and unbelief." These words came home to him—not that he was in darkness or unbelief, but that he had seen a light in the cross that was as the terrible crystal, a love that was a breaking hammer and condemning, consuming fire. Love had spoken a holier word than the mere heart could hear, and had revealed itself in the cross to conscience. He had seen men eating and drinking, marrying and giving in marriage, full of comfort, zest, and affection, and a flood descending to sweep them all away. And he had seen this flood stayed by the cross of Christ alone; while the hearty and the affectionate, even within the church, were for the most part ignorant of what they escaped, and to what they owed the security of their lives and loves.

Meanwhile his deacons, his inner disciples, shared the general bewilderment with special concern. They were good, devoted men, and they were overjoyed with the prosperity and promise of the church. They were happy in the paragraphs of the religious press, and some of them had begun to think this was he who should save Israel and give their communion a new lease of life. And they were responsible for the financial conduct of the church, and for the new obligations that had been or were to be incurred. Some of them had grown up all their lives under a system of pleasant sermons with a poetic garnish, whose ideal was a domestic piety, not too troubled with the human aches, and the world woe, and the soul's cry. It was an education which the new minister had promised to finish on more social lines. But it had really lulled the spiritual sense and closed the eye to more vital, searching, commanding truth. They did not know what to do. They thought the change was due to the minister's reading too much theology. They hinted once or twice that what a successful minister needed was an acquaintance with life and not theology, that an active ministry was a much more effective thing than a studious one. The man who said that had a son a rising journalist in London, who had opined in an article that if ministers would sell their commentaries and buy good novels they would turn their pulpits to better account. They would understand the heart in a way impossible to writers or preachers in the first century. And one of them, in his perplexity and disappointment, took the minister aside in a kindly way and warned him that he was on wrong lines. He said that that kind of old, strained, and hectic religion was very well for devotees and those who had not much to do with the world directly, but it was useless for their work with the new world. It was fatal to the prospects of the church, and to their various organisations, which could not be worked without the money that was leaking away. He pointed out that the only hope for the cause of Christ was in the Churches, and if they became feeble, if people were repelled, the kingdom of God must be indefinitely delayed. He was deeply attached to his minister, and he deplored the effect of this extravagant mood upon his future. And what a star of the Church would go out when that public career was quenched, and he subsided into ministering to a little church and living in a little house! He advised him, while not yielding of course to the spirit of the age, to make more use of it, and speak its language, and not go so far beyond its intelligence and its pet ideals. So Peter took him aside—kind, devoted, shallow man—and began to rebuke him.

I am not going to pursue the parable further. And it would be foolish to say that a full church is not compatible with a faithful gospel. There are cases enough to the contrary. It is only a possible and imaginary case, which I use as a modern translation in small type, of the situation between Jesus and His disciples when He told them what the Christian really meant when he took the cross in earnest. What I wish to leave on your mind is not the fable but the thing it would convey, the mind of Christ. There is no doubt that but for the cross Jesus would have been the most popular and effective prophet that ever rose in Israel. But for the cross Israel, through Him, might have been one of the great powers in modern history—greater than Islam, which is the Semitic civilization with Christ cut out. Jesus might have made Mohammed unnecessary, and given far humaner, subtler, and more commanding empire than Mohammed's to the world, at least to the East, if it had not been for the cross. Do you think He did not know that? Do you think He did not see what the empire that *He* could found without the cross might do for the kingdom of God in the world? And did it never occur to Him as a possibility that the cross might hinder that kingdom, or nip it in the bud? Was it never suggested to Him that His cross might prevent God's throne, which a forward policy would establish on the earth? Had He no misgivings about His inward policy? What else was His temptation? Are there not plenty of men, good men and lovers of justice, to day who are honestly of the opinion that if the British Empire could be made for all the world what it is for India, the kingdom of God would be here or near? And a British Empire, as Lord Lawrence might have understood it, or General Gordon, would probably do very much in that way. And yet none of these men were what Jesus was in natural power and kingly faculty.

Do you think He did not realise what He might do in this direction, and what an obstacle and fatality to it all the cross must be? What else than this feeling made His temptation. It was His distraction between cross and empire—empire of course as a means of blessing and not a field of ambition. (His very temptation to sin was of good, like the subtlest in His Church.) It was between these two that He had to choose; and the conflict was so awful that when a voice like Peter's, freshly endeared to Him by the great confession, spoke for empire again, it was like to stir to life all the dreadful strife with Satan who had departed for a season. Do you wonder that Jesus turned in agitation on Peter, and heard in him for the moment the Satan He had disabled but not killed? He did not, of course, allude to Peter's character, but to the position which Peter took for the moment to His conflict and work. He did not say Peter was offensive, but that he was an offence, a stumbling-block, a peril in His path. His very love of Peter made Peter a Satan, a tempter, to Him—as your dearest might be to you, or your ideal, or your success.

There was a danger for Jesus in the remonstrance of Peter which did not lie in the solitary temptation of the desert. It came to Him from one He loved, one of His own. It came pressing on Him what He must make them suffer. It was not His own suffering that moved Him so much, as His sure sense of the suffering He must bring upon those who believed in Him and loved Him. It was unmerited suffering that He bore and that He should cause.

Much of the cross of Christ was His sympathy with those of His own whom He dared not spare, as the suffering Father spared not Himself. None can be more serious agents of temptation than those in whom our heart is bound up. How many a man has sold his conscience for his family, has changed his Church to please his wife, has lost his spiritual ardour in the ease and affection of his home. And is anything harder than to have to go on and do the right thing in the face of remonstrances from those who are deeply and genuinely concerned for our comfort or our reputation; on whom our course will lay new burdens; who are sedulous or ambitious for us; and who are not thinking of themselves at all any more than we are, but of us, and even of our cause?

No prosperity of home, business, State or Church is serving our souls well if it dull our faith in the Man of Sorrows and His sin-made cross. You may view Jesus as the gentle, noble, just, and benignant man, the flower of righteousness and mercy, the incarnation of stately charm and loving goodness. Yet you have to enter—you have not yet entered—the holy of holies. You cannot take Him without His cross, nor without His cross as the crown and key of all. Your soul's king must be its priest. You cannot take Him for all He is till you have taken Him in despair to find Him an endless hope. You do not know what is in Him till you have lost hope of everything and everybody, and chiefly of yourself, and found Him come when all had gone, and come where none can come, and take what none could lift from you, and give you the life that all the world seemed to be stealing from you. You do not measure Christ duly till you find that you have committed moral suicide, from which you are saved by His atoning self-sacrifice alone. Nothing but loss brings home the cross. It is lost men that find the true Christ. Nothing brings out the power and genius of the cross like having all the world against it. "Night it must be ere this lone star shall beam." It is not itself till it is opposed to a world in arms. It is not truly your salvation till it has delivered you from the onset of all the world both in your soul and on your soul. They best know the cross who have been fortified by it against a world all devils o'er, and drawn by it from the lowest hell. God makes His great saints out of great sinners. The offence of the cross is not ceased. Nothing hates it like human nature. It is still and always a stumbling-block to the happy natural man, to the man who is good only because he was born good and likes being good. The cross is still a shock to the natural instincts and the ordinary expectations of respectability and prosperity, culture and common kindliness. I do not say you must for its sake surrender such things. But the cross has a higher law, another standard. And *when the call comes*, that is the law you must obey. And that is the real and final standard by which you must measure life. The cross is the real measure of life. You either stumble over it to spiritual death or you rise on it into newness of life. And if you are not called to bear it in its extreme form yourself, you must be ready with your chief sympathy for those who do, and your whole faith for Him who did. When there are none to bear the offence of the cross, there will be none to save us from the piety of the world, and none to hallow and uphold our ideal of a King. It is a moral revolution when you have learned to love the shame of the cross, and dread somewhat the ease and comforts of life.

Now return to the comfort, interest, and affection of life, to its love and its laughter, as I shall do forthwith; but do it with a new sense of the terms on which you have them and the price they cost, both Father, Son, and Holy Ghost. Eternity itself is moved for the coming of our simplest joys, and all the kindness of life is kept in place by the stern and crushing mercy of the cross of Christ.

8

Christ and the Christian Principle

Can an historical person be the object of an absolute faith? Can a human personality at once express absolute Godhead and exercise a true Humanity? In one form or another that is the modern question which it is vital to Christianity to answer, and to answer positively and securely.[1]

It is a question which arises partly from our modern interest in Humanity as one, partly from our new concern with its several stages; partly, that is, from our new sense of the Idea, and partly from the evolutionary tendency to judge everything relatively to the standard of its own age alone. We do not want to judge, indeed we shrink from going beyond explanation. The same motive as makes us tender with the vices of a mediaeval monarch, because he must be measured by his contemporary standard and not ours, makes us also sceptical about the holy finality of Jesus Christ. The same tendency as whitewashes the sinners takes the glory from the saints. As the world cools, things tend to an equalisation of temperature. The historic mind, it is said, which does not allow us to apply a modern code of ethics to a cruder time, forbids us also to find in any age what would entirely satisfy modern needs, to say nothing of dominating all possible ideals. History, it is said, not only carries home to us, with the eighteenth century, the vast

---

1. N.B.—It may be an aid to clearness if it is explained here that by Christ is meant the historic Jesus as the Eternal and Only Begotten Son of God, and by the Christian principle the idea of sonship taken religiously as the sonship of Humanity, native and inalienable however man may behave, and not secured by a moral redemption in Christ alone and for ever. The principle of personality is not essential to it, and not necessarily Eternal for individuals. In the one case Man is God's son in his freeborn right, in the other for Christ's sake alone.

organic unity of Humanity, but, with the nineteenth, reveals the action of evolution as ruling all that takes place; and it is therefore impossible to fix upon any one point in the past, and so to isolate it from the great stream as to give it an absolute value for every age of a race so vast. The twofold idea of the unity of history and of its movement as evolution affects religion far more than the once dreaded uniformity of nature.

Especially is this so, it is urged, with one like Jesus. He belongs to the past (it is said) in everything except influence; for the present He has not final authority; and He may be surpassed in the future. We can no more deify an historic person than we can crystallise an historic stage, or stereotype an historic creed. No man, indeed, it is allowed, has had such an influence on posterity as Jesus; but He has created a Frankenstein Humanity, which now escapes from His control, and turns to question, and even to dissect, its creator. Jesus had not to deal with an age like ours, an age with our knowledge of the past, and our rights over it. He belongs to the past which we command, and He must accept the same criticism as all the rest of the past from the age of historical science. We cannot allow Him absolute authority in any region, sensitive though we have grown to His spell. We may feel Christ more, but we worship Him less. And we contemplate with calm a remote future when His influence will cease, because it will have done its work and been replaced by other influences giving us all His best and more. We are told that if Christianity is to continue to be a religion when that time comes, it must be detached from all control by the past, though, of course, not from its causation, or even inspiration. It must be detached from Christ in the sense of being made independent of Him, except as He may be considered the prophet or symbol either of Humanity or of a long stage in the human career. The ideal Christ must be loosed and let go from the historic. Time, which was once His home, is now His tomb. We must, indeed, for long (till Nietzsche supersedes Him) continue to hold the Christian principle of our sonship, but that is independent of its temporary connection with the personality of Christ. Most Christians now admit that a distinction has to be made between the passing and the permanent elements in traditional faith. The question is where the line must be drawn. And among the passing elements, it is said, among the beneficent

Christ and the Christian Principle

but terminable illusions, we must include the deity of Christ, and the absolute, final, decisive value of His person and work for our relation to God and our eternal destiny.

Now it should be realised at the outset how far this deposition goes. With a supernatural and final Christ goes a permanent Church, and all its intimate involution in history. The Church has meaning only if the Christian principle is inseparable from the eternal person of Christ. The Church exists and endures in the faith that the principle if detached from the work and person of such a Christ would not have power to keep afloat in such a world; that Christ was not the organ or crystallisation of a principle, but that the principle is the explication of His person and the result of His work; that Christ did not regard Himself or His work relatively (for with all His humility He never contemplated being superseded); nor was that how He has been construed by whose who knew Him best, whether at the first or in the long history of the soul. On that the Church stands. And when the Church passes, the note of spiritual religion must alter. Its great manner of mastery over fate, chance, and change, will pass. Its attitude towards the world will be different; it will be less secure. The religious principle of man's divine sonship will not give that certainty of the Father which the Church's faith in the Son does. It may be noted also, that as the faith in Christ retires the "religion of Jesus" retires too. For the very historical reality of Jesus is now denied by the untrammelled evolution of criticism, to say nothing of His personal religion; and a totally different religion, fitted with all modern appliances and conveniences, takes its place as the religion of Monism. Christ comes to be viewed as the mythical symbol of a priceless idea, which is the real inspiration of religion. But in its own account of itself Christianity is not the expression of an idea. It did not so enter history. It does not condense and point a natural process in the spiritual region. It does not even incarnate the idea of the unity of the divine and human natures. Philosophemes like that cannot make a religion. They did not exude Christianity as a popular metaphysic. That Hegelian version of Christianity has served its day and fallen on sleep. And one reason why we think the Christian principle inadequate without the person of Christ is that the old life and work is found at last to ebb and fade without the old faith. We do not continue to get the Christian ethic or the Christian philanthropy without the Christian creed. A religion of Christian principle is inadequate, after a generation or two, to the work done in Christ, and needing always to be done, for such a world as this—the work of its Redemption, even from fate, to say nothing of sin. It might explain well enough the power of the God-consciousness in Christ as an individual saint, or among certain of His fellow-Christians. It would explain Christ as the filial completion of man's sense of God. It might even explain Him as a healer of souls. But it would not explain Him as Saviour. It would place Him among those whom the action of the principle saved, among His fellow sinners and pensioners of God's grace. But it does not meet the moral case of the world, or pacify the conscience really quickened and grieved. It would explain redemption as the action of an idea or an influence, or view it as the completion of Humanity when it bursts into flower and takes the full air of heaven; but it would not treat it as God's work, as a moral achievement and historic victory of a crucial kind in the region of man's prime need, on the scale of the race's experience and guilt. The meaning of guilt it always minimises. It protests, with a modern scholar, of singular eminence in the American Church, against the idea that "because one man feels his need of divine grace therefore all men must need it."[2] But the New Testament surely regards this as the prime, universal, and eternal need which Christ came to meet. And that intimately personal saving work is possible to a person alone. Here, as often, we see how indispensable the work of Christ is for approach to any true interpretation of His person.

Few thinkers are so luminous in their treatment of Christian theology as Eduard von Hartmann, and none more thoroughly destroy its foundations than he does with his deification of the Unconscious. But this is what he says on the subject in hand: "Christianity stands or falls with faith in the foundation of a new cosmopolitan religion of redemption by Jesus, and in the identity of this historic Jesus with the later idea of a Christ, *i.e.*, with the divine principle of redemption. None who view these as historic

---

2. Macgregor, *Christian Freedom*, 86.

fictions have any further right to the Christian name."[3]

The principle of Lessing, that historical truth has nothing final, and affords no warrant for absolute truth, has sunk so deep into the modern mind that it is worth while to examine it somewhat closely. Historical truth, Lessing and his school said, cannot prove the supreme truths of Christianity for two reasons. First, because the Christian record is not complete. Even as history it is defective. The evidence would not satisfy a jury of historical experts. At some of the most crucial points the data are lacking. We have nothing directly from Jesus Himself. We have from no eye-witness firsthand and tested evidence of an act so central as the Resurrection. We are also unable to reconstruct with complete confidence and modern effect the psychology of Christ, the pragmatism of His action, the motivation, or even the sequence, of His proceedings, or the context of His sayings. But, second (they said), if the record were complete yet it would not be effective for the purpose in hand, because the two kinds of truth are disparate. Historical truth is, by its nature, relative and accidental; whereas the final truth of religion must be absolute. Mere probability, which is all that history can reach, cannot be the basis of absolute religious faith. The soul cannot stake its eternal destiny, or cherish a complete and final certainty, on anything which is only settled by a balance of evidence, as history must be. An absolute faith cannot rest on a probable base. A faith which rests but on the probable has a root of sceptical bitterness which is sure to trouble it at last; and it is by so much the less faith. To faith's demand for absolute certainty history can offer but the probable. The only correlate of faith is God (when we use care about words), and faith in Christ must therefore mean that Christ is God. But a probable God is no God. Yet a probable God is the most that mere history permits in connection with Jesus. There is, therefore, a great gulf fixed between an historic figure and an absolute faith, so that none can pass to and fro. Hence the *penchant* of our critic-racked age for a mystic religion, or an ideal Christ, interior and superior to history and its

---

3. Preface to 10th edition of Hartmann, *Die Philosophie des Unbewussten*.

sceptics. "*Spernit Humum fugiente penna*"[4]—as Ferrier quotes and puns.

It is worth while, perhaps, to cross-examine the chief witness. The exact words of Lessing are these: "Accidental truths of history can never be proof of necessary truths of reason."[5] First, it may be observed how awkward, how ambiguous, how archaic is the expression "truths of history." It is not the truths of history that we have chiefly to do with now but its facts, and especially their nature. But Lessing belongs to a bygone day of noetic and propositional religion. Its orthodoxy was but the intellectualism of the right, its heresy the intellectualism of the left. Christianity was to him and his age a matter of truth more than of life, act, or power, and facts were but empirical; none could be super-historic, none sacramental. He belonged to the time when Rationalism, with a negative doxy, was attacking the positive orthodoxy in what is really a family quarrel. Both were entangled in the error that revelation was a matter of belief rather than of personal relation in living faith. But for us now, with our wider knowledge and deeper grasp of all religions, Christianity is not a complex of truths, either accidental or necessary, about God; it is a new and vital relation toward God, effected by Himself.

The second fallacy in Lessing's words is that history, by its very nature, contains only the accidental and probable. On the contrary, history is now seen to be in its nature sacramental, if only sacramental of an Eternal making for righteousness. Its facts are consecrated elements. They are conductors of the Eternal. At least for the psychology of religion it is so; and religion is now allowed to speak for itself, without a rational editor or chaperon. Such religion finds the core of history to be an act of God which is anything but accidental. As a matter of fact, rightly or wrongly, history *has* yielded to the soul a God in an historic act which is in its nature eternal. And with that tremendous faith running through history and spreading over it, it is not enough that criticism should declare the sources incapable of producing it, and write it off as an illusion with a stroke. Rigid historical science cannot extract all that history has to yield, any more than physical science can be the

4. ["Disdain the soaring wing."]
5. Lessing, "Über den Beweis des Geistes und der Kraft," 12.

complete hierophant of Nature. The scientific critic dogmatises if he says it yields no more than he finds, or no other dimension. His methods apply only to the accidental, empirical, relative element, which is not the whole of history. His machine only extracts the tin and leaves the radium in the debris. The words of both Lessing and Kant on this subject reveal them as antagonists only to an outgrown conception of religion, to a view of Christianity which regards it as a scientific system of truth made statutory for subsequent generations, and made also, in that form, a condition of future happiness. It all smacks of an age and a mood which is bygone, except in those marts where men deal in the cast-off clothing of generations ago, or those paths where the ghosts of dead ages walk the dim purlieus of the living mind. The sympathetic study of all religions shows that there are parts of the past so timeless in their inner nature that they can become parts also of our own personal consciousness. It is so, at least, that the Christian learns Christ.[6]

6. To be quite just, I admit this represents but one side, the conscious side, whether of Lessing or of Kant. They have another, which however becomes explicit chiefly in their successors. Both represent the great transition from the dogmatic to the critical era. But it was to a criticism that had in it the conditions of a new dogmatic, with a moral instead of an intellectual foundation, and, with a place at once more modest and more powerful in Humanity. Lessing is, perhaps, the supreme type still of the creative critic. He was, indeed, limited by the then state of historic study and the then analysis of moral and theological ideas. But he did grasp, as none before, the essence of Humanity; and he grasped that essence as action. He prepared the way for Kant, and, through him, for the moral, instead of the mystical—or the noetic—escape from the confusion caused by historical criticism. In so doing they threw the accent on the personal side as distinct from the principle, and they opened a new career for evangelical Christianity delivered from Orthodoxy and from Pietism. In viewing the work of Christ as the supreme and compendious moral act in history, thought places it at the creative centre of the new Humanity; and by making the true Christianity to be communion with this moral Re-creator it saves mysticism from the æsthetic for the moral experience. The result of this changed method upon the central doctrines of Christianity, and their restoration to the conscience, and so to the race, I have tried to express in certain volumes upon *The Person of Christ*, *The Work of Christ*, and *The Cruciality of the Cross* (Hodder & Stoughton). They represent an attempt to place evangelical belief, which has been accused of violating morals, upon an impregnable moral basis; inasmuch as Kant's moral principle, that supreme action is doing the right for right's sake alone, appears in the crowning work of Christ as the self-oblation of the Holy One to His own holiness.

But Lessing's theme tends to recur in a new setting at the hands of the current religious-historical school, led so brilliantly and sympathetically by Troeltsch, with his principle of the relative absoluteness of Christianity. Historical religion, he says, does give us the absolute, but in each faith only in a relative way, which is fatal to any unique position for it. In many quarters it is held almost needless to prove a principle so evident as the relativism of history. Nor, it is said, should we wish it otherwise. For it is even asserted that the effect of the application of the relative principle to religion is not only to make religion more rational, but more rich in its truth, more ethical, more human, more intimate, and more religious really, because nearer our actual case. The relativist principle in this more sympathetic form is held and pressed by men who yet cherish a deep reverence for Christ's person as the first, and still the classic, case of the true religion of divine fatherhood and human sonship. Hegel went so far as to say that in Jesus and His results the absolute became conscious of itself. We are bound to recognise at this point the unprecedented insight we have gained into the character of Jesus and the doctrines of the Church from the sympathetic labour and the divining scholarship of many powerful men, who yet cut the ground from the Christian Church and faith by resting them ultimately, not upon Jesus, but upon the ideas and principles for which Jesus stood either as sponsor, or as symbol. The sonship of man and the fatherhood of God, they hold, are permanent intuitions, which are only historically connected with Jesus. And this historical connection with His person is irrelevant at last to final conviction on the principle; so that the conviction would grow and flourish now, with the historic "way" it has accumulated, even if Jesus were forgotten. The spiritual truth itself would spread among men by its own appeal to human nature, apart from Him who historically introduced it, who first realised it completely in His human experience, and who fixed it for ever in the religious consciousness of the race. Christ was indeed the way, but we may forget the road when we reach home. It is even said that He Himself, in His old humility, would wish it so thought if He were among us now. He would not care whether He were remembered or not, so long as the object of His life was won—man's filial trust of a living Father in an Eternal Kingdom. The certainty that the

Great Power is Father is declared to be a matter of the spiritual experience and its intuitional witness, which, when it is as real and clear as Christianity can make it, may always be trusted to report the same Father as Jesus so clearly and surely realised in the name of Humanity at its best. If He had not done so, some other would. The Christian principle can now hold its own, whatever we may come to think of the person of Christ or His work.

The weakness of such a position is that it must rest on a certain psychological interpretation of our spiritual experience, and it has against its forecast of the future the whole experience of the Church of the past (*i.e.*, of the initiates and experts of the soul); and especially the profound psychology of conscience and sin by the great Reformers, who, however they parted from the rest of the Church as to the remedy, were at one with it in the diagnosis of the case, because they were legatees of the Church's long penitential tradition.

Of late years the Hegelian line of thought has not seemed so sure in the land of its origin as it did two generations ago. With the decay of the philosophy of speculative Idealism there has come a distrust of the great truths of the reason, or at least of their power to shine by their own light. God, Freedom, Immortality are, of course, secure enough in æsthetic or sentimental circles, and in the region of the domestic pieties, where the heart rises dramatically, like a man in wrath, against the reason's colder part, ends the case, and crushes the critic with "I have felt." This shows how subjective, how individual, how dilettantist the current conception of the problem is, how little it is conceived as the problem of the world. But where there is a more serious and more historic grasp of the situation, with a more adequate sense of the difficulties involved, where there is a due knowledge of problems, and especially a grasp of the world problem, then the happier intuitions of a literary and pectoral theology are not found sufficient for the race's eternal committal, and for an absolute faith that nothing possible can shake. And, if we turn to the philosophers, whereas the ideas used to be their own assurance, by what Hegel calls "the intuition of thought" at the cost of personality, the tendency of recent thinking has been to recall personality and its moral effect to a much more important place. Personality has come, even for philosophy, to mean more than it did when it was treated but as the vehicle of ideas in a mere accidental and detachable way, as the pipe conveys the water, or the "sacred penman" the inspiration. The personality is now coupled up with the principle, not as its duct, or its penman, but as its prophet. They interpenetrate in a far more organic way, as the current suffuses the wire, or the fire lives on the fuel, or the mind in the brain. This change has come about as thought has grown more ethical, more psychological, more sympathetic, and less intellectualist, as Kant has discrowned Aristotle in the realm of mind. We begin to hope that a personal Idealism is about to restore the kingdom to Israel, as far as any philosophy can contribute to that end, and to help the recovery of our old faith in the personal finality of Christ.

But just at this point thought swerves, under the influence of a cross-current which is also modern, and, for some, final—the filial formula, they think, at last—the doctrine (or rather the dogma) of evolution. Just as personality seemed about to step back to the throne of things its supremacy is challenged (or qualified at least) by Evolutionary Relativism. If the parable may be indulged, this mighty angel, with one foot on the earth and another on the sea, commanding all nature, proclaims his profound respect for the dynasty of Personality as hereditary suzerain of the cosmos, but his inability, at the same time, to allow any single member of it to mount the throne in perpetuity. No single personality must have eternal monopoly, no single king live for ever. Even were personality immortal, no single representative of it must be secured in eternal reign. For that would not consist with the relative principle. Immortal as the principle of personality or kingship might be, no particular personality of history could be absolute or final. He could be no more than a terminal president. And whoever for the hour took the throne must give constitutional guarantee that, as his resources began to fail, or when a greater personality arose, he would abdicate, consent to be superseded by a more spiritual right, and pass from the scene, or gladly take his place among the subjects of the larger lord. If it was Jesus that was placed upon the throne, the noble champion avowed with earnest tones his deep reverence and loyalty to His moral Majesty; but in the greatest of interests he could consent to His royal place only with a proviso which relativists could not forgo. It could not be allowed that He was an eternal King, or a King of all possible kings. For there were constitutional principles, bound up with the very existence of the realm of human nature, which were not dependent on any single personality (nay, they were imperilled by it), deeply as they were entwined with the personal or regal idea. Redemption as a process, for instance, was of more range and moment than any redeemer could be, and the particular monarch was otiose to the constitution.

The form of thought that I have ventured to describe in this parable is much more attractive than the line pursued by the old rationalists of the association school, it allows to personality a function higher than merely to convey the idea; and it finds personality more interesting than the idea. We are attracted also by the prospect of finding some means, however inadequate, of coupling them closer, and having the benefit of both. But really the new line is little more satisfactory than the old. For, if we do not concentrate on a single absolute person, are we not dissolving with one hand the connection we would cement with the other? To return to our metaphor, if it is only the dynasty we enthrone, the category of personality, and not a particular person, what are we doing but restoring the supremacy of the personal principle, of the idea of personality, and making a particular personality indifferent? We have only replaced a principle by a principle, a principle which is associated with personality by the principle of personality itself. And the result for faith, for religion, is not very different in the long run. What we come out with at last is the worship of ideal Humanity and the spiritual principle it embodies. We postpone personality and its moral action to a monistic power and its processes. We find movements promoted which, with the aid of extreme criticism, throw Jesus into a secondary place, and promise practically to dispense with Him, or historically to dissolve Him, on the ground that the great Christian ideas, like Incarnation, Atonement, Resurrection, Ascension, Regeneration, are not specific acts of God in history but movements intrinsic to collective Humanity, valuable indeed, but well assured to us as processes of man's native and inalienable spirituality at its best. Man makes his own atonement, and Christ but illustrated the fact. Man does not rise by the Spirit that raised

Christ, but Christ rose by the spirit that elevates man. These ideas, these experiences, are the necessary movements, phases, or effects of our spiritual evolution, which cannot be holden of death; they are not the contents of an historic revelation and act in Christ, on which alone our reborn spirituality must revolve. It may be questioned (in passing), and with some force, whether it is quite fair to use the New Testament words and ideas in this bleached and emptied sense. It may be said, with some truth, that a change from being theocentric to being anthropocentric means a new religion. It is, indeed, engaging and enlarging to the mind to mark these processes in human nature, as the premonitions of that which Christ fulfilled, and which He secured in final victory; just as it interests and expands us to mark the same thing in the convergence upon Him of other religions, and especially of those gnostic mythologies which lay round the cradle of Christianity. They were prayers that called for Christ, rather than powers that produced Him, and they are much truer as prayers than as powers. They were prayers that He had to answer rather than principles which He had to serve. They were, and are, impotent without Him. We may prize them as prophecies. But it is another thing to make them the prime movers, with Christ and His action but their classic case. That is not Christianity. At least it is not apostolic Christianity. It is certainly not the faith that made the Church. And it is practically another religion. Would it not be much more fair and fertile plainly to recognise this, and then go on to ask which of the two religions better met the facts of history, the record of experience, and the needs of the soul. Neither old truth nor new has anything to gain from confusing the issue.

Let us not refuse the truth which is so luminous to many of those teachers that it seems to them final. Let us not discard the spell of their ideal Christ, or deny the composite nature of some of His early theological photographs. Let us not despise their reverence for Humanity, even if we cannot adopt their faith in it. (For reverence is one thing and faith quite another.) The ideal yet human Christ of the modern age is, in its place, a real contribution to the enlargement of our thought of Christ, if the thought of Him were all. It corresponds to the step taken when, through the Reformation, a near God replaced a far; when

God's relation to the world began to be something more than accidental, when it became organic; when the world ceased to be thought of as one of several possible to God, when it became His form instead of even His garment, and a theology of immanence began to supplement and enlarge the mediæval theology of transcendence alone. Let us consent to learn from all we are told about the greatness of the Christian principle, and its supremacy to every other spiritual principle found up to now in the soul of man. We may then gain some hope of a fundamentally Christian ethic replacing a pagan in our chief centres of education. Let us, moreover, recognise the contributions that may have been made to the *form* of the first Christian theology by the theologoumena of either Judaism or Gnosticism. St. Paul incorporated several of these into his thought of the riches of Christ, adopting even some of the technical phraseology of these schools, as every reader of Colossians knows if he continues to assign it to St. Paul. I see no reason why, if it were proved, we should not recognise that St. Paul had a Christology before he was a Christian, and might even have believed in a Messiah pre-existent in the heavens. He did believe in a celestial Jerusalem, pre-existent as the Temple, the Law, or the Memra was also thought to be; and he might have shared a like belief as to the Messiah, if such a belief had existed. Which, however, both Bousset and Dalman seem to doubt. As they well might; for to a Monotheist Jew the pre-existence beside the one God of a person like Messiah would be a far more serious matter than the pre-existence either of law, angel, temple, or city of God. But, speaking generally, I see no reason why Paul should not have utilised the ideas of other religions than either Judaism or Christianity, to fill out and express what he found in Christ. But they did not base his faith, or produce it. In Christ they all fell into place, and were gathered together in one. Christ was the answer to their prayers. He stored in advance all possible treasures of wisdom and knowledge. In Christ all high ideals and moving principles were from eternity real and effectual. In Him they came back to their home. And therefore in Him they became not only powers in history but, what is the real point, they became *the* powers. They were put once for all in eternal command of history and man. Their final, visible victory, in due course, was secure, because they shared his secure place in God.

They became invincible as the Kingdom of God. The æonial issue of light and darkness, life and death, good and evil, grace and sin, was settled for ever in principle on the battlefield of Christ's person. And final omnipotence was secured, by, that person, for a redeeming principle which, however divine we may now call it, but for this victory might, for all we knew, have succumbed to some stronger malignant power ere all was done and the long historic strife closed. Fixed in that faith, we need be no more unsympathetic to the ideals of our age than Paul the aged was to those of his. Unless, indeed, they aspire to thrust the living Christ from His throne and sit there. Then they threaten the Church's life, as the old Gnosticism did. It becomes a struggle for existence. And our attitude might have to become that of John rather than Paul, because it is John's situation and not Paul's that we face.

The chief practical objection to putting a principle in front of a person is that the religious life thereby becomes a one-sided process rather than a mutual act, an evolution rather than a communion; and thus it loses its ethical value, and is relegated to the pensive and passive side of our nature. And when religion does that it practically goes out of life. The difference between a principle and a person is the difference between a process and an act, between a man that is carried and a man that goes. It is that the person has will and purpose towards some conscious act and end, while the principle moves but in a current which may be blind (because it does not certify its own goal), which bears us along on its course, and tends to submerge moral action and choice. Our very choice of a principle becomes then but part of the action of the principle, and our freedom is gone in a determinism the more fatal as it is subtle, and even religious. It is true our best faith is not of ourselves, it is the gift of God. But it is His gift, not in the crude sense that we are flooded, overborne and carried along on the current of something infused into our nature, but in the sense that it is the destined, yet not fated, response of our free will and conscience to the gift of God in a personal Christ who is morally calculated to affect us so since we were created in Him. The Eternal Life is not an infusion whereby we are coupled to a source and charged anew. That is a psychology of it which leads to magical religion, and the whole Roman theory of the sacraments;

and it means a religion that turns upon something else than moral personal relations direct and reciprocal. But grace is a relation of divine mercy, and not a process of high natural magic spiritualised. The new life is ours by a moral action and reaction, our moral reaction to the prior, moral, and gracious action of a God whose *will* is our peace. So that it is more exact to say that the gift of God is not the faith directly but that Christ who stirs the faith. It is the faith only indirectly, in the sense of our personal response to a Person's gift of Himself in a Person. If the principle be the main thing, then mutual personal action falls to a second place, and communion in the true Christian sense too easily sinks to be fusion in the mystic sense. Regeneration becomes at best a mere awaking to feel that we are partakers of a divine nature. And it is a process through which Christ Himself must also have gone. He becomes the greatest of all regenerates. Redemption, which has Christian meaning only as an act, becomes a process of increasingly pantheistic and Buddhistic character, including and blessing the Redeemer Himself. It is the release of the infinite from the finite, the process of absorption in the larger ideal, mere delivery from the limitations, causations, and controls of a hampering world; instead of being God's destruction of guilt by forgiveness, His new creation and restoration of us to moral communion with His holy Self. History becomes but movement, hardly action, and not at all a drama. It is a mere procession to a grand final panorama; unless indeed it ends in the redemption and release of the Absolute Being Himself, through the aid of man's ascetic sacrifice, from that most original fall wherein "He darkly blundered on man's suffering soul." And with all this the conception of sin accords. It becomes merely the most unfortunate form of our limitation, but it need not carry with it guilt. It is a back-water of the great current of process; it is not an act of the will's hostility or alienation towards a holy God. And the effect at last is that the principle, being detached from the person (except historically), sinks: it sinks either to truth of a divine kind, so that its revelation, as the communication of divine doctrines, is some kind of orthodoxy—a notion of revelation now well outgrown—or else it falls lower still and becomes but the manifestation of a fine sort of cosmic force, the flood of a stream of living water, clear as crystal, proceeding from the throne of whatever rules as God, and carrying us on its bosom, almost without action of ours (however much motion), to be lost in the infinite sea. In either case the dominant type of religion acquires a pantheistic and non-ethical cast rather than a theistic and moral. The principle may employ personality or drop it. It may appear and act as a personality, but always so that the person returns to be merged in it. And a person not identical with the principle could even preach it in a most powerful way and yet find his real personality satisfied elsewhere; or he might renounce it at a later date, and go on to another, and even contrary principle. But what we need is not a principle any more than it is a dogma. Principle-worship is but the modern form of dogma-worship. What we want is life from a life, conscience with conscience, and soul to soul. But what we get in a speculative system of interacting ideas and principles is a result like this. "The fathomless wealth of God's thought and act is reduced to the monotonous echo of an ontological machine in systole and diastole, pulse and counterpulse, thrill and chill."

We may, perhaps, put it thus: Religion must be not only subjectively sincere but objectively real. That is to say it must rest on a real objective, and one possessing the initiative to which faith responds. Religion is meaningless without something in the nature of revelation. There can be no real religion on man's side towards anything which is but the projection, or the consummation, of Humanity itself. The object of religion must approach its subject creatively. But if that objective be construed as a mere immanent principle, patent only as the various spiritual processes subjective to Humanity, like incarnation, atonement or regeneration, where does a real objective for the race and its religion lie? What is really initiative and creative? Of course, if Humanity is regarded, in the positivist way, as itself the divine reality, it has, collectively, no object of religion. Religion becomes but one of its subjective phases. Its initiative is in itself. Believing Humanity is its own object of faith. It is the object of its own worship. And the religion of individual altruism is a collective egoism on the vastest scale. Or if, pantheistically, Humanity be regarded as part or phase of a more cosmic reality, its experiences are still not more than phases. They, too, are but phases or processes of reality, they are not responses to it. They are parts of its huge subjectivity. And religion,

Christ and the Christian Principle

then, is not the relation of Humanity to anything real, but a mere phenomenon on the face of reality, having no necessary or eternal connection with its nature. The principle asserts or expresses itself in many forms, but it meets with response not at all. Humanity is a phase of reality, it does not greet reality. There is no revelation, and therefore no religion is possible.

But how, then, shall we secure a religious reality behind these experiences, processes, or ideas of ours? How shall we know they correspond to anything in reality, anything ultimate, and supreme, and victorious? How shall we get moral, holy, footing in the region behind good and bad? How shall we know that love or goodness in man mean the same thing in the region of the last reality? Is moral difference rooted in the Eternal? It has no religious, no eternal, value unless it is. Now there are various philosophical ways of answering this question, turning on theories of knowledge; but the theological answer is this—that the historic revelation in Christ is that the real is what we know as the transcendently moral, the holy. That is the meaning of the Incarnation. How the Church reaches that certainty opens two very great questions, as to the value of inspiration and the value of Christian experience. They are questions that evoke powerful answers, but they cannot be discussed here. The real, we say, is the moral, the historic. But now, if we work from the other end, and apart from such a revelation, can we say that the moral is the real, that the loving, the sacrificing is the real and eternal? Can we be sure that these moral idealisms or principles in history are upon the rock of permanent being? Can we be quite sure that moral excellence, which is at present the crown of things, will be permanent, victorious and eternal, apart from its establishment and re-establishment by a Personality, Holy and Almighty? Can a principle secure itself or prove itself to be Eternal? And if it cannot, can it be a base for religion in the great last sense of the word—a stay in the crash of a cosmos, or amid the collapse of our own self-satisfaction in guilt? Can a principle really reveal itself in any such way that a whole person can respond, and can respond with himself? We can respond as persons to a person, and we can discover a principle, or be taught it by a person, and we can acknowledge it; but can a principle *act* on us? Can a principle act in the moral sense of the word? Has it in it what constitutes the essence of personality? Can it create? Has it the power of self-determination? Has a supreme principle necessarily the power of absolute self-determination? Many minds are embarrassed, when the question of an absolute personality arises, by the fallacy that the essential feature of personality is limitation, that personality is no more than individuality—something marked off by a circumference from all else. Whereas the essence of personality is not that it is a closed circle, but that it is a radiative centre of power, of moral power, and especially in the way of self-command. A personality is a power that is lord of itself. It is not a power made personal by its limitations, whether in its volume, or in its spiritual energies, but a power that has in itself the secret of its own control. It is a power with self-determination and self-sufficiency. From this point of view there is nothing unthinkable in an absolute personality. With us personality is never a finished thing, but a thing in constant growth; and it is an error to treat it as a complete, limited, and standard thing, and then proceed to declare an infinite personality impossible. It is really the only form in which we can conceive intelligence or spiritual life—infinite self-knowledge, self-sufficiency, and self-determination. But a principle can have none of these. Its action is not self-determined, and therefore it is not moral. Therefore it cannot really act in the way of self-bestowal, self-revelation. It cannot reveal itself in any such way as to appeal to our moral personality and master it.

A person can by free action give or reveal himself to a person, and to a person he can also reveal a principle. But can a principle reveal itself to a person, if we really grasp what is deeply meant by revelation? Can there be any self-determined and free self-revelation on the part of a principle to evoke all that is free in our personality? Has it such initiative? Self-revelation, beginning as it must in free self-determination, is an act, a personal act; but is a principle capable of anything beyond movement in a process? It can assert itself, establish itself, absorb, overbear, organise, or submerge all else, like other forces—but can it reveal itself, bestow itself, open its inmost self and final purpose? It can develop itself, but can it save? It can produce resignation, can it win reconciliation? Can it provide a worship for man, who, as a conscience, needs forgiveness more than evolution? If it is but a principle that we have to do with at last can we speak of revelation, at least in any such sense of saving self-donation as Christ has taught us to associate with revelation? A person can reveal a principle, but not a principle a person. Is it not debasing a person, and robbing it of personality, to make it explicable as the vortex of a principle, as an atom might be a knot of ether? For a principle is not free in any moral sense. Moral freedom vanishes if it is treated but as a kink in a principle. A principle does not carry in itself its own origin or explanation. It may be a cause, an essence, the unity of a system, a uniformity of procedure, a universal, an idea, a notional ultimate, a logical solution—one of many things, which are all below a free and originating person in moral dignity and worth for life. It may explain much, but it initiates nothing. It organises, but it does not create. It is more of a terminus for thought than a source of life. It may order a world, but it does not love, nor is it loved. It may be owned, but neither obeyed nor worshipped. It cannot keep religion the personal thing it must be. And it can never effect what is the Christian relation to God, personal communion. Than this there can be nothing higher; and nothing less than this is the fulness of Christianity; which is not contact with God, impression from Him, or influence either from a God or a principle; but life-communion with the Eternal. This is only possible with a living person. And the faith that effects it is absolute and final.

No such mere principle can be the ground of a religion adequate to the highest practical purposes of a world of living men, or to the actual moral situation of such a world. It is not equal to the great tragedies, resolves, actions or consciences of a race of loving, acting, suffering, struggling, failing, conquering souls. It must have its sponsor and guarantee in a revelation by a moral person who holds of the last reality, and who is secured in a final moral conquest of such life and fate. For a world of men a man is the only fitting form of revelation. And the only question, then, is whether a man is a possible form of revelation for God; whether the great last Reality is so moral in His nature as to exist *in nuce* in a perfect moral manhood.

It may here be noted that the tendency to detach the principle from the person mostly goes with a tendency to reduce to something monistic the essence of God as well as of Christianity. And at its root is an easy confusion between the idea of immanence and that of incarnation; as if the divine Incarnation in Christ were but the luminous summit of an intrinsic divine immanence, *ejusdem generis*,[7] in the constitution of Humanity; as if Humanity were the real Son of God, with Christ as its most conspicuous individual case. But the Christian principle is not immanence, which is a philosopheme with little direct value for personal religion. It does not become religious till we are clearly sure that we mean *the immanence of the transcendent*. The principle of Christ's relation to man is not a natural identity by constitution. We can say little about that. But it is a self-identification by will, by Christ's eternal act of self-emptying and self-bestowal. A Christ who was the culmination of a divine immanence in Humanity might complete a process of divine self-realisation, but He would not perform an act of divine self-renunciation—meaning by divine such an act on the part of God. Principles may realise themselves, but persons alone can renounce themselves. A self-realising Christ would not carry self-sacrifice into God, as the act does which brought Christ here; which also underlies all the detailed acts of self-sacrifice in His earthly career, and which makes man's self-sacrifice in union with Him to be not merely Godlike, but really divine, "I live, yet not I but Christ in me."

Hence it is a defective ethic that works out of immanential theories even when Christian. They identify sin with selfishness in a one-sided and negative way. They ignore its positive aspect of hostility to God and aggression on Him. They invite sacrifice for others, but they give collective Humanity no eternal principle for its sacrifice, none to make sacrifice divine and not foolish and wasted. They may lay much stress on sacrifice to God, but they cannot carry home sacrifice by God. They set up in Christ less an act of salvation through self-sacrifice by God than a process of self-realisation through the sacrificial principle of Humanity, which, however, cannot be guaranteed as pleasing to God because it cannot be carried into the divine nature itself. The cross, that is, becomes but functional in Christ, it is not organic, nor constituent of His appearance among men; it is the effect of an epiphany, but not the principle of an Incarnation. And selfishness can never be extinguished by an ethic of sacrifice so long as sacrifice is not placed at the core of religion by its revelation at the heart of the

---

7. ["The same kind."]

object of religion. Nothing can continue to evoke self-sacrifice in Humanity which does not find in Christ the self-sacrifice of a holy God, and therefore the supreme moral reality. For nothing can be conceived ethically higher than that God should sacrifice Himself to His own holiness for love of man. The act of the cross is the very nature of God's self-revelation, which is His self-donation; it is not simply one form of revelation, far less one phase of a moral ideal. The object of worship in Christ's person is there among us by an act of self-sacrifice; He does not simply perform such an act upon occasion when He has come there. His connection with Humanity is not one of continuous self-realisation, as if He crowned the great human process, and used sacrifice as a means on due occasion; it is one of self-identification, by an initial and a compendious act of sacrifice possible only to a Person who has the absolute disposal of Himself. Christ was God giving Himself far more than man finding himself. The Incarnation is a moral act of this kind far more than a spiritual process. Therefore it cannot be monistic in its nature; for monism may stand many scientific tests, but it breaks down on the moral. Morality may undergo a process, but a process *per se* has nothing moral in it. Nor can man's response to the Incarnation be a mere mystic or subliminal spirituality, but it must be a faith as historic and ethical in its heart and genius as the revelation which stirs it; it must be a faith in that which once for all re-creates the conscience; and that a social and evangelical creed alone can be.

I have recognised that the old way of putting the rationalist position differed from the new. It said that the principle and its prophet had no necessary connection, but only one external, passing, and at bottom accidental; that the aqueduct did not necessarily guarantee the water; that the person might be most sincere and true but the principle wrong and false; and the person might even conceivably live, as St. Paul did, to promote a later principle quite antagonistic to his first. That view marked the early days of the narrower rationalism, when both revelation and its critics were preoccupied with stateable truth more than cognisable reality, and when the work of the person as prophet was to convey truths and doctrines, supernatural or natural, as the critics' work was to dissolve them. Everything, orthodox or heterodox, was a matter of truths. All was in the propositional region.

But we have changed that. The new way of putting Lessing's position abolishes that comparative indifference of the principle to the person. It couples up the connection and makes it necessary. The person is not charged with truth so much as with reality, action, life, and power. The charge is cognate, the vocation identical, with the person. The person is not the medium but the incarnation of the principle; whose first adequate realisation was in a person with a central place in history. The redemptive principle henceforth acted from Him, not as its expositor merely, but as its one vital historical source; and He became not simply its prophet but "both its pattern and its *Guarantee.*" The phrase is from Biedermann, one of the most powerful and pious of those who postpone the person to the principle of Christ.

But now may we stop a little on that word "guarantee"? I have had to use it myself already. And the ablest champions of the Christian principle as superior to Christ's person (like Biedermann) are driven by the depth of their Christian experience to use it too. But why? Is it not because, with their true religious feeling, and their masterly knowledge of religious history, both Christian and other, they do realise that the very element which distinguishes a guarantee from a prophet, a pattern, or a classic case, is for religion the one thing needful. What is the meaning of the word guarantee? Why must we speak of Christ as our Surety, with the old divines and these new thinkers? What have we in the expression that we have not in speaking of Christ as the type, prophet or promoter of the principle? Have we not in the use of such a word the surrender of the whole case, and the identification of the principle with the person? Is it not a confession that, however it may be with philosophy, yet for religion, for the soul's life, the person of Christ *is* the principle of Christianity and of the spiritual world? Could anything less serve the purpose of religion, and plant the soul upon eternal reality? Could a person, as a phase assumed by the principle, guarantee either its Universality or Eternity? If the supreme principle is to be guaranteed by a supreme person it must be identical with it. For a person not identified and co-eternal with the principle, but merely its exemplary symbol in life, word and deed, could only utter in a most impressive way, even in his martyr death, his own life-deep conviction of the principle. Further he could not go. The thing he could not do is to guarantee that what was such a conviction for Him is the eternal life, power, and master of the world and the race. He could not assure the man of to-day that the principle for which He died is always as mighty for the last reality of things, for God and Eternity, as it was for His own soul. That could only be if His soul and person were absolutely identified with that last reality and principle; if Jesus of Nazareth were living eternal Godhead. To speak of Christ as the Guarantee of an eternal principle, as Biedermann's religion makes him do, is to identify Him with it, as his theology does not.

An ultimate can only be guaranteed by itself. That is the basis of the certainty, supremacy, and autonomy of religion in the soul. God swears by Himself because there is none greater. Our final authority must be God Himself in direct contact with Humanity, *i.e.*, with History. He cannot be proved, because there is nothing more real and certain to which we can bring Him for sanction. And if the principle be that of sonship to a Father-God—that is surely a personal relation, if it have any meaning at all; and it can guarantee itself only as a person: not by assuming the passing form of a person for an historic purpose, but by existing as an historic but universal person in whom the relation is realised germinally,[8] perfectly, and for ever, by existing as the King of all personal sons and the ground of all sonship. If the word guarantee must be used (as those who are thinkers, and not historians simply, feel it must be for the effective base of a real religion), it can be used only to mean that in the historic person we have not the effect, nor the avatar, nor the intuition of the principle, but the principle itself. It can be used only in the sense that the person *is* the principle. And we are then left to choose whether the power identical with that person is the principle of Humanity, moving in fine spiritual processes, or a personal God bestowing Himself in a moral act. The person of Christ is an incarnation either upwards of the principle of Humanity, which is a Christianised positivism, or downwards of personal Godhead, which is positive Christianity. And between the visualisation of a principle deeply immanent

---

8. God appears in Christ *in nuce*, not *in extenso*.—Rothe.

and the incarnation of a holy God, religion will not find it hard to choose, if it rise to the ethical level of Christian faith. The key to the person of Christ is to be found not in an intellectual conviction, philosophic or theologic, nor in a romantic piety, part mystical part wise, but in a positive religious experience of Him and a crucial moral decision behind which we cannot go in the quest for life's reality. It is not a theory of Atonement that is the deep need of the hour, but the experience of it, the atoned soul. We need most, not a theology of religion, but a theology which is religion; not a theology of religion but of God; not a speculative theology, which has always broken down, but a soteriological and experimental, which actually solves the moral crisis of the world. All that speculation can do for a Christology is but in the way of prolegomena. It may survey the ground, and even build the house and staff it, but the tenant does not arrive. It may trace a general process, cosmic or rational, and mark it emerging in the history of man's progressive elevation and sanctity. It may note in the course of that history the powerful part played by various providential personalities, and even religions, that yet but stand and wait. Such geniuses may be as far above common men as these are above molluscs. But whether the principle of their service ever appears as a single person with the sole right to sign God's autograph to all their witness—that no speculative treatment of the world can guarantee; at least not powerfully enough for practical life and eternal committal in such a world as this is. It is a matter for a theology which is not speculative but dogmatic, on the basis of an historic experience by the conscience that He has come as God's gift of Himself. Speculation has its great uses (so long as it is schooled and competent, and not amateur speculation).[9] But at its best it has no gospel, it is not propagandist, it is indifferent

---

9. Till, for instance, a passage like this (from Treherne, before German philosophy was heard of) seems something else than absurd. "For His very perfection God needs what is not God. An energy working outwards He must possess. He must think his non-ego. And considering what thought is for God, He must posit the non-ego. But the non-ego is a negation, a limitation of God. And it would destroy His absoluteness, if that were not necessarily restored by His absorption of the non-ego as such, and His recovery of Himself in the Creation. Distinguish the two timeless functions—the positing of the non-ego, or its counterpositing, in Creation, and the absorption or surmounting of the antithesis, or its Repositing, in a Reconciliation."

to success, and it is not for the pulpit, or the people, or history. Idealism founds no Society. Not that it is for that reason futile, or even inferior. It is simply different. It has a different work. It can neither be a religion nor infringe upon the independence of religion. But when we have found our soul in an historic salvation then speculation may richly enter, and metaphysic may amply deduce from a Saviour's action for God a content of God in His nature and work. If for our faith Christ have the value of God we cannot help assigning to Him in our thought the nature of God. But the thought that affects faith is one thing, and that which takes the place of faith is another. The phenomenon of Christ is ultimate, and the faith that grasps it is the same. He is a final fact that cannot be constructed, and He can be construed but a little way, while He is received and trusted for eternity.

The effect, then, of the theory of historical development on religion is twofold.

1. Either it denies that any final revelation of the absolute and eternal is possible in history. All is in evolution, all is relative, all is temporary, and the generations must live from hand to mouth.

To which the answer is an old one, and a double—the identity of ground and goal. What is it that develops? And to what end does it move, so that we may know whether the movement is development, and the evolution is progress? What develops? How is it possible to think of development unless there be something that develops? And if a something be admitted, but a revelation of its nature and object be denied, then how are we to tell if its movement be development, *i.e.*, if its action be giving fuller effect to its nature? We cannot, unless we have some means, religious or philosophic, of convincing ourselves that the God of history is also its ground, and the person the principle. It is impossible to speak of all being in evolution, all relative, unless there be an absolute to evolve and to make relation possible and measurable. Two things, two stages, could be in no kind of relation except by virtue of a unity which made them comparable. There could be no relative without an absolute, nothing temporal without the Eternal. So far

That may be true, or it may not be true; but it cannot be dismissed as unmeaning.

from evolution excluding an absolute, therefore, it demands it for its existence; and Time is only intelligible on a foundation of Eternity.

2. Or, admitting an absolute reality brought within our cognisance by revelation in an evolutionary history, one may go on, as we have seen, to deny the possibility of its complete and final revelation at any one point of time. And this is the view which practically carries most danger to Christianity. Practically it is most dangerous, because to the generous amateur it seems religious and broad. It appears Christian by acknowledging a revelation, only it spreads it over Humanity. And it seems to promise an intimate spirituality by an experience of God in the depth of each soul which is a revelation to us in the same sense in which it was to Jesus. Which leaves most men to a subjectivity without a compass or a pole.

If the possibility of the absolute and final in a person be conceded it may still be said, as by Strauss, that such a person could not appear at the beginning of a series but only at its close. And to that the answer would be on lines like these. The statement is one drawn from physical evolution rather than psychical or historic. For all history shows some of the greatest triumphs of poetic genius, and especially religious genius, in very early stages of society. Moreover, we have to make our most crucial decisions early in life. And it is, still further, a statement too obviously bound up with the Hegelianism Strauss represented, viz. that creation took its origin, not from a personal absolute at the beginning of the series, but from an idea of some monistic kind which only acquired the self-consciousness of personality at the end of the series as Man. Finally, if a revelation of the absolute is essential for faith, and it cannot come till the close, then for history it cannot be a factor at all. It would be history's last product, and one dissociated from faith (which there was nothing to create). And to dissociate history from faith is to non-moralise it; it is to reduce all to an ideal process, concerning which we could have no certainty that any ethical revelation was to be more sure at the goal than it had been active in the course.

But it may be worth while before leaving the subject to ask here what it is that is really objected to by many who refuse a unique finality to Christ's experience and person. It is often the notion that the whole metaphysical being of God with all His divine attributes was identical with the human personality, Jesus. Now that is a statement that may mark certain crude Christologies at certain levels in the history of Christianity, but it is not the thing that is asserted by Christian faith; and it has no more sense than the new dogma at the other extreme which says that Christ was identical with Humanity.

What faith has to do with is the personal unity in an equal Godhead of Son and Father, a unity which is moral, because holy, in its nature, though it is much more than moral harmony; a unity also on the great moral principle that subordination does not imply inferiority. There must be a metaphysic of it, indeed, but that is deductive from the experience of faith, and not primary in producing faith, and not fixed in its form. Dogma, and especially metaphysical dogma, does not produce faith. It is only a temporary register of it. The function of dogma is to express the mind of the believing Church, not to prescribe to the inquiring world. The person of Jesus, however it may be metaphysically explained, has its first value as an actual and complete manifestation of the absolute personality as holy love. The necessities and implicates of such a revelation made to experience form the only sure foundation of a doctrine of the Trinity. For Christ could not be such a manifestation to the soul without sharing in that absoluteness in the way of entire and eternal continuity of life. He shares in that absolute life as a constituent person; He does not receive it into His person as a great unit of Humanity might, whose relative personality formed but a fit *receptacle* for the absolute Spirit. Nor is it as if other men were robbed of the divinity concentrated in Christ. For the greater a moral personality is the more room it has for others, whom it does not impoverish, but enrich and realise. And Christ makes real for those who enter communion with Him what without Him were a mere possibility, a mere bias to God. He *is* that which in them is only a destiny. He *is* the gracious destiny of all. He *is* the will and purpose of God for which they were but planned, but for which they are only in Him empowered. God truly was in Humanity before Christ was born, but as a presence and a power in contact, and not in communion; by His Spirit, but not, as He is in His Church, by His Holy Spirit. And

He was in a created Humanity, moving always to an increate but historic Christ as at once its ground and its destiny; in a Humanity created from the beginning with a view to that Christ as its free consummation; created as it were round Christ, yea by Christ, and not merely so as to eventuate in a Christ at some far end, which was to be remotely divined rather than trusted as near, and which closed a series it did not produce. The end was in the beginning; the goal of the Church is also its ground. That is what is meant by a Christ the same yesterday, to-day and for ever.

We cannot grasp too clearly the real issue of the present time. Since the death of Agnosticism it no more concerns the possibility or the reality of a revelation, but it concerns the finality of the revelation in Jesus Christ. The conflict is no more between religion and science, but between two forms of religion. The revelation is admitted both in Humanity and in Christ, and therefore religion is admitted, and a certain kind of faith has its due place. The Cosmos grows sacramental even for science. What is not admitted is the absoluteness, the finality, the cruciality for the soul's eternity, of the historic Christ as the saving revelation. By which again is not meant the existence in Him of all possible knowledge; for religion is not a matter of knowledge, but rather of the heart's conscience. Nor is it meant that we have no indication outside Him of God's thought; but indication is not revelation, which means certainty, and concerns not God's movements but His final purpose. It is meant that in Him we have that new moral departure which all the sequel can only unfold and enrich; we have a new Creation, the new Humanity round which the old dies like a corn of wheat; we have the turning-point of human destiny for all Eternity: we have the presence and act of God decisive for that purpose, a final salvation but not a final science of saving truth, a final faith but not a final theology.

9

Christ's Person and His Cross

I

When we discuss the historic foundations of Christian theology the question is raised by some whether it rests on the Cross of Christ or on his Person. The doctrine of seventeenth-century Orthodoxy, continuing a great Catholic note, rested it upon the Cross of Christ rather than his Person; but, by laying most of the stress on what it called the passive rather than the active obedience, it put its case in a way which has caused a good deal of reaction. The death of Christ was cut off from his life, and an excessive value was given to his submissive suffering at the cost of his moral action, after a pathetic fashion which detached not theology only, but religion also, from a salutary ethic. The chief agent of the reaction from this orthodoxy was Schleiermacher, who rebounded so far to the other as almost to lose Christ's Cross in his Person. By the stress he laid on the God-consciousness of Christ, and our union therewith, he certainly redressed a balance that long had been false. But he fell on the other side. He took from the Cross of Christ its objective and active value. He underprized both history and ethic for the sake of a mystic union; which must certainly be there, but which, if it is not to lose reality, must pass through these points and not go round them. And the history of this branch of theology for the last century has largely been an effort to adjust the two poles, to find the Person in the Cross, and the Cross in the Person, and in both the real moral action of a holy God, and not merely a manifestation or an influence of a God only spiritual.

In what I have to say two things will be indicated:

First, that the ruling interest of an ethical religion is personality. It is Christ.

And, second, that the crowning expression of a moral personality is action. It is the Cross.

There are certain elementary cautions as to words. By the Person of Christ of course we mean much more than his character; we mean something interior to it. And if we speak of the Cross being latent in his Person, we really mean more than latent. We mean active, essential, and dominant there—acting in his teaching as the call for repentance, and, still more deeply, in his death and resurrection as the power of regeneration; for the Cross meant more than that we repent—we must be born again. The Cross is latent in Christ's Person as the oak in the acorn. The acorn must end in the oak and come to itself there, unless it rot or be crushed. And the whole energy of Christ blossoms in the Cross not as a mere possibility nor as an idea, but as an entelechy, a ruling end, a destiny—as the result not of a mere moral process, but of purposed action. It matters much also where we begin—whether we start as wise men from the mystic East, as devout people seeking for their worship a King of Saints, or as desperate people seeking relief from sin's moral tragedy, and finding it in the tragic salvation neither of a soul nor of a group, but of a world. It matters much for our type of religion whether the central interest of faith is a piety or an action, a choice experience or a crucial action.

II

On the first head, then, the supremacy of personality, I would indicate the growth of that principle as a chief moral development in the history both of the Church and of modern Society.

We may start from the point at which the whole treatment of Christ's work started on its serious career as a part, and the central part, of theology. We may start with Anselm. He begins his scheme with God. For Anselm the first charge upon man or his champion is the satisfaction of the objective conditions in a God who was not only a monarch, and not only absolute, but absolutist. God's first interest was his honor. His wounded honor had to receive reparation for the lese-majesty it had suffered, and for the robbery of its rights. This was done by Christ. But it was done without reference to the moral nature of man in whom the benefit was to take effect. It was done entirely over his head, and he was to be only its beneficiary. The honor of God must be satisfied, and it was indifferent whether by man or another, whether the satisfaction regarded man's moral nature or not.

By the time we reach Protestant orthodoxy, however, the idea had changed. It had become moralized. The juristic development of the Middle Ages had not gone for nothing. For the honor of an arbitrary monarch had been substituted something more constitutional—the idea of a divine justice. The sovereign's private right was replaced by the notion of a public moral order, whose guardian the King was, and which was expressed in civil law and penal justice. From being courtly the ruling idea became juridical—which was ethically to the good. The interpretation of Christ's work on its large lines has always followed the ruling ethical idea of contemporary society; and during the Middle Ages the ideal had become so far ethicized that it passed from a king's dignity to the law's. The categories in which the matter was discussed were more or less forensic. The prisoner was guilty less of treason than of crime, less of imperial detraction than of infringing the moral order on which all law is based and all society secured. The monarch represents law, rather than law the monarch. The king reigned in righteousness. This was an ethical advance, because the making of the satisfaction was a concern not of the monarch's dignity, but of man's conscience as under the moral order of the world which God, its Creator, had to maintain.

It is here that the modern view attaches. While it prolongs the ethical strain, it is a more immanential view. God, even as guardian of the moral law and of public righteousness, does not sit deistically apart, with a watching brief for justice in the course of the world he had set going. He is personally and actively involved in the moral order which pervades society and the world. He is at least as near and intimate to the world as that spiritual order is which enmeshes and pervades every soul. The roots of this view of Christ's work go as far back as Abelard, though Ritschl, developing and repairing Schleiermacher, is its most powerful exponent in recent times. And it worked thus. We have seen that Orthodoxy made, by its jurism, an ethical advance on the absolutism that preceded it. It seems but another step of that ethical progress that the necessity for Christ's death should be sought only in the moral predicament of man's heart and conscience, and in nothing within God's own nature and claim. All that was to be considered was the change to be wrought in man and his moral history. The keyword moved from satisfaction to what would now be called impression, but it did not deepen to regeneration. The Cross was the grand spectacle of God's love; its action was on man only, and its object was to make him penitent (if not always regenerate). All that had to be met was the conditions prescribed for salvation by history or psychology, the obstacles to it in human nature and its fall. In these conditions the moral majesty of God had not to be negotiated in any way, but just displayed as mercy. It had to submit to these conditions and antagonisms subjective to us in order to reach and move us.

Here I say the old juristic necessity seems to become still more ethical. The public justice of the State, after all, is unwieldy to individual cases, as general law must always be; so it is replaced by that more intimate form of the moral order which we call righteous personality—by the norm, or principle, or genius distinctive of personality, by a *living* law. The Reformation, with its conception of personal faith, had been at work long enough to create the beginnings at least of the modern regard for personality, its supremacy, and its freedom from codes or institutions. Authority was not only constitutionalized, but personalized, only not now in a monarch's rank but in a Father's holiness, in a Head not of power alone but of love, of righteous love. Its methods, like its nature, were more ethical and less arbitrary than even Anselm's genius had conceived. The necessity of Christ's death was not theologized as by Anselm, but psychologized, if we may so say. It was called for by the moral psychology of sin. Even if it were not required juridically, as final satisfaction for the past, it would be needed teleologically for the future—*i.e.*, to bear in on men a due sense of the greatness of God's love and the gravity of their own sin in ignoring it—*i.e.*, to create a worthy repentance. On the same ethical lines even public government was on its way to be regarded as more educational than it used to be, and not merely regulative. A Lessing described God's object and function with the world as its education, its growth in moral personality. And the government of a God of love must go far enough in this educative way to produce that repentance so essential to the Christian idea of such moral growth. The death of Christ was the only means by which man's moral case could be dealt with according to man's moral nature as well as God's majestic, massive, and simple grace. To this end Grotius had made of that death a penal example; while Ritschl, less mechanically, made it a personal revelation, with a power, however, impressive rather than creative. The change by such theories was great, and it was largely due to the growth of the sense that the ruling interest in religion, the ruling power in morals, and the ruling influence in history is personality. Man's prime anchor and need, therefore, is not his adjustment to positive law, but his reconciliation as a person to a person—as a moral person to a person whose norm is not a formal righteousness, but a holy love, vital, mobile, and absolute. The doctrine of Atonement is for the hour withdrawn from action in the interest of a doctrine of Reconciliation. But its retirement from public notice is only for the purpose of its being rebuilt in the new perspective; it is a doctrine that can never really go out of commission. It is the condition of Reconciliation if man is to remain moral. When the moral nature of God as the Holy regains as much attention as has been given to the moral subjectivity of man, then interest must return to what his holiness requires no less than to what our conscience needs; and in the same interest of personality we shall resume an eager, not to say central, concern about the revelation by atonement and its redemption.

It may be interposed that Ritschl, much as he ethicized Schleiermacher, did not say the last word in this direction—in this moralizing and socializing of the divine relation to the world. This is significantly shown by the way in which some of his best pupils have gone back upon him in the matter of the exigent holiness of the divine love, to which Ritschl did no more justice than he did to the doctrine of a Holy Spirit. They took more seriously the idea of judgment, and pressed for a real atonement to God due to this necessity in his own holy nature. The Reconciliation is not sympathetic only, but moral; and its moral conditions involve not man's moral structure alone, but God's. Besides, it has to be not only shown, nor only offered, but done, and that means a change on both sides of the relation. It is the adjustment not of two hearts only making things up, but of two consciences making things good. And its necessity lies in both parties. That nature in man which required such treatment from God as the death of Christ is the reflection of God's nature as man's holy Maker. If there is a difficulty due to man's moral psychology, the root of it is really in God's, who so made man in his image that the transgressor's way is hard. The necessity is really to be carried back to the moral nature of God, *i.e.*, to his holy nature and its reaction in judgment, were it but automatic judgment, upon sin everywhere. We cannot think of anything arbitrary here. We cannot imagine God (in a Grotian way) reviewing several devices open to him for bringing man to his moral senses, and selecting the most judicious (as a college tutor might choose between gating and fining) out of many expedients otiose to his own nature. Whatever was done embodied a moral necessity for God, one which arose out of his free holiness, just because it had to adjust itself to a moral nature in man which was created in God's image. We have here a necessity which is solidary with that which made him create; and that was no whim. Unless we return there, to a real atonement required by God's nature and not merely by man's predicament, we hardly get beyond an expedient, and we do not really advance in moral reality and seriousness. We do not do justice to God's personality—especially as holy and absolute. We fall behind the old doctrines we want to correct. We do not take seriously enough either sin or grace. We do not find our data in the experience of the saints, but in the postulates of reason. We do not do justice to personality either in God or man. We reach, with Ritschl, the offering brought *to* God in the fidelity of Christ's love, but not to the offering made *by* God in the visitation of that love. The element of holy judgment is either ignored, as by liberalism, or it is severed from love, as by severe orthodoxy; and that cannot be done by either without damage to the moral personality which love is to reveal or to rear. The old view, so far as it went, aimed at something more thorough than that. And, when we are speaking of God, the more thorough is the more true. Deep Church means more than either Broad or Low. Deep Church is the only true sense of High.

My object has been to suggest the way in which the growing and ruling interest of an ethical religion has come to be holy personality and all that it implies. I now go on to discuss the true expression of such personality, its only adequate expression, which I will suggest is action, and not mere instruction nor exhibition. Christ was more the Plenipotentiary of Grace than its Manifestation, and especially so on the Cross. He did things, he did not simply state them.

III

The second point to be discussed, then, is this: What is the reality of a moral personality? What is sacramentally given us in it? Is it a substance or an act? What is its congenial function? Where does it "arrive"? How does it take effect? Is it merely spectacular, æsthetic, for our contemplation? Or is it ethical, and for action? Does it impress us or remake us? And the answer is for the latter alternative. The crowning expression of a moral and historic personality is action.

How do we get at the entire personality of Christ? The account in the Gospels is too meager for our purpose, and to many it has been made by criticism more or less unstable. With these data we are more successful in reaching the character than the person, though even the character cannot be depicted on modern, intimate, and psychological lines. The motivation, the pragmatism, cannot easily be traced, if at all. As we go into the Gospels it becomes clearer that they were not put there to depict a character, or to be a monument to a personality, but to lead up to the great crisis and victory which, for the first Christians, made Christ Christ before a Gospel was written, even in rudiment. The Gospels have a tendency. There is a movement in them. They hurry, with many a leap, to a *dénouement*, to a goal in which the movement "arrives," where the deep fire flames. They make for a crisis where the center of gravity lies. And, as the interest concentrates, the treatment expands. They are more ample as they draw to the close. They spend a disproportionate space on the passion, and on all the precincts of the Cross. Their stream is never so broad as when it enters the sea and disappears. The Gospels have the work of Christ on the Cross for their goal, as the Epistles have it for their center. Redemption is their *Leitmotiv*.

This is in keeping with the life of all the men who have been what we call providential personalities. I do not speak of the men of artistic or devout genius, like the poets or mystics, but of those woven into affairs as Christ was, and all the train of the Fathers and Leaders of Church or State. The personality is revealed as it becomes effectuated in deeds. It is incarnated in action. Its object is not just to reveal itself and give play to its powers, but to do something, or get something done, in course of which it is revealed. It makes for action, and for action which is more than mere activity, action for a purpose in a vocation, and not merely in the indulgence of a genius. The world is for the conscience, as for the heart, a tragic world. And the mere repose of a majestic personality, even of Christ's, does not meet that tragedy. It does not speak its language, nor return its note. It is something afar from the sphere of our sorrow. It is apt to produce a passionless Christianity, unequal to the color of life's vitality, the fervor of its fever, or its dramatic choice and issue. More than rapt adoration is called for by the tragedy of life. Personality is an energy. A great and royal world-personality must be gathered by passion into action on that scale. And a complete and vital personality like Christ's must come to a head in one Act, which in its nature is final. Its unity, its singleness, does not take form in a symmetry, but in an achievement. It is not statuesque. Its Reconciliation is not an æsthetic harmony of parts, but a moral union of lives. In the Act of the Cross the whole personality of Christ is thus condensed and brought to pass. The revelation is much more than a manifestation; it is a redemption. The Cross, as the Act in which God and man, Time and Eternity, Sanctity and Sin, meet, lifts Revelation above the mere exposition to our gaze of the rich beauty or spell of that person; the person has in it a vocation to action, both Godward and manward, in which alone it can come to itself. The Christ of the Cross was more than the wonder of the moral world, more than a spiritual splendor; and he stands amid the great moral figures otherwise than as the majestic head of Jupiter Ammon might stand among other fine busts. He was much more than the King of Saints, and more than the condensed Light of the World lighting every man. He was Action more than Light, except to such a Logos-theology as impairs a Holy Spirit and its ethic. He did and he does much more than shine or walk in beauty—he is of the Creators and Rulers. If he is

King, it is not in splendor only, but in moral power and effect. If he is Light, he is much more than illumination. He is more actinic. He warms, controls, and, above all, changes the world he lights. It revolves round him, it does not simply bask in him. He does not simply show the divinity of Love. Perhaps, after all that poets or other idealists have sung or shown (to say nothing of our heart's native instincts), it did not need the Son of God to show us Love's excellence or its lovableness. The central thing in Christianity is not to convince us, or to impress us, with the principle that God is Love, unless we are made certain that his Love is omnipotent. It is not love we worship in God, but the power of that love to make itself good for the whole world, to establish itself everywhere in dominion over its foes forever. He might love beyond all that heart can conceive, but can he love to any final effect, and does he love forever? Among men, love that has passed all speech has yet changed and faded. Or he might love with a fidelity that outlived all that mankind has yet done to try him; but is his Love capable of overcoming every possible enemy to it, of subduing the whole spiritual world, and beating down even Satan under his feet? Is it the eternal omnipotence? It might go far beyond our imagination, but does it go to eternity? Is it equal to his imagination? Is it universal, omnipotent? In one word, is it holy? Is it absolute? Nothing can really win our whole worship but the holy, nothing but the absolute Saviour justify our whole soul's faith. He might love us unspeakably but be helpless, after a point, against the hate that blasts, the malice that wrecks, or the cold that kills. Like the lovely Venus, it might be most moving in its grace but have no arms. We might die for the winsomeness of Christ, but what if in the very end he and we died together? Now, the Revelation that the Cross makes has for its object not simply the existence of God's love, but its power—that last conquest and that last certainty. The revelation was the very victory itself. It was not simply love at work, but love working its final settlement of all things. It is not just Love that Christ reveals there, but the absolute and eternal dominion of Love; and that cannot be revealed except as it is achieved. For our soul's last purpose a prophet's promise is of no use. What we have in the Cross is Love in final and decisive effect for the universe. It revealed not by way of a divine impression, but by way of an eternal achievement and accomplished fact. It was the Cross in its holiness that beat down Satan under Love's feet. It secured Love as holy, *i.e.*, as absolute, as final, insuperable, invincible for the universe. The Cross was the Act of that victory by the whole might of Christ's person; it was not simply a case of it, nor its symbol, nor its promise, at last far off, at last to all. And a Church without such a Cross, with a Cross moving but not regenerating, cannot help lapsing into an impotence it feels to its misery but cannot amend to its joy. I know it is a tremendous thing to say this about the Cross and what was done there. It seems sheer extravagance to say that the Cross was a mightier matter than the war, than all wars; that it was mightier to secure love in the world than war can be to destroy it. And indeed it is a belief beyond the power of individual faith. It is the matter of a revelation so great as to be a transforming act both for the soul it comes to and the world it saved. It is so great that only the collective faith of a whole Church can rise to its height, or open to its breadth. We cannot really believe it, if we grasp its significance, except with that vast and reciprocal increment of faith that comes from a whole Church believing together. And the Church's belief is one due to the faith of apostles selected and inspired for this supernatural purpose by the same Spirit as gives her power to believe.

Only in this sense is Christ King, throughout the whole height, depth, and range of human possibility or need, as that need is roused by the world problem on the one hand and by Christian faith on the other. If he is King, it is by action rather than by speech, and much rather than by the mere ideal he presents in his kind, stern, and stately soul. Christianity is not the religion of manifestation, but of redemption; not of the imaginative Ideal, but of the mystic Act, the mystic Will. Christ's religion is not a moral æsthetic, but a moral faith. And, for all its glories, the Ideal does no small damage to our action when it takes the place of faith. The ideal of what may be done can never replace for practical purposes the faith of what has been done for good and all forever. It does not bring an ought, and certainly not the supreme *ought* which always *is*. If Christ is the King of the world, he must act. And he must act, not in a series of minor acts, but once for all, with all his person, on the scale of the world, and indeed of eternity. Sure faith must have an absolute object. It is the loss of this absolute act out of our Revelation that lowers the pitch of faith, contracts its range, and is the source of so much of the public weakness in our religion, and of the powerlessness of our preaching with men of affairs. Unless it is the message, nay, the energy, the function of a thing done, preaching can do nothing but interest, lecture, or poetize. It cannot convert or control. The Cross was this Act, this pointing, of Christ's whole person. It taxed and focused all the resources of that person to die as he died, to do what the Church has found that he did in his death in the way of meeting God, effecting grace, winning love, destroying sin, and setting up the kingdom. Our only access to the Absolute is not philosophic, but religious. The Act of the Cross, realized by our faith, is the only sure point of the soul's final contact with absolute reality (which is moral reality); and it is the seat therefore of authority, and the source of mastery. That idea of authority is, at last, an Evangelical idea.

IV

We hear much (or did when we could hear anything but the din of arms hurtling in the air) about our loss of the sacramental idea—the loss of the sacramental interpretation both of the world and of the Church. The chief defect of non-Catholic religion, it is said, is the lack of the sacramental type. It is a charge to which we should pay due attention. Properly understood, the sacramental idea would protect us not only from hard, soulless, and trivial religion, but from the prevalent mysticism which bounds to the other extreme. The sacramental is the mystic element *in* things, and not over their heads, conveyed *by* things, not *round* them. It is a mystic influence which is inner-worldly and not other-worldly, working through the conductivity of nature and history, and not simply arriving by wireless. God is in Christ and in Christ's Church, and not just wherever we may recognize a Christian spirit coming by aërial post. He does not go round Christ, reach us by an intuition, and leave Christ and all history otiose to the soul.

But there is a reaction against the sacramental which is not without its ground. For the chief exponents of the idea have left it, for all the glamour on its face, too metaphysical at its heart and too little energetic. Their sacramental theory has turned on a metaphysic of being instead of energy, of matter instead of action, of essence rather than ethic. It has dwelt too much on the conversion of substance, and too little on the conversion of will, on the refining of flesh and blood to a celestial body. (Is it wonderful that, after all the Church has done, wills are so little changed as they are either within the Church or without?) Its sacraments have been therefore too static and too little dynamic, if these ungainly words may pass. They are apt to be more consoling than inspiring, and more perfunctory than effectual; working too much in the way of infusing into us the Saviour's heavenly substance, and too little in the way of creating in us his moral salvation. With the coming of the activist philosophies, however, both the scenes of Nature and the sacraments of the Church are now beginning to pass, the one into the revelation of an endless energy, and the other into a phase of the eternal Act, which (and not a supernal fluid) is Eternal Life. A sacrament is less a heavenly food than a spiritual energy, action, and gift. What has been lacking in the view of sacraments is the dramatic element. By this, of course, is not meant the histrionic, but the element of some positive thing done—some final thing done instead of some fine thing merely shown (as with Protestant Liberalism) or some rare thing merely infused (as with Catholic Sacramentalism). The lack at the religious center is the lack that we feel within much of the religion of cultured pietism or sympathetic rationalism—the lack of action, of power. We feel it both in preaching and in worship. They are spineless. Our preaching, at the least interesting, and at best inspiring, is yet not sacramental. It is not regenerative; because it has not the note and movement of a moral thing finally and creatively done as its motive power. In respect of worship, the Romanist at his Mass can always say to the Protestant: "I have, at the center, something *done*. Do your people leave worship with the same sense as mine of something really done, and done in the spiritual world? Do you feel that what you have been engaged in has left any mark on the world unseen? Your devotion is too little dramatic." But upon the Romanist himself it can be retorted that in his sacraments also there is too little that is really dramatic amid so much that is but spectacular movement. There is much that passes, but too little that is done. What is done is too metaphysical and too little moral. There is too much in the way of mystic alchemy, and too little in the way of moral transaction. I know the word "moral" here may to some bring down the whole matter in a sudden bathos. But it is not so. For I speak of the moral at its mystic height of holiness, as the very persons of the Trinity prosecute their eternal converse, communicate their eternal powers, and mightily and sweetly order all.

It is not simply action we need in our worship, nor only collective action, but sacramental action; not man's earnest prestation of praise, but God's full and passionate donation of himself. We need a revelation which is not truth, but action, and action which is not simply a deed, but an eloquent deed. We need more of the sacramental, truly, but a sacrament in a reciprocal act of persons, and not in the act of a person on a substance; not a conveyance to our nature of Christ's person merely, as a finer light in light, but a conveyance to our will of Christ's Act as the mightiest power in power—crowning, winging, and affecting all his person, and working by faith a response of personal, holy, and sacrificial love in us. The moral is the real. Reality is not a substance, but an eternal act. The transcendently moral, the holy, is the last reality. There is no higher gift than Grace at work refining Grace. An essence given is not so great as mercy given. It is not yet God as the gift. It does not rise above the first creation to the second. For the very self of God is not his essence all-divine, but his holiness and its Act of self-donation in the person and work of Christ—of a Christ not infused as the finest substance subduing our disease like a potent elixir, but as moral Omnipotence destroying guilt at his Word. "By his own will begat he us." The real presence in the worshiping Church is the presence of a real Christ gathered into a real act, conveying his holy deed of saving Grace, and not distributing the substance of his sacred soul. We become partners of his Act, and not merely partakers of his Person. We receive the Lord's death more than the Lord's body. Reality is an Act, and not an essence, and such is the real presence. It is Christ in action, not in elements.

V

A person who does not eventuate in adequate action is no true representative (whatever ornament), and certainly he is no king, of a community, whether it be nation or Church. The Church at least, as it arose from God's supreme Act, stands on that Act always. And the supreme Act was not simply Christ—that is too indefinite—but Christ crucified, and crucified not simply as the result of human crime, but in the exercise of his own will. Christ willed to die. His death was a deed. (Though the form of it was willed by man's wickedness.) And he willed to die because his Father willed it. He took death from God's hand with his whole active will. And, retrospectively, the Cross was the principle of all his ministry. The end was in the maker's thought. It was the supreme determinant, unconscious or conscious, indirect or direct, of his life. So that, if it was not his effectuation, it was his failure. For he put all his life into it. It either crowned his person or stultified it; for it did rule him. It was his crowning work or his crushing fate. If he was not final Redeemer, he was fruitless martyr. If his person did not destroy sin, it was destroyed by it. But it did destroy it. The Cross was the only place where sin was thus paralyzed—as the Resurrection showed. There is no sign that Christ took the Cross as a foreign fate, or raised a protest against its destruction of his real work. It was his vocation; it did not destroy his vocation. His word was Love, and sacrifice is Love in its native action. He died with all his heart—with all his broken heart, with all his moral soul, and strength, and mind. His greatest work was to triumph over the failure of his work. Forgiveness to the uttermost meant forgiveness for treason and desertion. It meant sacrifice to the uttermost, self-emptying to the Cross. His great victory was over his God-forsakenness; for it is easy to be good when God is a delight. So the Eternal Redemption came not merely as the fullness of time, but as an irony on time; not as the blossom of history, but of Grace; not as a fruit, but as a crisis in the standing miracle of Grace.

> For we gave Him the Cross where we owed Him the throne.[1]

VI

It need hardly be pointed out that if our attention is turned wholly on Christ's person and on our absorption into its consciousness of God, if it is diverted, therefore, from the effectuation of the person in an Act which settles and solders all, we have the result that appears in Schleiermacher and his magnetic line. We have no such

1. Jackson, *The Meaning of the Cross*, 40.

thing as Atonement; and that is to say we have a religious but no moral center of the world. Its morality does not come to a head in an effective act with an imperative in it, but remains at best an ideal. And the case of Germany, which disclaims a morality for the State, shows that, when the religion of a whole people deserts its moral source with characteristic thoroughness by discarding the creative center given in a real Atonement between man's conscience and God's, it loses its public ethic. The Cross, as such a real Atonement, is the source, standard, and dynamic of any ethic on a world-scale. This is the weakest part in Schleiermacher's system. And it flowed from the same defect in his idea of God as led him to abjure petitionary prayer. Our relation to God, he said, is absolute dependence; therefore we cannot act upon him either in the way of rousing his anger, or of obtaining our request, or of uniting with Christ's act (but only with his consciousness). Some, who are not with Schleiermacher in the matter of prayer, are yet with him in regard to Atonement and its place in the Christian type of religion. For them it is not central. To some young amateurs of piety it is a theological nuisance. The judgment of God is a mere parergon, a mere disciplinary device, outside the Cross of his Love, and irrelevant to a real faith. A share, or a copy, of Christ's personal sense of God is everything. This is bound to have a great effect on the moral quality of such faith, and in the end an effect not happy. It must soften it too much (especially among the young) to a mystic piety which is as attractive to the religious fancy as it is indifferent to conscience. I mean that the ethical element becomes but sequential to the faith; it is not intrinsic to its nature, as it must be in any creed where the Cross is the Act of *holy* Love. Piety of the kind I describe gravitates to think of Christ's person as no more than the mercy-seat, as the trysting-place of God and man; that is to say, as an inert area with an atmosphere instead of an active and decisive moral power, as a divine site rather than a divine Saviour. It misses the fact that Christ was above all things a Doer in and for man, that his supreme deed was toward God, and that this came to a head in the Cross, which, as it was the greatest opportunity for all that the person could do, was God's greatest gift to him. He came to give his life as a ransom, which was at least a degree above mere service, and many degrees above mere boon. To hold the Cross to be comparatively irrelevant, and to treat it but as the great instance of self-sacrifice is a temptation of that moral inexperience in youths and women which responds to heroism but does not grasp the nature of salvation because it does not yet know how heavy sin weighs.[2]

The truth is that Christ was bearing the saving Cross all his life. But that he could not have done except for the complete unity of his death with his personal life; and apart from that unity the Cross would have had no effect except as beclouding his person and truncating it. It was all one act; else, living or dying, how could we be the Lord's? When he startled his public by forgiving sin, it was the same shock as he gave his disciples by accepting the Cross. It was the same shock working two ways. Let us learn to think of personality as itself one grand and standing act, not as a mere vital entity. Human life is not a mere interplay of parts; nor is it a long process; but it is a standing act of resistance to death and defiance of it on the part of the race. So in the moral sphere, all Christ's life he was exerting the Cross, and growing in conquering personality as at every stage its domination deepened. But for the Cross that life would seem casual and unbraced, the life of a preaching friar or vagrant benefactor. It would seem pointless, planless, and without a ruling purpose. But it all shaped to the Cross, which was a *dénouement* not a *débâcle*. It was not but another incident in a life of activity, it was the culmination of a life of sacrifice, the goal in which all the prior energies found themselves. It was not but one action the more on a larger scale, like the ring at a chain's end, which you could drop without breaking the chain.

The matter of New Testament preaching is the person of Christ, but only as he is what he is supremely in the Cross—as he is the vehicle and crisis of God's Grace and the agent of his Redemption. He is not merely the great mouthpiece of that mercy, nor the infectious ideal of divine excellence. What makes the interior of his person is the redeeming Grace of God; and it works out sole and clear in the Cross as the point at which he bursts into his absolute Lordship and full universality. Only an act could destroy sin, which is an act, and vanquish it as a personal power, as the work of the Devil. Only a universal act could undo its

---

2. "In the dormitory we heard Dr. ——— on the Power of the Risen Lord. We were specially anxious to hear him, for he plays such a good game of tennis." (Letter from a student at a Swanwick conference.)

universal bane. The Gospels read like a triumphal procession of Christ through hosts of demons; or it is as if he were cutting a way through such a bodyguard in the kingdom of Satan to reach and dethrone their King upon the Cross. Only upon such an act of Judgment and Redemption could universal Love stand for what Christ revealed it—as holy Grace. Only on such an act could a Church stand, with the like differentia from every other society in the world—as holy. It could not stand or grow upon an inert person, nor upon one merely influential. Nor could it stand on a closed personality whose life-movement was but self-contained, however holy or lovely he might be to our contemplation. That were but an æsthetic figure, and could produce but an æsthetic ethic, a religion of charm and charity, a cloistered faith, and a sectional, not to say sectarian, community—like the winsome Christ, or the undergraduate's Christ, of whom we are apt to hear too much. The Redeemer is not in the first place the Christ of the young. Two things are not always well remembered—that the Church rests on the New Covenant, and on the suffering Saviour. Christ was more concerned about the founding of the New Covenant, the new moral relation with God, than about the founding of the Church. And the Gospel was not, Jesus is Messiah; it was the Gospel of a suffering Messiah who was Jesus.

We are apt to speak as if Jesus had no more to do than open up (though it might be even by the Cross) his capacious soul, and display the overwhelming wealth of his spiritual interior. But that is not the New Testament idea of revelation—which is the moral Act of redemption as the function of his entire person. How little, when we think of it, he does in that way of self-exposure! He was very reserved, not to say elusive, about the penetralia of his soul, about what was idiosyncratic in his own faith. What we reach of his inmost life we reach indirectly and inferentially, by making his teaching *yield* an autobiography it does not describe. To teach love and live it would have made a supreme saint, with disciples, but it would not have made Christendom.

We must escape from the limited conceptions of sin that are given by the personal lapses of the decent or the small circles of the pious. We must learn to view it in historic dimensions if we are to escape from the sectarian righteousness which ends in religious egoism, priggery, and futility. We must think of it imperially.

We must realize sin distinguished, subtle, cosmic; sin so universal that it needs a Church truly catholic to cope with it. Think of great sin, of world-sin, sin in the grand style, sin Machiavelian, national, warlike, sin past thinking of, and you must turn to the Cross. View the death of Christ as the self-condemnation of a people, of the select and chartered people, brought about by a society of religious, earnest, influential Pharisees, and not by a crowd of evil livers. Indict a nation. View its doom as the result of national sin. Israel did not fall by immorality, like drunkenness, or licentiousness, or swindling. On such counts Rome was much worse. Israel fell by a sin too great for most Israelites to call it sin. All its rabbis, even the Hillels, the whole scribal professoriate, its most interesting Sadducees, were against Christ and for a righteousness which the Son of Man called sin. It sinned much more against its light and its calling than Rome did—just as Christianity can be much more inconsistent than paganism. It fell by a corporate, and national, and constitutional sin, by the sin of a decent society as dense as it was cultured and as blind as it was sure, by the choice of its religious leaders and public representatives, by a political slavery fatal to the old genius, the moral soul, and the spiritual mission of the nation, by sin lordly rather than coarse or mean. The death of Christ is a revelation of sin such as we do not get from his life alone, of sin more deadly and desperate than arises from the mere neglect or dislike of his person. It was a revelation not of the common sins of the common man, but of high-placed sin—of illustrious sin, imposing, even dazzling, sin, of distinguished perdition and unsuspected ruin; the sin of a fine fearless godlessness abetted by earnest ecclesiastics, scholars, jurists, by party politicians, popular leaders, sentimental preachers, deserting disciples, and betrayers who kept all the commandments perhaps from their youth up, by spiritual wickedness in high and reputable places. It was over the city that Jesus wept, the collective center of his nation's culture. That is how we must see the deadliest sin to realize the saving Cross. It is how the saving Cross, as the compendious Acts of Christ's national universal person, opens our eyes to the perspective of sin.

VII

There is another way in which the sting and deadliness is taken out of sin, and so the Cross is moved from the vital center of the moral world. Some do not begin with the historic Cross and God's revelation of the holy, the evil, and the eternal there, but with the idea of a divine, moral, and spiritual order of the world, fundamental to its constitution, and condensed and incarnated in Christ. This means that he would have come to history in the working out of creation's destiny whether sin had entered or not, only in some other form. To this Christianity, coeval with creation, Christ is as the sun that gathers up the preexistent light. He concentrates the light that lighteth every man in his very constitution as man. He is not so much the center of life's tragedy and the Saviour there of its ruin and despair; he crowns a process, and represents the ripening, of a constitution of things which is imperishably good, and has an exhaustless power of self-recuperation. Man is the compendious summit of creation, and Christ of man; so that in Him we have the proleptic surety of the great ordered end. But it is not clear whence this idea reaches us with such power and certainty that we can make it the foundation of our interpretation of Christ and the basis of our faith. Does it come from Christ himself? If so, where? In his teaching or his Cross? Surely not from his Cross. It is most prevalent among people like the Friends, whose theology has never done justice to the doctrines of Grace, the cruciality of the Cross, and the fontality of its Atonement for all we are perfectly sure of in God's moral dealing with the world and its reconciliation. It is more like an importation from the religious theosophies, or the philosophic constructions of religion—more that than a theology that analyzes the moral reality of God's one historic Word—Christ crucified. It seems but an attempt to do no more than exhibit in the Cross an outcrop of all the antithetic tensions so finely balanced in the processes of Godhead, This is a version of the matter which lets personality and its moral action down in discussions about the make-up of the divine constitution, lowers the idea of sin as it lowers its burden, and reduces the value of Christ's conflict as the crisis of eternity and of the war in heaven no less than of time and of history. It is not just to the New Testament at least to regard Christ in the Cross as the supreme symbol of a humiliation and suffering which the Word undergoes in each individual. He is the Source and Creator of all the humiliation that is noble, and of the suffering which learns to rejoice.

10

The Christianity of Christ and Christ our Christianity

It is not uncommon today to hear the Gospels praised at the expense of the Epistles. The character of Jesus is set up in contrast with His redeeming work. And to His teaching is assigned a permanency denied to His person. Being dead He only speaketh; He does not reign and rule. St. Luke is called against his companion and master, St. Paul. And the mysticism of St. John is preferred to that of St. Paul because it is less definite and more idealist in its theology. The real reason, I suspect, is that St. John's mysticism is woven into a story, whereas St. Paul's has a more dialectic form. For I cannot see that the one is less theological than the other. Only in St. John Jesus speaks, while St. Paul speaks for Him; and there is a dramatic interest therefore in John which is not in Paul. What links Luke, and John, and Paul? Let us ask what is the common and permanent element in the New Testament? What is its unity? It is the grace of God as Christ's Cross. 1 Peter 1:10–12.

It has been generally and truly said that this element is the *work* of Jesus, what He did uniquely for mankind on the Cross in the way of altering fundamentally and finally the relation between the human soul and God. This has been the conviction of the Church as a whole, and the ultimate center of any power it has had upon the world. But to many this has become a piece of theology. It is not an active ingredient in their soul's life and their religious experience. They live more upon religious affection and sympathy than on religious faith. They say the prevalence of such a view is largely due to certain Judaic elements introduced into a simpler Christian faith by St. Paul. So they turn the Cross into the latest of the life-long series of self-sacrifices that mark the wonderful character of Christ; and it is upon the *character of Christ* that they fix for the permanent element in His religion. The affection, the wonder, the admiration, the imitation which such a character still calls out—these form the permanent influence which Christianity exercises on the world.

But then it is pointed out that His character is a thing of the past. It is simply now an ideal standing, though it towers and shines, in the far uplands of history. And what we need, they say, is some more positive action coming down and drawing very near, and laying on us a power and a command; not only attracting the soul but lighting up the soul, and searching it, and guiding it, and releasing it, and controlling it,—nay, what is more than all, remaking it. Now one section of those who demand Christ's actual touch on the age find it in the Church. The Church is the continuation of Christ, as it were, into our age, and Christ lays His hand on the soul of the age by the Church, its demands, its ideals, its truths and its privileges. Another section finds that Christ touches the age by a less institutional though no less personal rule over the spiritual world, and by His living access therefore as living Saviour to living souls. The eternal person of Christ is King of the unseen world which permeates the things that are seen. While another section still finds the real point of contact between Christ and the age in His teaching more even than His presence or example. They find the near, vital, and relevant influence to lie in the teaching of Jesus and its flexible actuality for the time. It is the principles of Jesus that the age needs, they say. The age can no longer believe in His living person as being very relevant to its exigencies. His work on the cross, they say, is a fine and typical martyrdom, but it is not the condition, the foundation, or the vital principle of the new soul. It may contain the moral principle of action in so far as that is sacrifice, but it is not the vital principle of a new spiritual creation. The character of Jesus is as splendid and influential as we should expect from One who crowned life with a death so tragic and noble, but it is still a heroic and remote ideal for today. And it is the insight of the teaching of Jesus in which He was so far ahead of His own time as to be for all time. It is the *teaching* which penetrates to the real sympathies and needs of the age. It is the teaching that is the most precious and permanent legacy from Christ to the world.

It is there, and not from a theological cross, that He really tells upon the human soul and human society. It is there that we hear of the Kingdom of God, and there that we learn of that love, sympathy, and pity which is the true health of the soul, and the true cement of souls into a society. No gospel (they say) is of first value for today unless it be human. And it is in the teaching of Jesus that we find the real humanity of His message—the teaching, coupled with whatever deeds of mercy may survive a modern criticism of the miracles. Of course, of the teaching also we can only take what criticism leaves.

Well, but is it not a wonderful thing that if His teaching was His great legacy He wrote nothing. He dictated nothing. He took no means whatever for having any authoritative version of it ready to survive Him. Socrates, to be sure, wrote nothing; but then Socrates did not found a society, or contemplate a line of disciples throughout history as trustees of the Kingdom of God. He did not contemplate changing the whole of history. Surely one who had that in view, and was before all else a teacher, might have been expected to leave something specific in his main line of work, if only to protect His secret, to keep it pure and powerful and to keep his disciples from quarreling. But He did not. If we were to be kept from quarreling it was not by an original code or record from Christ Himself. That was not His legacy. The Gospels themselves came there by an afterthought, humanly speaking. He did not commission their production. They arose as manuals of instruction. He charged His disciples with a Gospel but not with Gospels. What we have are memoranda, not always quite exact in every detail. Indeed, we often extract His *teaching* from them with so much trouble that an order of specialist interpreters, an educated ministry, is indispensable. He *could* have written had he pleased. He knew letters, though He had not passed through the school and college culture of the day. The craftsman and the scribe were often found in the same man. He was perfectly versed in the old classics of His race; He lived on them; they made His constant breviary. It was a literary age, too, with Josephus, Philo, and others on its front. What reason could He have had for not writing, but that He came for another work. He came to be His own Epistle, especially in His *parousia*, and to call out living reply from the world.

But let us take the teaching. Let us go to the teaching of Jesus as selected by evangelists, and even as sifted by critics. Let us ask there what the central, supreme, and permanent thing is in His intention and in His Gospel. May I suggest in advance what will be found, and then show by some examples how we are forced to find it?

We shall find that for Himself teaching was not the great object of His life but the setting up of a Kingdom and the proclamation of a message, the achievement of a salvation, and the delivery of its Gospel. He did not set out to solve problems either of thought or life but to perform a task. He spoke not for soul-culture but for change of soul. He was not a sage but a herald, not a teacher but a prophet, not an educator of men so much as a revealer of God. He was not a moral tutor but a holy redeemer. He was not among the men who say things but among those who do things. He was neither sage, herald, nor prophet, but King.

We shall further find that this Gospel, with all the teaching carried in it, was not the outcome of a student's work, nor that of a man of genius. What He uttered was not only, nor chiefly, the result of His observation of life or His insight into the moral world, but the expression of His own character and person. He found more in Himself than in life or the world. You cannot separate His philosophy of things from His person. You can with Shakespeare, for instance, who has done so much for the culture of a world that knows next to nothing about him. But Christ's gift was Himself. His message was the expression of Himself. It was a cast from His own spiritual countenance, and not from the face of the moral world. He spoke less from observation than from consciousness. It was by His knowledge of Himself that He knew both God and man.

Then we shall find that His character, His type of character, was, in His own view, based on something peculiar and unique in His person. The manner of life that He offered the world in His conduct was stamping (χαράκτηρ) on the world the meaning that lay in His spiritual constitution and His relation to God. His Messiahship rested on his Sonship. The character which the disciples appreciated so much from the first was based on the mystery of a person which they did not realize till He had passed away. The character which impressed the disciples was the outer garb of a personality which is as real, vivid, and active today and forever as it was then. Their *impression* from His *character* failed them at this great crisis. And what caught them up and made men of them, what turned them from deserting disciples to apostles that never looked back, was the *regeneration* from His *person*.

We shall find, besides, that the power of that personality today is something which was not only foreseen but purposed by Christ Himself. He did not make Himself everything just to vanish at the last and leave but a tradition. If He made Himself everything it was forever. The centrality He took for Himself was a centrality for the whole soul and for the world eternal. He was central not for His age or His Church but for mankind, for all time. "I am with you always." "The same yesterday, today, and forever." If His earthly life was all, it was a poor embodiment of His huge claims, a mere torso of His plan. His death was a beginning rather than a close, historically speaking. It demanded resurrection at least, it moved to exaltation, and involved eternal reign. He looked forward to being all that the Christians of today find Him and much more—both for them and for the world. He claimed to be both King and Lord of mankind, of time's history, and of Eternity's.

And we shall find, lastly, that this power and victory of His was in His own mind due to the one comprehensive, decisive, and final thing He did on earth. It was due to His work as the Redeemer. And I choose the word Redeemer because some of the more humane, liberal, and genial forms of Christianity are shy of it. They speak of the Saviour as the first born of many saviors of society or man. But they do not readily speak of the Redeemer because they are uneasy about the theological suggestions which certainly give it its distinctive meaning, and confine it to Christ alone.

The point, then, is that Jesus was more conscious of the uniqueness of Himself and His work than of the originality of His teaching. You can parallel much of that teaching from other faiths, and perhaps trace some of it to Hebrew wisdom. But you cannot trace or parallel *Him* and the power He gives to fulfill His own leading. His own faith was very humane, but it was more deeply rooted in His difference from men than in His likeness to them. His union with them was indirect, and it depended on His union with God, which was direct. He came to man through God, not to God through man. No one ever helped Him to find God. He was one with man by will more than by birth, by purpose more than by parity, not so much as a member of humanity but for purposes with humanity flowing from His unity with God. His relation to God was first; it determined all. And in His consciousness it was unique. It was one which He did not share with men, even with His disciples. He never prays with them, but for them. He does not say "Our Father" on His knees in their midst. He tells them to say "Our Father" "when *ye* pray". It was a lesson, not an act of worship, teaching *them* how to pray. He speaks of "My Father and your Father, My God and your God". His relation to God and theirs were different. He was not a beneficiary of the Sabbath, He was Lord of the Sabbath, and with it of all the things that were made for man. He was greater than the temple, for whose sanctity generations of men had laid down their lives, and would again. That is to say, He was greater than all the temple stood for—greater than the law, greater than the covenant, greater than Israel, greater than Israel's worship. He was the goal and object of it all, the Holy One of Israel. He was to judge even the world. His sanctity had no share in human sinfulness. He confesses His Father, and His own before the Father; but not His sin. It is our sin He bears, not His own. No trace in His words shows the ordinary fellowship of human sin. He tells His disciples that they were evil. "If ye, being evil, know how to give good gifts to your children." He does not say *we*. They are blessed in suffering only when persecuted *for His sake*. Nay, He ventured on something the sinless alone could do. His relation to God was so different from ours that He undertook to forgive sins—a function that belonged to holy God alone. Healing the paralytic, He said, "Son, be of good cheer, thy sins are forgiven". His meaning was clear enough to anger the bystanders. They were not left to suppose that He meant mere absolution. They did not understand Him simply to *declare* to the man a forgiveness general and ready, as we might now declare it to a world forgiven in Him. They quite understood Him to mean that He *exercised* the forgiveness of God; for they took it as blasphemy. And He accepted their interpretation of His words, and said that to forgive was as easy and proper to Him as to heal (Matt 9:2).

Again, He accepted the confession of His disciples that He was the One Messiah. He was not surprised by it, however gratified. It was a confession to which He had been educating them in the most patient and skillful way. It was His own object with them that was reached when Peter owned Him as the Messianic Son of the living God. That meant that He was the sole King of God's Kingdom; and who could be sole King of God's Kingdom but God? The indirect object of all His teaching was Himself, His unique and royal self, whom to serve was to serve God. He never plainly said He was the Messiah. His method of education was far profounder than that. He did not *tell* them, *He lived it into them* and forced their faith with a moral compulsion. All His teaching and healing, hearty as it was and occasional, was there for more than pity and passing relief. It was part of one overruling purpose, and with one ultimate goal. It was to prepare and to extort from men the confession of Him and His kingship as a spiritual discovery. And His joy when it came from Peter shows how passionately He had longed and patiently prepared for its coming (Matt 16).

Take another aspect of the matter. What did He die for? For His teaching? For His view of truth, of the soul, of the divine? For His Sermon on the Mount or His doctrine of the Kingdom? No, but for His place as the King. He might have preached the Kingdom and kept His life. Preaching of the Kingdom was welcome then. He was popular while He preached that. "We trusted that it had been He who should restore the kingship of the world to Israel." His popularity did not wane till He began to behave as what they thought a *faineant*. And it was that claim which roused the alarm both of Pilate and of Herod. It was a king they feared, not a teacher's spiritual idea. And what cost Him His life was His declaration upon oath at His trial, not that He preached the Kingdom, but that He was Himself the Son of God, the King. That threw Pilate into the hands of the Sanhedrin. If they reported to Rome that Pilate treated lightly a rival of Caesar that was the end of Pilate.

And what did He mean by that "King"? Was it a mere metaphor, as we call some hero a king of men, or a vulgar plutocrat a king of finance? No. He claimed the real, veritable, ultimate control of human wills as His right; and He set Himself on the whole world's judgment throne. "Many will say unto me in that day, Lord, Lord!" (Matt 7:22). "In that day if ye shall have confessed Me, I will confess you" (Matt 10:32). "All things are delivered unto Me of the Father" (Matt 11:27). "The Son of

Man shall send forth His angels to gather" the great harvest of souls at the last (Matt 13:41). "Heaven and earth shall pass away but *My* words [not *their* words, but *My* words] shall not pass" (Matt 24:35). He is the Judge at the great dividing of the sheep and the goats that ends human doings (Matt 25:31). His foes, He promised, should see the Son of Man sitting on the right hand of power (Matt 26:64). It has been said that it was the preaching of the Saviour as the Judge that did most to impress the pagan world in the years when Christianity spread so fast at the first. People were not used to a judge that was their Saviour, to a judge unpurchaseable but on their side. He laid down in a royal way the laws of the Kingdom, and He determined its conditions and its course; He began with the Sermon on the Mount, He went on through the parables of the Kingdom; He laid down that doctrine of the Cross as the true King's power in the answer which He gave to the ambitious mother of Zebedee's sons and to the angry ten in her wake. And what is to withstand the great utterance of Matthew 11:25: "No man knoweth the Father save the Son and they to whom the Son wills to reveal Him."

I know that the amount and detail of His teaching was about the Kingdom while the words about Himself are comparatively few. But they are the key to all the rest. If the *bulk* of His teaching was about the Kingdom, the *weight* of it was about Himself. The Kingdom filled the extent of His teaching but its significance was the King. In quantity it was the one, in quality it was the other. He taught the Kingdom as only the King could. And He so taught that the deepest impression left on His disciples was not the Kingdom but the King. From the New Testament, outside the Gospels, the Kingdom vanishes, being merged in the King. And for some today there is about the idea of the Kingdom something slightly archaic, but the King is vital, actual, experimental.

But the ultimacy and eternity of this kingship was due to its nature. He was a priestly King. It was a sacrificial kingship. It was by devotion that He won devotion. He came not born as King, not to proclaim Himself King, but to *make* Himself King. He had to conquer the realm and make subjects He should rule. He made a people He did not find. Like a great new poet He had to make His own constituency. His empire of the world stood historically on His salvation of the world. He came not to wear a dignity but to do a work. And that was not simply to administer a secure office, but to deliver, nay, to create His realm of the soul. He had to found the Kingdom He would rule, and redeem the race He would bless. He could not bless them till He redeemed them into the power to appropriate His blessing. He takes to Himself the great Old Testament promises of a Redeemer as in Luke 4:18: "The Spirit of the Lord is upon Me", etc. (from Isaiah 61:1); and He does it in the reply to John's messengers, where Matthew 11:4 reproduces Psalm 146:7 and Isaiah 38:5. This redemption was the work He came to do. It was not simply to exhibit His person but to put His person into an achievement, to put all His person into one, great, decisive, redeeming work *which was God's even more than His*. What else than this is meant by His saying that He came to seek and to save that which was lost; and (still more expressively) that He came to give His life a ransom for many; and that the great fruit of His death should be the remission of human sin and the power of Eternal Life.

The teaching of Christ carries us into the person of Christ. His person carries us into His Cross, and it is out of His Cross that all the kingship springs to which His teaching moved.

It is not possible for criticism to destroy all these passages. I have not quoted others that criticism challenges. But to sweep these out of the record would not be criticism but laceration. It would be cutting the story down to the form and pressure of our time. It would be using the Bible in the most violent way to prove a foregone negative theory of Christ. And that is just what the critics accuse the Church's positive faith of doing—of fitting the historic Jesus to a later theology. But we have no more right to trim the Bible to a shriveled Christ than to an inflated Christ. The day has gone by among responsible scholars when the Gospels could be reduced to legends of the second century. You find such views now only among the derelicts of amateur rationalism, or the mother wit of the cheap secularist press. Christ did say such things about Himself as I have quoted.

If these passages hold, the teaching of Christ Himself carries us much farther than His teaching. He taught His person, His Cross, His reign. He taught as one who had a unique sense of Himself, a unique relation to God, and a work to do for man which all humanity could not do for itself. He taught as He lived—royally. He lived with other men and loved them, but He did not class Himself with them. He knew the solitary value of His life and death, and we only know that He knew it by what He Himself said. What we have been going on is not theories by His disciples but words of His own.

And we are shut up to one of two conclusions. Either we must accept Christ's account of Himself or else treat Him as a crazy fanatic, a "megalomaniac", filled with a restless lunatic sense of His own imperial importance, and the homage, the worship, due to Him by other men. You cannot separate these teachings I have quoted from the rest. You cannot cut these out as morbid and yet leave the rest as sane. If He is wrong here, where can we trust Him to be right? If wrong and deluded there. He fails even as moral teacher. If He is not more than a teacher, He is less. The Christianity of Christ is Christ as Christianity.

We are driven thus if we turn to the impression He made on those nearest Him, on the first Church, on the New Testament writers and the Christians they had to do with. It is sometimes urged against the godhead of Jesus that He never claimed to be God. But that was not His way. We saw it was not, in His education of the disciples up to their Messianic confession. He did not proceed by way of direct claims. I allow I do not much like the word "claims". When plain men asked Him to say plainly if He was the Christ, He did not indulge them. Christ often disappointed the plain man—the plain man being often but the man impatient for immediate solutions. But He did make the final recognition of His Messiahship inevitable. He forced the confession as a spiritual necessity from their souls by acting on them with His own. So it was with His *godhead*. That word did not belong to His vocabulary. And the idea is not like the Messianic idea—one that filled the thoughts and hopes of His time. Quite the other way. The idea of a man they knew being God was repulsive and blasphemous to these Jews. It was foreign to the Hebrew mind. It was much more natural to the Greek or the Indian. He was used to incarnations. But the passionate monotheism of the Hebrew left no room for such a thought. To be equal with God was a blasphemous suggestion, and they called it so when they heard Him forgive. Yet this utterly unsemitic idea—so unsemitic that that race has suffered everything rather than admit it—was forced upon many Jews, and on a Jew like Paul besides, by the compulsion of the spiritual situation, by slow, subtle, spiritual logic. The love of Christ constrained them when once they had felt His holy spell on their Spirit and read history with their souls. His godhead was forced in on them by the impression, revelation, and work of Christ on them and for them. Their theology was experimental. They did not give up their monotheism. And yet they held to the godhead of Christ. They did not express it in the elaborate and metaphysical forms of some centuries later. They held it as a religious certainty; as the result and action on their construction of the Gospel, of the Cross, and not of speculation; for who could forgive and recreate but God only? But hold it they did, in the profound, natural way of a spiritual conviction, or rather, a spiritual relation to God in Christ. Paul, writing to the Corinthians (1 Cor 8:6), says; "To us there is one God, the Father, and one Lord, Jesus Christ." Christ was their one Lord. But if He was not God, then they had a sole Lord who was not God, and God was not their Lord. So again there are "diversities of ministries" but the same Spirit, the same Lord, the same God (1 Cor 12:4–6). That Trinity was the ground and unity of all the ministrations—not three unities but one. They "call Jesus Lord to the glory of God the Father" (Phil 2:11). The godhead of Jesus glorifies the godhead of the Father. They use the word Lord of Christ in the full Old Testament sense as applied to God. "If thou shalt confess with thy mouth Jesus as Lord" (Rom 10:9). "Whether we live we are the Lord's, or die we are the Lord's." "Christ died and rose that He might be Lord both of the dead and the living" (Rom 14:8–9). That means more than their master. It means their God. It was much more than a title like "the Lord Serapis" in the papyri. And so in Phillipians 2:10: "That in the name of Jesus every knee should bow and every tongue confess Him Lord." They apply to Christ (not defiantly, nor in the way of adventurous speculation or dogmatic novelty, but in the way of spiritual *naivete* without being self-conscious over it), the very expression which the devout Jew used of God. They invoked Him as God. They describe themselves as those "that call upon the name of Jesus Christ" (1 Cor 1:2; Rom 10:12). This means worship. It was not taking His name as descriptive of themselves—like calling themselves Christians. In the Old Testament to call upon the name of the Lord was to pray to Jehovah for salvation (Ps 116:4): "Then called I upon the name of the Lord; O Lord, I beseech Thee, deliver my soul." So Joel 2:32: "Whosoever shall call upon the name of the Lord shall be saved." This very verse is deliberately applied to Christ in the New Testament twice—Romans 10:13 and Acts 2:21.

Paul certainly prayed to Christ and spoke of it to his Corinthians as nothing startling. With his thorn in the flesh he prayed the Lord (meaning Christ, as always) thrice that it might depart. It is hard to see what element of worship to God is omitted in their attitude to Him. They recognize His universal sway. For them He is Lord of all. They give Him absolute, final, unshakable trust, and they commit their eternal souls to Him. They ask and receive from Him forgiveness. They pray to Him. And their ideal life is a walk according to His will. For them the work, the will, the spirit, the Kingdom of Christ are the work, will, spirit, and Kingdom of God. If all this is given to Christ, what is left to give to God? Has Christ not monopolized from God the worship of the soul? If He be not God, can He be other than God's rival for man's heart? But if He had been, could the apostles write and speak as they did of Him and the Father together? Everything they give and do to Christ, their worship, is given to the glory of God the Father. Is there any doubt that the New Testament, unformed as its doctrine of the Trinity may be, at least is full of the godhead of Christ? He is not identified with the Father but He shares the godhead of the Father. That was the faith of these men, of that Church. It was not yet a system with them; but it was a faith. It was an irresistible, spiritually natural, religiously inevitable, movement of the Christian soul. It was just the congenial response to the touch of Christ on them. It was the impression His word and work made on them—especially His redeeming work on the Cross. It was the effect of His regeneration of them by His Spirit. They had no alternative but to say "God was in Christ reconciling the world"—not using Christ but present and acting in Him. It was this reconciliation, this redemption, that forced them to this huge and, to them, most solemn spiritual step. It did not grow out of doctrines about the Logos. These came after, as mere philosophical ways of putting it. It was the identification of the Redeemer of the Cross with the Redeemer in the Old Testament—God Himself. God was in Christ in such a reconciliation. It was Christ that reconciled, and it was God in the same person and act. God came. He did not send. Not God spoke by Christ, or acted through Him, but God *was* in Christ; and not tending, helping, pitying, loving, lighting, and warming the world—but *reconciling* the world by dealing with its sin atoningly and redemptively. All our systems of incarnation or atonement are but necessary efforts to give a clear account of that faith. They are faith trying to account to itself for itself. But the faith is always greater than the account of itself it can give, greater than the theology. And the redemption as a reality or a power is greater than even the teaching of Christ Himself about it or about the Kingdom. The Redeemer *did* more than He *said*. His great work was done almost in silence, without strife, or cry, or voice heard in the street. No man heard the sound of the world's creation and very little was heard of its redemption—and least of all from the Redeemer. What really preached His death was not His teaching but His resurrection, His exaltation. The resurrection was the great word that proclaimed to the Church the value of His death and not to the world the evidence of His survival. And the resurrection itself was silent. It was a silent discourse. It was an event speechless like His death, but like His death a deed. It was retired, and to many doubtful, like all the chief steps by which He has impressed His personality upon the world He taught the Kingdom but He acted Himself. The supreme truth was not the Kingdom; it *was* Himself asking, and it could not be uttered; it had to be lived and died; and the silence in which Christ lives and saves at this moment is only a portion of the great silence round His whole redemption. The silence of the spiritual world is the sign of its unspeakableness rather than its impotence. It is the token of awful action often ironically still. It is ominous silence. But it is the most blessed omen for us; it is auspicious silence. The silence of the whole earth about God is the sign that God is in His holy temple, that He dwells with man, and that His eternal redeeming work is going on with sure and mighty power.

We do not do Christ's teaching justice till we worship Him. We owe Him that as Redeemer. His great claim on us is not that He loved us, nor is it for our love. It is not that He has blessed us, nor is it for our blessing of Him back and our thanks. Had He only loved us He would never have been the Christ for the whole world and for the soul's deepest, darkest world. Would that more of us loved Him and loved Him more; but we can never rest there. We must do more even than trust Him; we must trust ourselves to Him. He is more than our lover; He is our Redeemer. The point is the moral omnipotence of His love. It was not helpless love. And we are not just to our Redeemer if we but love Him. There is something in modern piety that is a little too free, and possibly familiar, with its expressions of love. The love of Christ may be too awful for the ready expressions of affection. The forgiven sinner should be too full of His repentance to be very free with expressions of His love. Let him *worship*. It is his Redeemer that is before Him. It is so with every one of us. Let us worship and bow down, let us kneel before the Lord our Redeemer. It is He that hath saved us and not we ourselves. We are *His* people and the travail of His soul. For us He poured out His soul unto death, and the whole silence of the world is His intercession for the transgressors.

"Do you love Christ?" Sometimes we hardly know. I like that hesitation. "Do you trust His love of you?" "Yes, to whom should we go?" That is faith, living faith. "Do you trust Him as your Redeemer?" "Yes, trust and praise." "Trust yourself to Him?" "Into Thy hands I commend my spirit." That is worship—trust and praise for His blood, and death, and might, and majesty, and dominion forever.

11

Regeneration, Creation, and Miracle I

What do we mean when we not only speak (as we do) of the doctrine of the new creation in Christ crucified, but speak of it as being inevitable to a spiritual veracity,[1] an ethical thoroughness, or a penetrative moral imagination?

It belongs to the type of doctrine that is most frequently challenged by those who claim the special custody of such high interests as I have named, and who would rescue for their own idea of positive truth the intelligence that they deem wasted in theological fantasy, or perverted by dishonest accommodations. In many such cases it turns out that our adviser betrays no sign of the experience which is involved, and indeed that he has never studied the ultimate philosophy of *any* experience. He knows little of the history of theology, and nothing of its inner history. And he has no knowledge of the revolution effected in theology through the historical treatment that makes and saves its modern phase. The ethic that he knows, when he knows anything of ethic as it should be known, is apt to be the natural ethic of conduct or virtue, and not the spiritual ethic of the soul of the good, of the holy; or it is the ethic of a distributive justice, and not of a regenerate personality. It may be but a branch of sympathetic sociology. It is not Christian ethic; or, if it is, it is the ethic of the Christian ideal, and not of the Christian revelation and its experience.

But it is impossible to allow the monopoly of either veracity "lucidity," or positivity, and the credit of "thinking to a finish,"

---

[1] It need hardly be said here, perhaps, that by veracity is meant not the habit of telling the truth, but the passion for thinking it, and thinking to a finish and resting in Reality—what Matthew Arnold called "lucidity."

only to minds whose ideas of truth have been formed but on a natural ethic, or on an acquaintance with the sciences often called positive and their logic of research and induction. Nothing can be thorough in its veracity or lucidity which does not take the soul seriously as the greatest of all facts; that is, which does not deal with it as it is before the last reality, where that is supremely revealed as its God. Even, when scientific logic rises to the scale and range of a philosophy, we may but find ourselves consigned by it to a system whose data are only the five barley loaves of the senses, without any miraculous action upon them. Against all this we have to urge that moral history and the experience of the spiritual world supply data no less positive, and much more live and pregnant, than those of the natural world. An urgent and earnest veracity will not consent to have its attention arrested on the empirical aspect of human nature. It presses on to factors which do not reside there, but only emerge, and emerge by an action which is much more in the nature of divine inspiration from a creative fullness than of subliminal eruption from congestion and crisis. The doctrine of a new creation in Christ is central to a theology which, from its historic origin, is no less positive in its unique data than any science, and no less inevitable and sequential to moral and intellectual veracity. No monopoly of that virtue is held by the abstract rationalism that reigns with equal force and fatality in rigid scientific positivism and in strict theological orthodoxy. The reign of law may be in its tone physical with the *savants,* or forensic with the orthodox; but it is in both equally destructive of that element of life, freedom, and faith, which is at least as potent as force or fate in the history and experience of the race. "The proof of man is in the reproof of fate." There is an historical positivity which is at least as positive, real, and effective for Humanity as the scientific, the juristic, or the economic.

Let us approach the matter from another quarter, from the history of modern thought on the subject. The great theological influence which broke the ban of a forensic orthodoxy and a cultured rationalism was Schleiermacher, whose appearance in this science is comparable to that of Darwin, or even Bacon, in another sphere. The fundamental principle introduced in Schleiermacher was the return to nature and experience. Only it was the new nature and the new experience of the Christian who has not only touched but tasted the last reality, and who is a Christian in spirit and in truth, and not by mere courtesy, or as an ethical type. And yet there are whole regions of religious thought, not to say whole Churches, hardly touched by this principle. I say nothing of those scientific trippers who take an occasional vacation in theology, as they would in an attractive country whose language and literature they do not know, and then write about their travels. But the effect of the great movement I describe has hardly reached the Anglican Church, for instance. The Anglican Church, with all its splendid piety, does not strike the full chord of New Testament faith. It is too Catholic in its quality, too æsthetic and too little moral. It is too patristic or too scholarly; or it is too philosophic on belated Hegelian lines; or too scientific, as science goes in the middle register of things. It is scriptural in the Erasmic, academic sense; and it is too little scriptural in the massive Evangelical sense to have taken its proper place in the moralizing of theology, and therefore of life, and especially of the life of culture or affairs. Its genius, like all Catholicism, is more æsthetical than ethical, as its cultus develops dutiful reverence more than filial worship. It is not quite at home in the language of the great Christian paradox of grace, which is the great moral paradox of reality. And it is too exigent of the simplicity and clarity that goes with the æsthetic or classic idea of a perfection more symmetrical than saved, more harmonious than reconciled. Some of its most fine and eager spirits can write a delightful, vivid, and liberal volume[2] on the deepest things, which yet has not in principle outgrown the extreme æsthetic of Hegelianism. It is too unfamiliar with spiritual seismology. It has taken to heart Green and Caird more than William James. It has little trace of the moral crisis in Redemption. An afterwash of baptismal regeneration blinds it to the moral wealth and theological resource in conversion. And it shows no trace of commanding spirits in modern theology like Schleiermacher or Rothe (whom it names, but in a quotation from some one else in a note). It still rests its Incarnation in a metaphysic, subliminal or other; and it does not found it, as the New Testament does, on the work of an atoning Redemption whose experience founds the Church and all its worship and thought. We wonder sometimes why that great

---

2. *Foundations*. Oxford, 1912

and glorious Church as a whole (for we allow for the great social work of Green and his disciples) is so much less than it should be a moral power, leader, and guide in the tense new situation of the society around it. And the answer is, in part, that the foundation of its creed is metaphysical rather than moral, and the genius of its broad effect is but too true to that Catholicism, with its defect of moral initiative and its excess of æsthetic culture, its defect of motive and its excess of sedative, its lack of great gospel and its extravagance of good form. And this acts in another way. It drives its Free Church critic into protest from the ethical side, but a protest robbed of the power and mass which Catholicity could supply if the contribution of each were pooled, and the Nonconformist conscience thus protected from its tendency to a hectic note and its danger of mock heroics.

The rationalism of orthodoxy and that of philosophy both gave way a century ago to a vast new influence, corresponding, on the one hand, to the new cosmic sense of Science, and, on the other, to the new sense of Humanity in the revolution. The cosmic form of the Revival rose to its height in Hegel, with his dialectic process of the developing idea; the humane side of it took shape in a new recourse (rising in Kant, led by Schleiermacher, and developed thoroughly through Hoffmann by Ritschl) to moral history—the history of the moral soul in its most crucial experience as the locus of revelation—and to a new experience as the answer to such revelation. If modern philosophy was born there in Kant, so also was the modern view of history in religion, as revealing not the ideal process but the spiritual foundation of the world. A theology of revelation, faltering on the now hollow ground of Scripture infallibility, was but the more broadly based upon a new historical interpretation of the Bible, of dogma, of the world and the soul. The old supernaturalism, resting as it did, with one foot, on an impossible theory of verbal inspiration, and, with the other, upon a metaphysic of things instead of personality, society, and history, fell down. The tradition, indeed, still continues to stand in some of the more closely organized Churches, and in those secluded from modern influences by immersion in a false conception of authority in Church or Bible. But they are hollow shells of ruined towers that let heaven be seen through their cracks rather than their windows. A theology, free and independent both of philosophy and of scholastic, now comes to its own. Its watchword is, Back to the saving facts that created both the Bible and the Church, that gave a new life to the old philosophies, and that have their continuity in the Church's experience of the Spirit. Back to the facts and powers that made Christians, that made them Christian, and that carry the distinctive power and genius of the faith in them always. Back to history, to a history that *created* in us Eternal Life, because it sprang from the eternal power in His supreme, practical, historic *miracle* of Grace. Theology had been (what it still is very powerfully in many quarters) too little historical and too much national—whether the notions were those of metaphysic, or those of jurisprudence. Slain by the notions, it must be raised up by history, by the saving facts rescued from the saving schemes for their free saving power. It must become the exposition of its own unique and creative fact by that fact's intrinsic light and power. The creative historic Reality must be expounded by a mind that has experienced its creative change. The autonomy has been declared of religion altogether, and especially of the Christian revelation in the soul of Christ and his Gospel. The Bible is the history, not of Israel, but of redemption. It is the record, not to say the sacrament, of an historic new creation; and it is not an arsenal of proof-texts for a system which it is salvation to receive on some other authority—that of the Church as infallible or of a literary miracle like a Bible verbally inspired. Revelation is identified with Redemption; it is no mere manifestation, or the deploying of an ideal process; it is God's practical intervention as a person for personal regeneration. And the supreme authority for the soul, and therefore for the world, is one to be felt and owned only by the redeemed. The real saints are the judges of the real world.

In this view Christ is not a functionary of salvation, but the Saviour, by the universal act and finished victory in his own personality. He is (by a fundamental mystery yet richly to be explored) a life at once historic for us and experienced by us—the Lord the Spirit, a positive, historic, warring, and creative person, achieving in his universal soul the timeless act of moral victory which is the last stage and exercise of Creation. He thus becomes (and not merely produces), by the moral mysticism of regeneration, a new experience in his believers. The key to his incarnation is not in speculative theories, but in the achievement of an absolute moral victory, racial and final, which functions in us as his regenerative work.

Within the historic Christ himself Schleiermacher broke down the barrier set up by orthodoxy between his life and his death, his active and his passive obedience. His death was not a *dingliche Leistung*,[3] detachable from his life, a quittance compensatory and preliminary to salvation, a something merely factual and ponderable, which could be put into the scale opposite to human guilt (treated as a like entity), and could more than weigh it down. Rather, his death made the moral consummation and crowning triumph of his whole moral life which executed sin in human nature. His personal conflict and victory was the essential thing in his work. As the perpetual achievement of holiness at every trial in a rising scale, it was the one offering pleasing to God, and supremely so in his death where the tragedy of the universal conscience rose to become the theodicy of God. It was in line, though not in kind, with all spiritual heroism, and it effected (in a way I shall shortly try to show) a new creation in history, at once moral and mystical, individual and universal. It was not the lodgment with God of a forensic preliminary or deposit, but a crisis in the nerve and marrow of human history taken as the conscience writ sharp and large. It was not a further fact, in a series of other facts in Israel's career, which formed an historic postulate of God's grace; but it was the present action of that grace itself. *It did not procure grace, but gave it effect.* It was God at this gracious work, not waiting to be gracious. It was his grace in historic and decisive operation, it was not an external and prior contribution which made the action of grace possible. Christ's office was much more than official; it lay within his own personal and moral vocation. Into the fellowship of that act the Christian soul was taken up in the congenial act of faith; and he was entered, by such faith, as a freeman of Christ's consciousness of God. The supreme function of Christ was not to suffer a penal necessity, as in the forensic theories. It was active. It was freely and fully to obey, and only thus to honor God's free holiness. The suffering was divine as an act, as an act of holy obedience and not mere heroic submission, as a moral act and not a mere resignation. Mere suffering and mere resignation to it is not

---

3. ["Real achievement."]

redemptive. Christ offered to sinful man's holy God the only satisfaction holiness could receive—a moral satisfaction, a complete, answering holiness on the scale of the offending race. It not only came into line with all great moral action in the men and nations that make history, but it was the divine core, and became the divine source, of such action everywhere. Man's one evil, godlessness, was met by man's one good—God with us. The moral nature of God, the divine holiness, was placed at the center of all the righteousness of history, and all the spiritual triumph of the race. It was from henceforth set at the source of all that man should do in the one thing where (for all his triumphs) he was becoming less and less able to do anything—in the matter of facing God, meeting his judge, and even rising to confidence and communion with him. Man's evasion here is the cowardice behind the great heroisms, the fear that cankers his earthly valor, the failure eating out the heart of his fine achievement.

There is indeed a vast courage in our race to face nature and master fate. Man is indomitable.

> Many the powers that mighty be,
> But none is mightier than man.[4]

To the forces around him his spirit rises, and he has waged with wind, sea, fire, famine, pestilence, and sword a most gallant war. He has conquered both Poles and is mastering the high air and the deep waters no less than the broad earth. By the practice of a long, long history his courage has been developed in cruel tests to a heredity strain. It becomes a precious entail and racial asset. And it breaks out at times of great crises like battle, accident, or shipwreck, in people whose normal habit of life had given no sign of such resource, or indeed had been morally weak—in a Nelson or in a nurse. It is perhaps less their personal virtue than the outcrop of the national strain, the spurt of a reserve of power gather from a wide ancestry and stored at a center interior to individual volition. All this rises, rushes, to meet the antagonism or untowardness of nature, man, or fate. It is the courage to face fate, to war against necessity, to suffer or die as man for man.

But the supreme courage is to face God—not death nor pain, but God. It is the courage of the conscience before its last judge.

---

4. Sophocles, *Antigone*, Ode I, line 333.

And for this, natural resource fails whensoever the conscience has risen to realize what it means. The solidary reserve of courage in the race does not reach to this; for it has been little exercised or exercised under peculiar disadvantages. This is a valor which is not stored in Humanity, but given in Christ. Man's supreme fear was conquered by man's supreme faith—the Son's faith in the Father. Drawing on him we do not draw on essential Humanity, but on God's grace to Humanity. He is our treasure and steward of confidence in this kind. He is the creative Source for an achievement for which man in himself has mostly but a great void. And it is by drawing on Christian resources, on a courage gradually becoming immanent in Christian society, that we have either heart or power to stand, to say nothing of glorying, in God's sight; and in Christ's victory only have we, despite our guilt, communion with God. It is the courage of the Holy before the Holy that rises in us by our union, conscious or unconscious, with a Christ in whom the Holiest was always well pleased. He is the deeper Deity in all the divinity of the race. The divineness we share, the deity we receive. He is as to God what racial power and valor are as to nature and man. The heroes in this vein are such as those who, by faith in him, gather poor, weak, dying people around them in the hour of calamitous death as a hen gathers her chickens. A simple stewardess in a wreck calls a crowd of frantic people around her as the ship goes down in the wild twilight, lifting them, in her hymns an in prayer and its power, to commune with the Unseen that walks the stormiest waters of the world.

This righteousness, this holiness of God, was shown by the modern departure to be the redeeming and saving thing in Christ's personality and its action. Its sphere was his own moral conflict, in which his real victory was also the victory of the race and for it. Man's one evil was mastered by God's one man in the Armageddon of His soul. And the effect was not simply the repair, but the consummation, of what creation began. It was the new creation of creation. It was God at his most godlike work. It was the founding, by a moral re-creation, of a new Humanity as high above the old as that old, by its natural creation, was above nature. In a word, reality, salvation, theology, was moralized and sublimated in the act. Metaphysic, and especially traditional metaphysic, was shown to a second place. It was not banished, but it did not lead, and it did not prescribe. Life, experience, with its reality, took the place of the speculative quest of reality. The doctrine, for instance, of the two natures in Christ, if it was not dismissed, was put aside till it could be interpreted by a metaethic rather than a metaphysic, by a metaphysic of personality instead of substance, drawn from moral experience rather than Hellenistic thought. This is a change so great that it has not yet had time to work out its moral consequences on society, even the society of the Church, and its social consequences are very great. The effect of a central mobilization on such a scale is bound to be great upon society everywhere as its influence comes to be felt. It is but slowly making its way.

But a serious obstacle to a positive and ethical doctrine of the new creation is presented by the doctrine of the baptismal regeneration of infants. This is bound to have a blinding effect on uncorrected eyes, on the vague general mind, affected by a tone rather than a conviction. It is a metaphysical and nonethical idea which is more dulling to the moral sense of the multitude than the forensic conceptions of atonement. For these have, like all jurisprudence, an ethical genius, though it may be ethic arrested at a partial stage. And the tenacious nature of the metaphysical tradition, with its moral astigmatism is shown in the attempts made by distinguished men to evade the real core of the Incarnation in the Atonement by seeking its locus, not theologically in the ethical nature of personality and its supremely holy action in the redemption of the conscience from guilt, but psychologically in the subliminal cellarage of the soul.

As the result of the new movement which spread from Schleiermacher, and flooded the theological sky with light during last century, we have secured the conviction of the supremacy and fundamentality of history, the hegemony of personality and action, the retirement of speculation before a positive experience created by history, the creativity of the saving facts, the organic personal unity in Christ's life and death of active obedience, at once crowning and creative, and the conception of the history of the race as a moral unity and a moral organism, destined to a corporate personality round the public person of Christ.

Now if we take these last two results, the organic and personal unity of Christ's own life and work along with the organic and moral unity of the human race as the crown of creation—we are driven to seek the relation, if there is any, between them. What, on the one hand, was the reality in the unity of Christ's person? Nothing less than his holy soul and conscience—a moral reality, conceivable only in personal terms of conflict and victory in a moral warfare which is the true human tragedy. And what, on the other hand, is the reality of Humanity as a unity, the true continuity of the race, the central nisus and issue of history? Is it not also a moral reality and a moral issue? It is not mere civilization, but moral personality. Is anything so central and potent for the race as its conscience, however splendid the sphere of imagination or achievement may be around it? Is Butler not on the firmest ground when he says that morality is the nature of things? Goodness is reality.

And, if we so judge, are we not ready for the next step? Are we not forced to it? Is the holiness of Christ not the ultimate nature of morality, and therefore of things? Is not the conscience within the conscience, the conscience of God himself? Is it not his absolute righteousness in an historic person, judging all the earth? Is it not the outcrop of the moral stratum on which all creation, all being, rests, and which every evolution or convulsion is bringing to the top in a kingdom of souls, of righteousness, and of God? Was Humanity not there presented before God as what it essentially is, is in its divine purpose and destiny, is in the creative Will—as perfectly holy and humane? Was the unity and sanctity of Christ's lifework not in central, moral, organic connection there with the unity which we have recognized a moral humanity to be? His achievement was a personal victory; was it for his own person alone? Did it not anticipate, condense, and insure the moral victory also of that Humanity with which it was his Divinity to be in such perfect sympathy and continuity? Was he not there as central to man whom he saves as man is to the universe that he understands? Was Christ not thereby the reality which permeates and subdues by its eternal moral act the collective personality which is the reality of man? Subdues, I say, and not merely consummates. And I say by his moral act, and by no mere magic change, and by no mere infusion nor infection of a metaphysical substance. It is no accidental connection, no mere parallelism, no mere arbitrary or external relation, between Christ in his triumphant agony and man in his guilt and grief. The Reconcilement of the Cross is the fundamental moral crisis of a world which is at last moral *or nothing*. Only it is a crisis and a reconcilement effected and not merely illustrated, in this its greatest case but also its greatest cause. Christ's person was creative and not expository. His work was in the nature of moral achievement, not of necessary process. And it was concrete with living history and organic with the new Humanity. It was a real fact, a thing done and not merely handled, done under the conditions of a *free* social evolution, as personal development must be; done under the conditions of personality, individual or corporate; not therefore a thing presented but a deed performed, not (that means) taking place under the relations of necessity, but under those of moral freedom, and its social triumph, and its creative worth.

For moral victory by holy obedience *is* both a social and especially a *creative* thing in the nature of it. It increases the power of the race. It increases the moral weight of the universe. No such victor conquers for himself alone. He adds to man's permanent power and value. Is it not so, more or less, in every case of it? It is not simply a transmutation of existing energy, nor is it simply the gain of another fort by the rising tide of an evolutionary process under necessary law. It has the specific quality and *differentia* of a moral achievement. And that is not a mere resultant of antecedent forces, tendencies, or powers. It has in its center and essence something creative, something new and additional. Moral victory means new power that was not in the soul before. Thought is not creative, but moral action is. It has to do, not with new insight, nor even new combinations, but with a new energy and direction of will. It really enriches life and the world. It draws far more directly than any mere force does from the Creator's distinctive action. It is truly creative, in the only sense in which creation has any meaning for our experience.[5]

5. The contention that real moral action has, in the initiative which is its distinctive mark, an element of the creative may be put otherwise thus: "My Father worketh, and I work," said Christ. If, then, God's work is preeminently creative, so is Christ's. Now by our Christian union with Christ we share his work, his activity. For our relation to him is not merely passive. Therefore in our own way we participate in his creativity. And we do so by that which puts and keeps us in union with him—by our faith, which is an active thing. But our faith is essentially obedience, the obedience of our will to his saving will and work, obedience to him as his was to the will and work of God. That is, it is our supreme moral

I have been trying to show that the work of Christ was a moral victory, and that the acquirement of his own soul was in the same act the new creation of the race. I have claimed that such victory everywhere has a creative element in it, whose foregleam was in the natural freedom of will (however restricted) which makes man a responsible being. But with a perfect and unsullied victory like Christ's we have that freedom made absolute, *i.e.*, perfectly holy, and therefore final, as in perfect union with the last reality of things. He realized, in obedience, the glorious liberty of the Son of God. But the perfectly holy is the Creator; so that Christ's work was above all creative. It had not simply a creative element in it, as our moral victories have, but it was the crowning act of the Holy One on a first creation's wreak. It was the work of the God who created man for the active commission of His own holiness, and who carried creative action to its last form, its true close, and its inner significance by the Cross; so that Christ's work was the new creation for which the first was made, and not merely the last wave of the first. He did not simply pour a new stream of the old divine vitality into the current of history, but he did a thing in its course more crucial than when the first chaos was ended. The true image would not be the influx of a great tributary, but a tremendous cataract negotiating an abyss, and at the gorge of the fall the river turns sharply in a new course. The whole drift and religion of the race are changed. It is not acted on by new forces, it is taken possession of by a new spontaneity of the moral and not merely the vital kind. It is invaded and occupied by another personality, whom we not only own but welcome. We yield and cooperate with the tragic, crucial, glorious conquest in which His whole personality, dying and rising, forever acts. "The very citadel of personality is invaded. An *alter ego* appears where before the *Ego* sat enthroned. And the *Ego* loves to have it so."[6] "There is a *degree* of intimacy

---

act. Our great moral act, therefore, as Christians sharing as it does his work, is in its nature creative. It is a fresh contribution to the moral wealth of the race and the moral assets of the world. And we have in this supreme moral act the key to the true inner nature of moral action everywhere. The paradoxical combination of entire selflessness and supreme will-power was the secret of Christ for our new creation. And it is our secret also in all the action which prolongs his and reflects the new creation.

6. Rev. E. A. Burroughs, Hertford College, Oxford.

at which a difference of *kind* appears." As, when we fall in love, one, who before was but *a* personality beside us, becomes *the* personality within us, and through us, and for us. We are something higher in the scale of life than a mere human being—we are Christians. There is a new life for us. We are born again. "The Christian is a human personality of which the Head, Center, and Completion is Christ. He lives in so far as Christ lives in him. Not that he loses his own individuality; for the 'twoness of the One' is as essential to spiritual life as the 'One-ness of the two.'"

The death and resurrection of Christ was his taking possession of Humanity as a fellow-soul takes possession of our own, to be a mere fellow-soul no more. And the analogy is specially close when the capture of us is not like natural love, a case of mystic instinct without necessary moral action on us. But it is as when we owe to our benefactor's concern and sacrifice our rescue from ruin. If the soul of Christ was as great as the race (and it must have been, to cope with *the* evil of his race), his sinless self-mastery and his achievement of perfect obedience to a holy God was the divine holiness itself at work (since only the Holy is self-sufficient for the Holy). It was the divine holiness in its central nature and creative action within the race, on a plane which by the first creation was only prefigured and prophesied.

Creation, miracle, and prayer, are all powers in this strain and in this train. The theories that take the life of one of these destroy also the rest; and it is another universe we then contemplate, another world we live in, another religion we cherish—if indeed anything is still left that should be called a religion at all. For miracle is creation. There is a "creative synthesis" in the very recasting of the causal chain, its deflection, the determination of existing forces in a new direction. It is an addition in kind to the causal chain, an insertion. The old forces are all at work, but what causes their convergence to a certain point in experience? However close the causal tissue may be, it is not impervious. A due respect to the causal conditions is yet not abject. The Kingdom of God comes in through the interstices of all other causality. And the answer to prayer is lawful miracle. Even if we do not go beyond what is called the reflex action of prayer, what we have there is not an auto-suggestive sedative, but the appropriation of creative power. It is a supreme exercise and experience of a quite new life, in which we draw on the power distinctive of God and share it in our relative way. All these great things have their meaning in that life, in the new creation in Christ. That breach with the old life in the new birth which is the fontal Christian experience tunes the mind to the miraculous idea. The radical rent in the natural soul makes credible such invasion of the natural world. They are explicable, only if we start with the life really new, only if we carry with us the experiences and the categories given us there, only if we refuse to begin with an empirical and mechanical universe, or even an ideal process. They belong to a view of the world which is, above all, life, and neither sense nor thought. And, above all, it is dramatic life. Life is determined by its collisions and crises more than by its order, by action more than process. Every now and then we meet views of the world and methods of treating it which are of immense ability and interest, and which do much to modify or illuminate certain regions of our conception, yet missing is—what? They have not the eye. They have purview, they have new combination. What they have not is insight; or, if insight, then not faith, not the one great moral venture; being full of *Geist*; even of genius, but not full of the Holy Ghost—which yet either fills the world from depth to height or is an empty dream. Much of the inability to associate creation, and especially the new creation, with the idea of reality is due, first, to the impossible assertion that it is a creation out of nothing. That is impossible, because, if God is in any sense all and in all, there never was a nothing out of which the creature should rise. Besides, we have no faculty, nor any analogy, to give, as the least conception of what an emergence from nothing could mean. And, being thus meaningless, it is unreal to us.

But the chief reason for the unreal nature, to many, of such an idea as creation, lies in the fact that we think of it as an arbitrary act of God, as something he might have done or not, just as the mood took him, or the idea occurred. And whatever is thus arbitrary, not to say whimsical, is unreal, no matter on how vast a scale.

Here our standpoint is everything. If we start, as the sequence of life starts, from the empirical, the mechanical, or even the idealist view of the world, our mind must be a blank as to anything real corresponding to a word like creation. But, if we start, as the *principle* of life starts, with what is prime rather than what is prior, from the view of the world which makes personality and its distinctive power—action—to be the supreme category; if we start with personality and its crucial action as the one created thing, and the multiplication and nurture of moral personality as the purpose of all we see and feel, all the scaffolding we call nature—then we are not quite without an expedience which can give content to such a notion as creation. (Unless, of course, we banish the order of experience called moral experience as no real datum, and treat the supreme form of it, the Christian, as illusion, valuable in a way but only as fictive ideas are—as formulæ for the manipulation of life, which can be dismissed when we reach a result.)

As we view the first creation from the experience of the second, and its principle, it is not arbitrary, it is anything but whimsical. It is, for such a God of Love as Christ reveals and we answer in the spirit, a moral necessity. As God and Father he must create—by no brute necessity, but as a necessity of his personal spiritual nature. Yet by a real necessity none the less, though by a necessity whose action is perfect freedom. There is no necessity so urgent, irresistible, and universal as the pressure of moral freedom. And creation is the action of an absolute, universal freedom, charging its area with entire and concrete fullness. It is freedom, not only free but rich. It is Love.

For what was the Redemption itself, which drew God from heaven to earth, but the necessity in the one and only tree to establish the perfect freedom and fullness of his life for his world, a free fullness in material and not only in form, in a wealth and not only a range, as holiness and not mere amplitude, as holy Love.

The freedom of God, therefore, was not a freedom to create or not create. That were a freedom very elementary, arbitrary, and for him unreal. It were to introduce something accidental into him. And the relation between him and his world is not accidental. His world is not merely the best possible, perhaps but a second best. He did not deliberate, pick, and choose among possible worlds, and then decide on the fittest. That were too anthropomorphic. Within a created world indeed diverse possibilities might be presented to him by himself as means to an end, means contingent on the free behavior of the creature; but he could not present to himself worlds good and less good for his own selection as ends. If he could but choose the best, he could but think the best. And we cannot suppose that he had to adjust himself and his action to the thought of another. When we say that he made the world by an act of will and choice, we mean to deny that he did it from any external coercion, internal poverty, or blind instinct. His freedom is the freedom of his own full and self-sufficient nature. His determination was self-determination. No necessity lay on him from without. The other that he needed and created in his world was still within himself. It was his own Other, not an other in any rivalry. He was determined into creation by his own self and nature alone—which is true freedom, if we have taken pains to understand what personality and its distinctive freedom are.

The necessity that moved him was the freest power we know, or the power most creative of freedom. I have named it. It was Love. Love, which is always at the origin of new existence, and is always the matrix of new birth, was the motive power of the first creation, as we know it to be of the second—Love, where, if anywhere, true freedom lies, and the need to create it in responsive personalities. His Holy Love would not only be perfectly met in his Uncreated Son, but really multiplied in his sons create. Creation was the creation of personality capable of answering Love in its manifold freedom; all else in creation is but the machinery to carry out that work, and may disappear when it is done. This is a view which is supported by the modern conception of matter as energetic in its constitution, as energy under intense condensation, as more or less spiritual, therefore, and congenial to spiritual purpose.

The one object of creation is souls. We go in quite at the wrong end when we start with our interest preoccupied with the creation of matter. The soul with its freedom is the only truly created thing. It is the key of creation, especially in its re-creation. It is the true asbestos which survives, and which profits by the fire of all the timbering used in its construction. Nature is the divine alloy which enables the soul to be worked; but it is dissipated by something equally divine when the soul has been shaped. Nature, therefore, may be God in immanence, in a sense in which he is not immanent in Will, and cannot be without extinguishing its freedom.

God's immanence stops, nor indeed at the constitution of human nature, but at its will and freedom. It is the moral soul (whose creation is the miracle of a conferred freedom) that alone realizes God in his free transcendence. Only freedom can understand freedom—only our transcendence of Nature can appreciate God's transcendence of us. God must create if he is the Love that redeemed. If his supreme gift is redeemed freedom, the base of that is created freedom, which (natural yet supernatural) is the only created thing. Love is true life and its infinite increment in souls. The whole world is the ascending scale of God's creative Love, "arriving" in the freedom in which alone Love is itself.

12

Regeneration, Creation, and Miracle II

I

There are considerations that aid us when we are afraid of being committed, on the lines of a modern and liberal theology, to something pantheistic. If God be held to put himself into his creation in the immanent way we must now welcome, do we not set up an identity between him and it which leads to some kind of Monism, tends to erase moral distinctions, and makes goodness but nature on its top floor?

And at the outset here we must of course say that any conception of the case, which erases the unique quality and sanctity of moral ideas, destroys creative power; since it destroys a God acting freely, acting from the moral necessity in his holy Person to establish itself in holiness everywhere, and to cover existence with its response.

But, further, we may say that such a simple identity would result only if we treated creation as the last stage of the self-completion of God. If we thought of him as arriving at perfection only in his world, and there at last drawing the deep, infinite breath of self-realization, and heaving the sigh of eternal repose, because he had now found himself fully in his own work—then, indeed, the danger would be great. But such a God would be no holy God; who is forever all he is, whose holiness is the moral aspect of his self-sufficient Being with his life in himself and no darkness nor impotence in him at all.

Creation is not the perfecting of God by the last stage of an evolving and tentative process. Its light is not a new thing to him.

Its joy is not his fresh delight at the discovery of himself. The world did not reveal God to himself as a growing genius acquires in successful production a faith in himself or the mastery of his soul. For then another world would be to us no faith, but only a hope—a hope that, when God had pondered the anomalies of this world, his maturer power might produce with the old materials another no longer the work of his prentice hand. But, whatever we mean by another world, we do not mean that—another experiment with completer success, another approximation more worthy of his instinct of what it was in him to do, or his sense of what should be done.

No religion were possible toward a God who was but a growing God, coming to himself, through the stages of an ascending success, in a series of masterpieces each more masterly than the last. Who could say when such a God might end, or when the creating arm might falter or decay? Faith would not be possible in a God who might end anywhere, even in an ethic that reversed all his past, as many artists have outgrown the moral restraints and principles of their early manner.

For religion the world as a whole is an expression of what God forever is, and it is not a phase of his becoming. It is the result of Divine Will, not of eternal process. He is not the mere possibility of what in the world becomes actual. He is not the infinite germ or preformation of a reality to be deployed in the world. He is the ever holy, the morally self-sufficient and self-complete. The world is his work and not his growth, his offspring and not his completion. He is the ground of the world, or its cause, but not its process. To call him the world-process is no more true than to call him (at the lower extreme) the artificer of the world. He did not emerge and come to himself with the world. The world came there to express the fullness of his power, and not to make good the poverty of his condition. It reveals him to us, not to himself. The world is not his self-achievement but his self-expression. Especially is this so with the world of persons, who reflect God but do not form the field of his self-realization. However we interpret the immanence of God, it must always be so as to give the more effect to his perfect transcendence. Let it also be remembered that a deistic God, insulated from the world, could not transcend it (which implies some relation to it). He would simply be irrelevant to it, and therefore no God for it. So that deism readily develops either to atheism or agnosticism.

II

If the world is the end of God and the completion so far of his self-realization, we cannot escape some form of pantheism; which again cannot escape moral *débâcle* at last, because then creation does not proceed from a free moral necessity, but from nature process. But, if God be the living end of the world (as he was its beginning); if he is the latent teleology of the world, its immanent purpose, rather than its immanent presence and pressure; if he is the subject over it rather than the substance in it, then we have a true Theism, with the immanence of God's transcendence and the ethic of the holy at the root of all creation.

All this if we have a God for whose Love creation is a moral necessity.

But also such moral necessity ends in creation and its freedom. If the pressure of nature, rising to the structure and evolution of society, forces us upon the moral issue (as it does), much the more are we driven, as we rise in the quality of this moral issue, upon the creative element in it. Here lies the supreme dignity of the moral world—in its creativity. The holy Love cannot but create. And if, on the other hand, our experience, individual as well as social, convince us that the chief feature of the race is a need, and that it is a moral need, then the more experience deepens by actual contact with that need, so much the more shall we discover that moral necessity to be Redemption. If, then, the moral necessity of holy Love issues in creation by its very nature, and if, empirically, the same Love's moral necessity ends in Redemption, it is not violent to identify Redemption and the new creation, and to view the one as the nature of the other. "Thy Creator is thy Redeemer." Sin being what it is in intent—the destruction of the holy—nothing less than a Creator could be a Redeemer. And it really calls for more; for he has to make the holy not only out of a non-holy chaos, but out of an anti-holy crisis. This new creation in our Redemption is the only creation we can experience. It is for us the supreme creation; and it gives us the key to what all creation is.

Regeneration, Creation, and Miracle II

The drift of the argument is this: Religion exists by a right of its own. It is deduced from no other experience of life, and it holds its place from none. It is in the context of life, but not under its control. It is not a utility in life, nor is it the bloom on its face. In neither case were it holy. But as holy it is the key of life, and not a consequence from it. It is the supreme thing in life, therefore it is our starting-point for the measure and meaning of life. As the key of life, it is the key of thought, which is but one aspect and exercise of life. It is no product of thought nor its licensee. Therefore the supreme religious idea of the new birth, the new creation, is the key to the first creation where thought starts, and where much thought is pent. The new creation is *the* creation, and the key to what all creation is. The second creation is the inner destiny of the first, not its result. Hence the first both is and is not continuous in it. Man is born to be reborn, to come to himself in a new self. The experience of the new creation does not mean the appearance of personality where there was none before. It is rather what we might call the puberty of the old than its replacement by a new. Everything changes that it may be more truly the same. The new personality is not created out of nothing, nor does it mean a new rational or psychological constitution given to human nature. It is an ethical experience and an ethical reality. It means not only new impulse to our will, but still more, a new complexion and a new perspective in it, and its world, a new hope with a controlling interest, and most of all a new sense of self in its loss to the Divine Self, a new sense of freedom and soul-possession—when, indeed, we think at all of a self that we only find by losing it and taking no thought. We never knew before what the soul was, nor, therefore, what the world was to which the soul gives effect. The new creation, as creation *par excellence*, reveals all creation to be a moral act of God in respect of another moral being. The Creator's *vis à vis* is not a cosmos, but a conscience with a cosmos for its arena. The cosmos is but the prolegomenon of the true creation. It groans, being burdened. It travails. And its unfreedom has its meaning only in its destiny, which is to evolve freedom by a perpetual creation. The true creation in which creation comes to itself is the appearance of that freedom and that personality, that soul, that conscience. It is all the time the *nisus* of nature, and the first charge upon it. But all the same it is a gift to it by another creation.

Creation is thus, in the light of the new creation, a moral act of God, whose holiness does not isolate him, but surrounds him with persons destined to reflect and share it. The new creation, therefore, with that reality in which morality is so much deeper than rationality, makes the growth of persons to such holiness fundamental reality and purpose of the universe. It lays course for all development, and shows all the evolution of the race as creative of this moral goal, issuing from this moral source, and proceeding by this moral way of an immanent righteousness, whose genius and destiny are to subdue all things to itself.

III

We can, thus, perhaps soften the difficulty felt by some who are not clear about the relation between the "old man" and the "new" in respect of personal identity. It seems to them out of place to speak about a new birth where the matrix is not another person but the same, or where we pass but from one form of conscious existence to another, and do not come into being for the first time. And (if they do not learn to speculate about trans-migration) they tend to minimize the greatness and the cruciality of the change that takes place—as it is the fashion also to do as to the crisis in death. They urge that the old personality is not extinguished and replaced by another; and they dwell on the action of memory, the persistence of idiosyncrasy, the permanence of responsibility, the prolongation into the new state of all the old psychical processes of the race, not to say some of the mannerisms of the individual. Can you call that a birth which is so continuous? Or, if you do assert any moral continuity in the new birth with the past life, what fatal objection is there to treating every birth as the sequel of some previous life of the same individual, however forgotten?

The first thing to be pointed out here is that the essential feature in the idea of birth is not continuity, but dependence, obligation. I will only allude here to the fact that we have in the Bible no reflection or theory as to the nature of creation old or new. We have the naïf power of the mighty fact. This is so, whether we think of the way the new word of Christ was related to the Old Testament, or the way the new community of the Church rose from the wreck of the old community of Israel. Regeneration is more of a religious than even a psychological term, and the ruling idea in it is our absolute indebtedness to God for the infinite change. It is entirely his gift. Any act of ours is but taking home the gift in the way appropriate to it. That subjective side of the matter is represented by conversion, of which regeneration is but the Godward side. They are not two things, but one, given and taken. Questions about the psychological continuity of the individual are secondary, an may wait for more insight into the regenerate experience. The twice-born may well discuss them, and indeed they are the only people with due data for such a discussion. But they are not considerations constitutive for the fact. The gift is taken, it is ours, before we can examine its behavior in the context, or the crucible, of our psychic nature. It is in the light thus shed by an absolutely new departure and a fresh beginning that we read the past. Is is in the power of the new life that we find the constituent idea of life, and of whatever begins it, either for tune or for eternity. The religious principle of all history, at least the Christian principle, is that it is from eternity that it has its destiny, and therefore its meaning; that it is the invasion by eternity which gives us any standard to measure progress, or to command the life which birth but begins.

But three things further may be said in this connection.

1. The change takes place in the will, and not in the constitution of the individual. However we construe the Fall, if we leave it any real meaning at all, it did not directly affect the constitution of human nature; which remains capable of very great and godlike things in the way of spiritual, rational, affectional, imaginative, and civil life. It is full of heroisms in various kinds. What was directly affected was the harmony of man's will and God's, the personal communion, love, and trust. What was lost was communion, and the power to recover it. It is a case of total impotence of relation, and not total corruption of nature—however, that latter might come to be the *dénouement* when the moral perdition had run its full course. For the moral canker kills the finest gifts at last. What Christianity denies is a power of self-recuperation native to humanity in relation to God and to that communion with him which is at once man's loss and his destiny. Therefore, when God reclaims us in a regeneration, it is by a re-creation of the will, and not of what might be called the paradigm, constitution, or machinery of human nature.

2. The change must be a gift; and, as it affects directly the will (richly conceived, as in the Scripture word, "heart"), it is therefore a gift of power much more than of light, or even pity—not new machinery, nor new opportunity, but new life. And it is life not as mere vitality, not as a mere driving force, but life with a quality, life as something positive, carrying in it not mere impulse, but content and directive. And especially it directs the current of the personality outward to a saving God instead of inward to a rising self. It reverses the machine. And still more it concentrates it on God, and so makes a spiritual organism of it, whose limits develop to their new function as the parts of a machine could not.

3. The mode of regenerative action is therefore one appropriate to a will in contact with a will. It is the effect of one personality on another, and not of a magician on a substance. It is not transmutation, not spiritual alchemy. It is within the region of consciousness. In that respect the metaphor of birth is misleading. Of our natural birth we have neither memory nor any other function that can tell us of the nature of what takes place; but in the second birth that is not so. We do not indeed take its measure in consciousness. It does not appear what we shall be. But we do realize its nature— the mystic morality of it, its nature as holy. Its center of gravity is not subliminal; that is not its native land. Which would sooner or later make it magical, and would open all the theosophic subtleties that underlie a baptismal regeneration. It is the result of a personal will acting on our own in moral categories, however exalted and refined, rare and unspeakable.

But that means, in the circumstances, a forgiving Will, a justifying Will, who puts us, without desert, in living and loving *rapport* with his own holy self. It is not the pressure upward in us of a process working in the dark; it is the intercourse of two living and spiritual beings, with all the consciousness of the sinful and the holy. As conversion, it is choice on our part; but under and within our converted choice of God is his holy choice of us. It is his choice of us that we choose, not simply his excellence irrespective of us. All begins there. It is that which moves our choice. We love because he began it. If Pilate could have no power *against* Christ but what was given him from above, still more is it true of any power we have *for* Christ. The very idea of regeneration is that it is not an ever-laborious effort of our will to reach and rejoice in a higher

Regeneration, Creation, and Miracle II

goodness; but that it is an enthusiasm in which we are carried up as by a rarer kind of natural force, which yet has all the moral world and its conflict with nature overcome in its holy heart.

IV

The great movement of revelation is in a crisis, and not in a process merely. And what differentiates a moral crisis from a process is the new departure, the new element, which we call creative. The deflecting, releasing, eliciting touch on the past is not its product, but it is a creative act upon it, however minute or delicate. In this region that is not true which is true of art, or even education, that

> Nature is made better by no mean,
> But nature makes that mean.

The core of an ethical revelation especially is a new creation. It is essentially miraculous. The life of the Holy Spirit in the conscience is a standing miracle. Its genius is conversion, and not evolution. Sanctification is a series of conversions. The fact that the Christian revelation is in a crisis, that it is struck from a collision, that it issues from a tragedy, that it rides a sea of trouble, and emerges from a great shock, gives us its real inner nature all along the experient line of the faith which answers it. A creative, miraculous quality is immanent to the true nature of Christian faith, whether it is felt in every experience of it or not. Those fine souls, that grow to all goodness like flowers in the sun, yet grow in a climate, and prolong a tradition, created by stronger souls, who broke with self and the world in some crucial and memorable way. And this feature presides at every new stage of the development of the religious experience. Its nature does not always come to the surface, but, when it does, it is revolutionary. In that experience the supreme and absolute spirit comes home not as the transcendental ground immanent in a process of the world moving on in terms of the natural order; but it breaks in, and breaks open in a collision, will with will, spirit with spirit, which means a crisis, and at bottom a creation. There is not simply a procession, but an invasion. Without this there is no religious life in the proper sense—only a self-withdrawn religiosity. But, with it we have the key to our inner, ultimate, and interpretative relation to the world. We are in immediate relation with God, and find this entry to mean not simply but a clash between the natural spirituality and the moral, is an antithesis, rising to an antagonism, not to say antipathy, which only a creative act can resolve into peace. And the crest of the crisis is the special, moral experience made by the impact of such holy revelation on the guilty conscience—it is repentance and redemption. We have here the true nature of miracle. The true inwardness of it is evangelical. It is really explicable by salvation only. The miracle, which underlies miracle, is the new birth. To believe in miracle to any purpose is like writing an epic—we must have lived one. This is the obstinate experience which explains the inextinguishable vitality of the idea of miracle.

All the more outward miracles are valuable as expressions or harbingers of the indestructible miracle which makes the soul's true life by way of a re-creative revelation. Grace does not prolong nature, but descends on it, acts on it, changes it. It contradicts it rather than continues it when we come to the last issue. Here is the true supernatural—not Nature's extension upward, nor its refinement inward, but its conquest. This is why miracle is Faith's true child. All miracles exist and are cherished in the interest of a spiritual revolution, and to protect it from slipping down into mere evolution. They are outposts of God's creative action rather than his rectoral. They become the symbols, not to say sacraments, of God as not only a moving but a *living* God. The idea of miracle is bound up with that of a living God. It is somewhat sterile to disprove miracles; it is iconoclasm. We must evaluate them, treat them as sheaths, reliquaries, monstrances, as preludes or outposts of the one invasion and creation that our experience really knows—the new birth. And we must prove them less by historical evidence than by their organic connection with the grand regeneration. The best proof of miracle is real regeneration. We should go in at that end; we should view the evidence with that eye. It is a mental climate in which we approach them with the partiality that belongs to true justice, and call them probable to begin with. The regenerate are divinely prejudiced for miracle. To begin here and think down is more fruitful than to start upward from the laws of nature where the mind's youth begins. It is not for miracles as infractions or as mere prodigies that we need contend, but as ancillaries of a supremely miraculous grace, as servants of the king's court, to whom the ordinary traffic gives way. They are entrances, through nature's pores, of the last creative power. Spiritual miracle does not dispense with physical, just as physical miracle does not dispense with natural law. But the lower end of the chain hangs from the higher. As we interpret genius by its *magnum opus*, so we explain the world by miracle rather than by a causal chain. It is not enough to say poetically that we find miracle everywhere in nature, and then transfer the observation in a special way to the sphere of the soul. That makes spiritual miracle too naïf, too much of an inference. If there is any inference, the soul infers it in the other direction. And for it miracle is not only possible, but is bound up with the action of the reality which is its supreme revelation, and the one thing it knows better than it knows itself, the thing which gives the law, *i.e.*, the *nisus* and destiny, to all the prior stages. *Heilesrath ist Schöpfungsplan*.[1] The purpose of salvation gives the scheme of creation. Such at least is the Christian religion when it does not shrink from covering the cosmos. And, as God's salvation is the greatest miracle of which the world is capable, the scheme of creation is fundamentally miraculous with a crust of order and a coat of law. Miracle is the fundamental principle of a world created and redeemed; and it leaps to light at the closest touch of its Creator and Redeemer.

V

Our business therefore, is not to refute the current negation of miracle by scientific intellect. Apologetic grows more sympathetic as it grows more understanding of the world of science. I hope science would be more sympathetic if it knew more of the world of personal faith and its principles in theology. William James made a good departure in this respect. Our business is not to refute but to realize, to show that the *élan vital* in nature comes to itself only in supernature, and the new creation is the old gone to heaven. And it is not as if it only escaped there into a spacious air, and could breathe deep as last. But it comes *home*. It discovers there the spiritual principle which was its own birthplace, its deep life and onward bent. Yet miracle is not simply a new and higher phase of

1. ["Holy counsel is a plan of creation."]

that first creative power of God which put nature there; it is rather an expression of his new creation—not a thrust forward of nature, but a thrust backward, a retroaction, of grace. It is crude to say that the first creation is followed by the second. It is less crude to say it develops to it. But the ripe thing to say is that the first creation was posited by the second, that nature is not sacrificed to grace, but created by it. The service for which we were made is no sacrifice. A mighty God could never justly have created a free world, had he not done so on lines that really arose in the mighty *Grace*, by which he could more than repair freedom's wreck. The *cosmos* was created in the Redeemer. Creation had from the first Redemption in reserve. And nature's first charter is but leasehold—"occupy till I come."

VI

The question is raised by an increasing number of people today, what the connection is between the historic Christ and the Christ of experience. *There* stands an individual two thousand years away, and *here* stands the individual of to-day. How can they ever come into the relation expressed in the supreme forms of Christian faith (for we need not trouble about the average form; it must adjust itself to the supreme)? How can I directly experience the historic and distant Christ? How can he be more my life than I am? How can a historic person, as a historic person, and not merely as a posthumous influence, become a constituent of my own soul? How is an *actio in distans*[2] possible wherein he not only affects me but takes possession of me, and creates me anew?

Much depends here on what is meant by the historic Christ. If he is but the spiritual splendor in history, to whom our relation is the æsthetic one of contemplation and impression, then the intimate relation consecrated in the long record of Christian faith is not possible. Or, if we start with the inner light and find the light that lights every man condensed in Christ, as the first created light was at a stage condensed into the sun—then also the classic forms of Christian faith are extravagant, and he is not our Redeemer, our new Creator, but our superlative only. And we do not really

2. ["Action at a distance."]

outgrow the æsthetic point of view, which is so attractive to the younger stages of intelligent faith.

The ethical point of view is the true one. It is, indeed, in the ordinary sense of the word, ethical, inadequate to the spiritual life. For that calls for an ethical mysticism, a mysticism of the conscience and its action. But I mean the point of view where we begin not as knowing a passive object, but as known by an active and searched by a holy; where there is a personal, a moral, relation; where we begin with God, with a holy God, and a God whose holiness is not simply immanent in creation, but is its source and destiny; who is there, and who is energy there, not as mere process nor as mere vitality, but as personality; in whom energy rises to be an act, and personality itself rises to spirituality.

The secret, in such inquiries, lies mostly in the form of the question, in the half-conscious presuppositions which rule our expectation from God, and prescribe our form of relation to him, and the manner of our interrogation. We must begin with his movement to us. Our inquiry must make for that point. In religion we must court and construe the relation between God and the soul from what he has revealed himself to be. For Christianity, that took place in history. And it is a revelation of himself not as the absolute *ens*, but as the personal energy and power eternal. But personal energy is action, moral action. His infinite redeeming Fatherhood in Christ's cross gives him to us as the *actus purus*, and not merely the *élan vital*, of all existence. We must therefore cease to treat the relation between his soul and ours as a mere contact of individuals, whether in contemplation or in mystic immersion. We must found, consciously or unconsciously, on a metaphysic of energy and of history instead of substance and thought, of action instead of either contemplation or sympathy alone. That will put a special complexion on the continuity of the Christ in history with the Christ in us. But even if we ignore the metaphysic (which cannot really be ignored, because it underlies the faith even of believers who scorn it), we start with objective revelation rather than inward experience, with an act and not an impression, with God's self-donation rather than with the subjective frame of our soul, in which, of course, it emerges. We must begin from the eternal act of a World-Redemption, which is the supreme function of the New Testament Christ. We begin as Christians, and not as people who are cross-examining Christians; and we begin therefore with creation of the New Humanity by the energy of Christ's whole life and person imparted in the greatest act within human knowledge, in the many-sided act of cross, resurrection and ascension. Our relation to the cross of Christ is not the relation of a soul to an event, nor even to a personality, but of an act to an act, a soul's act to a world act, faith's act to the act creating it, the cell act to the organic and cosmic.

We fail to connect the Christ without and within, much as we fail to connect our own *ego* with the *ego* of our neighbor. The defect that destroys brotherhood between personalities parted by space, is the same in kind as the defect which destroys the relation between us and a personality like Christ's removed by time. In the case of our neighbor we make the mistake of starting with an atomism, a discontinuity, between individuals. We ignore the fact that the other man's existence is a factor, and not merely a feature, in our own. It is the other man that makes me possible. I discover myself, possess myself, just as I come up against my limit in him. The individual is not a spiritual reality; he finds himself only in a society of individuals. The cohesion of souls is constitutive for the existence of souls—for the individual's life as a soul or person. I and my neighbor are not two atoms, absolutely independent, who mate by contract. That is a notion which is responsible for almost all the failure of Christian ethic. We do not coalesce like two dewdrops, nor do we engage in a covenant. We each partake, for our very existence, in a corporate personality. Only so is life, and especially action, possible. It is love that makes personality. The egos have to be homogeneous before they can cooperate.

In like manner, I say, we think to begin by approaching Christ from without, unprejudiced, judiciously, with a life and intelligence independent of him—as no Christian's really can be. We cross a space. And, of course, two millenniums are more than we can leap. And we fail to reach him, because we do not start from the faith and sense that he has reached us. We try to answer a religious question without what creates life-religion—a standing act of revelation.

So we fail to connect the Christ without and within, because we start from a long discrete process of nature, and not from a universal act of grace where duration is lot. We put the inquiries of nature, and expect answers which come only to the questions of grace. We ask in three dimensions what we can have but in a fourth. We begin as men who want to humanize, not to say rationalize, Grace, instead of beginning as Christians who seek by Grace to humanize Humanity. We start without the fundamental relation with Christ, and then ask how it is possible. It does not seem possible, till we have it. On the humanist and merely historic base, it is impossible. We start with a discontinuous individualism, Christ's and ours, with a historic series of such discrete points, and we naturally find no *nexus*. The same principle of procedure reduces society to atoms and anarchy. Whereas we must begin with the *nexus*, the indivisible, we should start either with a metaphysic or a faith of personality and its act. The continuity must be already in our hand there, as an oversoul in who we live; but as an oversoul not of mere being but of energy, as an inter-soul where the energy is no mere *process* but the *act* of a universal person, not flowing through all things but functioning in them. Monism loses its terror if we cease to think of a substance pervading all, and realize an energy acting in all as only personality can act, and producing agents of a like free and responsible kind. The unity with which we begin is the unity that makes any thought possible, the unity of one person—the unity of one thing that cannot be broken up—personality, corporate personality. It is personality existing in a supreme, absolute, and eternal act, which does not coalesce with other acts or souls independent, but in their existence and action takes effect. We then view the historic Christ as that act *in petto*, the eternal act which gives us our spiritual existence. We view him as that timeless, spaceless, immeasurable act in bulk, so to say, "once for all." While the Spirit is that same eternal and universal act in multitude—the Spirit being notably the individualistic power on Godhead. We view Christ as the Doer, with all his Person, of the one eternal act to which we owe, and from which we draw, a growing spiritual existence, which it, on the other hand, never ceases to posit. All of which is so palpably absurd as to be certainly true. We shall never answer the question how he can become our life so long as we treat him but as figure of history, or as the luminous outcrop of a spiritual entity. We must begin by taking him at his own valuation—as, by his life-act, the true universal of the soul. He is the Doer of the one eternal act of all moral existence, and therefore of all existence whatever at root; the historic focus of a God who is eternal energy; whose holiness, therefore, owing to the historic situation in one conscience, is an eternal redemption, only conceivable as between persons; who is the ground of all personality, and of the supreme action of personality—its action on personality; and who, in Christ, takes, in such action, the new creative departure which is distinctive of the holy. Christ does not condense the inner light; but as the Holy One he creates the New Humanity, wherein the soul (which comes to itself only in action) comes to itself by coming to him. By the incessant functioning of that eternal and absolute act, which consummated Christ's whole Person in the cross and resurrection, man is born anew. There is new creation when any man is in that Christ. And the relation between the historic Christ and the soul is the relation not between the primal diffused light and the sun, but between the personal world-energy of the New Creator and the minor centers of personal energy in which his absolute act takes relative effect. The doctrine of the inner light is not at last compatible with the doctrine of grace, unless indeed (as light is a mode of motion) we go behind the illumination to the energy, to the personal, and crucial, and eternal act of which it is a minor mode.

13

Veracity, Reality, and Regeneration

Bishop Gore complains that the huge perils in front of the Church of England are due to a refusal in recent years, and among all classes, movements, and offices, to think clearly about principles. He would welcome Disestablishment as forcing the Church to consider its first principles. But his remark applies to lands where there is no Established Church, and applies as much or more. It is a vice of the Church everywhere, and quite conspicuous in the Protestantism whose special charge a spiritual thoroughness and mental veracity is supposed to be. It is not easy to see what is to shake to its senses sections of the Church which never have been established, and to do for them what Disestablishment may do for Anglicanism. It is part of the general blurring of the features of truth in a nimbus of pious impressionism, or in a mist of social sympathy which impairs the individual conscience.

Other effects of this frame of mind are apparent in the type of preaching which pervades the pulpits of the hour. The preachers were never more able, and the sermons were never more interesting. And yet they do not win the public; or it is more than they can often do to hold it when won. The lack is penetrative power and inner moral passion. It fills one with a sense of waste to mark the able men whose ability is only running at half speed for the lack of a power to seize them, to unite and vivify all that is in them, to bring it out and get it home. It is doubtful if anywhere so much ability is going to seed as in the pulpit, if so much toil, ingenuity, intelligence, and feeling are being wasted anywhere as in the thousands of sermons that go to their drawers as to their last cradle and long home, week by week, to haunt as feckless ghosts the preacher's soul. Hence the restlessness that is observable in the ministry in various quarters, the sense of ineffectiveness, the desire to try a new soil with the same seed, in the hope that the Spirit may at last reward the effort and bring back His sheaves with Him.

But it is not a change of sphere that is required most. That may but foment the unquiet, or else become the soul's narcotic. It is a change of note that is needed, and a change that no new place can bring. If the lack is power, the cause of the lack is the absence of a definite, positive, and commanding creed which holds us far more than we hold it, holds us by the conscience, founds and feeds us on the eternal reality, and, before we can do anything with it, does everything with us. Every Church and every preacher is bound to run down without such a creed, and no amount of humane sympathy or vivid interests can avert the decline. In every direction, the Church is suffering from the inability to know its own spiritual mind, or to strike a stream from its own rock, and from its indisposition to face the situation or its impotence to fathom it. For a generation now we have been preaching that experience is the great thing, and not creed; till we are losing the creed that alone can produce an experience higher than the vagaries of idiosyncrasy, or the nuances of temperament, or the tradition of a group, or the spirit of the age. The older preachers complain that by their education they were set afloat alone on a wide, wide sea of thought and question, without the pole that alone can adjust their compass or lay their course. They were not started with the modernized dogmatic foundation that could enable them to carry their age, and so they were carried by it. In various seminaries the dogmatic was either antiquated, amiable, or absent. It is cruel to the preachers, and it is fatal to the Church. The ministry becomes more restless, and missions break down in our hands. And all through the lack of power from the highest or of footing in the abyss—all because of the lack of a positive, fixing, ruling belief, with its train of security and blessing, most effectual often where most indirect. The surest and securest have often won no right to be either. The current claptrap against theology is only an advertisement of the lack in religion of that passion of spiritual radicalism and mental veracity which will settle nowhere but at the very roots of things, and must draw its strength from the last realities of the soul's intelligent life. The result of the defect is a vague sense of insecurity as to foundations and an insidious dubiety which, unconsciously to the preacher, conveys itself to his flock, and generates a *malaise* that nobody can explain. There is too much judicious detachment and an absence of that passion and conviction which the preacher should utter, whether he is welcome or not to a people blinded by the god of the period, and whether they will hear or forbear. He may be too anxious about the impression he makes, and too careless about the sound source of impression—too little the agent of a searching truth that makes him by comparison indifferent to the cheers.

A positive, creative, and controlling belief of ultimates, a ruling and resting theology, drawn from the nether springs, is the goal and the seal of spiritual veracity, of that lucidity of soul which, though searching, is not sad but strong. It is not a thing that comes easily or swiftly; and it is readily underprized in a day which is the day of the young, and of all the crudity that that connotes. But it has the staying power, and it can guide, temper, dignify, and command. These are powers that the Church needs and the ministry much craves. But the laity are little interested in such truth, often will not have it. They are still too much the belated victims of a revolt against it which at the upper end of intelligence now grows obsolete. Yet they too feel the effects of its absence, though they have not skill to trace the trouble to its true source. All the other needs of the Church's hour, social or aesthetic, fall into insignificance before the Church's need of a positive, personal, powerful, and creative belief. It is the one thing imperative in a score to be desired.

Yet as soon as that is said, there is a chorus of angry resistance to the re-establishment on the Church of an Orthodoxy long outgrown and for ever now impossible. There is nothing more depressing than to hear such protests from the ministry itself. What is to be done with teachers who have learned so little in their plastic time as to learn no more after years of ministerial life than leaves such stale *clichés* still possible! They at least ought to rise above the common criers in the press and elsewhere, and to know what words like Orthodoxy or Positivity really should mean to instructed minds, and to minds especially that are saturated in New Testament thought and its rich continuity in history. That discernment of essential reality and expansive truth through the ages is the minister's stay and standard. It is the knowledge and the passion *before* the pulpit that give reality to the passion *in* it and save it from sentiment, melodrama, and lusty *blague*. The power in the pulpit always has its source outside the pulpit—a statement which I reinforce with the remark that the preacher will not be a failure, whether he be an idol or not, who thinks as much as he speaks, and prays as much as he preaches.

But such reflections will tempt some to say that the true object of ministerial training is to make preachers and pastors, and that for this purpose a good deal of instruction could be spared it only piety and sympathy were cherished as they should. And no doubt knowledge, or even thought, is too dearly bought at the cost of these. But men from certain sections of the mission field, for instance, who and went so far equipped with but the pious passion for souls, come and ask me for some guidance in their belated study, telling me they are no longer competent to guide the churches they gathered, that their field threatens to revert to prairie again. The fact is that, even if a man equipped with due attainments gather a Church, to prevent labefaction it must grow in grace and the intelligent knowledge of Christ, and of what Christ is for the moral soul of God and man. And especially it must grow in that knowledge of Him which is relevant not simply to personal and domestic needs but to the intelligent *milieu* in which the members of the Church find themselves even in every local paper and every public meeting. If the pastor and teacher have no power to handle such things, and no ability to do more than show that he buys the minor books, reads the little paper, and knows the little mind, the influence of his piety alone will not do the work of Christian faith. His sympathy, losing in intelligence, will lose in value as time goes on. And a veil will gradually fall between him and his people, which a devout dogmatism can neither lift nor rend. He will cease to be the preacher he was, because he was never equipped to be more than an impressionist, because at the most he only learned to be a reader and to know the questions. He never learned to be a student and master the answers. He has not learned to go deeper than those who ask the questions did, because his reading was but part of the luxury of his life and no part of its toil; because his thought but occurred to him, and was not dug from a mine; because his truth cost him nothing but a little mental exposure, like a sensitive plate, in an easy-chair to the printed ray; because it therefore was not dear, as the things are dear that cost much to master, and powerful, as the things are that by our wrestling prevail; because he had learned the habit of valuing truth but for its effect, and often its first effect, of pursuing but its impressionist side; because he had not learned to love and worship it for beating himself small; and because, therefore, in the true spirit of a sect, if only he could move an audience, he had less concern for what could win the age. He had but the tangential mind; he centralized, he bottomed, nothing. The result is that in due course he wears out; and he becomes a burden to the Church because he had no touch either with the great world facing it, or the last reality founding it. He did not even know his Bible, because he knew nothing else. This is not a plea for scholarship, but for the culture of that blended mind, heart, and conscience which is the keynote of apostolic faith, and which will not let us alone till it has fired our clay at the burning foundations of the moral world in the Cross of Christ with its revolution and regeneration of all natural things.

The plea for a radical and positive belief is no plea for a repristinated orthodoxy, as its critics ought to know. It urges the only way to escape from Orthodoxy without falling into spiritual vagrancy and mental anarchy. A man may be very positive and creative with a gospel that permits many reputed heresies as to the Bible, the Church, Christ, and the Eternal future. These views may be peripheral; but he stands in the dynamic centre of the grace that creates Bible, Church and salvation, as well as views about them. And to reach that position he will spare neither thought, prayer, nor humiliation. He will be thorough. He will sell all the pearls of old tradition for this pearl of infinite price, which has all Christian doctrine, and a new career for it, sleeping in its deep, rich, and creative heart.

Again, a positive belief is not only not Orthodoxy, but it is not the same as current pietism. It may consist with such pietism, which is largely a matter of temperament, being as natural to some as to others it is alien. But it does not run to coteries, introspection, or the "language of Canaan"; though, if it do, it possesses the great antiseptic for such complaints. It gives power to the sweet, and to them that have no light it increases understanding.

Once more, a positive belief is not necessarily an ecclesiastical, nor has it a Church seal for an authority. It makes the Church rather than is made by it. Some who are strongly positive do not much court the accent of the current Church. And some who have the accent strong are anything but positive, so far as a gospel goes. A Church note and a Church spirit can be very strong and exclusive among some whose theology is Sadducean; and some, on the other hand, whose gospel is highly evangelical, do not disown their obligation and sympathy to circles that refuse to come into a Church pale.

Nor is it always positive to be religious, spiritual mystic, magnetic, or so forth. Christianity is much more than spirituality, mysticism, or idealism. It is the moral rescue by grace of religion from religiosity, of faith from mere spirituality, of piety from temperment, of creed from the idiosyncrasy of either an individual or an age. It saves Christianity from the aesthetic note and the poetic style that blows through an age; for what is often called inspiration may be nor more than the result of "sitting in a psychic draught." Much religion is not faith but inferior poetry, or it is mawkish fiction which sells by the ten thousand and is worse for the soul than the virility of *Tom Jones*. It is certainly not believing. It is but the willing suspension of disbelief for the moment, in a warm air. A positive faith is so far conservative that it stakes the salvation of history upon history. It therefore finds the core, crisis, and spring of eternal life in a divine action. If the first creation was by a word, the second was by an act. It can therefore be moral and powerful, and not simply true and charming. Revelation has its field in the conscience and will. Given or taken, it is a moral act; it is *the* act and crisis of the world-conscience. So that the root of all human morality, the principle of all historic ethic, the foundation of a new Humanity, is in the Cross of Christ and the action there by the divine holiness and upon it, the crisis there of the moral world, and therefore of the universe. *There* is the decisive thing for the soul and for the race, the one vital issue of God's conscience and man's; *there* is the node where Time and Eternity really intersect (if we may escape from the notion of mere duration in these words).

Here we come upon the element missing in so much of the preaching which is found both able and interesting, and which desires to be large and liberal. It is humane, sympathetic, *vif*, optimist, and in a sense Catholic; it touches us at many points, and we respond; it was its object that we should. But we go away and we know that at the depth and at the centre it does not touch us. It is as if we were translated into a land where every desire of the soul was satisfied, one here and another there, but we were left with the soul itself unsatisfied—unfed, unfathered, and even unreached. And the secret sorrow in the life of many an earnest preacher of the kind must surely be that he is too clear-eyed not to know this. The message (if message it be) may be interesting and able, but it has nothing powerful, creative, miraculous, revolutionary, crushing, and regenerating in it. And yet at last Christian faith is faith in a miracle of re-creation, or it is little. Preaching may be impressive without being regenerative. Some would harshly say that much of the popular preaching of the day is such. But the impression fades. The interest strongly roused, being but interest, wanes. The elation subsides, and we slip into the grey light of common day. We look back it may be to the hour of uplifting, but it is only as a happy memory, not as a fixture of choice, not as a permanent deflection, and a foundation of life or a replacement on rock. We look back as to a memorable play, or a moving symphony, or something equally aesthetic, not as to the crisis of our own life drama. We felt greatly, memorably, the better for it, but we did not live anew, we were not changed and re-settled after the inmost man. We were flushed on a mountain-top, but not glorified in heaven. There was a transfiguration of life, but not a resurrection from death. The grand moral lack of the soul and of society is a regenerating plant for forcing ethic into religion. We need a religious atmosphere laden with the germs of a fundamental and immutable morality which kill the old man and his deeds by a new life in Christ. What we need is not the regularizing of our natural connexions but their revolution.

If the central issue of Christianity is in the Cross it is a moral issue. What we call the Passion was not merely passive; it was active, holy, and passionate far more. It was the passion of One with the prophet's insight of the righteousness of God and the King's function to establish it, the passion of one whose first charge was to set up and secure the holiness of God in face of man's sin. If the issue was more than moral it was because it was moral on the scale of eternity, moral with all the mystic air that makes the ethic of heaven that makes holiness, Dealing radically with holiness it was the moral crisis of Eternity and the root principle of human society.

We do not school our conscience at such a Cross. We are afraid it would be a lapse into Orthodoxy and a preaching of the Atonement a thing now too antiquated for public use. Our moral passion is all used up in the preaching of social righteousness, in proclaiming respect; for the moral personality of man as man, and in the denunciation of abuses. Even the Church has but little left for the radical appropriation of our Redemption by our conscience, and the appreciation of its moral essence and its moral cost. Our faith becomes a matter of sympathy and sentiment. And so we have that blend so deadly, from Pharisaism down to Tammany, of a popular manner and a moral vacuity—a natural ethic of the interests and the egoisms with a sentimental religion. From which wars and rumours of wars—foreign war let into a background of civil discord on the like huge scale. There may be little to choose between the mere nationalism of the awful war that paralyses Europe, and the mere labourism of that which was (perhaps is) threatening to paralyse England by the greatest strike on record. As Industrialism comes to be in an age of competitive egoism, when the spiritual control has gone and the humane has not yet come, militarism is but commerce in mail, and commerce is but militarism in mufti. A catastrophe so wide as the present war is the result less of a political situation than of a moral situation common to all the nations. It means a day of judgement and the end of an age. It goes back in the last remove to a religious situation, one with more religion than God in it, and more God than Christ. The Kaiser's belief, for instance, is much more Jewish than Christian. He holds but to a Lord of Hosts, the tutelar of a conquering race.

It all means a paralysis of Christian Ethic through a demoralized Christian religion which is more concerned to consecrate a natural ethic than to create a new ethic from the fountain of the New Humanity in the Cross. The source of the one war is the same as the source of the other in principle. It is natural and egoist Ethic baptized with religion but not regenerated by sacrifice. And can we escape the divine judgement on the aggressor, be it capital or labour, which in this present war is falling on the whole naturalist competitive God-oblivious structure of society? So far from its destroying faith, faith might well shake if no such judgement came on a loveless world. What is to make religion the creator of righteousness and the moral revolutionist not of society but of human nature? What is to change its passion from success to service, from grasp to give? Nothing but the Cross of Christ coming home as the New Creator, not directly of the social order, but of the social will, which means the moral soul of each individual man.

Let us approach this whole matter on another tack. We have two kinds of admiration, one for the man that can do much better what we are always doing not so well, and one for the man who can do what we never can do or hope to do. We have an admiration for the teacher who is far beyond us, but who may hope in time to make us his own equal, rival, or even superior; and we have an admiration for the man who has a divine something, a *mirum quid*,[1] in him which parts us from him by a great gulf, and makes him do, with ease and by a touch, what is for ever beyond us and all our toil—a something which belongs much less to its possessor than the inferior gifts or aptitudes do. We have the man of talent, that is, and the man of genius, the man who spurs us as an ideal and the man who is a wholesome humiliation to us, the man who has more than most of a certain endowment and the man who has an endowment that puts him in another kind, who does not simply offer us our ideal, but comes with a θεῖον, and lays on us a spell of magic difference, as speech owns music, man woman, and woman man.

It is the latter kind of power that is the analogue in nature to the object of our worship in the spiritual realm. The genius is nature's prophet with a special inspiration, as the apostle is the prophet of grace. The reverence for genius is in the natural world the counterpart of the worship of Christ in the spiritual. Genius promises that which grace *is*. As the genius is to other men, so Christ is to all men, including the genius. He is as far above the spell genius lays upon us as that spell is above the talents we can toil to emulate. We do not compare here, we capitulate. We do not argue, we adore, and we come to rest. His region is creation; the other, inferior and prelusive, is evolution.

Having made this distinction, let us carry it forward on a wider scale. There is a way of regarding all religious history, and Chris-

1. ["What a surprise."]

tianity in particular, which views it as the superlative of that evolutionary process immanent in the race (though, perhaps, by God implanted there); and there is a way which views our spiritual history as made and moulded by the invasion of factors transcendent yet not alien, and creatively divine though not the less truly human. In the one case the movement is a process, which may or may not be moral—only civilized; in the other it is an act, which is moral or nothing. In the one, the prime interest is that excellent creature man, to whose expansive eminence of soul Christ gives vast aid and superlative effect; in the other the striking thing is not human excellence but human impotence, deepening to human guilt; and Christ brings not an ideal consummation of our best, but a moral Redemption of our worst. For the one view Christ is the greatest symbol, not to say agent, of the natural evolution of the spiritual; man comes to himself in Christ, the pride of the race. For the other view, the greatest thing in the world is not an evolution, but a miracle. It is the miracle of its salvation by a Christ whom we worship as all we could never be, and do not merely revere as the ideal bloom of all it is in us to be. The one view starts from man's fullness the other from his need. And, while the former finds in Christ the incarnation of a humanity glorious amid all its defect, the other finds in Him the incarnation of God's grace to a race whose glory without Him is, in the end, hollow, doomed, and lost for lack of spiritual power to carry its natural success. For the one view our religious experiences are products of man's natural, though latent, destiny to rise to the higher triumphs of a soul of goodness in things evil; for the other, they are chiefly the result of a special visitation and creative action of God. For the one they mean a higher stage, for the other a new creation. For the one they arise, at most, out of a divine love, ample and imperturbable as the Zeus of Phidias, which our sin cannot agitate or deflect, and from which we are never severed, as our representative Christ never was; for the other, these experiences are such response to God's creative grace as takes in earnest the holiness of His love, and the tragedy of man's guilt. This view finds in the historic Christ something far more tense, real, dramatic and triumphant than a revelation of kindness unruffled and unweary. It finds there something that is more in the nature of history, will, action and agony, yea, an act and crisis within Eternity (not to say the divine Nature) itself, a new creation, more creative than the old, the last creative Act, of which the first creative Word was but the preamble, and which recovers us for living and mystic union with God in the moral crisis of the holy Christ crucified, risen, and royal for ever. In a word, the difference between the two views is that the one rests on the evolution, however divinely guided, of a spiritual nature indelible in us as children of God in a natural Fatherhood; the other rests, not on spiritual evolution and education, or coming to ourselves, but on spiritual miracle, absolute crisis, death turned life, new creation, and an eternal redemption which is worlds more than another step in the evolutionary series. We have there spiritual evolution, expanding under a natural but infinite fatherhood, and here moral miracle and re-birth, worked by the creative grace, and not the mere nursing kindness, of a Holy Father. We have there sympathetic intuition as the key of the world, here the soul's moral experience. In the Cross of the Holy Son, Jesus Christ, we are created anew, and our impotence is empowered to all the good works that we could dream for our torment but never reach for our rest. The heavenly thing was latent in Him and not in us.

These are the two issues—evolutionary idealism and new creation—which dispart to life and to death for the Church of the day. They should be clearly grasped, for they make the great watershed of Protestant Christianity development or redemption. Their difference is more vital than that between Rome and Luther, more vital than any difference in the world, except that of evil and good; of which, indeed, they are the heavenly counterpart and eternal crisis. They differentiate the liberal Christianity and the positive, the Christ of excellence and the Christ of Grace.

It is the latter of these alternatives that alone does justice to the searching passion of veracity and reality, piercing indomitably to those moral issues that form the central tragedy of a tragic world and the crucial area for human destiny. Man turns on his conscience; and it is the conscience also that goes to the heart of Eternity, and is, therefore, the organ of the holy. For if morality is the nature of things, the crisis of things is man's relation to the Holy. It is in man's sin. For the classic consciences the certainty of salvation is inseparable from the sense of damnation. It is there, to that arena, that we are carried by the most unsparing spiritual veracity, by an insatiable moral realism, by the radical pertinacity of moral thought and the energy of moral imagination that *will* go to the root of things in a spiritual world, and rest only at the deep centre of a universal whole. It can rest but where Eternity rests—in the Being, Will, and Act of the Self-existent, Whose Being is Holiness and Whose Will is Grace, and Whose Act is the New Creation of the New Humanity. The theology of grace is the higher realism of that conscience which makes life real and growth radical.

So the whole idea of veracity deepens for us beyond mere truth-telling with our neighbour to a veracity with our self, and passes on from speaking the truth to thinking to a finish. We are driven to ask the relation of the self (when its speech has become as honest as you will) to reality. Let us talk less of conscious hypocrisy and think more of unconscious unreality. Is our most intimate experience contact with reality, or is it a mere symbol? Is the highest we feel or think to be God, really God, or may it be illusion?

To illustrate. In the realm of religious truth, we may consider that the kind of veracity represented by the great critical movement has about done its work and nears its term. There is, for instance, in Germany (if we can at present give our mind to Germany's better self and true world power), a standstill for the moment in the region of pure theology; which is explained by the fact that the critical stage is as I say, and that the theological mind is taking in the new situation and preening its wings for a new departure in the direction of depth. The deeper mind would then take its flight from the sifted critical results, and view the old powers and truths in a new constellation of facts and ideas. We owe the modern passion for veracity largely to modern science. But the veracity of science (and especially critical science) casts us upon the veracity of philosophy; and, as philosophy is now in a new flux, through men like James, Windelband, Eucken, or Bergson, that is again driven to a veracity, deeper still, which adjusts all truth no longer to the metaphysic of substance but to the metaphysic of energy, to the last reality not of thought but of active life—an absolute personality as a holy and creative God. The veracity of range casts upon the veracity of depth, and seeks the last depth in the abysses of action rather than the recesses of thought. The interest of truth (as it were), from being horizontal, grows vertical; and from vertical it grows energetic. The positivity of science passes upward into the positivity of reality; reality is action; and the last reality is dramatic and personal. Generalization gives place to intuition. And yet for contact with the great reality something more activist is needed than Bergsonian intuition, something more lifelike and dramatic, more of the nature of will and deed, more in the way of personal faith, and the metaphysic of that. A growing conviction arises, from the study of scientific method on the one hand and the modern sense of life on the other, that reality is beyond science, which can only handle the demeanour of reality, and not its purpose or its nature. Our attention, chained and disappointed in soul by the movement of order, is loosed and fascinated by the movement of shock. We ask what it is that is objective to our objective world, what is within the cosmos and makes its goal, to what reality we are brought by all the stages of illusion; and we wonder whether its nature is not given us by something which does not so much crown the same procession of law, or dawn as a clear warm inner light, but rather arises from the collisions that seem to defy law, and from the tragedies that rend the soul itself, and shake and eclipse the light within. We have the collision of life with ethic, of reason with will, of morality with happiness, of the will to evil in us and the will to good. We have the deadly blow of the Cross on the normal world. The last veracity, far beyond the placidity of mere peaceful evolution, may well be a veracity of tragic crisis, of reconciliation, and not merely of expansion. For there is a flatness even about an expanding and evolutionary series, which levels life as fast as it enlarges it, and takes depth and power away, as it increases breadth. We lose in value what we gain in order. And the plan of creation may be found, by a due sense of *all* the facts of experience and insight, to be an active and personal purpose of redemption with which the whole world travails. The great metaphysic may be (as I say) a metaphysic of energy rather than substance, of will rather than of pure being, of soul rather than science, of personality rather than of reflection, of history and its action instead of thought and its repose—a metaphysic of society, of the Kingdom of God rather than of entity and essence. As against the plea that the notion of miracle unsolders all order, disturbs all harmony, destroys all forecast, and unsettles all life, my point is that miracle, spiritual or physical, comes nearer to the root of reality than Evolution, than Law, since it partakes of the nature of the incalculable and inexplicable act which founds the world—creation.

This movement of our interest cannot stop short of a fresh interpretation of what creation means or involves as its own consummation. It is even suggested whether a due and new philosophy of the act of creation must not have for its condition a new creation of the philosopher; whether religion does not autonomously grasp and hold a reality which for philosophy is but an asymptotic mirage; whether the nature of evolution is not travail rather than process, a new birth rather than a new stage; and whether regeneration is not the last goal, and therefore the master key, of the cosmos itself. Men like Wendland and Troeltsch, representing the recent and foremost influences in the philosophy of religion, claim for religion its own metaphysic, independent of a scientific, but not in conflict with it—a metaphysic not of science but of faith—a metaphysic not of substance but of power, in which the leading part is played by a personality reducible to no logical or calculable scheme, and felt by life's experience and action rather than reached by the method of the schools. Is it absurd to think that it takes a creation to understand creation; that the change which perfects and crowns creation in holy personality must be qualitative, and therefore itself a creation; that it is the *process* of the first creation coming to its true self and secret in the supreme *act* of the second, in something which is creation *in excelsis*, and the only creation we can experience; that it is something which is more than the final automatic stage of a process set moving by an initial creation on one plane? This last, this automatism, would make the closing scene but the final step in a series of necessity; and our moral victory would then be only the self-assertion over our head of a latent spiritual nature, or the dénouement of a processional idea which carries us on its crest. Whereas the closest, the crucial relations of person to creating person can be no such evolved and coerced thing. Our moral best is not a great wave's crest. It is a victory crowning the free kind of energy peculiar to will. It is the consummation of a process of *creation*, of a "creative synthesis" of powers, as Wundt calls it. By that suggestive phrase he means that in the world of life the new thing formed by the synthesis of converging forces or causes is more than their resultant. What causes the convergence of causes? There is a real novelty in the effect, a fresh contribution there, which is in its nature created and creative. The process is thus one whose inner nature all along is creation, fresh contribution, and which is, at its close, not less of a creation but more, than at the first. It is with a creation that the whole creation groans. Thus the grand reconciliation issuing in the new Humanity must be the supreme creation, the most excellent and characteristic act of a power whose native action is creation, and is more creative at the end than at the beginning. The beginning only exists because of the end, and exists to be glorified in the end. The world which begins in a creation must end in a creation, but in one far greater if evolution means progress at all. It is an evolution of creativeness. We were created to be recreated. The new creation is the destiny of the first. And it is the experience of the new creation crowning all that gives us any key to understand what creation everywhere is and intends, what it was at the first in a mystery, and aims to be in a manifestation.

In a world such as scientific thought presents to-day, whose atoms are nodules of power, whose reality is energy, and of which energy is the true substance, a distinct stream of that energy enters (according to even Ostwald) to raise the inorganic to the organic, with its power of evolution on the one hand, and on the other its metabolism, or change in the atomic parts. To make atoms behave in cells postulates a special and peculiar cause. In like manner, as life ascends to personality and society, a still newer stream of this energy flows in; and, most of all, as personality rises to spirituality, there is required such an agent and action as Christianity brings in the Holy Spirit, the new birth, *the* new creation. This is the last reality; and it casts its light back on all that went before. It illuminates its own wake, and lights up its origin. For its uses all things at bottom were and are created, and the course of their long stream does but roll to the top what was its deepest depth. The spiritual or regenerate person is the key of creation, as being its burthen and "truth," as being in the most direct contact and final relation with the ground of all things. The second birth is the final solution of the problem offered in the first. To understand creation requires a creative act. Why Nature was born is known only to the twice born soul.

This new creation is an ethical matter, but much more. Regeneration is not merely sanctification. It is not merely ethical in its method. It is ethical, indeed, in its inmost nature, since it is a union with the holy; but its method is not just the development of character by putting it upon action. It is an ethic not of spiritual self-culture but of divine redemption. It goes below sane character or conduct, behind ordered growth or process, to a birth, an irruption, which is the root of both. It is a transcendental ethic, and can never be reduced to an immanental. Order is kept up by the incessant initiatives and fresh departures of perpetual creation. It is a matter of personality, which is the only energy or initiative we really know at last. Though it is now well recognized that moral personality, as distinct from crude and elemental egoism, is a matter of life-discipline, growth, and acquirement, this very growth postulates an autonomy of the personality; which again means an origin of its own, a new departure by a creative power acting on it directly at its incessant source. Such an autonomy is, like all the highest freedom, a divine creation. It implies a departure of a religious and super-rational kind, breaking free from the causal nexus that holds the natural world and much of the moral, and that controls the instinctive or natural man in so far as he is instinctive or cosmic and nothing more. It involves, therefore, our decisive release from the tyranny of science or its causality, on the one hand, but also, on the other, our release from an extreme social obsession by sympathy, which is apt to stifle the sense of personal responsibility and judgement before God, and so stunts the moral man. Moral culture, as the development of the real and moral personality, is something greater, deeper, more mysterious and divine, than the training of character. It is therefore a religious more even than an ethical matter. Yet it is the practice of action, and not mere behaviour, the practice not of the presence of God merely, but of His supreme divine Act. It is a thing of the living soul itself in its will and conscience, and not merely of its features. Great and mighty religion is the solution of an intolerable contradiction by a spark it strikes, rather than a light that dawns over it. And it arises in a creative act breaking in with a new nature on the instincts of nature (which carry us more than we carry them). It masters the necessities of this world with the miraculous power and command of another. Ripeness is not all. Our spiritual destiny is much more than the procession and expansion of a moral order to its flower and fruit. It has choice in it and responsible action. And it is impossible, amid the conditions of the world, without the invasive, creative, empowering act of a Creator whose chief creation is our freedom. This Eternal act (and not mere movement) is His vitality; which emerges for history in the Divine Person and holy work of Jesus Christ. This is, as Troeltsch says, "an abruptly transcendental ethic," an action far more revolutionary than evolutionary in its nature, and therefore more creative—though its introduction may be as imperceptible as the force that forms a curve. It makes men more thoroughly and radically than anything done in the first creation. It is a greater act of creation that Paul has to speak of than *Genesis*. It founds the real, personal life, individual or social, which is organic in itself and whose organism "is the life system of personality," as Eucken calls it. And, with a creative selection, it builds up this life by a constant appropriation and assimilation of that in the natural and instinctive egoism which was getting most ripe for such distinction. Amid the vegetating vitality, the ferment, heat, and friction of the protoplast region of Humanity it starts a new process, a new departure (Wundt), which is not the action of previous process or causal entail, but of God's subtle will and choice. It attaches to that in the natural man which is most supernatural, most near the frontier of the divine, and most of a prelude for the last creative action of God—it attaches to the moral will in its freedom, or at its height in the sense of the holy. The natural exercise of that free will is not yet the new creation, but it is the postulate of it, its anticipation and point of entry. In this supremely new departure we are delivered from the bondage of the ethical, or rather from the ethical as a bondage, into the ethical as the *milieu* of the new power. We are saved from the love of law to the law of love. We are lifted even from the pressure of the ideal, or its mockery of us and our impotence, to its resurrection of us by the Spirit of Holiness into our distinction as sons of God. We rise, by a new spiritual upheaval, to a life that is ethical because it is so much more. It is "beyond our good and evil"; it is the holy. And the old prophecy in our free-will then receives effect and fulfilment, it comes to its own, by the moral regeneration in evangelical faith. Psychological freedom becomes true moral freedom in obedience. Such Faith *is* a regeneration, it is not a mere condition of it. For it answers a God who is not only credible but creative, and creative above all of that true, free, and holy personality which is freedom set free, which is in command of the world, and which has the reversion of all things. The Christ, who stirs our faith, does it as no mere passing impressionist, but as the soul's new Creator for good and all, the source of that which only a Creator can produce—a new personality within the lines of the old, but with another centre and another note. This alone also survives, ruling the death and dust of the old assertive, egoistic, self-destructive self. Christ is, indeed, our new spiritual world, "become our universe that feels and knows."

Hence it is no true worship of Christ to treat Him as differing from ourselves but in degree and not in kind. And it is below the authentic note of Christian faith to regard His person apart from the Cross, to treat Him as Jesus, the soul's dear friend, or as the gracious figure of certain artists and happy pietists. Christians are those in whom there works the power of that personality who, by His redemption, creates from creation. They carry the mark of the second Creator, who works with a finer clay, but from a worse chaos than the first. They are made neither by divine dignity alone, nor by kindness alone, but by the grace of the Father holy and royal in the Son—in the attracting and offending, the saving and judging Son, with all the strange, mastering, stern, melting, majestic, and adorable features of Eternity in His conquering face.

His redemption is the redemption of *the race*. And, being of Christian quality, being perfectly holy, it is the action of that of which the holy is but the moral name—it is final, eternal, and absolute. But the relation of the absolute to the world is that of Creator. Christ's Redemption is, therefore, God's second and supreme creation of the race into the communion and likeness, not simply of His freedom in Nature, and dominion over it, but of the ulterior liberty and final wealth of His personal holiness.

The divine unity is the unity of an organism, not of a unit but of a whole, whose positive and creative energy is constantly subduing everything negative to itself. It is the unity of a life triumphing in a standing conflict and paradox. For without paradox and absurdity, no religion. It is no simple unity that we adore, either domestic or monistic. And the relation between the personal unity of Christ and the racial unity of man is of this dynamic kind. It does not merely confront us as a divine essence might. It masters us. It is a process of collision and conquest, which is the movement of a new creative act of Reconciliation between the Holy God and

Veracity, Reality, and Regeneration

guilty man, an act, therefore, supremely moral. This is the final theodicy and harmony of good and evil, ineffable as a creation must be, and beyond all reason we can set forth. It takes effect in no adjusted system, not in a symmetrical scheme of eudemonist teleology, but in the communion of living persons. It proceeds in the communion of the holy and the sinful soul on the whole scale of God and man.

Such is a shadow of what is meant when we speak of the new creation as the necessary belief of a radical moral consciousness when it escapes from the platypod type of thought and works with the depth, height, and urgent passion of a penetrative spiritual imagination. It is the discovery of such ethical and ample veracity, such searching and sweeping intelligence, or else it is such stuff as dreams are made of. It is either fundamental or fantastic, according as it is our deep moral soul that gives the last anchorage for eternity, or as our ethic is the mere adjustment of the day's conduct in a way that seems to work out—we know not what.

When we come to view things thus, we may discover what the element was that we so vaguely missed at the outset in much of the able and interesting preaching of the time. For all its zest, it left us untouched where to be touched were to have loosed in us the spring of a new life-joy and a ruling power. What we need for our worship is the kind of power involved in a religion whose inmost nature of freedom and wonder is miracle, i.e., creation. The thing we missed is the one thing that creates worship as the crown of faith—the contact with a miraculous God, a holy and gracious God—a forgiving, regenerating, commanding, and pacifying God. No amount of delightful talk about the love of God can do for a sinful race the regenerating work of the miraculous grace of God; nor can the tender recreate and rule as the holy does. Though we need comfort much, we need command more. There are, perhaps, more moments in life when we need kindness; but, in our few great and decisive hours it is much more than kindness we need. "With everlasting kindness—will I have mercy upon you." It is more that must rule in a gospel which proposes to change the heart, reverse the will, and take command of the social conscience on the scale of a whole Humanity. A fatherhood without holy sovereignty is not adequate to the world's conscience; and it is in the holy grace of God that the sovereign authority lies of that

Fatherhood whose grace goes deeper than all kindness to touch with moral tenderness and healing the sorest and deadliest regions of our guilty need. The world's need is far greater than its power and glory. And the supreme proof of Christ is His power to treat that need wherever it is felt with the unsparing keenness of the last moral veracity and the creative mercy of the last moral reality, whose judgement leaves nothing unsearched or unsounded, and, therefore, nothing unforgiven. It is His powerful patience to wait till a disillusioned world come to drink of Him, despairing of every other spring. Only the infinite power of a world Creator has at command the ageless patience of a world Redeemer.

14

The Conversion of the "Good"

I

Both John and Jesus regarded the public which they addressed as a unity. Their appeal was collective. When they did not speak to the nation itself, they addressed themselves to single communities within it, which were, like Capernaum and especially Jerusalem, capable of common action; and such was the action they demanded. Their audiences they did not regard as sects or groups, but as patches of the whole people. To this unity came the call and the condemnation. It seems sometimes sweeping. Yet Jesus was not indiscriminate in His impeachment. He was searching. He challenged a solidary system and an ambitious programme. And He was public in His note. He did indict a nation. He did save a world. He did think in wholes. The keepers of the vineyard were all bad; there was no distinction between the true and the false among them, the better and the worse. But that was not say that there were no good and devout people in Israel, even among Pharisees. When we denounce Germany as the world-agent of Satan we do not deny the many fine and worthy lives in that land. We judge it as a collective unit with a solidary policy and ideal. It was a national unit that was in Christ's mind. It was an evil and "adulterous" *generation* (*i.e.*, a recreant age of Israel, false to its husband God, not a generation of adulterers) that was warned and judged. In that national unity and action the better suffered with the worse. Jesus was preoccupied with the national self, with the general will, as we should now call it, and with the way it worked down into individuals rather than was made up of them.

The call for repentance in particular was directed both by John and by Jesus to the community perhaps even more than to the individual. When Jesus was told of the massacre of some Galileans by Pilate for an outbreak of religious fanaticism He said to His informants (who thought, in the popular way, that a violent end was a judgment for the victim's special sin) that Chauvinism, however religious, was not the line for Israel, and that revolt was hopeless. He said that a nation in arms was not Israel's *rôle*, that Messiah was of another spirit, that for this people, with its election, grace could do more than force, that they must all (collectively) repent of their perversion of God's purpose with them, and turn to a policy of moral permeation as His will in calling them, else Pilate and his legions would do for the whole nation ("likewise") what he had done in the *fracas* in the north. The "you," whether of John or Jesus, was not a group of scattered individuals but the collective people, with its common will, national policy, and national guilt. Each audience they had represented that people. The same line, of course, was taken by the Rabbinate, which both prophets withstood. For them also the unit was the nation. For all that age, indeed, the basis of religion was collective, national, racial. Israel before God was a quasi-personal unity in mission, destiny, crime, and doom. Still, as for the prophets, it was the nation that was God's *vis-à-vis*, rather than the soul. But John and Jesus took this ideal fact seriously and crucially as the true reality. Their call to repent went to all alike, while with the Rabbis it was directed but to a part. These leaders started from the idea that Israel, as a whole, *was* obeying and serving God, and that obedience was its total, normal, and deserving condition. No doubt (they said) many came short, but these, with their need for repentance, were only a deplorable section. Repentance meant no more than a revival of enthusiasm and observance; it did not mean a new birth and a new public spirit. The nation was substantially sound. Its spiritual gentry, its religious *Junkerthum*, was right, and it set the public pitch. Its collective state, therefore, was right and meritorious. Israel as a whole, by its correct service of God's law, deserved God's blessing, and, from God's promise in its election, the lead of the world. Its officers were working for this, with extraordinary faith in an eschatology of Empire, and with the closest attention to preparatory detail in their way of ritual drill. But John did not exempt the most religious from his call, nor did Christ. Indeed, they pressed it on the "good," the eminently religious, in particular, for whom religion and patriotism were one, whose piety, therefore, had lost the true God and his true Kingdom. With these churchmen especially they had their quarrel. Such were the Pharisees. The really and deeply good Christ found in the silent and obscure saints, the humbly devout, the meek and lowly in heart (as it might be the old Germany of the hymns and the heights), with whom so far He ranged Himself, weary and laden as they were with ritual requirement and its religious eminence. Here lay his private affinities. If not in the Kingdom they were not far from it. (Strangely enough He did not take His twelve from them.) Those whom the people held most pious both Christ and John found most wrong (because most in earnest), and most in need of repentance. And, if the religious representatives were wrong, then by solidarity the people as a whole was. It was the good chiefly (understood as I have said) that Christ called on for the national response he never got. It was the "good," the believers in chief, and the well-doers of repute, that disappointed Him most. Both He and they believed passionately in God, His will, and His Kingdom. It was those with whose creed and its passion He had most in common that He broke.

And how did He wish this unity, this community, to act? Through its government? That government, indeed, stood condemned clearly enough in Herod; but it was not such rulers that preoccupied the two prophets, and were specially called to repent and change. If it had been, Jesus would have been more popular. For the rulers, whether political or pious, were not beloved. When Jesus exposed the Pharisees the common people heard Him gladly (though many of the poor were of the Pharisaic party). But His prime demand, though public and corporate, was nothing that a mere government or a court could meet. Christ was not the mouthpiece of a religious party with a forward policy, nor of a Socialist movement. He was extraordinarily conservative of the national past—as Luther would have taken the Pope if he would let him preach the Gospel. He was not the prophet of reform programmes for either belief or action. He was no idealogue. He did not detach the rulers from the whole people who accepted their lead. "Unless ye repent, ye shall all likewise perish"—rich and poor, good and bad should perish in a national enlargment of the Galilean massacre. The only morality He knew was the deep kind that culminates not in conduct but in repentance, and still more in regeneration. He had no class interests. The demand was charged upon the whole nation as a unity, upon the common temper of the society around Him, its non-moral type of religion, its low-pitched decent conscience, its vigorous programme, and its common will for a forward policy. For throughout the public religion of Israel the *vis-à-vis* of God (I have said) was not the soul, but the people.

What to do? To repent as a nation. To flee from nationalism, and save their true nationality. The repentance demanded was not personal lamentation but moral action, private and public, not misery but change, and a change not in religious zeal but in their heart of hearts, and so in the national note. Was it to live for the Kingdom of God, then? To choose the Kingdom, the Sovereignty, the Empire of God? But the Pharisees were doing that passionately. It was their whole zealotic programme, about which they had no misgivings. No, it was to choose Him, and His reading of their past, their Bible, their call, their mission. And, as the result of that contact with Him, to repent, to so change in heart as to change their public ambitions. Things had so gone that that meant a moral revolution on a national scale. To have no misgiving about current religion was, to an eye like Christ's, the last perdition of a people with the Old Testament in their hands. The true genius of that Law for which they were ready to die was their condemnation. The crucial issue was not between the Kingdom and the World, but between the Kingdom and its King, between two different views of the Kingdom—the imperial, with a tutelary God and a belief in power, and the moral, with a belief in grace, and with a God of holy love to whom righteousness was more than sacrifice. The issue was not between a domestic and a world policy for the nation. The call was to choose goodness and reject evil according to the deep principle of the Kingdom as it stood out in Him. It was to choose public excellence as it was in Him, His principle of national righteousness, His version of Scripture, His manner, the manner, not of precept, conduct, rigour, vigour, and force, but of grace, repentance, faith, and love, the note not of Empire but of the Kingdom, as He, its true King, in its true spiritual succession, made it. This, He said, was the true

The Conversion of the "Good"

genius of law and prophet, and the true vocation of Israel. "This is the work of God," *i.e.*, the action required, "to believe in Me." He, and not statute, not prerogative, not conquest, was the soul of Israel, He and not the tradition of the Fathers. It was faith freed from patristics, faith regenerated, faith moralised. The ethical was to be the first interest of a nation.

Those chiefly responsible were less the political authorities than the ecclesiastical (if in Israel they could be severed), the "good," the prominently pious, the active Churchmen. They were the counterparts, for that day, of our "eminent Christians" in Victorian days, the representatives of national, reputable, prompt, public, and bustling religion, the leaders of the religious world as the press might select them. For Israel was, above all things, a religious nation, which owed to its religion the unity of its existence, the reason for that existence, and the policy of its social leaders. The State had become a Church, and a law Church. Of such a people the publicly religious were bound to be the public leaders. And it is on the religious *élite*, the *haut monde* of observance, the cynosures of the Church, that Jesus places the fate of the public. *To these in chief goes the appeal for repentance*—to the "best" people of His religious day. For to His mind they had taken the moral core out of religion, as they showed by their treatment of repentance, which to Him was the root of all morality. And the Orthodoxy of the leaders was in this respect abetted by the sentimentalism of the crowd (Luke 11:27). To a large section of the people Pharisaism was the pink of piety and policy—to Jesus it was its blight. Its falsehood was so unreal as to be unconscious. There was nothing for it, therefore, but a fundamental repentance. For the unconscious falsity was sinking into conscious hypocrisy. A religion severed from the last moral reality of grace was becoming a religion of the worst duplicity. The ideal precepts of the Sermon on the Mount were really a part of this call to repentance. Nothing but despair of fulfilling them could qualify for their fulfilment.

Of old the pure Jews had perhaps always been in a minority in the population of Palestine, amid a crowd that easily gravitated to the indigenous cults and conduct; and even now in every considerable place there was a Brahmanic ring, a junto of religious Rajpoots, a group, or even party, of Pharisees, high separatists from the general public, and respected as such—for the position they took rather than the piety they felt. While at the other end was a mass of common people, too poor to be pious in an expensive religion of observance, passing as "sinners" because sectaries, and disowned by the notables of faith and their set. And Jesus meets both of these extremes, not with a call for more zeal, nor for grave amendment, far less with the promise of reward for patriotic fidelity, but with the demand for a repentance as deep as their zealotry, and the message of a moral kingdom based entirely on grace and forgiveness for all alike. He was more at home with the penitent than with the excellent people; but He came to all not with the invitation to inherit but with the call to repent, to change their mind and ways, to take from Him a new religious type, nay, a religious new birth deeper than repentance, deep as the Holy Ghost and His searching fire. To both classes alike the call came. But chiefly to the chief. The objective of Jesus was the nation through its heads. He did aim at working through Israel on the world, like the Pharisees, but not with the Law. His central religious ethic was national in its note, though more than national in its scope. And the nation was not to be converted only when the "sinners" came to Jesus, but, still more when the "good" came, the reputable, the "righteous," the nation's head and front. He was not so sweeping as He was thorough. It was His searching moral realism that was so unsparing, not His wide sweep. He was always more deep than broad. He blamed not many but much. If all the "sinners" had come to Him one by one, Christ's first call would still not have been met, nor His work achieved. That would not have been the vineyard staff receiving the Son. It would have been a response too atomic for His full call. Israel would not have been saved; nor could it be so long as the lawful representatives of its religion stood out against Him as such. They had the authority, and they determined the temper and destiny, of a community which was religious or nothing, which had been God's elect, and which was still His true goal. Christ always recognized them as its proper organs. It does not appear that those known as "sinners" were at first singled out by Jesus as specially needing His grace—though they responded much better. "The blindness of the religious was visited with a sterner condemnation than those sensual transgressions which are punished more obviously by both their own consequences and by social censure." But it was one Salvation, as it was one Saviour, for the nation as one. The lost sheep to whom He was sent were the whole house of Israel. When He said the Kingdom was impossible unless their righteousness exceeded that of the Scribe and Pharisee, He meant a qualitative difference, and not more of the same. He meant Redemption where they revelled in piety. He meant a new birth, which was to the Pharisee a foreign idea, one which could only have its place in passing from Paganism to Judaism. For the Pharisee the resurrection meant no more than the replacing of that death took away, not a new life with a new hunger and an unearthly food. But still more, Jesus was not thinking of a group severed from Israel—whoever He might have been addressing at the moment. He was thinking of the true Israel, of the nation as He desired to see it and make it. It was the Cross that first universalised the Gospel, and also finally individualised it. The nation said it was religiously sound as a whole; Jesus, Who, as its very Salvation, was God's Judgment upon it, said it was as a whole hollow. He brought a larger forgiveness and judgment than covered a class or a section—and a more historic visitation. He and His call were on the whole public scale of a nation which had a long life of calls, deliverances, and destinies behind it. Such Grace is the great leveller—and unifier. To every man this penny, even to the best. In the Gospels the great example of a penitent is not Matthew the publican, not Magdalen, nor any other such sinner (as sentiment has selected them) but the rock Peter. And the members of the earlier Church were all alike objects of Grace. There was not an inner circle of the penitents.

As to the vital nature of this repentance for which Christ called, this may be said more particularly. It has been pointed out that the Pharisees, no less than Jesus, believed that it was the Spirit that quickened. This only shows that Christianity is much more than spirituality. It means more than the belief that God is a Spirit—more even than obedience to such a God. It is obedience to God where and as He has pleased to express His heart and work His will. The Pharisees believed in a Resurrection by God's Spirit—as they believed in some way in many, not to say in most, of the things intimate to the faith of Jesus. But it was a Resurrection which only restored the previous state of things, with new facilities which gave more freely what death had taken away. It replaced the old egoisms and ambitions on a new plane, and substituted an egoism of more culture for one more coarse. There was no dream of being born again by pure grace as the grand destiny of life, the grand necessity of the soul, the grand purpose of death. The spirituality of the Pharisees involved nothing which fundamentally changed the soul's deep relation to God. His intervention meant but a restoration, and in no sense a regeneration, whether personal or national. The national consummation especially, the public perfecting, was to be by a divine *coup d'état*, which should bring Israel world-power without a world gospel, without a new moral principle or spiritual ideal. The Pharisees, full of culture, earnestness, and efficiency, mocking rather than worshipping a God publicly holy, and waiting only for the right moment, were all agog for a great new state of things for the whole earth. It was to come by such a miraculous augment to the national force that Rome should be beaten with its own weapons. Their one business was to get the nation perfectly ready by ritual drill and machine morals for the hour that God would strike. They were not on God's side, but He was on theirs. They were to have Him for their ally against all the rest of the world, and His Messiah for their Emperor and idol. This God was to extend infinitely their will to power which had totally ousted any call to world service. Were they not God's elect, and therefore made to crush and to rule? The result was to strip from the messianic figure of their lordly age all moral features. He was simply to be national, irresistible, imperial, and magnificent. There was no room for the idea of Humanity. The Almighty was to be but a tribal God, in command of the world by a viceroy at Jerusalem instead of Rome; but with the same weapons to secure everywhere the dominance of the Law, which was Hebrew *Kultur*.[1] The *pax Judaica* would just replace the *pax Romana*—with the more vigour and rigour as its impulse was religion, and its fidelity intolerance.

But the principle of Jesus was not power, far less force. It was Grace—the Omnipotence of holy Grace, *i.e.*, of moral redemption. It was not force but love—sympathy between souls, and between nations the righteousness of sympathy and its service, flowing

1. ["Culture."]

from the faith and love of Himself as holy. He contemplated therefore the hegemony in the world not of Israel but of Humanity, under the Kingship of man's God. There was nothing inhuman or phantasmal about the Messiah which was the historic form of His Sonship. Because He was Son of the God of holy Love and Grace He was the Son of Man. Because He was the holy Son His Kingdom was moral rule; and because He was the King of love it was a universal Kingdom. We may see from the inhuman and unethical programme of His opponents why He mostly presented His Sonship of God as the Sonship of Man. To rule the world was, for the Messiah of such a God as His (the true God of their national Scripture and Charter) to love it in His name and die for it. His power was the power of holy Grace in a land of national egoism and coarse ideals.

The difference between the two programmes is fundamental. It coincides at last with the difference of Good and Evil. It divides mankind into two great sections, one under the prince of the world and one under the King of Kings. These sections may lie down together when the issue is quiescent, but they meet in blood whenever it becomes acute. There is no discharge in that war except by blood—either the blood of the Cross or the blood of the nations. Between these two moral halves of the race there can be no peace but by surrender or by judgment. Power which trusts power and discards conscience, and Grace which glorifies conscience in atonement can never agree, and the righteousness which triumphs triumphs in blood. And this, unless for Pharisees, is as true for a nation as for a soul.

It was this choice that Christ forced upon His nation. This was the nature of His call to repent. This was His challenge to Pharisaism. And it was one in which He came to see He was destined to fail, and to be God's last doom where He had come to be His last boon. So that the legions which His providence in history marshalled against Jerusalem in 70 A.D. were ranged by the same Christ in judgment as came in mercy a generation before. They were as surely an exercise of divine force as those catastrophes of physical and social convulsion in which He predicted their present aeon would sink, and the last judgment take place. No wonder some find in the destruction of Jerusalem His Second Coming. We can understand, even if we do not quite agree. The blood of Israel's rejected Salvation became its final doom. If Cyrus was God's servant to judge Israel in earlier days, Titus was Christ's in later days—if we still believe Christ to be the King of history. When He comes to judgment thus He comes *with His angels*. He uses the nations, even if they are but comparatively righteous, to execute the judgments He inflicts. If war can in no sense be Christian, we must give up the idea of any providential connection between the national murder of Christ and the destruction of the murdering nation.

This style of condemnation by Christ was like His manner of salvation—corporate. It is the kind of judgment, as of salvation, fitted for such a great crisis as His mission made in the history of a whole people, or of a world as a whole. The good are condemned with the bad, the bad are saved with the good. All were shut up unto judgment that mercy might be on all. Christ judged in wholes and saved in wholes. In wholes, but not in masses. The individual has his place in a whole, but not in a mass. In the mass he is but a unit, in the whole he is a member. Christ, on His way to dealing with the whole world, was not dealing with a mass of individuals, but with a nation. But it was a nation content to be led like sheep by a religion organised round a racial God and an egoist ideal, while the revelation it professed to honour and serve was that of Grace and Humanity. There are those to-day who beg us, at an hour like this, with a flickering will and a charity foreign to Christ, to think of the good features in the Kaiser, or of the many souls in Germany as Christian at least as ourselves. They bid us admire the self-sacrifice of individuals for their country there, or their patriotism, which has as good a right as our own. As if absolute loyalty to Satan were a title to regard. If they find little to choose between the combatants it is because they have lost the faculty of moral choice (or never had it) in a religion of mere sympathy and its irresolution. They may be reminded that the judgment we have to inflict in God's name on Germany, like Christ's on the Pharisees, since it means business has nothing to do at such a juncture with individual cases, and can not tarry on exceptions. They may be urged to escape from a trivial piety, and to acquaint and accustom themselves with this Christianity in the great style. They may be invited to grasp, with New Testament Christianity, the idea of a whole nation's perdition and judgment; its racial solidarity too

The Conversion of the "Good"

tribal to emit Christian protest at moral enormity; a whole public too tractable and gregarious to be trustees of Christian principle, liberty, or Humanity; a national soul lost, in its own idolatry, to the Kingdom of God; and, falling on these, a national visitation from God which avenges, on the best of the people as well as the worst, their common neglect to watch the Government with a brief for His Kingdom.

It is not hard to make caricatures of Pharisaism, and to waste powder on such guys, to picture obvious humbugs and pillory them. The view of those who so regard the old Pharisaism is quite unhistoric. It is quite blind to its religious earnestness, so faithful in its faithlessness, so false in its truth, so sincerely and sacrificially devoted to its egoisms and ambitions, and therefore so much the more deadly. The real Pharisee is the last person to be able to put his finger on real Pharisaism. It is easy to voice the obvious verdict, which it needed no Son of God to pass, on Pecksniffs and Chadbands; while the subtle judgment of His searching and startling Spirit on themselves or their age people evade, along with the bracing repentance, the revolutionary ethic, the mental reconstruction, it would stir.

II

The conversion called for by Jesus was thus a conversion from the most reputable and national Churchmanship of the day. And to be quite explicit we may observe two things.

(*a*) It was not the sin of the *wicked* that troubled Jesus so much as the sin of *goodness*.

(*b*) Nor was it the *sins*, or lapses, of the good he was most severe with, but their *goodness*, the kind of goodness that left such sin possible, as troubled Him most, sin public or social.

Bad religion may do more mischief than none. There are worse things than ill-doing. The morality that urges reform was worth less to Christ than the morality embedded in repentance. It was not so much the glaring sins, nor the social anomalies, that Christ denounced—the things everybody could see to be wrong and cheer their denouncer. He did not delight in shaming men by the exposure of single sins, nor of individual sin, or wrong, or inconsistency, in the way of the slashing preacher. Love prefers to be somewhat silent in the knowledge of such things. Christ was most popular, not when He was preaching His Gospel, but when He was bearding the upper and more religious classes. It was only on such an occasion (as I have said) that we are told the commonalty heard Him gladly. They cheered the attack rather than the message. The context of Mark 12:37 makes this quite clear. And this was the class-popularity that forsook Him and fled.

As to (a). Judgment begins at the House of God, and Jesus was more severe with the leaders of His native faith. There are demagogues, even Christian demagogues, and champions, who never once have turned to rebuke their own side or to criticise their own followers; these are always fine fellows and always right. Those champions would lose their lead if they did. They have criticism but no insight; they are partisans but not prophets; tribunes of the people rather than eyes of the Spirit. They represent party egoism. This Lover of children, this Magdalen-Blesser, whose words to her were richer than her oils and tenderer than her tears, was almost as rough with His disciples as with the Pharisees. And this mind of His was a spirit that the first Church quickly caught. The Evangelists are at least as careful to record the rebukes of Jesus which judged the disciples as those which condemned the Pharisees or the outside world. And these Gospels make it clear that it was Christ's judgment on the "good," the pious, of His day, coming to a head in His clearing of the Temple from their commercial monopoly, that brought the Cross to pass—as it is Mammon that has precipitated, if not made, the judgment of our present war.

As to (b). Jesus called the religious to repentance not merely because He condemned their sin, but because He condemned the goodness that left it possible. It was egoistic religion, whether in the individual or the national form. It was really egoist, though it thought itself devoted to God. It was seeking security while God sought service. This was the fundamental hypocrisy, which bore its fruit in due season, when the self-delusion worked out to delude and betray others. The wickedness of the world is not so hopeless as the self-satisfaction of Christians can be. The self-sure Kaiser, the Antichrist of the hour, is head of the German Church.

Not that Jesus denies the goodness of the "good," and calls it an evil effort. He does not, any more than He calls the sinners saints. The objectionably good really believe that obedience is the one thing needful, and that they obey with all their might. If only obedience were all! But it can be public perdition. It is so. It is His insight they lack into that God whose revelation gives obedience moral value (Matt 9:13). Obedience is no virtue unless the command be such as makes it a duty. The Pharisees differed from Jesus less by their spirit of obedience than by their insight of what should be obeyed. They had not moral imagination or sympathy. On the other hand, the "sinners" really sin, and know it as well as the "good" know their goodness. But it is far more hopeful to know well that you are a sinner than to be quite sure you are a saint. It is the sickly sentiment of the *littérateur* to say that the "sinners" were really the sound at heart, and that the "religious" were rotten; that the "bad lot" is at bottom "a good sort." Jesus never extenuated evil because those who did it were also likeable people, and did some good with tempermental kindness. That is modern and maudlin when it is made the ground of moral judgment. The Bible aggravates evil, it does not extenuate it. Jesus never said that badness is good, or that it was not so very bad; only that those who were sinners and knew it were more hopeful and tractable for His purposes of mercy than those who were good and who knew it. But "except ye repent, ye shall all likewise perish."

The "good" specially need conversion, not because there was sin mixed with their obedience, but because their type of goodness was, or became, or tended to become, sin. What they lacked was moral insight. They did not know majesty nor mercy when they saw it. They were right in a wrong way. Their hardness was as demoralising as our softness. They were as keen as Christ about God's righteousness; it was their conception of it that debased and ruined them. Paul owned that they had a zeal to God, but not according to knowledge. The earnest piety was that of a blind asylum. So it will not do to say of a vendor of spiritual poison that he is a good earnest fellow. The need is not the religion of good fellows, but true positive religion, and the discernment it brings.

In Christ's teaching, the good, who are sure of their goodness, are in more peril than the bad who are sure of their badness. The damnation is greatest of those to whom it will be most of a surprise. The goodness, that stops short at a point satisfied, with its moral education finished, is more dangerous, because less practicable, than badness that does not think its education begun. The occasion to sin that rises out of self-satisfied goodness, unbroken and unhumiliated, is a worse temptation than that which rises out of passion. Well-doing becomes such a temptation because it may create a stronger sense of self than even passion does, by bringing Heaven in aid. Self then has God for guarantor. So the devotee may be more hopeless than the debauchee. The self-will of the popular saint, or the spiritual "side" of the cultured pietist, may be an almost incurable malady.

There is a Pharisaism of culture which has had an appalling apocalypse in the war. To say nothing of intellectual priggery, there is a Pharisaism of the ideal, which has a Greek ethic, a Jewish regard for proud, good form, and the incorrigible self-respect of those who have never seen the Holy in His burning bush. This also the prophet of a searching grace and a living faith must sweep into his call for the repentance that is the foundation of the new morality and the source of the last religion. The doctrine of justification by faith, says Wernle, is the one meeting point of ethic and religion. The Pharisees who made the Antichrist in Israel were as religious, scholarly, earnest, and efficient, and they were as much devotees of the Union of Church and State as the German Church to-day is—and as false to the Kingdom of God in any sense that Christ would have recognised. They worshipped power at the cost of grace; in their modern antitype the barrack goes for far more than the Church in the schooling of the public. Surely a Church which has so definitely rejected Christ's Kingdom of God, and so de-ethicised religion as to abet the official repudiation of morality for a nation has ceased to be a Church, and must become a pariah among the Churches of the future righteousness. This is the end of Lutheranism, and its reversion to an Antichrist worse than Rome.

15

The Cross of Christ as the Moral Principle of Society

At some risk of being misunderstood I will venture to say that the chief of the wider needs in current religion is the moralization of the idea of God through His Kingdom; its translation to experience, and to the central experience—that of the conscience. It is the standing need, indeed, of an atonement—to do justice to the holiness of God in the central human situation. This is the chief interest of the New Testament. And it is the element in any religion that fits it for such a moral crisis as history has reached.

We all feel the impotence of the Christian Church in the national and European situation into which we have come. And the remarks made on it are various—in the image of their makers. We may state the case briefly by noting that the State at its best is a body and an interest mainly ethical, while the Church has become a body with a concern mainly mystic—whether the mysticism take the high and sacramental form or the broad and rational. Both of these mystical forms tend to lose the preeminently moral note, the note of reality, the note of the conscience, and of the guilty conscience; the note of the true catholicism, which is the evangelical. But that note involves a moral restatement of the human problem in its present phase, and of the Christian redemption which solves it. The supreme and central problem ought to be adjusted to the world's actual case, and presented as the problem of man's historic wickedness and God's historic holiness in modern terms, man's public unrighteousness and God's public kingdom. But both sides of that collision are moral quantities above all else, whatever fashion they take in each age; their adjustment, therefore, is an ethical one. So far it is relevant to the chief interest of the State. But is it relevant to what has become the chief interest of the Church, whether as its piety or its sacraments? Has the mysticism there retained on either side a moral genius in command? Has it risen from being a mysticism of the imagination to the mysticism of the conscience, and of the conscience on the world-scale, the scale of the Eternal, of the moral Absolute—in a word, of the holy? It handles the holy, does it realize it? There are those who think that in this direction the Church has much failed. It has lost the ethical note in the mysticism either of the sacramentalists, the rationalists, or the pietists. Revelation with its authority has fallen from being moral redemption to be but a deposit of sacred truth. Whereas at its center, the Cross of Christ, we have neither an instruction nor a ceremony, but sublimated moral action—the supreme moral crisis of the soul, of society, of the universe, of eternity; and the creation of the last moral realm, the kingdom of God. (I speak much of notes, much more of notes than of programs, or even doctrines; for in acting on the collective public it is the note that tells most, and most determines influence.) That note of the Cross—ethical, holy, atoning, and redeeming—the Church must recover as its grand dominant. Its mysticism must be moralized at its source, and on the scale of its source, if it is to regain the ethical tone which States can understand and own. That is to say, the Church must become more true to its New Testament genius, where all turns on the Holy One's treatment of sin, or rather of guilt; that is, on the solution of the human problem as the problem of the conscience, man's and God's. All turns on the kingdom of God in history as in heaven. This is a view of the case which the writers of this world know not, and know the less the more fluent they are, especially in fiction, about the human problem. Did they know they would not treat life as if religion were foreign to it, nor crucify by silence the Lord of glory, or put him off with a mere historic admiration. We may venture to say that the decaying public impotence of the Church coincides (to say the least) with a mystic curiosity on the one hand, and, on the other, with a growing shyness of the only moral solution of life by a deep and positive grasp of atonement, or God's own moral adjustment for society. The Cross of Christ was the moral Armageddon of the race. It meant more for God than all the battles of man's history. It meant more for man's moral destiny. And the moral principle of that victory must mystically pass into the fiber of the Christian conscience if it is to speak with divine authority to the peoples as such. The Church's public influence will not return till its apostolic succession recover the great prophetic note which makes saints to be also statesmen of the kingdom of God, the kind of saints that judge the world.

I venture to speak of the bearing on the nature of society of this Cross which crowned the person of Christ. If would indicate how the very structure and course of society carries, and even hurries, us into the theology of the Cross as the one eternal crisis and focus of the moral powers that make society possible. There they all gather to a head. Indeed, that theology, as the first thing it did, created in the Church a new society, which is, with all its faults and crimes, the finest product of history—not to say the final when it is perfected. The Cross, which is central to Christianity, is inseparable from the kingdom of God, and that Kingdom is the truth of society. Yet it is the power chiefly left out of account by the philosophy which would explain history, or the politicians who would repair it.

If the race is an organic whole and not a crude mass, it must have a center of moral power. Authority there must be, and government; and the more so, the more spiritual we are (if there is anything moral in our spirituality). But there are governments many and authorities many, appealing even to our conscience; what is the government for all governments, and the authority for all authorities? What is the last center and authority of the human spirit? Is it something we take to the Cross or something the Cross brings as the kingdom of God? Is there a kingdom of heaven, and is there a King of kings? Is not our very freedom an imperative? We *must* be *free*. That which creates even freedom is it not an authority?

If mankind is not atomic, and if this organism is not a mere organization, not merely mechanical, not one of force and empire, then it is in its nature moral. Its foundation (as the family shows) is not a unity, but two at least; it is a relation; and it is a living relation—sympathetic, indeed, but still more, authoritative. Certainly it is a matter of heart, but still more it is of conscience. The moral interest is the ultimate interest of history. The chief problem of the latest form of society—democracy—is its moral control. If mankind is but a mass of units, if there be no society but what these make by a consent or contract, if the ultimate thing is the individual, and if society is but individualism clotted, then it is false to speak of the moral interest as central and supreme. It is not only false by tyrannical and Puritanical. And there are other interest, such as the æsthetic and cultural, which claim control; they repudiate moral control as a usurper, and resent moral considerations as interlopers. They demand independence and equal rights with morality—art for art's sake. The same claim is made by the modern State, which in Germany insists on discarding morality when it interferes with the power of the egoist State. We have then not a society but only a culture, which is concerned not with the whole but with the exploiting of the whole for the development of the individual, the genius, or the State. It issues accordingly in the superman or the super-State, above and beyond good and evil. The æsthetic life, or the life merely national, is an egoist life. And it is the curse of modern life that its very ethic becomes æsthetic for lack of authority. Therefore, it is non-social. But if, on the contrary, mankind (like the Church) is a society by its nature, and not a mere coalition at its choice, if it is not a compilation but an organism, then its very essence and ground is moral and not æsthetic; it rests on what is good and not on what looks well, on what we trust and not what we enjoy; it is made of consciences and not mere atoms; which consciences cohere in a moral reality; so that the individual does not come to himself as a true person except as he finds himself in this moral milieu, and develops a good will there. The State then does not arise simply from individual need. Like the Church, it is not a club where the individual utilizes for his own need similar needs is others. It is not simply a self-improvement society. It is not a poise of egoisms, a balance of interests. But it exists through the social necessities intrinsic to a moral or spiritual life. The analysis of its phenomena by any psychology, individual or social, which takes account of all the facts arrives at last at something beyond analysis, which forms the ground of these phenomena, and explains their why and wherefore. (This is preeminently so in the greatest society of all—the Church.) The man in his inmost nature is not a unity but a member of his society. His very substance is notched into it. He is built like a house meant to grow into a row, with projecting bricks to tongue into next door. The influence of society on him is not simply regulative but in a sense creative. It makes him what he is. It constitutes him, so that he is not a man if he is not a brother. It is inexplicable but it explains all. It is beyond analysis as the creative synthesis of all. It does not police him merely but develops him, comes out in him—yet by free action on him and not by ideal process. It gives him certain rights, which are valid simply as the conditions under which his moral development to a personality can proceed, and his passage, therewith, into the kingdom of God. That is his true and only liberty. But you ask if I really mean that he has no rights but what society gives, none in whose name he should resist society. I do not mean that. But if he claims any rights as not conferred on him by society, rights which society can only recognize, they are yet not intrinsic to him as a sheer individual, but they are given him by God as himself the supreme world in which he lives, moves, and is. And a prompt Trinitarian would say God was the supreme society, where I have just said supreme *world*.

The final, the ruling, interest of a society supremely moral must be personality. For such a society is itself a quasi-personal thing. It has a corporate personality, a common will, which does not come into existence just by pooling wills. A race of growing persons cannot really cohere in anything which is just put together, or whose nature is lower than indivisible personality. The moral nature of man cannot grow either in a vacuum or under mere compression, whether the squeeze be by force of arms or force of numbers. Majorities we must work with, but they are only the expression, crude as yet, of the collective personality of the nation. They only give effect to this, they do not produce it. The State which works with them is fundamentally a moral being, and reflects a social *morale* whose education is from moral sources. Where are these sources? Are they within the resources of the State itself? Is the State so self-sufficient morally that it can provide all the moral education its members require? Is it the moral standard, and ultimate for its citizens? That is good German, but it is bad English and fatal ethic. Where, then, shall the individual go to find the chief source of his education into true personality, so as to become the kind of individual that makes majorities beneficent for a nation, or a nation for a world? To his national history? But, even if he had better means than his schools provide of reaching the true genius of his nation, and owning it in his loyalty, he does not thereby become a man. He may only become a patriot, worship nationalism, and sacrifice the whole of humanity to its juvenile egoism. Where is he to find the ethos which is the true nursery and happy climate of his personality as a man. Where at last but in Christ and Christ's kingdom? That kingdom every democracy, every republic, must obey.

The supreme interest of a society essentially moral we should all agree is personality. It is absurd then to think that a real person (and not the quasi-personality of a race) must be the creative center of society, that it is a person who must educate the unit into the humane personality of membership? It is true the subconscious effect of the State and its atmosphere is great. "The State," says Bosanquet, "is not merely the political fabric. The term State accents, indeed, the political aspect of the whole, and is opposed to the notion of an anarchic society. But it includes the entire hierarchy of institutions by which life is determined, from the family to the trade, and from the trade to the Church and to the university. It includes all of them, not as the mere collection of the growths of the country, but as the structures which give life and meaning to the political whole, while receiving from it mutual adjustment, and therefore expansion, and a more liberal air."[1] Or, take Green: "The State is, for its members, the society of societies, the society in which all their claims on each other are mutually adjusted."[2] And, we might add, they are not simply composed but organized in a creative way. It is history crystallized, the past incarnate; and we must include the past in humanity and own the educative influence of the dead especially.

The spirit of such a body, the genius of a nation with a great history, certainly acts upon us very strongly and nobly. But it acts in away too general and too subconscious to reach the most intimate and influential springs of moral personality. It surely cannot be, as William James says it is, that "in these crepuscular depths of personality the sources of all our deeds and decisions take their rise, and that here is our deepest organ of communication with the nature of things."[3] Surely we do not get out by the cellars. Surely the determinants of our will are more in the open than that, else

---

1. Bosanquet, *The Philosophical Theory of the State*, 150.
2. Green, *Principles of Political Obligation*, §141.
3. James, "Is Life Worth Living?," 62.

there is, making us, more of a process than a choice, and more of a pressure from beneath than an intelligence from above. It cannot be that the roots of whatever is most divine in man are in the subconscious rather than in the conscious region of moral vision and decision. For the creation of the moral personality we need something more than the subconscious *élan* and gregarious influence of our nation. That is not pointed enough, not personal nor moral enough, and on the other hand not large enough for the race. It is not subtle enough, for by itself it gravitates to material force; and it is not wide enough, for it tends to national egoism. To escape mere nationalism must we have not some incarnation of humanity? But is that possible? Is it not if mankind is but a heap of sand. Nor is it if we regard humanity (with Strauss) as but the effectuation of an idea. Ideas do not become persons, they come from persons; they are a person's ideas. Ideas do not incarnate, only wills. But if the essence of human society is more in the nature of an energy, if it is a common will, or a common conscience, then its incarnation is not impossible. The incarnation of an idea, or even of a national history, is not what is offered us historically in Jesus Christ. At this moment I say nothing of him as the incarnation of God; I will only speak of him as the mightiest of the dead and the focus of a humanity which is above all things moral in its nature and center. And I suggest that the more humane, the more ethical, the more of a unity society grows, the less it finds its account in an egoist culture, the more it presses a freedom of citizenship instead of atomism, the more stress it lays on the moral soul instead of the imaginative or even the sympathetic—so much the more is it driven to rally upon the personality of Christ, whether it interpret it theologically and really or only ideally. Jesus Christ is the historic center of the race, whether we regard him æsthetically, as its ideal figure, or historically, as the cause to which ethical society and modern history owe more than to any other actor in its course. But he is only the center of the race if the race's center is the moral center, if its region is the conscience as the suzerain of every other interest. If the intrinsic value of society is its moral value, if this moral region is really the creative, where men are made and not ideas only, then the most precious and potent factor in society is Jesus Christ. And a faith in him full of ideality takes the lead of all idealism, which by itself is now a social danger. In him both the destiny and the ethic of humanity are gathered up. The common will, the moral core, the spiritual genius of the race, receives in him such a condensed expression and permanent control as no man has ever given to any nation from Cæsar to Luther, from Luther to Washington. And he is, therefore, so powerful for humane personality that the reign of his humanity is bound to take command of all nationality, and to give to it, no less than to the soul, its true and tributary place in the reconciliation of the world.

But will that not put him in front of God—obscuring more of God than he reveals? Must we not take two more steps? He is not dead but alive. How can we speak in any real sense of his taking command if he has himself already been taken into the command of death? A beneficent influence on the race does not necessarily take command of it. How can the quite dead rule the living? Is it possible to regard the first figure of a living race as only dead? His effect would then be but æsthetic; and could an æsthetic influence be a conscience for our moral life? Could it create such a conscience? If Christ deserves the praise of many doubters who feel his spiritual spell to be supreme for life, can he be but the first of the dead? He is a living Christ and a living King.

But we must go farther still. If Christ be the living center of mankind, what is the center of Christ? Where does his personality have its full and final power? I have tried to suggest that if it is in his person it is in the act in which his whole person took effect. It is in his Cross. *There* is condensed the moral crisis of the race. (Or, if you object to crisis, I will let that pass, for the moment, and say that there is the grand node so far of the race's moral development.) Now, what was the nature of the moral issue in Christ's Cross? It is no true account of his mind, in so far as the Gospels allow us to reach it at such a time, to say that he was engaged in a tremendous struggle to impress mankind with his Father's love. It was not a struggle merely to *impress* at all. At the great crisis he was not trying to impress the public, even with a gospel, and quite a worthy one. He was engrossed rather with doing something—doing something for that public with God which it takes ages to impress upon it in any adequate way. The very difficulty we have in reaching Christ's mind at this solemn juncture would seem to show that something else was going on there than the effort to impress men. Had that been his principal object it would surely have been much facilitated (especially as the world grew older) but a completer revelation of the interior of the soul that best realized how God loved the world. But the very silence of Jesus on his own inward experience, then and always, would seem to show that it was something else that chiefly engaged him than the effect he was having, or was going to have, on men's conscience and heart. He was certainly not engrossed with his own soul's adventures, his own spiritual pilgrimage. He was engrossed with the conscience of God and his own relation to that as the Son at once of man and God. Here was the crux of the Incarnation—the collision of the Son of man and the Son of God. Here was the paradox, the miracle (far greater than that of man's freedom in God's sovereignty) of the Holy One made sin for us. The supreme moral issue here is the engagement of the representative of sinful mankind with the holiness of God, and the adjustment between them in one personality. The supreme issue of the racial and sinful conscience is its issue with the divine conscience and that perfect sanctity. It is no adjustment of finite and infinite. That is to say, it is a matter of atonement in some real sense as the base of reconciliation, and it makes the final miracle of all we can know. But this we must say: the atonement was only possible by the offering of the perfectly holy to the perfectly holy. That is, the Saviour was not only the living Christ but the living God. God was in Christ atoning the world to himself.

We have plunged some way into theology. But is there any means of avoiding the leap into that buoyant air without discarding our beginning and adopting another than the ethical view of society's foundation? If society is no mere contractual product, no mere compilation, but, if it is, in its essence, an organism, more or less personal, creative of moral personality, then its moral secret is not to be reached by either an analysis or an induction performed on its historic career, neither of which can give its destiny. And it is its destiny that prescribes its ethic; its goal makes its law. But that secret, that destiny, emerges in Christ, where universal personality appears in its classic and normative case. We may differ about the precise interpretation to be put upon both the mind and the action of Christ. But surely we must own that a person morally so complete reveals more of the conditions of personality, and of its last social ethic, than anything so indeterminate as the historic ethos of a nation or a race. We may take the many new studies and disciplines whose rise has given such interest and promise to the last century. Biological analogies, the principles of political economy, the study of jurisprudence, psychology (and especially the psychology of society) together with the vast broadening and deepening of historical science—all these have lightened up the complex nature of the social organism in a unique way. But the real science of society (except to the young) is an ethical study. It is the study in social form of life's last values and powers, of the things that, from the soul's inner castle, make and mold life in its most precious and personal worth. Ethical study is the study of living personality and its relations, not simply of moral laws and their pressure. We have to do not simply with a universal moral order but with a universal moral personality, if such an one can be found. Where look for him? The true universal is not the natural man but the spiritual. It is not elemental personality but moral. It is the man of conscience, of the universal and absolute conscience, the Holy. The last morality is our relation to the Holy, to the moral absolute, to infinite Love. It is our religion. "The one morality is loving thee." And the religious-moral relation of man in his guilt to God in his holiness must surely be an Atonement. We have run into the Cross of Christ. The form of love is sacrifice, the form of holiness is atonement, the form of holy love is atoning sacrifice. And the Christian revelation is that it was an atonement made by the love of God we had most reason to fear. If all life runs out into morals, morals culminate in repentance and in confession. But not chiefly in the miserable confession of sin but in a glorious confession of the Saviour, of the holiness that forgave it at his own sole cost and inmost sorrow; in such confession as the Holy alone could make, in such atonement to the Holy as consists in sacrificial holiness alone. Mere suffering is no expiation, only perfect holiness in conditions which involve suffering.

But Thou giv'st leave, dread Lord, that we
Find shelter from Thyself with Thee.[4]

The Cross of Christ is the moral center of society, being especially the creative center of that society in which morality rises not only to public righteousness but to eternal holiness. It is the center of the Church—the greatest society on earth, the trustee of the New Bond, the consignee for the New Humanity of the righteousness of holiness, so penetrating, commanding, sympathetic. And what is the moral principle of the Cross which satisfied and delighted the absolute conscience of God? Is it not obedience to begin with? But it is not obedience to end with, obedience *per se*. It is not obedience as a subjectivity, not simply a spirit of obedience, which might be but resignation and merely docility, Teutonic and immoral. But it is obedience as action, obedience with a content, obedience moralized, obedience with a moral value which flows from its object and his demand, obedience to holiness as the nature of the action of the supreme power to which it is due. It is obedience which that power does not exact but inspires. It creates what it requires, *dat quod jubet*.[5] Why have I had so little to say about the love, sympathy, and sorrow of the Cross? Because it did not lie in my direct line of argument, which started from the moral basis of society and the adjustment of consciences. And my line was suggested by the crisis of the time. It is the form of love as righteousness that is the grand concern of the hour. Another line might well be found on these kindly things, whether they carry us to finality or not. Truly the one morality is loving—but loving the holy. We must lay stress on the holy. For a social nexus merely sympathetic will not stand the strain. Mere fraternity will not, nor mere idealism. We must come back to the kingdom of God, round the authority of the atoning Cross. What is to save when love seems to give way? What is the last victory of faith? It is not so hard, nor so triumphant, to conquer when we delight in the joy of God's love and the warmth of his communion. That was always the restoration of Christ's energies—more than nightly sleep. He could sleep in the storms because he waked of nights in such prayer. But obedience and trust come to their crucial trial when the comfort of love is felt

---

4. Cranshaw, "Dies Iræ Dies Illa," lines 25–26.

5. ["He gives what he commands."]

no more, when it holds and lives only to that in love which is truly almighty and eternal—the absoluteness of it, the holiness of it, the power of dominion and finality in it. That was the very crux of the Cross, the spot of final victory. It was to love and trust love where no love was *felt*, where love was doing everything except rejoicing, when all his lovers failed him and things that had long gone from bad to worse reached their worst. It was love as faithful obedience to the holy, love to God when all reason for loving treacherous man had gone, love to God as the hallowing of his faithful name when even he seemed to have gone, love where it was not felt as sympathy, where the sympathetic side of it was beclouded, and the righteous side alone survived in a sacrifice which was a fidelity more than an inspiration. Love as righteousness, when it is on a scale too great, and in a crisis too deep, to be felt as sympathy—that is the moral principle which is the stay of society when love as a feeling is impossible or unstable. Righteousness, holiness, the kingdom, is the most social form of love. We cannot love all men in the affective sense in which we love those who are our own elect. But we can in the effective sense of righteousness to all. That is the more public and civic form of love. We cannot love all men with all our heart. God alone can do that. But we can so love the God who does it as to love them with our conscience, to behave to others as if we loved them—which in God we do. If the love of Christ do not make us lovers of our kind in a repentance (however reserved) we do not know that love as it is truly revealed—in grace. To whom much is forgiven the same loveth much. If he love but little his forgiveness is small. But the forgiveness of Christ is a full salvation, a final social righteousness.

The Church may live on love as kindness. The State lives on love as righteousness. And both the kind and the stately, both sympathy and righteousness, mercy and holiness, meet in the Cross of a love sacrificial, holy, and by holiness, atoning to the holy. The Cross of Christ taken at its true moral value is the principle of the State at last, as it was the foundation of the Church at first. Is our type of religion equal to the part we propose to play in a great old world, complex and tragic?

16

Faith and Mind

I

It is common to-day to hear a protest against theology, on the ground that it is an intellectualizing of what is really a religion of heart and conscience; that it is the capture of Christianity by aristocracy of mind. But it might arrest some of this mindless protest, if time were taken to ask what theology really means. We might then note that there is theology and theology. There is what may be called a primary theology and a secondary. And they are thus distinct as from speculation so from each other. The one is the statement of revelation, the other its exposition. The former belongs to the very nature and definition inseparable from Christian faith as soon as any attempt is made to pass beyond mysticism and convey it; the other belongs rather to its scientific and expansion treatment. The one can be verified by experience, the other only by study. There is truth which produces faith, and truth that faith produces.

For instance, if we say that Christ died for our sins according to the Scriptures, or that God was in Christ reconciling the world to himself, we are stating the source and marrow of Christian faith; and since every one of the terms is theological, we are at the same time confessing that without theology this has no meaning, and becomes a mere mystic and lonely intuition, as sweet, perhaps, but as mute and powerless as the daisy, "whose great bright eye most silently Up to the throne is cast."[1] Every word of statements so simple and essential to a social Christianity carries on its face

---

1. Coleridge, *The Rime of the Ancient Mariner*, part VI, lines 7–8.

the theological truth, and without it religion becomes mere rapt religiosity, mere individual spirituality. Of course if we think only of religion, and not of faith, we may be content with some expression of our subjective attitude—like "the sense of dependence," where (with most of the favorite modern religion) we state something about ourselves rather than about our God. But when we rise from our subjectivity to speak of faith, some truth about its object and creator is inevitable. And it is equally inevitable that that object, and not our attitude, should be the main matter. The truth in faith, therefore, can only be theological at heart. It makes theology of the primary kind, without which faith is not faith, nor Christianity Christian, but we are left with mere religiosity, or spirituality, or humanism.

If, however, we go on to draw out the exact thing that was done by the Son in relation to the Father in redemption, or the science of Christology, or the (trinitarian) conditions under which the Eternal proceeds *ad intra*, then we enter upon a scientific, or secondary, theology. It may be theosophy (strictly speaking) rather than theology. It handles not so much the power, but the wisdom, of God; not his grace, but his psychology. It does not directly belong to faith, however inseparable from a Church, and it is not presented in faith's first passionate account and confession of itself.

Now it is the neglect, or the refusal, to distinguish in this way that has caused some of the resentment felt when the plain Christian is summoned on his life to believe in a theology. There often included under the name theology matters on which he knows himself incompetent to pronounce, which are outside his, or perhaps any, experience. And he naturally objects to be called on for assent to such matters with a pistol at his head. Neither he nor, perhaps, the authors of the demand realize the difference between such remote or speculative points and those that are bound up in the very statement of the faith which, to our experience, does save us from our peril. But, for all that, Christian experience is not possible without Christian intelligence.

It is not to be denied that often a saving theology has suffered from its too close association with a scientific theology. In Germany, particularly, this has happened. In the training of the ministry there, for instance, an extravagant regard has been had to the latter. The education for the pastorate has been organized far too much in the interest of theology as a science, and the culture of the practical, ethical, and religious side has suffered accordingly. This must always be a danger when theology is made a mere university study, and is dissociated from the Church, its pulpits, its pieties, and its occasions. Most Churches can never hope for a learned ministry—if only we could preserve an educated and a competent. It is upon the primary and experimental theology that our pulpits work, our faith lives, and our Churches thrive. It is in an intense but generous grasp of the primary theology, rather than by an accomplished interest in the secondary, that we have our future. And this is true, indeed, of the whole Church, which otherwise becomes but a school. It is not easy to say which danger is the greater, pietism or rationalism. Faith may soften into the mere sentiment of religion, or it may stiffen into the mere rationalism either of amateur heterodoxy, or of a crustacean orthodoxy which loses the perspective of theological values, rates all Christian truth alike, makes scriptural form final, and includes all its hard science as essential in its faith.

Now the primary theology is not vaguely mystic for lone emotion, but positive for thought and action on the world; and it therefore makes demand on the mind. It exploits world ideas and aspirations. It appeals to the spiritual understanding, in the great, penetrative, and sagacious sense, in the sense in which we speak of the vast understanding of Dante or Shakespeare. The secondary theology is rather the work of the acute, speculative, or architectonic intelligence. The one goes with insight, the other with purview. The one is more creative, and is associated with a revelation; the other is more deductive, and goes with a system. The one draws on the ethical, the other on the rational mind. The one goes with moral greatness and its synthetic grasp, the other with intellectual power and its analytic range. The one gives a heaven, the other a horizon. And as the one may degenerate into the goody, the other may sink into the clever; while the one may decline to futile mysticism, the other falls to the level of the religious witling.

II

The contempt for any theology is really a symptom of the philistinism which goes with that pedantry of actuality, that morbid devotion to outward things, calling itself healthy-mindedness; or it is a sign of the levity which goes with much of the temperamental and subjective religion of the hour. It betrays a poverty which has only to go far enough on the same line to end in Church bankruptcy and moral pauperism, if the Church's history has anything to teach us at all. Let us be clear. Theology has no special claim to the general attention of Christians unless it is a part of our religion, the objective element of it. It has no claim on the Church as a scientific hobby—like, say, the geography of the Holy Land. If the doctrine of the Trinity is merely the ideal physiography of the divine nature, without any direct connection with Redemption, and therefore with religion, we can leave it to the speculators whose philosophic interest moves that way. But if theology do represent that element in religion which gives it footing in the Eternal and preserves it from a subjectivity atomic and flighty, it is vital to the Church. For the Church's first requisite is an objective, intelligible, and stateable Gospel. And the contempt and neglect of theology would mean that the sons of light should roam the hills as children of the mist.

Theology is not always an academic interest forcing itself pedantically upon a practical Church; it affects the fountains of life and work. Why should any Church work but for those ends of the kingdom of God whose very statement is a theology? The theological interest is not for the Church like the programme of a social class struggling for a place in the sun; a class which feels how great a lever for its purpose the Church would be, and tries to capture, exploit, and even monopolize it, with a jaunty and juvenile indifference to everything but a new sociology. The society that most nearly concerns the Church is itself, as the only society created by the Gospel; and its belief is its most intimate affair. Its theologians are therefore an essential part of its ministry. It is by its theology also that Christianity is superior to every other faith in the world. Judaism, which comes nearest to it, has no theology to speak of—nor has Buddhism, also very near. Christianity is superior by an element in it which to express is to state a theology, and to expound which has produced the only really great theology in the world. Of course it is not meant that every Christian must be capable of discussing or teaching scientific theology, nor indeed every minister. Like the Bible, it is the property of the corporate Church, rather than of individuals. Individuals should not be called on to assent to its scientific forms; but they ought to be called on to respect the place of these for the great Church and the great faith. They ought to be subdued to the frame of mind which is interested in interpreting the systems, instead of rejoicing in the ignorance which despises them. That is true of theology which the Reformers said about the Sacraments—the deadly thing is not ignorance of it, but scorn.

The misfortune which dogs us here is the fruit of individualism and sectarianism pursued as permanent ends, and not as temporary means or expedients. Church and theology are inseparable correlates. But in so many cases the independence of the single soul or sect has been cultivated till all sense of the great Church has gone. And in words about the One, Holy, Catholic, and Apostolic Church people cease to hear a solemn music. To their too suspicious and protesting minds such words carry but suggestions of the Pope behind every bush. Very many are in more danger from the abuse of their own liberty than they are from the authority of Rome. It is an extravagant and *insouciant* liberty that drives many to need and to welcome Rome. We do not need more liberty—at least in the circles nearest the present writer. We have won what we need, and more. What we most need is some authority for whose sake we may use it, and by whose guidance we may keep it from credal nihilism. We may, and do, so use our precious liberty that we both lose a center for the soul and drive the public into the most imperative Churches to escape an anarchy we do not seem able to stay. The fate is sealed of any Church whose creed is the region of its anarchy instead of the order of its mind. Free lances raid, they do not conquer. They keep the district awake, and even rob it of due sleep, but they do not bring life from the dead. It is impossible without a common, credible, and liberal type of belief to fulfill the Church's mission to save society. She cannot make herself respected, to say little of being trusted, still less of being nobly loved. We must have over individuals an objective which saves them from mere singularity. Let us keep in his proper place the man whose one argument for the Gospel is that it does him good and he feels it. He would say the same thing for some hours after a tasty meal loaded with ptomaines. The Gospel which fills human need is not to be measured by it.

We must recover the sense that we are all constituent members of the great federate, historic, universal, eternal Church, and all servants of a Gospel which would be true if it cost every man his happy comfort, as it cost the Saviour his in the dereliction which saved us on the Cross. We are the agents of a grace which our sects and communions have to serve and not exploit. And with that sense must return a new solidarity of generous belief, if we are to speak in the gate with the mind of a growing age, to state our message in terms commensurate with an educated world, and to confess our faith in the form of thought which strikes a kindred chord in those who think on a world-scale, and who do not simply peddle notions or dream with a raw and flamboyant ambition.

III

But let us view this matter of the intellectualism of religion from another side.

We can never have a biography of Christ in the modern and impressive sense of that word; and therefore we cannot get at what is known as the inmost religion of Jesus. By the religion of Jesus we may mean one of two things—either the staple of his teaching which we try to follow, or the manner of his experience which we try to reproduce. If we mean the former, we have it only in the New Testament, *i.e.*, in the apostolic interpretation which pervades even a Gospel like Mark. No other interpretation was ever known in the Church till the over-critical and artificial constructions of to-day. The whole history of the Church has been made on a totally different idea of Jesus from these, and one he printed on those who knew him best. We can never get at a religion from Jesus which can stand on better evidence than the apostolic Gospel of Him. How can we? We cannot get behind the Gospels, *i.e.*, behind the Jesus of the oldest Christian community, so far as documents go. (I do not forget Q, which was apparently found inadequate by the Church.) And this is a Jesus who is also the Christ (*i.e.*, the King), whose atoning, redeeming death was the crisis of history, and whose risen and regal life was the surest of spiritual things, as sure as catastrophe, death, and judgment. And either we have no historical Jesus, or we have him in the picture of his personality presented in the Gospels, written by men permeated with the evangelical interpretation of him. The same evidence which gives us the Synoptics gives them to us saturated with the apostolic Gospel, the Gospel common to Paul and Peter and John. The earliest community was that of Jerusalem, one therefore too Jacobean, too little creative, to give ground to doubt the fidelity of their version of Christ. They were nearest to Jesus, and they did not feel they were false to him in interpreting his Gospel as an atoning one. This is the plea of a critic so able as Jülicher, in his *New Lines in the Criticism of the Gospels*,[2] who also points out how little critical results, or efforts at a "religion of Jesus," can do for what the Cross and its evangelical theology serve so richly—the production of new religious life.

On the other hand, if we mean by the religion of Jesus his personal experience of God, his soul history, his inmost life, his spiritual psychology, this is beyond us—from the very nature and purpose of our documents, deep though we may now go on this track compared with our fathers. We can divine much as to his inner life, but not as to his inmost. We can never analyze his deepest motives, nor follow up either the causation of his resolves, the pragmatism of his acts, or the secret of his personality. Nor can we pursue where his life was hid in God. In this respect he is too elusive, and our constructions are too poor, too artificial. Who would venture to reconstruct one of his midnight prayers? "Others abide our question, He is free."[3] The story is too meager, and his told in another interest—in the evangelical interest, and not the psychological. Therefore as our interests begin to leave the simplest and broadest features of his life, as we seek to penetrate and refine, we are less and less impressed (however interested) from this interior source. We are in the region of conjecture, of imagination rather than revelation. So that we return to the other aspect of the religion of Jesus as the source of the impression made on us after all—what Jesus pleased to express in his teaching.

But if we do that, if we make that the gauge of revelation, are we not back again with the spirit and method of the Orthodoxies, though in a simpler and more gnomic form? Aphoristic orthodoxy replaces systematic. We are dealing with revelation as if it

---

2. Jülicher, *Neue Linen in der Kritik der evangelischen Uberliefrung*.

3. Arnold, "Shakespeare," line 1.

were a matter of truths and precepts (however kindling) instead of a matter of action, personality, and power, as if it were a theology instead of a grace that was revealed. We are responding to truths and statements, to Christ the prophet, rather than to Christ as God's personal presence and redeeming deed. It is the historic fact of the whole person, and especially the act (not the mere incident or casualty) of the Cross, that guarantees and continues for us the objectivity and reality of revelation. It is such spiritual history, such ethical effect as the eternal act of the Cross, that must save us from intellectualism—whether it be the intellectualism of Jesus the gnomic sage, the intellectualism of the credal systems, or the intellectualism of exact historical science. It is an historical theology, a theology whose shape is history rather than system, a theology whose interest is moral rather than dialectic, a theology crystallized in a Church rather than a creed, a theology of the immanent, ethical, and dynamic act,—that is what must save us from an intellectualist theology, old or new. In like manner, in philosophy, what we are now concerned with is not a hypothetical metaphysic of thought, but an energetic metaphysic of experience; not substantial Being, but universal energy; not a static entity, but a creative and evolutionary power, which does not furnish the ground of Being, but the fountain of life.

The kind of mind therefore that concerns us, our faith, and our future, is the mighty practical understanding which grasps, in a holy Redeemer, the whole moral situation of the race and its sin; it is not the capable intelligence, the ordinary, able, but often dull, intelligence, that correlates truth, or reforms the correlations of the past more or less aggressively. As Christianity is not a science, truth (in the modern sense of truth) is not its first charge. And, as it is not literature, it is not primarily concerned with an impressive style, or a neat and telling knack of putting sacred things. We have, above all, to do with life, with reality,—moral reality, which is the chief sense that the word truth has in the New Testament. We need more mind in our religion, not less, as the pietists plead: but it is the massive moral understanding, not the clear, crisp, and thin intelligence. We want the powerful dramatist, like Ibsen with his sense of guilt, not the smart playwright, like Bernard Shaw with his sense of incongruity and his elfish delight in its exposure. (Though even the cynicism of Mr. Shaw is better than the blind sentiment, or the stodgy naturalism, or the moral stupidity which exasperate him.) It is just this intelligence in one dimension, this flat intellectualism basted with sentiment, that so many of the new and glossy theologies promote. And what they neither show nor create is the searching moral understanding, taking joy in divine and saving judgment rather than delight in merciless analysis and exposure. This massive moral understanding is the greatest lack in the culture alike of our press, our pulpit, and our stage. They have not the sense of the moral tragedy of history, nor of the final *commedia* of God.

Theology becomes a matter of public moment, it ceases to be a mere pursuit, only when it becomes a piece of religion. In Christianity it is always that implicitly; and the present juncture has made it explicitly so. We have to call out our reserves. To ministers of the gospel especially, their theology is an essential part of their religion. To discard the theology is to "pith" the religion, to extract its marrow. Hence for us the cause of Christianity is practically the cause of Paul. What is challenged to-day, in the interest of what is called a "lay-religion," is the substantial Paulinism which contains the *differentia* of Christianity, and the note of its permanence, absoluteness, and finality. There is less question raised about the subjective religion of Christianity (except among those who follow the wild lead of a genius like Nietzsche). The whole issue is its theology. It is not its ethic, except in so far as its ethic is concentrated in the new and holy creation of the Cross, and made absolute in the New Humanity. It is there, in its Christology, for instance, that the battle must be fought which either saves or sacrifices its future. In a true sense I say it is a battle for Paul more than for Jesus—in the sense that, as Paul saved the Gospel of the Cross in the first century and in the sixteenth, so he must in the twentieth. And I will venture to express my sorrow and failing of heart when I hear this matter of our Christian creed treated, even by preachers, with an indulgent smile, as if it were an academic hobby instead of a believer's crisis: when it is dismissed with a veiled assumption all intelligence is wasted which does not go into religious sentiment, passing politics, or the social reforms of the hour; as if Christianity were there chiefly to magnify the child, the woman, or the workingman, rather than glorify God. These interests are indeed urgent, but it is a creed that is essential, it is a living creed about God and his grace that is the Church's greatest need. The first question for a Church is not what it does, but what it believes. It does too little because it believes too little. To denounce a theology is to announce atheology at last (if the truth will carry the quip). And it is for a creed rather than a programme that the trustees of Christianity in our pulpits are really crying out. They are crying out for it with an earnestness proportionate to their sense of the situation, and to their discovery of their own inadequacy to meet the situation when the vague young ardors that made their first capital are consumed in the fires of experience.

IV

That the creeds and theologies are the deadliest influences in the way of intellectualizing Christianity and removing it outside the pale of warm human interest or ethical concern, is not a view which the history of dogma will sustain. The whole *nisus* of the historic Church in this direction cannot have been a vast stupidity, unless the Church was abandoned by the Spirit in its early youth. And the whole inner object of the Reformation was to bring the religion of the Church back to its fundamental theology.

It is not the creeds that are intellectualist, but their idolaters or their critics. It is impossible to rise from a study of the Augsburg Confession without feeling that it is another than the intellectual interest that is supreme there. And even in the Athanasian Creed it is Redemption, and not metaphysic, that is the chief concern. That creed is the confession of eternal Redemption in the language of the hour. It is not the theologies of the Church that are academic, but some of the theologians—especially the amateurs and the half-educated among them. Also it should be noted that an intellectualism has followed on the great confessions (as in the seventeenth century), when they were taken in hand by the gospel-hardened successors of the great confessing age.

But there is another intellectualism that precedes the creeds—I mean the intellectualism of the heresies. It was the heresies that called the creeds into being. What is a creed? It is a necessary, but not a spontaneous, product, *non ut diceretur sed ne taceremut*. Every formal creed is an effort to adjust the positive faith of Christianity to the challenge created by some heresy. The heresy itself arose at certain points where secular history and natural thought came in contact with the surface of Christian faith or life. For Christianity has often as much to do in resisting the formative influences of an age as in absorbing them. Now the genius of natural thought is intellectual; and the genius of Christianity is voluntarist; it is moral. This means that its appeal is not to logic, nor to science, nor to any close thought or single idea, but to the will, the conscience, the personality, the life—to the region, that is, which defies and eludes our efforts at a perfectly coherent scheme of the world, to the region which transcends "sanity," and which Kant called the "Irrational." Christianity refuses to be explained by causes, or to take its rational place in a complete unity of conception. Its great and vital paradoxes, like the Trinity or the Cross, mock commonsense, and all that kind of preaching which is like stating a case clearly to a judge, or making a secretarial report on Christianity to a meeting of its shareholders. It deals with purposes, ends, and destinies rather than causes and coherencies; its object is neither a vote nor a verdict, but a venture of faith; and its unity is the unity of effective reality rather than of consistent truth, of telic purpose rather than organizing idea. It is as far beyond the intellectual grasp as our moral freedom is beyond scientific analysis or philosophic construction. Deep within the form of the confessions the reality and continuity of living Christian faith has been flowing on from the beginning.

> In Xanadu did Khubla Khan
> A stately pleasure-house decree,
> Where Alph the sacred river ran
> In caverns measureless to man.[4]

Our systems are such stately fabrics—and especially on their apologetic side. They are like great bridges thrown, at successive points, across the river of life; they are like palaces whose casements open upon the infinite sea in fairylands. Or, to change figure, in the interior of the Christian realm the life and business of the kingdom of God has been going quietly on, while a long series of frontier wars have engaged the energies of its apologists and the attention of the public. These apologists have only been called in

---

4. Coleridge, "Kubla Khan," lines 1–4.

to delimit a scientific frontier in the face of surrounding human nature. Often they have engaged in peaceful negotiation, but sometimes it came to a fight. And at intervals the situation became serious enough to compel a reference to the central government, a great (and sometimes unseemly) debate in the parliament of the Church, and authoritative action from its government. It was thus that the creeds came into being. They were indeed created by the Church's faith, they were not perversion of it. But they were not so much spontaneous expressions of the great realm's massive life as they were considered and strategic assertions of it in the face of a situation created from without. We have these inspired expressions of the Church's deep life in her liturgies rather than in her creeds, in the *Te Deum* rather than in the *Athanasium*.

In so far, therefore, the creeds were neither complete nor final. Nor could they be. For, in the first place, they must be psychologically inadequate. Faith must always fail, more or less, when it tries to give an account of itself, especially to the world.[5] It is so much more than it knows. It fails thus even in respect of its own time, far more in respect of a later age. And in the next place, they are for us intellectually inadequate. They were the verdict of Christendom on the mental junctures of a time now outgrown. They were conditioned, on the one hand, by that aspect of the Christian idea which happened to be uppermost at the hour—it might be Redemption, it might be Reconciliation, it might be Incarnation—and, on the other hand, they were determined by the form of the challenge from without. Now this challenge came mostly from the philosophies of the natural and rational man. It came mostly from some form of rationalism. Therefore the reply had to speak the same language. It bad to be intellectual and rational. But in the creed that was only the language. In the challenge which provoked the creed it was the matter, but in the reply it was only the language; in which another matter, a super-rational matter, strove to take an expression that could only be intelligible by being partial. The creeds are intellectual not in genius, not in substance, but in form—in so far they had to speak with intellectualism in the gate. In the Athanasian Creed the matter at issue was the reality, supremacy,

---

5. One reason why the Reformed Confessions are so much greater and deeper than the Ecumenical Creeds is that they were made to the Catholic Church, while the creeds were declarations for a pagan world.

and finality of Redemption, but the language, the form, was the metaphysic of the day. These creeds are replies by men of a new spiritual race (tracing, by a second birth, from Christ, and not from Adam), to men who for the most part were but once born, and who did not seize the personal, volitional, and regenerate nature of Christianity, but were arrested by its external, humane, and rational side. The life of Christianity has never been dependent in the first degree upon the power of its believers to commend and adjust themselves to the day's philosophy, to those constructions of the world that prevailed in the surrounding civilization. For Christianity is not a part of culture. It is not one of the tributaries of civilization, nor one of its products. Its history refuses to be explained by the science of comparative religion; its nature and genius is intractable to any other science than its own. It is a main stream, perfectly independent and unique, rising in the miraculous heights of a fresh divine causation; and if it ever join with the stream of civilization, it receives that stream as a tributary, and absorbs it into the vaster volume and power won from the moral heights where it rose. Its history is a positive and autonomous thing. So is the Church, as the only society that faith directly creates and controls. It rose far and high, directly from God in his Son. And it is fed all along its course by the influx of rivulets innumerable that spring from the less direct action of the Spirit upon the wills of men in natural society. The line of its course through history is indeed determined by the features of the country through which it flows, by the geology, so to say, of the natural man; often, too, it is discolored from its banks, or deflected by nature's convulsions. But its volume, power, and quality are all its own. And its total direction and purpose are prescribed (with whatever windings) by the hills where its life rose and the sea to which it goes. To drop metaphor, its intellectual variations have been, and must be, great; but the moral genius of its life-power, the action of its Holy Spirit, remains autonomous, positive, continuous, and imperative. There is a great creed within the creeds, and a persistent spiritual burden and vital purpose, which ought to recast them rather than discredit them. Its face wears countless expressions of sympathy, and it is the fruitful mother of a thousand more. The note of moral deliverance, of guilt and its holy conquest, the note of Eternal Life, still sounds and dominates these to the attuned and cultivated ear, on the scale of a whole complex humanity. And the faith that triumphs is not, in the first degree, a faith that adjusts in a scheme the many colliding forces of the world, or presents a *Weltanschauung*[6] systematically complete; but it is a faith that issues from a central act of world-reconciliation met by repentant personal faith. That is to say, it has its element in those moral powers of the new creation, the new birth, the New Humanity, the new world, which confound our logic; and it has its consummation in the final redemption of souls reconciled, far more than of forces harnessed, or thoughts harmonized. It has to do, primarily, not with saving knowledge or its sum, but with a saving Personality and the Church which He saves—saves, and does not simply impress. There lies reality, not in thought, but in experience, in regenerate experience, which replaces man's dislocated center upon the eternal center of the moral universe, and in a corporate experience. Experience is a concourse of Egos, of wills. Reality, therefore, is a kingdom of will, personality, and action. Its world is far profounder, more elusive, and more intractable than the world of processional or conflicting ideas. It is a kingdom, not a process. It is a world of warring wills subdued into a cosmos, and not a mere congeries. Its end is not a resultant, but a conquest. And its goal is a new world wherein dwells not consistency, but righteousness, yea holiness; a world which demands, for the gauging of it, far more massive mind than the idealisms do, and ever so much more than the systems; a world incomprehensible except to the will of the Spirit in whom it was created, reconciled, and redeemed.

The supreme concern of Jesus was the love of God to sinners. It was not God's general kindness to weak men, but his gracious love to sinful men. It was his merciful kindness and not his genial spirit, his forgiving and not his benevolent love, his grace and not his pity. God's revelation was not his kindly care of his creature, not his shining sun nor his helping hand; but his redeeming will of holiness, and its absolute power to overcome and rule the whole of history at the center and at the last. The news of the Father who makes his sun to rise on the evil and the good is, as a gospel, incomplete—like the story of the prodigal, which was not a gospel, but one illustration of a gospel at one great angle of it.

6. ["Worldview."]

Neither message could have established itself in the world without the atoning Cross. There was too little tragedy in them to cope with so tragic a world. But the parable comes the nearer to the heart of grace. We must always interpret Christ's Messianic consciousness in these terms of the Cross, and its theology, of the living grace latent in him always. It sent him down among the people with his healing word, instead of out of the wilderness with John's trumpet tone. And it brought him to the Cross, charged as a subverter of the divine order of society, and a supplanter of the elder brother in the father's regard; so bitter against grace can religious nature be. One keeps meeting, within the Church itself, frequent surprises which, by their avowed sympathy with the elder bother, show the lengths to which respectable nature will go in its *nisus* against grace, the "righteous" against the repentant, the prosperous against the prodigal, society against the sinner, the rational against the wretched, the happy possessors of the kingdom against the outlanders grace reclaims from the world.

V

Nothing but the eternal act of the Cross, and no analysis of it, can convey what Christ came to bring.

It is true that Jesus *taught*, in every way suggested by his rich mind at the moment, the love of God to sinners, the love that seeks rather than enjoys, and delights to find even more than to possess.

It is true, farther, that he not only taught but *felt* the love of God to sinners—never indeed to himself as prodigal sinner, but in himself as perfect saint. He felt to sinners as God felt. His love to them was as God's love. And his compassion was as God's— chiefly for their sin—deep for their sorrow, but deepest for their guilt.

Farther still, it is true that he not only felt this gracious love of God, but he *exercised* it. He was the high steward and plenipotentiary of God's saving love. He was not simply its voice, nor its reflection, nor even its agent, but its sacrament. He dispensed alike the pity, the judgment, and the forgiveness of God by life and deed. And especially the forgiveness. It was his forgiveness, more than his denunciations, that roused the hatred of the Pharisees. Forgiveness is exasperating patronage if we do not feel we need it.

All his acts of pity and healing were exercised by him as acts of forgiveness (as the Church's philanthropy is but a fruit of its Gospel). To the sick of the palsy he said, "Thy sins are forgiven thee." That was his reading of the central, radical situation of suffering humanity. And this is the greatest function of his Cross—to convey God's grace to sin in a sacramental way, as the radical, final, eternal remedy of the Almighty, All-searching Eternal for human ills.

But we must go a step farther. He not only taught, felt, exercised the love of God to sinners: he was not only its sacrament, nor its symbol, he *incarnated* it. He conveyed it only because he incarnated it. And to incarnate the love of a God who is love, is to be God. All our previous terms have been too poor. Even sacrament. We have sacraments of him, but he was more than a sacrament of God. For a sacrament is a created thing. All these terms are too poor for the work love has to do with us sinners. Even the sympathy they convey, close and warm as it is, is a sympathy too detached for the need of our case. He was love; and he believed with all his soul in God's love. But was his love actually God's? It is one thing to say it was as God's, the divinest we know, what God's love would be if God loved. But does he? Is God love, and is this the loving God? Is this utter man inmost God? It this man, who is the last word of spiritual humanity, the Eternal Word of Holy God? For the redemption we needed, we needed a God not only near and warm but identified with us, and therefore *sure* to us in a certainty that nothing but Incarnation could effect. The Christian faith gives us an intimate Christ who was, in deed as in word, the very Son of God, in the sense of being God the Son. If he be not God's incarnate love, all he does is to *report* on God's love, either by word or deed, to give us God's truth where we needed God's life. And that is the bane of intellectualism, orthodox or heterodox. It is something more than a witness borne from without God that we need for our absolute and certain faith. It is the very presence and action there, in us, of God himself. To deny this is to fail to grasp the moral situation which for religion is a fatal failure. But this presence and action of God in the conscience of the race is what the Gospel of Christ gives. As a matter of experienced fact we do get God there, touching, seizing, judging, saving, and changing us. This interpretation is the only possible justice to such religion of Jesus as we can reach. The faith of those first Christians who were in closest contact with the religious Jesus was that he was much more than religious, that he was the object of religion more than its subject, that he was the Son of God, with a title to their worship like God's title, and an action upon them which drew that that worship from them in spite of themselves. Were they wrong? Was his real action upon them so poor after all, so false, so unsteady, that it could not protect them from an error so tremendous as that of worshiping him as God, which they certainly did, and setting him with God on the great white throne? So to worship Christ is to treat him as other in kind from all mankind besides.

The only utterance which can grasp the whole actual moral of an active sinful world is a personal act of the Holy One, and an act of more than mundane scope prolonged within the experience of the Church. The salvation must share the nature of the sin in so far as this, that it must be an act, and an act at least as great as the moral solidarity of the race. It cannot be any statement about God or grace by the word of the wisest sage, nor even any reflection of Him mirrored in the life of the humanest and purest saint. For Redemption, prophets and saints were failures. Christ himself failed as prophet. The moral reality of the guilty world can only be dealt with as it is grappled by the personal act of a Soul more than commensurate with the world; by the act, therefore, of one essentially greater than the world of nature or man; the act of one with a greatness more than human or cosmic; the eternal, saving act of one so adequate to see and do as the Son of God. Apart from this, if he overcame the world it was only in himself and for himself, as we all have to do. It was only in his section of the world. But he conquered and saved on the scale of the whole world, nay of God. And no less a Soul than that, vaster than man and the peer of God, could, with all he saw of the total situation of man and history, possess and command himself in such power and peace as made him master easily of every passing situation, free to play his foes with the wit, the dialectic, and the irony of the Most High, and able to forgive as only he could against whom we sin, and to save as he alone could from whom we were lost.

17

Intellectualism and Faith

I

One of our Premiers once said that the sterling British mind neither liked nor understood cleverness. How true it is! How fortunate that it is true! We do take to Samuel Johnson; we do not take to Mr. George Bernard Shaw. The saying indicates a real source of our peculiar place and power in the world. We have a healthy dread of Intellectualism. We have, of course, the defects of that quality, which are revealed in time of war, whether on the veldt or in the soul. We have a fatal fear of knowledge and of education. We are bewildered as problems grow subtle, and our stupidity turns silliness. But suspicion of the clever is a great quality, rightly taken. Judgment is a greater gift than ability. The world is neither to be understood nor managed by sheer talent, logic, or knowledge. The greatest movements in the world have been irrational, or at least non-logical. And the irrationality of the world, the faith of a principle which flows underneath reason on the one hand, and of a power which rises beyond it on the other, and even seems to reverse it, has done more to keep religion quick and deep than any sense of the world's intelligent nature or consistent course. Faith, which is the greatest power of history, flourishes, and even exults, on the offence of the Cross, and the paradox of the spirit.

Is there, then, for Briton or for Christian, a premium on stupidity? Must piety be humdrum? What concord has faith with dullness? or what fellowship has Christ with the dunces? What enmity has Christ with mind? In what sense must we become fools for Christ's sake?

In the first place, it may be said, no mere fool can see how foolish the world's wisdom is with God. Of course, any fool can gird at a scholar, but it needs an able man to realise the insignificance of mere ability; while the worship of prompt intellect is a sign of intellectual poverty. The pestilent wit is the man who spends himself on wit. The merely clever man has no idea how little cleverness goes for in affairs, how different it is from a powerful sagacity. Cleverness seldom goes with greatness; it is not dramatic enough, for all its love of effect. The course of the world mocks the mere acuteness of man. And, says Pascal, the man who lives for *bons mots* has a bad heart. He meant Gallic wit, and living for salons. For *bons mots*, in the sense of the just, pointed, *frappant* phrase, abound even in the New Testament, and especially in the Gospels.

One thinks in this connection of Christ's dialectic, so easy and so effectual, in His controversies with the religious dunces and quacks of His day, the readiness of His wit, the happy skill of His fence, the deadly stroke, and the ironic parry. One recalls His deft handling of every situation, the aptness of His phrase, and the incisiveness of His epithets. "You solemn mummers!" "You quacks!" "You brood of snakes!" "Tell that fox." We note His paradoxes, His epigrams, His "lose your life to save it," His "serve to rule," His "give to gain." We mark the congenial way in which a witty faith appealed to Him, and fairly mastered Him, in the reply of the Syrophœnician.

His wit is well recognised—His gracious wit and His wounding wit; but He is charged with the lack of humour, of an element so great, if not essential, in humanity as humour. And some of His servants who possessed the gift have thought it stood in their way for His work. But it is not that Jesus had none, but that he had not the Western, Shakesperean, modern type. He had the type that goes with the prophet's genius, with the genius of Israel, the genius of ethical insight and exaltation, the genius of Isaiah, of Socrates, of Paul, of Pascal. He had irony, as all these had. He not only saw the irony of the world, but He exercised upon His foes the lofty irony of God. What was His silence before Pilate? Or "those ninety and nine just persons that need no *repentance*"? It betokens the deepest foundation, and the repose of unearthly power, to be able amid crises to play so freely about life as His insight and irony did. The odd thing is that, while the sunny Shakesperean humour, or the genial humour of daily life, is not felt by most Christian people to be foreign to Christ, or at least to Christian faith, the ironic humour, tending to the bitter, is so felt. As if Jesus was never bitter and sarcastic! How bitter was that, "It cannot be that a prophet perish out of Jerusalem"! The Bible has much more room for the humour of Carlyle than for that of Scott, for the grim than for the sunny. Nothing could show more clearly than this soft horror of irony and of scorn for the quack, how far the popular Christian mind has gone from the Christ of the Gospels, how the conception of the loving Jesus, being overdriven, has demoralised the Christian public, how false is the mere genial Jesus, or the merely domestic Jesus of fireside faith, how greatly we need to be forced back on the virility, what I might call the firstrate-mindedness, of this passionate Man, on His moral realism, on His sense of law, and holiness, and wrath, and of the bitter shams and incongruities of life—and of the religious life not least. It is not quite wonderful that men like Carlyle and Meredith should have been consumed with contempt for the "parson-opium" of the Victorian Age. We need to be urgently reminded of that in Him which so grasped the eternal verities that He could apply them to each juncture with an incision that made even His own afraid to ask Him any questions.

We note, further, in the Epistles the extraordinary felicity, pungency, and pregnancy of expression, as well as the acumen of the dialectic, to say nothing of the sacred pun. We recall Paul's exultation in the irony of the Cross in 1 Corinthians 1—the foolishness of God is wiser than men. In many respects the Bible is the wittiest book in the world; it is certainly not the most lucid, matter-of-fact, or simple of feeling. Jesus was not a plain man. We follow up with the brilliant style of many of the Fathers, and no few of the Reformers—to name but Tertullian, Augustine, Zwingli, and Erasmus. And it becomes harder than ever to explain the popular idea that Christian goodness should be monopolised by the dense and the slow of heart, or that the trusty must be the dull. We do not forget, of course, the patience of Christianity with the weak and slow, and its destination for mankind, and not for a cultivated *élite*. These features of it help to explain the association that has grown up. Something is also due to the recent substitution of mere piety for faith, and to the common use of religion as a refuge when we have so spent ourselves on the world as to be fit for nothing else but a rest-cure as we turn to God. No doubt other factors of the situation would emerge if we gave ourselves to its analysis. But that would perhaps be more interesting than useful.

The dunce, of course, will always see in the witty only the acrobatic or the smart. But is there not all the difference in the world between the mind-play of the moral master and that of the mental elf, between swift lambency and nimble coruscation, between the beam of the burning sun and the flash of the manufactured spark, between the lucid and the fulgid, between the lustre of paradoxical truth and the phosphorescence of freakish wit? Do we not all part the man who sparkles like a rich diamond at a chance angle from the other man who crackles like a made-up firework? There is the man whose good points drop from him accidentally while he addresses himself *ad rem* rather than *ad populum*; and there is the man who speaks on commission, and evidently in order to make a setting for the phrases he concocted to fetch the surprise. Is it not one thing to hunt for epigrams and antitheses, and another to see all things set one against another, and so deeply to read the paradox of existence as to be able to be briefly just to it only by phrases that compass two worlds? Is it not one thing to play the fool, and another to recognise our human need of nonsense—as Hazlitt was the first to note that Shakespeare did? Is it superfluous to point out that intellectual agility is one thing and moral acumen quite another, that mental vivacity is not effective grasp, that the keenest sight will not do the work of insight, and that we live by insight and not by sight? Carlyle speaks of Mrs. Mill as possessing a great deal of unwise intellect. It is not a rare possession; and it may be the cause of more failure in life than stupidity. What life has chiefly to do with is not a world of truth sharply presented to us, but a world of reality deeply working on us, and intimately experienced in us. And in religion above all things it is with reality we have to do more than with truth. Faith lies far nearer the dramatic sense than the intellectual. It is an act of ours answering a creative action in God—but a pointed issue, a crisis, an epigram of action. Truth may be a matter of vivid perception, but reality is a matter of intimate practical penetration. The God who is denied as an intellectual truth may be worshipped as a moral reality, as every Kantian knows. And faith lives in a vast antinomy.

II

Such observations open up for us the whole question of the place of mind in faith—either as the play of mind upon an occasion, or the grasp of mind upon reality.

It is frequent to-day to hear a protest against theology, on the ground that it is an intellectualising of what is really a religion of the heart and conscience, that it is the capture of Christianity by an aristocracy of subtle or ingenious intellect. But it might arrest some of this mindlessness if time were taken to ask what theology means in each case. We should then note that there is theology and theology. There is what may be called a primary theology and a secondary. And they are thus distinct. The one is the statement of faith, the other its exposition. The former belongs to the very nature and conveyance of Christian faith, the other belongs rather to its scientific treatment. The one is verified by experience, the other by thought.

Our first task in life is not to see a clear truth but to grasp an actual situation. We have not to perceive so much as to realise. We have not to watch the procession but to march in it. Religion especially has to do only in a secondary way with truths, statements, aspects, and co-ordinations, however clear or however pointed. With all the scientific side of things, with the way things lie, its concern is secondary. But it has in the first degree to grasp and deal with the way things work, with a practical situation, with the reality involved in our personal situation, historic and bequeathed, or experienced and intimate. And as that is a moral and actual situation of life, and not a scientific construction of truth, the intelligence required for life, and for the faith which rules life, is not intellectual, and not academic, but it is active and sagacious. The great matter is not the intellect but the understanding. Who speaks of Scott's or Shakespeare's intellect? It is their understanding, their grasp of life, that tells. Many a man who is slow in his wits has a wonderful power of gauging an actual situation. Many a man devoid either of science, taste, or the faculty of expression yet has the understanding that bottoms affairs, masters life, and commands his fellows. He is of the quiet, awkward men who do things. He has the instinct for what matters and the capacity for what rules. If he have not pathetic humour, or Gallic wit, he may have ethical humour, dry humour, or even the irony of the prophet. With such minds the chief use of the intelligence as the servant of personality is not in adjusting facts but in weighing them. We use our mind better in asking sin's weight than its origin. Our mind is there not to give us a centre but to lead us to a spring. It does not give us our bearings so much as couple us up with our source of power. The intellect is, for the purposes of life, an organ of estimate, far more than of mere cognisance. It makes value judgments (as the phrase goes). It assesses things rather than places them. And it sees in them a value which may be in ironical contrast with their actual place. That is its great function for *life*—appraisement, and not orientation. And the order of mind that runs to that use of the intelligence is the order that effects most, whether in history or in faith. But intellectualism on the other hand is intellect detached, acting outside life without being morally involved or committed, without practical judgment or grasp of complete situations. It is intellect either at play, or at mere exercise, or on parade. It is at sport, gymnastics, or pose, rather than at actual work among things. It is the literary rather than the parliamentary intellect. It loves to criticise from platforms but not to act on committees. And that is the cleverness, superior and doctrinaire, or elfish and irresponsible, which is so alien both to our national and Christian temper. Would, indeed, that our intelligence had more alert play and abandon about it! Would we were less dense, dour, or grim! Would we could laugh at our enthusiasms a little without losing them, and be intensely in earnest without taking ourselves so very seriously! Would that we were less the victims of the merely serious, and more of the truly sagacious! But only so long as that improvement is not secured at the cost of moral judgment, practical insight, and command of affairs.

It is not with truth that our intellect has chiefly to do, I repeat, but with reality. And reality is in the nature of action. It has to do with experience more than thought. We study, not in order to become pedants, but to go into action properly equipped. To cope with final reality and be adequate to it, our intelligence must be capable rather than clever, ethical in its nature rather than rational, experienced more than able, theological and not theosophic. The question we have first to meet is one which so many people will do anything rather than face. It is, "Where are we?" As business people we take stock and balance books periodically; as religious people there is nothing we shirk more. And that question does not mean, "What is man's place in the cosmos?" (which, as it keeps us from self-examination, is a very marketable line of inquiry), but, "What is our actual moral condition with reality? How is it with our soul?" (an inquisition which, as it makes us take ourselves in hand, has not ready sale). The question is, What is our actual, habitual, personal relation to the last reality? How do we grasp that with which, as living souls, we have chiefly, radically, and eternally to do? It is dreadful how little fear we feel before that to-day. If there is anything more formidable it is the way some pietisms can fondle it. But no nimbleness of apprehension can seize it, no alert ability can handle it, nor indeed welcome it. And accordingly some desperately or idly think that what cleverness cannot do here must be done by ignorance, that the good man need know little, that he may bungle the utterance of what he knows, and that the true illuminate must be illiterate. This is a delusion so current in religion because religion has to do with the greatest of actual situations and realities for all men, therefore with a region where the race is not to the swift, and mere mind is absurdly at fault. But for all that there was never a great thing done yet by a stupid or ignorant man. If the great thing was done it was done by one who had enough intelligence to grasp the situation, who had the practical wit to grasp with two hands its opposing sides, and who had enough practical knowledge to cope with it. Many great things have been done by illiterates, but none by fools. There is no beatitude for the dunce.

Every ray of intellectual light we have is to force, and enable us the better to put, the question, "Where am I?" "What doest thou here, Elijah?" It is not a question, "What do I hold?" but, "How do I behave to what holds me?" It is not, "What can I make of the world?" but, "How do I stand to what is given me in a world?" It is not, "What do I know?" but, "How far do I realise that I am known?" It is not, "How do I conceive the divine truth of the world?" but, "How do I meet the divine action in the world?" Not, "Do I see the cohesion of God's great truth?" but, "Do I gauge and answer the bearing of God's eternal act?" Not, "How do I feel about God?" but, "What dealings have I with Him?" Our first concern is not with the riddle of the Universe: it is with the tragedy of the Universe. And, in faith's name at least, we may only complain about poverty of intellect if it leave the Church unfit to grasp the moral dimensions of that tragedy, and therefore to gauge its gravity, or its redress—which things it sometimes seems slowly, and often incompetently, even flippantly, ceasing to do. It is here that concern for a theological religion (as distinct from a theosophic) becomes of prime urgency for a Church that claims to know where it is, or to gauge the moral world. For what is theology (as based on revelation) but a spiritual grasp of the moral, the human, tragedy, in God's terms and with God's power. So when I hear it charged that the theologians wish to make faith the victim of intellect, I want to carry the war into the other camp. The complaint we have to make is that the modern world is becoming the victim of intellectualism for lack of theological faith. And under a shell of ethical interest it is becoming hollow in moral power and judgment, for want of a moral theology.

This may readily seem to such victims one of the paradoxes by which ingenuity amuses itself at the cost of seriousness. So little do they realise their situation, so slight is their world. But I will try to make the statement good.

III

A favourite form of that reaction from serious faith which makes the amateur dislike of theology is this. It falls back from Christ the Victim and Atoner of the world's moral tragedy upon Jesus the Teacher of spiritual wisdom. It disowns, sometimes with cheap anger, the sophistication of this loving and devoted Jesus by the intellectualism of the divinity schools. It dismisses the cry of the conscience for a day's-man, and explains it away as an extravagant perversion of the natural ache of finitude, produced by a tradition of monastic self-torment. The need of an Atonement it gets rid of by tracing it to crude Jewish notions about sacrifice, aggravated by pagan mollifications, and accentuated by mediæval jurisprudence, with its ideas of compounding for the damage of an offence. And it recurs to those simple interests of the heart which (it says) are so warmly and really met by the words of the Master. (For St Paul we may note that Christ was his Owner, but for modern self-respect He is only our Master, when He passes beyond our Brother.) It has recourse, therefore, to the teaching of Jesus. And my case is, that in doing so it retires from the living present we experience to the remote past of which we learn, from the living, reconciling Christ to the merely historic and hortatory Jesus. It leaves the region of spiritual reality and moral experience in the classic protagonists of the conscience, and it succumbs in the name of history to the intellectualism which has been the note of orthodoxy and the death of religion. The cry for the simple teaching of Jesus, the simple religion of Jesus, is a piece of fatal intellectualism and orthodoxy. That is the absurd statement I have to try to make good.

What I am saying is that every denial of the central, final, crucial, and saving value of Christ's death, both for His life and ours, is based on this vicious, intellectualist, and gnomic idea of revelation. Sooner or later it reduces Christ to a teacher. It denounces doctrine in the interest of the doctrinaire. And I will put it thus. I will suppose that you recognise that Jesus came to deal with the conscience and its sin, and not merely with the heart and its aches. He had to do with our tragic guilt more than our tragic lot. You then go on to say that He did so deal with sin by telling us (with supreme impressiveness) of a loving, forgiving God instead of a holy, judging, redeeming God. He makes statements, with convincing magnetism, of a loving God who is ever ready to forgive when we repent. He does this, instead of really bringing a God who is carrying our sin, meeting His own judgment, actually redeeming, and creating repentance in the process. You say that Jesus replied to our laborious morbid concern about our soul by telling us of a better way, urging us to take it, promising us divine help in taking it, and assuring us of its safety, with all the force of a most earnest personality. Now, what is that but intellectualism? It declares that our case can be met by something in the way of fervid information, by something urgently exhibitory, by the goodness of God being made to pass vividly before us, by something we are sublimely told about God; that is, by certain statements, certain truths which Jesus supremely, and even authoritatively, declared as His convictions. But wherever you have salvation by truth or truths, however warmly opened up or kindly declared, there you have intellectualism. It does not matter whether the truths be simple or complex, whether they are those of a gnomic sage or of a reasoned system. If the prophet has no more than his intuition to give us, backed by his character, if he do no more than avouch his experience, and if he do not give us himself, or his deed, in a real, positive, and effective sense, then it is but statement he can give us, however luminous, however glowing. It is a statement of his experience or conviction of God. Now our experience we can but state or express. We cannot transfer it. It can only be created in others at the same source—unless it be the mere epidemic of a crowd—and all we can do is to bring men to that source with a certain will to believe. Therefore it is that we preach not ourselves but Christ—Christ, and not our experience of Him—not even the religious experiences of Jesus Himself. For we should then be saved, not by Jesus, but by the teaching, the testimony, the recorded insights and impressions of Jesus, not by the truth which is Jesus, or which He achieved, but by the truth which (rightly or wrongly) impressed and engrossed Jesus, according to His statement. And it makes no difference to the case whether the doctrine be gnomic or dialectic, sententious or systematic, nor whether the statement be scientific or sympathetic, cold fact or hot gospeling. It is dogmatic all the same. It is salvation by statement winged by personality, by doctrine incandescent in a prophet. It says that Christ's testimony of God was quite parallel to the testimony of Christ by Apostles or Fathers. In principle there is no difference whether the doctrine be the Sermon on the Mount or the Athanasian Creed.

But surely, it is objected, one of these is ethical, the other metaphysical. But the one is as ethical as the other at root, when we consider that their real matter and shaping interest is salvation. And when we consider their form or method, each is doctrinaire. Each is in the form of statement, of preaching, of theology rather than religion. In each we face a mirror of God and not God's gift of Himself. Each assumes the mode of statement congenial to its place and hour. Athanasius did not teach metaphysics; he taught the Gospel; but he did it in the language of metaphysics. But, allowing for the metaphysics, that is what the Sermon on the Mount is. It is statement and appeal—it is not action. It is mere preaching, it is not saving. In the Sermon on the Mount Jesus speaks as yet but as a religious sage, *i.e.*, as a saintly moral theologian, rather than as personal Redeemer. He speaks about life, conduct, and God; He does not mediate them. In the Sermon He faces men as a prophet; in the Cross He comes to grips with them as a Saviour.

Truth or truths about the spiritual life, if they stand alone, are intellectualist however impressive, or, to use a word fitter in some ways, they are æsthetic however penetrating. They may produce the certainty of knowledge but not of salvation. The speaker is not the object, he only has his eye on the object, with more or less power and veracity. He is a percipient rather than an agent, a hearer rather than a doer, or, as it would be put in the language of art, an æsthete rather than a poet, a seer rather than a maker. He is a reporter of his convictions rather than a creator of reality. His person is not the life, but only points to it or mirrors it. His personality may be a great dynamic for his principle, but it is not itself God in a gift, the Resurrection and the Life. He may talk of the living God with extraordinary power, but he is not God in life. He is still the preacher, the helper, he is not the Saviour. He is God's organ for effect, but he is not with us and in us as Life. He has something to tell us which has a great influence in making us; but it is not he that makes us, it is we ourselves, with his help. He is not the new Creator.

For those who would take this line in New Testament criticism the great effort is to get back as closely as possible to what Jesus really said. If we had that in its original form (it is held) we should have the best and greatest that He brought. The value of His personality was to give wings to His message, to feather His arrows of light. That message would be the real revelation, which therefore would not be in Himself but in His truth, His report. What is communicated to us is not God but doctrine, or even enthusiasm, about God. We receive lofty, urgent, or gracious exhortation on that basis, and deep impressions from a prophetic personality. Imaginative intellectualism and impressive conviction on the supreme subject is all we then should have. The revelation is in the doctrine, not in the historic person, facts, or acts. That is the point. And that is the bane of orthodoxy. No facts of revelation have then special value as facts, but only as they are incidental to the activity of Jesus as a Teacher who drew death down on Himself by the unpopularity of His momentous doctrine and the courage of its expression.

And this intellectualism, this orthodoxy (aphoristic or systematic), runs through much that is known as up-to-date theology. Modernism, dropping much even of the teaching of Jesus, and almost indifferent to His history, seeks to keep the Church alive on its dogmas taken as ideas, on truth emptied of the person yet treated as the power. But, however modern, that theology is simply exchanging old lamps, old clothes, old views for new. For it is a case of views or truths either way, new or old, narrow or broad; and it is not a case of act and deed in the heart of universal reality. The Cross appears as an exhibition, an object-lesson, an enacted statement, a crowning testimony, and not as a final achievement for the race. God reveals Himself in truths rather than in acts, in divine doctrine rather than in divine deed, in statements rather than in history, in instructive activity rather than in a sacramental or a creative act. His object is the most effective publication of His truth. His organ is the most gifted seer rather than the most effectual doer. And, where Jesus is the organ, salvation is through the impression He makes by His martyr death rather than by the work He achieves, and the world-crisis He solves, by His redeeming will. Jesus is the great figure in the history of religion rather than the great power in the religion of history. He talks aptly to the nature of the religious soul, but He does not handle aptly the total and eternal situation of the moral soul in the universe, nor deal with it for good and all. He speaks to the need of the heart; but He does not assure us that He is its food, and that He has the final disposal of a universe which is warranted to fill the heart's needs, and not flout them, at last. He is simply convinced in the deepest way that all things work together for good to them that love; He is not the guarantee of it, the ground of it—Himself the agent and anticipation of it. He appears in history, but is He the focus of the historic crisis, of the Lord's one controversy with man? In Him God reveals Himself to history, rather than in history, and through it. His revelation inspires action in us rather than forms the decisive action by God. His person preaches to us rather than re-creates us. Jesus diagnoses the soul's deep condition and prescribes for it, rather than determines its final destiny. He speaks powerfully to the question rather than takes command of the situation. His work is æsthetic rather than dramatic. The anti-theologians are thus the intellectualists—only they intellectualise in saws instead of systems, and by maxim rather than method.

The cure for this intellectualism, whether old or new, orthodox or rationalist, drastic or dreamy, is history—but history treated religiously not scientifically, morally not psychologically, and answered by faith and not mere assent, history as *Geschichte* and not mere *Historie*. It is history as the soil and series of revelation. It is a history whose old Jesus is our Eternal Christ—the Lord the Spirit. The prominent thing in Christianity is not a seer's eternal truth but a Person's eternal deed and gift. It is not the doctrine but the Cross. In the beginning was the endless Act. And the Cross is here taken not as the closing incident of the martyr life of Jesus, but, first, as the supreme action of the Son of God, and the supreme crisis of man's fate, and, second, as the eternal act of a Person thus present with us still. Revelation is only Christian as redemption, and not as mere manifestation. It does not say things, it does them. Its effect is not a belief, nor a school, nor a mood of mind, but a faith, a church, and a kingdom, all living only because Jesus Christ lives in them in this eternal act. The great historic act leaves for its great historic product a living society in which it "functions." Its first-fruits are not theologians but believers, not disciples but a church of active confessors. Its answer is not the mere resonance of assent but the response of faith, not impression but regeneration, not mere correspondency but commerce with God. We are not Christ's disciples merely, but His subjects. And we are not so much Christ's subjects even, but His property, by conquest, by purchase, by redemption—phrase it as you will. In living faith we are not simply loyal; we are in no respect our own. Loyalty is but one aspect of faith and quite incomplete. Loyalty mostly means fidelity to a king who yet has no business in our conscience. But the kingship of Jesus is much more Oriental than that. He sits, by a right He created, on the throne of conscience, in absolute command of our whole moral self. It is His, for He made it in our new creation. We are not quickened but changed. You may have the most impressive addresses for the deepening or quickening of the spiritual life, yet they are all but flushes brought to our face till Jesus Christ enter our history for good at its core and crisis, live in our heart by faith, and Himself become our new life. They are but impressionist, not sacramental. The way the Church invites this seer or that to lift or revive it on some particular occasion may or may not be wise and proper, but it is a confession of the absence of this life, and of a starved preoccupation with views and interests rather than facts and powers, with impression rather than regeneration.

Intellectualism and Faith

I know that some feel the inadequacy and the danger of the mere teaching of Jesus, but, as they will do anything rather than call themselves His δοῦλοι, and take that yoke of the Cross which has made theologians of the most thorough Christians, they seek to escape from their rationalism by going behind the doctrine of Jesus to His life and character, as revealed by a scientific historicism in the Synoptics. (Scientific historicism—it may be observed in passing—when it is made the basis of faith, is a piece of intellectualism or mind-worship.) They view Him either as a powerful example, or as an æsthetic source of the deepest impressions—only not as absolute Redeemer and rightful Owner of our wills.[1] It is in vain, however, that we seek to escape the intellectualism of Jesus the doctrinaire by the impression of Jesus the hero or saint. Ethical magnetism will not deliver us from the bondage to mere knowledge, nor from the cult of the religious genius and his illumination. The choice between Jesus the prophet and Christ the Redeemer is in the long run imperative and sharp. If He preach by His character, it is yet but preaching, so long as we are preoccupied with His life, so long as His person is not consummated in the saving act of a death which has its chief value for God, and is decisive for eternal human fate. Did we regard Him as the complete saint, and the divinest lover of His kind, He would yet be but one *from whom we learned* and not one *in whom we believed*—believed in the serious sense of putting our souls into His hands for ever as the hands of God, which is the Christianity and the faith of the New Testament taken as a whole. By the very perfection of His silent character He might be no more than a reporter of God, in the sense of a witness, a reflector, instead of God with us, and working in us. And wherever Jesus is but God's supreme prophet you have religion sinking in due course to a rationalism, Pharisaic or Sadducean, orthodox or heterodox, from which all the prophets were found unable to save Israel. Prophetism cannot in perpetuity moralise intellect, or worship, or action. It did not do so in Israel, nor has it done so in Islam (in spite of the Spanish Moors). It could not do it even in Jesus as prophet. That is only possible to a Christianity of redemption and reconciliation by the Cross.

---

1. I do not think Herrmann's noble and vivid picture of the action on us of the inner life of Jesus really lifts us above profound moral impressionism; it does not give the regeneration.

Now the dilemma between these two views of Christ may slumber unrealised without doing serious harm. But it cannot always slumber. And when it is forced into consciousness the choice becomes a matter of life and death to Christianity and its future—nay, ere long, to personal religion. For the wrong choice places Christianity simply in the chain of religious evolution, with a promise of something better one far day. The right makes it God's last but eternal Word to the race. The wrong view believes that Christ came to serve Humanity, by improving its fundamentally sound position in the Universe; the right believes that He came to recover it from its fatal moral tragedy. The difference also represents the great and hopeful advance in the negative camp from Strauss to von Hartmann and Nietzsche, from a religion of life concerned sanely only with the untoward, to one which grasps life dramatically as essential tragedy.

Finally, I am liable to be told that I have done more in the way of stating my position than of arguing it. But that is the very nature of my plea. Theology must be dogmatic, and it is only a choice of the right and wholesome kind of dogmatism. Theology is not syllogistic—that would be theosophy. It is not ruled by the logic of an idea. It is empirical in the great sense, in the soul's sense, the will's sense. By its nature it is dogmatic, as conscience is, as science is about nature's uniformity, or as society is about marriage. It is not the deduction of a system from an innate principle which Christ brought to the surface, nor is it the analysis of the Christian consciousness, but it is the exposition of what the living conscience of the Church finds in the fact and act of Christ, creative and historic. It is not progressive argument so much as enlarged statement, not the movement of a dialectic but the exposition of a corporate experience. Everything turns on what the soul does, or does not, find in the objective fact of Christ as the self-donation of God to our case. No otherwise do poetry or science deal with the gift in nature. We are always more sure of the reality than satisfied with the rationality of the matter. Living faith is always more of a moral miracle than a mental sanity. It is a will's mysterious choice and not a mind's lucid flame.

18

The Moralization of Religion

If we were to carry our thought back for, say, a century of this country's religious life we might mark a succession of influences issuing in movements which could be classified thus. They all mean, of course, the modification in some way of the traditional Christianity. First, there was the effort to *rationalize* faith, whether in the smaller way of the mere critical understanding, or the larger way of the imaginative reason. This was quite necessary in its place. But it was not all that was needed, nor was it the main thing. Accordingly, to balance matters, we had, in the second place, the effort to *spiritualize* religion. The foremost representatives of this were the evangelical and the sacramentarian movements, with which may be coupled the aesthetic and the intuitive, passing at a later date into the whole mystical tendency that is still so strong, and that degenerates into occultism. Thirdly, we had the effort to *humanize* religion—the humanitarian movement, when literature, and especially poetry and fiction, began to tell strongly on faith, not to say on belief, when people took their theology from Tennyson or Browning, or even MacDonald and Whittier, and positive creed was lightly doomed if it collided with the best instincts of the kind heart. Others, with a more scientific bent in their humanism, are engrossed with our mentality rather than our poetry, and their great desire is that religion should be brought home by being *psychologized*, as a new style of fiction might do it. Fourthly, there arose the effort to *socialize* religion, with all that rich crop of movements which led some to various schemes of Christian socialism, others to social reform, others to attempts to commit the Church to economic remedies and ideas, others to identify the two great types of Church with one or other of the political parties, others to manifold fraternities and fellowships apart from the Church, others to treat the Churches as no more than religious clubs, or to turn their work from evangelistic to social, as in the striking case of the Salvation Army. All this without a clear and ruling grasp of the social idea dominant for Christ—the Kingdom of God. And, fifthly, we have, working through all these out taking a form of its own, the effort to *moralize* faith and belief, to recognise in Christianity the "hegemony of the moral," the creative centrality of conscience. It makes the moral experience the ruling feature of Christianity as the religion of moral redemption. It means the tendency to treat the moral and not the rational as the real, to recognize, as the principle of all Christian formations and reformations, that Kingdom of God which dominated Christ in life and especially in death. It seeks to reconstruct all the forms of faith, social or intellectual, by that principle as the authority which is intrinsic to Christianity and is not an imported dynasty. It would open Christianity with its own key. It says that we loose with the power that binds. Freedom rests on control. If we are to speak of the reconstruction of belief the first necessity is a reconstructive authority. Mere liberty can reconstruct nothing; it only gives due play and honour to the reconstructive power. In this country, moreover, the battle of liberty has now been mainly won. And for the sake of liberty itself we are forced to recognize that its very first interest is authority; which must be an authority both moral and re-creative, one which new-creates the conscience, and, from thence outward, recasts, in so far as may be necessary, the forms of creed and conduct. He that sits on the throne makes all things new. The first charge upon anything that flies the flag of the Kingdom of God is not liberty but righteousness, and the apostles of spiritual righteousness are the aristocracy of faith. All this means at last the primacy of the moral, the finality of the holy, the recognition of Christianity as the religion which answers the revelation of holy love. This is the new Evangelicalism, for which reconstruction means at root *moral* redemption, redemption of the social soul by the last powers of the moral universe. We can moralize Christianity only by evangelizing it, and reviewing its orthodoxy by its own good news and great gift of a Kingdom of God. There is something which must precede the reconstruction

The Moralization of Religion

by religion; it is a reconstruction of religion. It is the kind of reconstruction, for instance, which does not leave it possible for a man to be an evangelical pillar and a public profiteer. It is a reform of evangelicalism by the gospel of the Kingdom, where salvation means something much else than safety.

I venture to illustrate this by discussing the relation of three ideas in particular—sacrifice, righteousness, and obedience—in the process of this moral revival. The great war has cast them all into the forefront of our moral concern, and it may do much to correct things in the religion it has done so much to shock.

For three years now the air has been full of the spirit of sacrifice. It is a good and a great spirit. It is capable of great and good things—indeed of the best things. But not in itself. In itself it is neither good nor bad. It may be used both ways. It is no monopoly of one side, either. It abounds among our worst enemies. But we believe that in Germany it is the servant of national unrighteousness, and the adjutant of Satan. It is the sacrifice of the citizen to a State which disowns moral obligations, repudiates for State affairs the moral world and its controls in the passion for national power, abolishes international law, and seeks to live in a region beyond good and bad. Such a Machiavellian State is the trustee of unrighteousness. It is the protagonist of Antichrist for the hour. So also with those who serve it. Their patriotism, however sacrificial, is a world curse.

Sacrifice by itself is morally neuter. Taken alone, it is more useful in poetry than in morals. It is more aesthetical than ethical. Let the war help us to this lesson, which had become so needful when sacrifice was coming to be regarded as religion, when religion was coming to be measured by the sacrifice we make instead of the Sacrifice we trust, when martyrdom was idolized, and was consequently falling into contempt because it was exploited without supreme regard to the moral nature of its aims. We needed to be sharply told that the sacrifice by love as a passion might be sacrifice to demons, that reputation was not well lost for such love, that a mere cause did not keep martyrdom noble, that to lay down life for the love of our country might be offering ourselves to the enemies of the race and of the Kingdom of God. Satan too has his sacrifices. We needed to be called above a religion which is one of sacrifice only or in chief, even of sacrifice for love's sake. It is not easy to be explicit here without seeming to disparage high and gallant things. But indeed, I am concerned with the principle of their permanent increase. Let me press it, then, that a soul may sacrifice everything worthy for a love illicit and ignoble. Or the spirit of sacrifice for comradeship may abound among men who are entirely pagan at heart. Romantic love is a stuff that will not endure. Love is eternal as it is holy. Righteousness is the last solemn music of things, as it is the keynote of the Kingdom of God.

One thing the war has done, especially for youth as it is represented at our Universities. It has turned them from a life of sport, good form, and general dilettantism to a sense of reality. It has destroyed for the time ethical ritualism. It has, indeed, cast us all on a deeper sense of reality, and the religious especially. It has given a blow to the kind of idealism that retreats from history, dreams in the lily gardens of peace, cultivates a sublimated religion, lives upon the brave, and eats the sacrifices of the dead. It has discredited the type of religion that cultivates a piety more or less aloof for fear lest the soul should be sullied or captured by the world. It has shown moral purism to be something else than moral nobility. It has done something to set the Church on a way of righteousness, leaving to God to keep it pure. Righteousness—that is the most real form of reality. I would put special stress on the enthusiasm for righteousness as a sounder thing than the passion for sacrifice, or even the enthusiasm of humanity.

"Offer the sacrifices of righteousness." The higher we rise in the scale of love the more it becomes a question of what the authority is within it. Love cannot live on mere liberty. In marriage it rises to responsibility. Its sound and permanent liberty flows from its authority, the authority itself obeys. The opposite of the egoism from which the higher love delivers us is not sacrifice but obedience. We have to be saved not from selfishness only—the essence of sin is more than selfishness—but from the self-will which so often goes with even self-sacrifice. People may sacrifice themselves in a way so self-willed that they can work with nobody, and they do much to set other workers by the ears. Patriotism, for instance, can become faction. The divine thing in love is not the operatic intensity of it, but its moral quality, including its power to convert even unselfishness from selfwill. Christ did not die for love alone but for *holy* love, for love whose prime passion and power was righteousness eternal, for love of the Kingdom of God and its righteousness. He died for that Kingship which dominated His whole life of love. It would alter considerably some of our time-honoured theories of His death to construe it by His own ruling principle of the Kingdom of God. That, in some form, is what makes all sacrifice divine. For self-sacrifice, I have said, may be practiced for ignoble, and even nefarious, means—as in the case of avarice. We have to ask what sacrifice serves. What is its loyalty? What righteousness does it own? To what do you sacrifice yourself? To die for country is not necessarily to serve the Kingdom of God which was Christ's end and is Christ's realm. So to die is not serving God's Kingdom unless your country is serving God's Kingdom in Humanity.

There is, therefore, a greater thing than self-sacrifice. It is obedience. That sounds less romantic; but it is really much harder. It may be less heroic, but it is more holy. We all know that sometimes the hardest form of self-control is to obey duty and abstain from self-sacrifice. But obedience does not always appeal to the romantic age, or the romantic half, of mankind. There are more people eager to sacrifice themselves, or to lyricize sacrifice, than there are who have the spirit of obedience. Real humility is less easy than martyrdom. Yet true obedience to the righteous or holy is what makes sacrifice fruitful, saves it from being thrown away, saves it from being ridiculous. Sound sacrifice is sacrifice in obedience to a righteousness we have taken due pains to understand, and which we have come to an age to gauge. One tires of being asked to respect a belief for which many have suffered; that witnesses less to the belief than to the believer, and not necessarily to his credit. The gospel no apostle need be ashamed of is that which primarily reveals the *righteousness* of the God of holy love (Rom 1:17). Here again notice that it is not a case of obeying conscience only. Nobody ever obeyed his conscience more faithfully than Torquemada. All the cranks obey what they are pleased to call their conscience—many being more preoccupied with their conscience than with their duty, as people have been more occupied with religion than with God, with their faith than with the grace of God which it lays hold of. To treat faith as merit is quite parallel to that idolatry of conscience which replaces the worship of the duty that conscience should grasp. The divine sacrifices are the sacrifices of righteousness and not of conscience merely. Which means that often the form of sacrifice that conscience needs most is a long course of discipline instead of a public martyrdom. The real destruction of egoism is obedience to the righteousness of God's Kingdom. And this is the spirit of the true International.

Since spirituality can destroy faith, the practical reform which religion needs is less its spiritualizing than its moralizing. And, within that, it is the change from the supremacy of self-sacrifice to the supremacy of obedience in the sacrifice, from the worship of love alone to that of the righteousness in love, to the worship of holy love. So we rise in three stages—*sacrifice, obedience, righteousness*—righteousness, obedience to it always, sacrifice for it at need. If the world needs to be converted from egoism to love, the Church needs conversion to *holy* love—from love sacrificial to love holy, from sacrifice for its own sake to sacrifice "for My sake and the gospel's," to sacrifice for the Kingdom of God, and not simply for any cause that happens to kindle us—and that may blind us with the smoke. There can be self-willed sacrifice, but not self-willed obedience. The Cross of Christ was the greatest sacrifice in the world because it was the greatest and deepest obedience. We have dwelt much on that Cross as love's sacrifice for man; we must go on to prize it most as love's obedience to God and His righteousness. We must return to think of the Cross not only as the sacrifice of love for man, and not as the supreme case of the sacrifice that adorns human nature; for the sake of that very love we must grasp the Cross anew as the sacrifice of love for God and His Kingdom. When Christ died, was He thinking more of God or of man—of God and what He required or of man and what he needed, of His gift to God or His gift to man? It was Christ's perfect and obedient sacrifice to a God of holy love that saved man. So we are not saved by the sacrifice we make, but by the sacrifice we trust. That is religion, that is faith. Self-sacrifice is not religion. Salvation by self-sacrifice is but ethic; and it may be poor ethic till we know its inspiration, its principle, and its object.

Now is it not true to say that at the present moment there is more of the spirit of sacrifice than of the spirit of obedience in this country? Perhaps we have exported too much of our sacrifice. The more of the spirit of sacrifice we have in connexion with the army, the more egoism and insubordination we may seem to find in other connexions at home. Soldiers may be dying while commands are quarrelling. We have the spirit of faction in public affairs, the spirit of profiteering in business, and the spirit of uncontrol and "don't-care" in the youth of both sexes.

Hence when the war is over and the enthusiasm of sacrifice has died down, when we are in the trough of its wave, we may have to face something little short of civil war. People mutter about revolution. And all for lack of the spirit of obedience (by which of course I do not mean mere submission). The war called out the latent sacrifice in the country; will peace call out a spirit of latent loyalty and obedience? Is it latent? Is it there? Of course, remembering how we were surprised by the revelation of the spirit of sacrifice, especially in the youth, we must take care not to dogmatize hastily in our answer to these questions. But is that spirit of obedience to righteousness the solemn temper in which classes promise to face the dangers internal to this country, and peculiar to its love of liberty? That love is constantly trembling on the verge of licence. Righteousness tends to degenerate into mere recalcitrance, and independence to mere self-will. And all for the lack of an authority which has the right to rule freedom because it creates it.

Take three of the chief discoveries of last century. They were the woman, the workman, and the child. But recall the years just preceding the war. Recall the attitude of these sections of the community. There was a degenerate tendency to believe in lawless force as the engine of a cause. The women were leaders in defiance and destruction. They hoped, in a Teutonic way, to gain by terrorism what better women have really gained by service. The workmen, copying perhaps the egoism of capital, broke loose from loyalty or obedience to their own organization and representatives; and they seemed to entertain the idea of war on society by a general strike. The young grew more and more insubordinate to parental and other control, especially where they became premature wage-earners or premature prophets. And this last feature has been strongly aggravated by the war.

At present we are united in a loyalty to country. But when that has done its work, and we are exhausted morally, physically, and economically, when the country is divided against itself as capital and labour will sharply be, where are we to find the object of loyalty and the source of obedience? Our wise and prudent men are, for the inevitable reconstruction, devising the machinery of a joint board to adjust the two interests, and to enable them to work in fairness and reason. But what will any such machinery be worth if it have not behind it that love of righteousness in the community which is the true citizenship, and which is something greater than fair play or loyalty to sect or party. In a Christian land that passion should be the enthusiasm of God's righteousness. It should be the Kingdom of God. I do wish some phrase about the enthusiasm of the Kingdom might catch on as the enthusiasm of humanity did in the seventies. That international of the Kingdom which we long to see ruling between the peoples should also take the lead within them. But is it an idea which has much power with us? It is a pulpit theme; is it a public power? Of course if it is a mere dream, another Utopia, a mere obsolete Christianism, one could not expect it to rule. It would be an aesthetic ideal without ethical control. But then if it is a mere dream, how was it the staple of the most potent, the most public, and the most inexhaustible figure in history? How could a visionary found what is, after all, the greatest institution of history—the Christian Church? The idea ruled Christ absolutely; does it rule Christendom? Does it rule the political and social relations of a nation of Christians? Is it ever alluded to by our very able publicists? Is it a motive which our political and social leaders can use on a platform with any expectation of response, or in Parliament without impairing their effect? Yet would a population of God-fearing people, true citizens of God's Kingdom, not solve the social problem? The Church does of course speak of the Kingdom of God; but a chief source of her need to be moralized is that her egoism does not seem to grasp it. How could an egoist sect preach the Kingdom of God? It means, for High Church, the Church itself as a polity; for Low Church it means missionary enterprise, or benevolence more or less sectional to history. But the Kingdom of God is greater than any Church or mission represents. The Kingdom of God is the supreme power deep and driving in the whole moral order of history and society. It is the destiny written in the very nature of the moral universe, mounting to the image of God. It means God's eternal and re-creative act for the humane conscience of all history and society which set up His Kingdom in the Cross. And, with all the great things the Church has done, it has not grasped that, nor taught that, as the public crisis requires it.

Which means that the chief part of the reconstruction of religion, theology, and the Church is the moralizing of them by their own central power duly understood by the gospel of that Kingdom of God. Let that be grasped as the moral intent of the world of history, as it was the dominant power working in the world's Saviour, and flowing from Him. It is not a matter of conversion alone, as the pietists thought. It is not a flight into a better world, but a step forward into it. It is a matter of righteousness and its policy as well as of piety and its philanthropy. It is more than the machinery of beneficent love. It concerns society and not only the soul. It is the whole realm of moral and social ends, not just developing to the ideal but converted from progress to worship. It is a work and gift of God deeply, mystically, practically realized by those who worship in love the public kingship for ever of a holy God in Christ. It is the doom of the exploiter and the sectary, of the honest old Pharisee with his moral dullness, and the devotee with his spiritual egoism. It is the glorification of God's holy and sovereign love by man's personal dignity, social righteousness, and brotherly sympathy. It is not a morality but a religion. It is not sectary; it is the last catholicity. It comes not as a moral demand but as a moral gift, a gospel, a good news. Above all else the doctrine means that the best things are not ideals of ours but powers of God. Life's dominant is not an attractive ideal on the horizon of history, but God's achievement working as the expansive power within it. It means that all the best things ideal to the soul are by the Christian gospel already guaranteed and real. Christ's redemption never can or need be redeemed. Seek first the holy and the catholic will be added.

That may be called theology, but would it not be the greatest reinforcement to public ethic were it active in every conscience? Communion with God, the divine value of the soul, the development of all its powers, the fellowship of love, the joyful exchange of spiritual wealth, grateful delight in nature's good, the passion for righteousness in the power of the holy, the sacred family of nations, the common conquest of earthly sorrow and social anomaly—such things are not heavenly *ideals* of ours but *powers* of God, already *given* freely, fully, and finally, always at work, as already victors in historic things, whose consummation spreads into the world unseen. It is an unspeakable moral asset when supreme ideals of ours are converted into final achievements of God and dominants of the moral universe. On this rests the gospel, and this way lies its public path. The root of public ethic is the rule of the King of the Kingdom of God.

What are we to do for an obedience, I have been asking, when sacrifice has done its work? And the question, I have said, is the great question that returns, and returns again, to our door, and to our scanty welcome. It is the question of authority. We have been the devotees of liberty so long that we resent the idea of authority; we certainly resent the notion of devoting to such a quest or interest the enthusiasm and sacrifice we have spent on freedom. Yet freedom itself demands that we should attend to it, and attend supremely, freedom which begins to feel serious tremors in the ground she has secured. It is no question of an authority which requires our submission *sans phrase*, but of an authority which is identified with the last righteousness, the last stay, and the last liberty. It is an authority which means the expansion of life much more than the security of a tradition. It is that will of holy love worshipped in the life of the single soul, embalmed in our growing Society, and honoured in our public life—till the instinct of it grow into the insight of it by the civic conscience, speaking in our most gifted men. It is an authority whose answer from us is the grand quest for the public and historic will of God, and the living out of it *con amore*.

I could not go farther on this line without passing into the theological region and speaking more deeply of the divine emancipation which underlies all the moral freedom of society, and is called redemption. We can really moralize only as we truly evangelize. We must ask ourselves, with new knowledge, courage, and conscience, what evangelical really means, what it has to do with a double ethic, what ails its moral note. The religion of the future must be more and more the religion of the moral soul and its reconstruction; the religion, for the soul, of a *holy* Father's grace, and, for society, of the kingship of the righteous King. The royal law of such liberty much orthodoxy has travestied. But the reconstruction of our spiritual world—of religion, theology, and the Church, is not the rationalizing of it but the moralizing of it. It is the social moralizing of it—as when we insist that the worker's due wage is the first charge upon industry.[1] And it is its moralizing by the central principle of religion, of Christianity itself—the Kingdom of God. It is moralized by that gospel, and the supreme moral act of the Cross at its heart.

The object is not to make religion more plausible. It is first to make it more sympathetically righteous by carrying it deeper than rational systems go. And beyond that it is to make it more imperative; for we need a command as much as a sympathy. But it is also to unite the elements of command and sympathy in a realm of holy love, redemptive and creative for the moral soul and the righteous society. Righteousness as a creative power—we are not grasping that, because it is not at the heart of what makes Christianity Christian for us. All this of course means more than that, by the aid of our scholars, we should realize Christ as a historic person more freshly and vividly than the Church has mostly done. That is a welcome thing. But it would be still more precious, if it made us that we could read for our mere delight no more; if it made us, with these fresh and living results, to pass to His moral depths; to ask what a personality so quick and powerful came to do and make us do; to pierce to the centre of His one moral purpose and work; to realize, in the new perspective of the Kingdom of God, His function no less than His person, His office, as above all His character; and to lay hold of Him as the Messiah and King of the moral universe in its crisis, and of all society at its moral spring. "Add to your faith moral proficiency" (2 Pet 1:5).

The passion for the world righteousness of God's historic Kingdom is the best antidote for the war-weariness which now so easily besets us. We have gone too far and too deep now to turn back, without walking into a calamity worse than the war, and a moral infidelity like the German. God has taken a hand in the game, and we are not free to refuse to be His partners. The issues have become widened and exalted since the war began. The war itself has undergone a certain conversion. It has risen morally

---

1. It was with horror and fear, and not simply with astonishment, that I read recently in the column of wills one item. The head of one of the largest industries of its kind left about a quarter of a million, and of that he bequeathed £1,500 for distribution among certain of his employees. No other public legacy was named. It was time we had war. No hell could be worse than the unavailing passion of such a soul to return and give it freely away.

in its course to be a crisis in the world righteousness which is bound up with the Kingdom of God. It is no more only a clash of patriotisms. It is a judgement of the Kingdom.

If there are good reasons why the Church should not control the State, yet the same social power in Christianity which makes the Church in its conditions—namely, the Kingdom of God—must also make society in *its* conditions. The moral power of society cannot be different at last from the moral power in the Church. We have but one conscience. There is really but one ethic; the supremacy of the Kingdom of God means that; and it is gathered up in the Cross of Christ and its righteousness of holy love as the crisis of the whole moral and historic world. The moral centre of our civilization and affairs must become identical with the moral centre of our religion. There will be recurrent war till this come about.

19

Unity and Theology: A Liberal Evangelicalism the True Catholicism

I

There cannot be many people really Christian who are quite indifferent to union of the Churches in some form more obvious and effective than the preset map of the Churches shows. But such people are certainly to be found; who say, "Let us alone. We are doing well enough with a general sympathy growing on the whole, with occasional fraternising on common ground, or with co-operation in neutral regions." But is that not as if Christian unity were no more than suburban neighbourhood, pious proximity, or a collective egoism modified rather than converted? Sanctified egoism may truly do much, but it is only a halfway house. However it be with the private piety of such people, are they more than sectarian in their Church mind? Do they rise above group egoism in the public relations of their faith? As a matter of fact the spirit, not to say the passion, of real union, union effective and not merely ideal or sympathetic, is in the Christian air; it is also, and far more, in the Christian Gospel; and the only question is as to its focus and forms.

But these conditions do create a very real difficulty, with which many who are keen for the idea do not yet see how to deal. Many of the idealists seem to think that the notion and its eager sympathies are enough. They hold that the obstacles are gratuitous or even factitious, that they are morbid growths which would dissolve if the heart's action increased and the temperature rose. Now we cannot do too much to cultivate the common sympathies—

unless we do it at the cost of a Christian intelligence and conscience. But all the good will in the world will not settle the merits of the case. What is the cardiac remedy we should take? In these great and venerable problems solutions are not simple, else they would have been found long ago. Answers to age-long questions are not to be given offhand. Ideal ardours without historic sense will not suffice. They may mislead. They will certainly disappoint. We cannot deal with history by wiping the slate and starting afresh. We cannot treat tradition as a perfect fool. Agitation will not bring life or liberty for the Church at least. These come from the nature of its creative source. We cannot deal with division by charging it on theology, and executing the culprit out of hand. We cannot make a mental solitude, and call it Christian peace. The problem will not yield to amateur good feeling. If union come, it is a sympathetic theology, but also a positive one, that is to bring it. The Church rests on its belief, which it is constantly clarifying at the spring. And that is why the scholars of history and the thinkers of faith are coming to play such a part in the matter. From being polemics, they are turning to be among the chief eirenics of the day. Parties may join for expediency, but Churches can unite only on principle. Here the ways of the State are not those of the Church. To develop a State from a general principle may seem academic and Teutonic; but with a Church it is inevitable. A State is not founded on a special revelation, a Church is. The charter of the Church is a gift of God in a sense which is true of no State. Let us not shrink from cherishing for the Church a foundation principle such as it might be pedantic and even fatal to apply to the State. Let us beware lest our political success lead us to the philistinism of applying to the Church those standards and expediencies which work so well in national affairs. The Church was created at an historic point by a final act moral and divine; the State, however divine, was founded in no such way; it grew by a series of adjustments in an ascending scale.

When we lay stress on the past, and on a point and act in the past, we are only pressing one phase of the standing difference between objective and subjective religion, between a religion of faith and one of piety, between religion of the historic and religion of the intuitionist type, between a religion of the saving facts of history and a religion of the consciousness. It is a difference which much in current religion tends to erase or ignore. With a democracy whose education has just begun there is a fatal impatience of anything beyond brotherly sympathy, immediate impression, vivid views, sharp alternatives, and hard extremes. There is a dangerous confidence in empirical conviction. Now this is all very well for an individual, but it will not carry a society, and least of all a Church. A crude mass of such impressibiles is easily convinced that there is nothing which they cannot grasp, do, or undertake, from a scheme of drainage to the control of the Fleet. And they are abetted by the cocksureness of practical success. The valuable man of business, for instance, is often quite prepared to run the education of the country. So the impressions or opinions of a religion individual and subjective are made to do duty for the realities of objective and historic revelation; and what is called life with its realisms is set up to overbear all the best verdicts of history about reality. The trouble becomes acute in the public attitude to theology, which is now probably the only great subject in which special study is held to be a disqualification, profound truth an enemy to the soul's life, the man in the pew a competent critic, the man in the train an authority, and the Press a court of appeal. It is even held in quarters, not only that a Church of energetic piety can do quite well without a creed, but that a creed is a useless survival, which, like the appendix, can become a source of danger to the body.

Now in view of all this it is necessary to say, with much respect, that the Union of the Churches can never be brought about on a basis of subjective and empirical religion, *i.e.*, of religion which is more full of its experience than of the source which creates the experience, and creates the Church. It can never be brought about just because it is in the air, nor because it seems to meet democratic aspirations. It does; but these will not bring it to pass: "I will hear what God the Lord will speak; to His people He will speak peace."

If I may supplement our vocabulary in this region by a clumsy word, I would say that the divided Churches have become weak, and even futile, through the excessive growth of religious subjectivity. "That must be true which does me good; that must be real which impresses me." Religion indeed is not possible without experience; but we have worn the idea of Christian experience thin.

Truly orthodoxy of an intellectualist kind had made the movement to experience imperative. But we have gone farther than that—farther than a due recovery of balance; we have made experience a test. We judge of truth or reality as that which we feel does us good like a proper meal. We have sought the test of truth in the degree in which it is vouched for by immediate, or individual, or group experience. We have not stopped to ask "Whose experience?" nor "Experience of what?" Nor have we found a criterion by which to select from a crowd of experiences the reality which gives them a scale of value. Experience tells me that I am saved, but could any experience assure me the whole world will be saved? Such theology does not pierce the depths or grasp the certainty of a divine purpose; it becomes but spiritual psychology. We have no science of God, but only a science of religion. We pursue a theology of consciousness, not one of fact, of history, of gift, of relation, of power. We infer God and His ways from our consciousness; we do not explain our state of consciousness by God's treatment of us to begin with. We believe in God's fatherhood by a mere analogy from man's. We postpone revelation to religion; which is an entire inversion. And that does not make for unity. For we are not one as religious but as redeemed, and especially from petty piety.

As we develop the modern subjectivity I name, we grow weak, trite, and trivial. Every Church feels it. And the frank Churches own it. We begin to realise that a ruling objectivity, a creative authority, is the one thing needful both for Union and for life and its liberty. The power to which we owe our life gives also our liberty and our unity. Union must be what our faith is—an act less of sympathy than of obedience to the authority of love's moral and sovereign Gospel. Experience is one thing, and may be but fraternal; faith is another, and must be royal. Faith is a matter of experience, but experience is not faith. And the difference is that in faith we are more concerned with the object than with the experience. "We preach not ourselves but Christ crucified." Faith is much more than piety. It is more concerned with the nature of the object than with the mood of the subject. It is more interested in our justification than in our peace. It is more anxious that God should come by His own than that we should be safe. And it is on faith that a Church rests, and not on experience. It must begin with God. It must found on God's self-revelation, though it may take shape in our appreciation of it. Experience, piety, makes but a group; what makes a Church is faith, and its self-oblivious engrossment with its object, as Creator and King. Our justification, our forgiveness, is an act of God before it is an experience of ours. Therefore it is not answered by experiences which come and go, but by faith, as a standing act, which has its sunlit patches of experience as God wills. We are surer than we feel about the Cross of Christ as the thing that puts us into the Kingdom of God and its righteousness. We are surer of His knowledge of us than of our knowledge of Him. We forget ourselves in a godly sort. Moses coming from the Mount knew not that his face shone. We are not members of the Kingdom of God just because we have gone through an experience. We believe far more than we are conscious of, but experience is limited by our consciousness of it. The unity of the Church invisible is beyond all our sense of being one. It rests on the act of God and our faith of it, our committal to it. And it creates its own recognition.

Experience is not valuable in itself; all turns on its source and object, which gives it its quality, and which we apprehend by faith. Otherwise it could easily produce but an æsthetic religion which consists more of impressions than of life committal. Experience is as our temperament is; faith is as its object, which is grace, holy love as grace. Experience answers suggestion, faith answers revelation. The one may respond to a *movement* of God, to His Spirit, the other answers His *action* and above all His *act*—to His *Holy* Spirit of our redemption. The one is concerned with God appearing and speaking, the other with God coming and doing. The one is luminous, the other new-creative. The one places itself æsthetically, intelligently, reverentially before a manifestation of God, the other ethically, personally, worshipfully, within His saving act. The one depends much on God's gift of a prophet, the other wholly on God's gift of Himself in Christ crucified. And it is on this last that the Church lives, since it was created by it. The Church was created by the redeeming blood and not by the edifying sacrament. Moreover, the source of the Spirit which makes the Church is the Cross and not Pentecost, a world crisis and not a group experience. The distractions and bewilderments of the Church are due to a departure from the Cross of our justification, and a recourse to the Christ of our varying sympathies. The creative faith is faith in the

Christ of the Cross; but the sympathetic experience may feel the attraction of Jesus more than the redemption of Christ. Experience thinks of God moulding us or changing us—words which contain natural notions. But faith thinks of our justification as a new creation—which is the supernatural power. Evolution moulds us, grace remakes us. We are born again in Christ, and not merely shaped or altered. And it is because the Church has ceased to realise itself as a new moral creation that it has lost its moral power over the created world. It may become but a humane institution, a friendly society. It does not feel its existence to be a miracle, therefore it can perform none. It believes in nothing contrary to experience, nothing but what comes in the warm air of experience, therefore its experience is not adequate to the contrary experiences of the world.

Does it not follow that the message for the time is not one that merely seeks to enrich, or even interpret, experience, but one that aims to create faith? Faith is not a new interpretation of life, but a new life to interpret. Genius can give the one, the other needs a Saviour. Faith in God's grace is a thing more moral than experience, less temperamental, more universal, more catholic. And being so moral it concerns first a God of *holy* love, and then our conscience, its sin, and its righteousness. It begins with God's forgiveness and justification of us. Christ the Redeemer is more to it than Jesus the prophet or the paragon. And Redemption is the burthen of the Apostolic gospel. So the unity of the Church rests on the apostolic succession. But by the apostolic succession is not meant merely the historic. It means a succession to the apostles as sacraments and not mere heralds, far less as officials—the succession to them as interpreters and not publishers, as trustees of an experienced Gospel and not of a canonical technique. The Apostolate was the Sacrament that made the Church, men prophetic for a Gospel and not ministrant of a rite. The Church rests on the evangelical succession and its unity in the evangelical solidarity. The interpreter of the Gospel, the real successor to the Apostolate, is not the Church but the Bible as the precipitate of the apostolic message. What opens the treasures of redemption is not a warranted priesthood but regenerate apostles. Is the Bible chiefly the record and sacrament of Redemption, or is it a quarry for orthodoxy, or is it the trust deed of a ceremony?

II

The foundation of any real unity must lie in the nature of our creative source. Religion is just what revelation makes it. What unites individuals into a Church is not a common experience but a common revelation. It is a common Lord, or Spirit, who creates a faith of which its experience is but a phase, who creates a soul whose experiences are but its chapters or even clauses. I believe with all my heart when I feel nothing, or am engrossed with my day's duty. It is an objective bond and not a subjective sympathy that is the real nexus. The circle is made not by the contiguous points in the circumference, but by their relation to the centre. And the same is true when it is a case of uniting Churches, and not mere units.

And more. The authority, the kind of power that makes our unity, is historic, but it is historic in a focus and not career. I mean that what is chiefly involved is not just the objectivity of the *course* of history, our canonical tradition, our official continuity, nor even the mottled record of our moral efficiency in affairs; it is the nature and action of the power that, from a *point* in history, creates both the faith and the tradition. That is, it is not objectivity alone, not canonicity, it is theology that is needed. Religion is made what it is by the *nature*, the interior, the dynamic, the theology, of the revealing act.

It is made a revelation which is energetic, creative, and not merely exhibitory—by revelation as redemption and not just as truth, as an act moral enough to set up for all conscience the Kingship of the holy God. If our cohesion is not there, it cannot be *permanently* anywhere. Fact, history, is quite necessary, but it is the nature, the interpretation, the theology, of the historic fact, the nature of its purpose and action, that tells. It is the eloquence of the fact, or let me rather say its vitality, its conductivity, its conveying power. It is fact as sacramental. If it were suggested, for instance, that the episcopal polity should be made universal and necessary for the Church while any theory of it was disclaimed, the two things would not seem to march. Could we claim monopoly for any spiritual fact or institution except on the authority of its rational interpretation or moral monarchy? Could the unity of a Church depend on even the highest convenience? Could the highest practical utility or historic prestige found unity in the

Church of an absolute Gospel? What will win the world is indeed a union of the Churches, but a union in virtue of the Gospel that unites them. It is the Gospel that looses and binds, divides and heals—not the Church, and not its ministry.

A theology then is not an adjunct nor a luxury of a Church, but it is creative for it. The Church did not arise out of the character of Christ, nor out of His historicity as a prophet, but out of the loving nature and moral work of His person as Redeemer. It arose out of a Christ not merely historical but theological, out of a creative theology of Christ's work, which made the spiritual power of the Gospel and Church something more moral and permanent than the religious impression He produced. He impressed many whom He did not regenerate and did not keep. I am not speaking here of a systematic theology, as I am not speaking of an official Church. Both of these have, to be sure, been treated as sacral, *i.e.*, as of first moment for the soul for their own sake. But I do not mean that organised theology or Church. I am speaking of the prime theology, which is dynamic, and not the secondary, which is scientific—of the theology which is ethical and economic and not logical and æsthetic (if we may use Croce's terms). I speak of a prime, seminal, creative theology, which does not handle themes but powers, a theology of God's action rather than His truth, a theology of final, moral redemption, which (and not precept or statement) is the centre, power, and characteristic of Christianity. It is the mysticism of moral redemption.

When we realise that such a theology created the Church at the first, we must realise also that it makes the life, liberty, and unity of the Church as it goes on. These things cannot be had from a creed that begins with neoplatonic notions of Logos and Incarnation, but only from one that rises to an Incarnation which we cannot experience, from an Atonement which we can. The Church is made and spread by a continuous creation of the moral kind, which sets up the Kingdom of God by the holiness of His love—by His grace. The creative act is eternal whether in the first creation or the second: and in the second it is a moral creativity. The unity of the Church lies in the moral act of love which created the Church, and continues to create it. Such a prime theology is not an expression of faith, it is the origin, creator, and norm of faith, with a simplicity massive, profound, and wealthy. It is a revelation; and the religion does not make the revelation. This revealed foundation of the Church's life is also the power and principle of its unity. Such unity is not to be found in waves of sympathy which sweep over its membership, nor in a heirarchy of its officials, but in the "organising surges" from its Redemption, which at once create and control its life, and which develop a constitution flexible enough for life.

I have said that that unity is more than an organ of Christian fraternity and sympathy. Take Democracy as an example. Take the American Constitution. Is that just the expression of Democracy? Is it just is organ? Is its value the facility with which it gives effect to each flush of movement that spreads through the population from time to time? Nay; from the President's power and veto downwards, (more thorough than anything we have in king or peers) is it not an elaborate and sagacious system, not for registering democracy, but for correcting it and protecting it from itself and its subjective humours? A democracy, of all forms of government, needs that safeguard most. And this should be well considered by those ultra-democratic Christians who live in an atmosphere of suspicion of central authority. Without that central authority nothing of moment or stay can be done in the region of affairs, of public affairs. The more democratic the Church is, the more it needs a source of life and control, and not of mere energy released from control, and misnamed freedom. Its great movements must be inspired, and permitted, and regulated by its creative principle. The free Churches do not merely register the subjective affinities of an age or of a piety. They rest on a faith. And the difference between a piety and a faith (have I not said?) is that the former, like filial piety, need not take prime account of the character or action of its object, whereas for faith these are prime, and produce worship and not mere reverence. The great committals of a Church must be moved, or at least countersigned, by a faith charged with solemn and formative beliefs. Sympathy is not a sure sign of inspiration, nor has it its power—though as the power rises, there rises also the temperature in which it works. Faith works by love. The moral dynamic works in a sympathetic medium, with which it may be said to be consubstantial. As structure is vital to melody so is holiness to love, atonement to reconciliation.

Some urgent creed, however brief, written or unwritten, subscribed or supposed, is therefore not only of the Church's *bene esse* but of its *esse*. Indeed, the Church's central account of its faith is not simply its explication of a Logos common to God and man, but the self-expression of a divine Redeemer. It is a creative necessity from His indwelling. It is a necessity. It represents the rock the Church stands on, or rather the trunk it springs from, its eternal conservatism. And it is a creative necessity. With the Christian Church its conservatism is creative. The more it is the same, the more it changes. The God of the Church and its Gospel is, but the subtle Spirit, the grand conservative power of the world; but it is conservative in method rather than in results. As creative it has the secret, the *élan*, the adjustment, the safety and continuity of all true progress, which is a wealthy self-realisation or moral, holy, and redeeming grace (Eph 1). For progress must always be measured by reference to the living identity of Christ, which is the nature of its fixed standard. A moving standard is none, as, at the other extreme, an iron standard is none. Christian progress is measured at last by the redemptive and ever creative principle, which makes Jesus the Christ; by the principle of the moral redemption and the new creation, which is the Saviour coming, if not to Himself, yet to His own. Movement is not necesarily progress because it seems desirable or strategic at a time. It must have a standard working from a higher plane with its own coherency; and for Christianity this standard is an objective revelation of a living, creative, and yet final kind, with all the implicates of such a vital source. It is not a matter of subjective religion with its affinities, but of an objective revelation with its holy miracle of Atonement on the moral side, and its creative reconciliation on the sympathetic. How do you know that Church Union is according to God's will? Because your heart moves you so? But many a fraternal ardour has cooled and subsided. Because it is filling the Christian air? But the passion of the disastrous crusades filled the Church high and low for a very long time. They had with them the heart of Europe, of civilization, of Christendom. Take, on the other hand, the Reformation. Did it take effect because it was popular, or because it was true and touched the moral reality? Something of the kind had

Unity and Theology

long been popular. The rank and file of the Church were aching for it, like the best of its elect. But the desire was impotent. The landslide only came when it came as the imperative of a positive and liberating Gospel for the conscience. The breach in the Church came from the principle of its Gospel, and not from a vague feeling pervading it, nor from religious nor humane insubordination. The dividing sword was the creating Word. And the healing of such breaches must come from the same source. "Thou turnest man to destruction, and sayest, come again ye children of men" (Ps 90:3). But is must also come as a corporate conviction and not merely an individual, as a conviction of the Church and not of its units alone; and it must come as the Church's conviction about what makes it a church, even in the wilderness, and not about what just develops its belief or range for culture. (I might withdraw my interest from the doctrine of the Trinity and nobody would be much the worse or the better; but if the Church ignored and neglected it, would all its sympathy or its philanthropy save it from subsiding into the world of mere culture and its sequels? That creed of a Trinity saved Europe from the Moors. Athanasius saved the world from Mahomet. He commanded at Tours, Poitiers, and Roncesvalles. And if you do not see that it founds the true unity of the Church, you might at least be led to admit that the unity of the Churches could not exist without it. Still more obviously would this be so in connection with the doctrine of Redemption.) The wickedness of the present war indicates that the belief which is to unite the world, and *a fortiori* the Church, must be one which deals first and effectively with the moral evil in the world, and not merely with its ignorance or its looseness of thought.

My case is that Church unity is fundamentally a matter of the central power in its theology—and in the theology not of individuals, but of the Churches concerned; that the difficulties to be met are not just soluble in fluid and warm sympathy; that, with a final revelation of *holy* love, moral principles and powers are more determining than affinities; that our first charge is the Kingdom of God and His righteousness, for which the Church exists; that difficulties must be worked out and not hustled out; that they must be worked out morally; and that justice must be done to the truth which each Church or its leaders feel they have in trust from a saving God. Those who are most intractable to us, the best and the high Catholics, are not moved by sheer love of prerogative, prejudice, and obscurantism. Far from it. They have a charge to keep, against even the piety, or fraternity, or democracy of the hour. There must be not only a sympathy, but a moral understanding arrived at. The matters must be thrashed out by the kind of knowledge and conscience concerned. It is not on the platform that the Churches will unite. Nor in philanthropy only. Not even in the secret oratory alone. But, with all these, largely, perhaps chiefly, in the study, where the fontal act and oracle of the Gospel is interrogated anew, and appreciated not simply as a charter but as a dynamic. The truth will create the conviction and impression which is its own driving power; but no amount of either impression which is its own driving power; but no amount of either impression or conviction will create truth.

III

In a question like this we need to be positive. We need to come to the point, the creative point. I am almost sorry to be so insistent on this. It is not enough to say we rally on Christ any more than that we rally on experience. We rally on faith, not experience. We preach not ourselves but Christ. And we rally on faith in what was the centre even for Christ—on the work given Him to do, and done—on His redemption of us into the Kingdom of God, on the Kingdom and the righteousness on which He put everything from first to last. *Ingens iterabimus aequor*.[1] The vital power for the reunion of the Churches, the Catholic power, is the evangelical, the last moral element in all the Churches, even in the Mass. Reunion must be planted deep, as deep as the reunion between God and man, far deeper than any reconstruction even of the Churches. It must rest on the unbought universality of redeeming grace as the greatest moral act of the universe. It must rest on the atoning Reconciliation, on a Reconciliation whose first concern was to do justice to a holy God, if justice was to be done to His love. It cannot rest on a deposit preserved with fidelity, but on a Gospel of grace prolonged by faith. The unity of the Church is supernatural in its source and nature; and it is in the moral region that the true

---

1. ["Tomorrow we shall plow the mighty sea." Horace, *Odes*, 1.7 lines 21–22.]

supernatural lies. Union must rest on the permanent, the eternal, element in our living faith, which is the saving element. It is not the element of sentiment on our part so much as of certainty, of the last certainty. And the last certainty is not a certainty of intuition but of conscience, of its redemption, of its miraculous redemption, the Kingship of the Redeemer as such. We must have a foundation more objective than sympathy, an authority more miraculous and creative, one more owned in our last crisis than felt in our calm culture. By authority is meant one moral and not formal, a power whose act for us and in us leaves us no more our own. I prefer the word formal here to the word external. For all authority must be external, if it is to save us from a mere masterless subjectivity. Externality to our egoism is of the essence of the word. But there is all the difference between an external authority which is formal, statutory, dogmatic, and one which is personal, moral, intimate, kindling, and creative; and this is neither a Church nor a theology—though it can only be described in terms which are theological and not merely humane.

But if the unity of the Church rest on Christ's supernatural and eternal—shall I say—seizure of us, which is our great certainty, it rests on it as personal and moral action on the part of God. The Church holds together by the moral and eternal act of free and triumphant grace which created it, and which is always functioning in it by the Spirit of holiness, which raised Christ from the dead. Its cohesion lies in its moral redemption. Its unity is its Redeemer. We are not vaguely in Christ as a spacious person, but in Christ in His central function, in Christ as the Creator, by redemption, of the Kingdom of God, and of the Church as its trustee. The real unity of the Church is the Kingdom of God, founded and set up in the Cross, and living by Christ as its King. The Church can only cohere in that reality, in the new Creator of its conscience, in the perennial and *holy* grace of Jesus Christ, in His grace taken as His mercy, and not chiefly as His food to us. It is not the feeding of the Church that makes it one, but its continual creation, not its sacraments but its Gospel—its sacraments only as they preach its Gospel. Its true food is its continued new creation in love's moral passion of holiness. And that is not an infused influence but an incessant moral regeneration, a constant conquest of our pagan egoism, private and public, the prolongation of the saving act of history which gave it birth. The Church is not the prolongation of the Incarnation, but of the Redemption for which the Incarnation is a postulate.

Therefore the unity of the Church can be in no mere polity of life or system of creed. All organisation, whether social or credal, is but provisional and opportunist. Living faith is not faith in a fabric whether of order or doctrine. Christ did not come chiefly to teach truth, but to bring the reality and power of eternal life. Till this is heartily owned, the moral power of the Church is lamed and pinched. Christ is divided. The Gospel is bound in the cerements of legalism. It does not come to its own as Gospel. It appeals more to the canons than to the conscience, to a certain technique, priestly or sacramental. It is neither national nor international, for it is righteousness that exalteth a nation. The real unity of nations is in their conscience. It is in a conscience schooled to the righteousness of Christ's holy Kingship, that the unity of the race is secured; it is not in a mystic or fraternal thrill. Man is one by the unity of his moral redemption, by his destined citizenship of the Kingdom of God, and not by the continuity of any fabric, social or intellectual. And a Church which appeals first to something else than the conscience, with its redemption, cannot at long last appeal to a nation or the race.

IV

That retreat into the permanent, eternal, and truly supernatural thing in Christianity, such realisation of its Gospel, is the true prerequisite of any Church unity which is to be other than forced, fanciful, or fleeting. It is a point on which the position of a liberal Evangelicalism is clear. The rallying point, the creative point, is not Christ's *teaching*. I am astonished that so many of the leaders of the Church should keep rotating, on the amateurism which stakes all on that. And it is not the *character* of Christ. I am again surprised that so many should not have surmounted the fine stoicism which often passes for the religion of an English gentleman. This type is liable to drop to one which reduces Christ to an imitable splendour, or teacher, working by reverence instead of faith. It reads His Cross as an unhappy arrest on powers in Him which seemed to mark Him as the Messiah of spiritual culture, or as the incarnation of a cosmic Logos. He is made to promise the Kingdom to an Israel of sweet reasonableness, shot with prophetic warmth. But the vital and indestructible thing surely, if one half of the New Testament is not to deny the other, is the redemptive work of Christ for the moral universe, as the Gospel within the Gospels, as the last interior of His person, and the full consummation of His task. It is Christ's person as morally redemptive for Humanity, and creative for the Kingdom of God. When we are put upon the last crisis, it is not even the person of Christ as a capacious haven for the world alone, nor as the source of an emotional devotion alone, nor as an unfailing manna for the soul alone, nor as a living epitome of what we are to believe or practise. He may be any of these things at certain stages of the soul, but not for a Church's end or being. For this He is more. The wealth of His person is all gathered up and all put into His redeeming work, as the creative crisis of the moral universe (cf. Eph 1:7, where the redemption in His blood is the fountain of the Church's moral and spiritual wealth, and not an item of it). His real and unique divinity is that He takes away the sin of the world by a new creation in righteousness and its saving judgment; it is not that He can be shown to incarnate the spiritual Reason, or to display the calm, sane dignity of the eternal Son of a passionless Father. The character of Christ may be made to seem so imperturbable as to be more superior than mighty, more dignified than royal. The permanent and binding element in Christianity is thus not the static keystone of a Logos or culture theology, but the creative power of a new and endless life in the holy Kingship of tragic judgment, spiritual victory, and moral reconciliation. The article of a standing or falling Church is the evangelical.

V

Only we must loose our evangelicalism, and let it go with its own moral power. We must save the Gospel from the backwash of law. We must release it from the Bible, for instance, as a bondage, just as we had to release it from the Church as a bondage. We must release the Gospel from the Bible, as the spikenard was released from the broken box to fill the world, or the lamp from the pitcher to overcome the world. We must release it, but never detach it. We must treat the Bible as the Sacrament of the evangelical power, and not the document of a canonical system, an orthodox creed, or a pious type.

The unity of the Church rests on the evangelical succession and not on the canonical, which is legalist and Judaist, and which ties up the Church more than it unites it. The real power is the evangelical confession. The real authority is the evangelical Redeemer thus confessed in a faith as miraculous as the grace it meets. The real unity is the evangelical solidarity. And it rests upon moral and personal conversion, real but not standardised. It rests on a new birth; and on baptismal regeneration not at all. It is in the last resort, a matter of a new centre, a new heart and conscience, and not of a common egoism, common tastes, or common theories in spiritual religion. It is not æsthetic at all in its nature, it is of a deep and transcendent ethic—of the deepest, most searching ethic we know. It rests on the readjustment of the moral universe, in a holy atonement of the evil conscience of man and the holy conscience of God. It treats this power as the norm of all Christian ethic no less than the source of all Christian experience and Church unity. It moralises all experience by the victory of God's holiness in His love.

The only thing then that can unite the Church is what subdues and reconciles the world. It is the world in the Church that divides us so. I do not mean by that the worldliness of existing Christians. I mean the importation into the faith for a long long time, of a divisive paganism, of a kind of thought that had not tasted the reconciliation nor owned the new creation. It is the afterwash of the effort by the early apologists to treat Christianity as a finial upon the fabric of natural religion, as a new storey built upon the natural man, as an annexe of revealed philosophy where nature's philosophy fell short; but an addition still philosophic in its nature, and more rational than miraculous, more orderly than creative, in its spirit. It is the attempt to give the natural man a pious finish instead of a new creation. As if natural truth, with all its value as a point of attachment, could ever be the basis for a religion of grace, whose radical rebirth goes to the last depths of the soul.

The only power to reconcile the world is not Jesus but Christ. It is not the spiritual Jesus but the atoning Christ. It is not youth's calm hero and high gentleman, but the tragic Judge and Redeemer of a world grown old and wrinkled in wickedness. It is not the wonder of His aspect, nor the sageness of His truth, but the miracle of His historic, universal, crucial and invincible grace. The reconciliation of the natural world rests on God's recovery of the moral world. The reconstruction of public society turns on the redemption of the moral soul; and this the Church is not getting home. It all turns on the supreme crisis of the world-conscience in the Cross. To say so is not to reduce religion to morality, but it is to lift it from ethical monotheism to moral redemption. That is the whole movement of Bible history, both in the Old Testament and the New. It is to make morality transcend itself, and find itself in a religion of holy grace. A moral religion is not just a religion of morality. And to expound the moral interior of the holy is not a piece of speculative theology. It is morality in the grand style, the moral action proper to the whole destiny of man, to the whole rebirth of conscience, and to the whole nature of God as the Holy.

It is not the Bible, I repeat, that we rally on. The Bible can be, and has been, so treated as to reduce it to be the dull code of a new law, instead of the living organ of an old Gospel. Taken by itself, idolised like a Koran, and treated like a document whose meaning is to be deciphered rather than divined, treated as a script rather than a Scripture, the Bible may well become a bone of contention and a shibboleth of exclusion. An obscurantist treatment of the Bible is a heavy handicap of the Gospel. The effective and conservative Evangelicalism must be more abreast of things than it has often been, both as to the Bible and the Church. There is little hope for anything but a liberal evangelicalism, one which casts off a "language of Canaan," which is sympathetic with sound and illuminative criticism, which has the historic sense, which outgrows the old individualism to magnify a corporate redemption, and which rises above a conventional and "proper" ethic to understand the moral psychology of the new time, and the moral interior of the new man. And it is essential that these liberalisms should not be reluctantly allowed as concessions, but that they should be joyfully proclaimed as corollaries of the principle of the moral emancipation on which everything hangs for evangelical Christianity.

To gather up and make an end. Real union must be planted deep. It must rest as deep as the union between God and man. It must rest on the world-salvation by God in His Cross.

We unite with more force, and to more purpose, when we know it to be God's historic will and achievement, than when we feel it to be man's eager wish. Our binding authority is our Redeemer in His redemption, and not in His instruction. He who redeems us leaves us with nothing we can call our own, but with everything in having Him. He destroys our self-will and our self-salvation, all our punctual compliances as such. Our rock is our Redeemer redeeming us, and not legislating about redemption and its social technique in a Church. That against the Canonist. And, against the pietist, the main thing is not the experience of being redeemed, but of a Redeemer of Whom we are more sure than we are of our experience. We shall never have the right experience of Christ till we are more concerned about His experience of us, till we look on Him Whom we have pierced. In the same way duty, where it is revealed, is a greater thing than the conscience, which is but the candlestick and not the candle. There are plenty of egoists of conscience, but too few of duty. You can cosset conscience, but not duty. Duty quenches the egoism that conscience often inflames. And so the Church is one, not in our Christian experience or conscience, or work, but in the Redeemer as creating the experience and the duty by His redemption. Experience is no authority, it is only the region of authority or its reflection. It is but the territory, not the throne, far less the King on it. And when we take stand on Catholic or Evangelical faith we are not transferring the venue to subjective religion any more than to individual. The Christian Reformation was not a change to individualist religion; that came with the pagan Revolution. It was a change to personal religion, to a religion which was not a relation between our person and an institution in which the moral Saviour was lost, but a relation between our person and our Saviour's, in whose Cross our egoism is lost and He is our all. Evangelical faith is truly a religion of experience, but it is the discovery there of the object more than the subject, of the object within the experience as its creator, and of the King in whose faith and worship we humbly forget to think about our own loyalty at all.

This faith is the focus and the principle of the Church's unity amid all varieties of polity or creed. And in this way the union of the Churches and the League of the Nations are set on one foundation, which is the moral bond of the conscience and the Kingdom—the conscience redeemed in the one case and enthroned in the other. For the Kingdom of God set up in the universal moral crisis of the Cross is the goal and the ground both of all religion and all ethic. As the great Church is to all the Churches, so is the Kingdom of God to all the kingdoms. And the Great Church and the divine Kingdom are one.

20

Religion Private and Public

It takes a very great deal to make men believe in the reality and cost of moral Redemption, to wean them from a supreme faith in their own reconstructions, and teach them to rest these on a supreme faith in God's new creation of the moral soul. It takes much of the real insight which religion tends to lose to believe soundly that redemption is a more real, urgent, fertile, and permanent thing than reconstruction. Not to see and hold that is to cherish the seed of war, which is man's self-confidence, and self-idolatry, and self-disintegration. The first interest of history is the moral; and the moral is the real. The redemption of the moral soul is the first reconstruction of the world for value and effect. The strife for it is the *nisus* of the world's last moral reality, labouring to the top in the convulsions of the new creation, and travailing with its latent glory. We need deliverance from the demonic element in society, progress, and culture, more than from its misfortune, weakness, poverty, crudity, or vulgarity. Devilry is more deadly than vulgarity. It is not deliverance from our weakness we need most, but from an evil power exploiting our weakness. What ails us most is not the lack of power but the non-moral, the anti-moral, power we obey. It is the Satans, human or other. The evil is not in wrong systems so much as in wrong souls. It is not in systems, whether of belief or of society, but in the souls that work them, or the demonic egoists that the weak souls serve.

We certainly need new systems, and much ability is working at them. But still more we need new hearts, in a way that few realize. We can make new systems, but God alone can make the soul anew, and His Church alone has His secret for it. Civics will not do it, nor social work—nothing less than the kingdom of God. It is regeneration we need more than revision, more than reform, more than culture. We need to be re-written and not just re-edited. We need a new creation of the conscience from its cultured egoism, a new moral relation of dependence on God (private and public), a new sense of the Father royal in His holiness and righteousness, a new and personal faith in His moral Passion and historic kingship. The average Christianity does not realize the kingship of God, but only His patronage. But the kingdom of God can never be set up on earth except by men in whose hearts is set up the kingship of God, which takes the instinct and the religion of egoism very effectually in hand. Christendom, if it is not to be at heart as pagan as Junkerdom, must unlearn the habit of exploiting God for its progress, its efficiency, or its other instinctive passions and pieties. It must wait on God, and not make God wait on it. It must worship and serve Him as life's chief end. It must repent, it must change the direction of its mind and its theology, as the first condition of the ideal redemption. And repentance is not decent regret nor a manner of conventional modesty. The new life of reality is not complacency, nor is it aspiration; it is the passion and homage of the forgiven. When it is thorough it is worship by those to whom the kingdom comes as the creative forgiveness of God. And it has its national form in a new public righteousness as well as its personal form in affection.

> It is not the case that any considerable number are longing for religion, and unable to find a form of Christianity to satisfy their craving. Those who feel the longing almost invariably find a spiritual home in one of the organized religions. What there is to be found is a deep hunger for a better and happier world. And the misery of the war has made this both keener and more widespread. But there is little desire for God in it. There is little interest in, or care for, the unseen world.
>
> And the irritation that is felt against religion is very largely due to the fact that religion puts God and the unseen world in the foreground, and not the happiness of men in this life. What they are aiming at is something that will ensure the future happiness of the world, not something that will ensure present commu-

nion with God and the priority to everything of the kingdom of God.

It is its demand for real and penitent contact with God that is the chief obstacle to the kingdom of God, especially in public affairs. For without national conversion and penitent reform we should not have a Christian nation, were the mass of its population converted next year. We should not have yet the reversal of our national egoism.

In a certain sense we need the conversion of the good—not into spiritual security, but into the kingship of God over every part of life. Everything Christ did was for the sake of the kingdom of God in history and eternity. Our salvation is our part and lot in that conversion of the race, both in its units and its kingdoms. It is our religious type that tells immediately on affairs; and we need a regeneration of our religious type by a new grasp of the belief which makes the type, a grasp which construes every item from the kingdom as the creative centre. It is not the spiritualizing of our personal religion alone that is chiefly required, nor the mysticizing of faith, nor "the deepening of the spiritual life"; it is the moralizing of religion, and especially of public and corporate religion. It is the moralizing of the revelation which makes religion. We need a new interpretation of grace and of belief in terms of the kingdom of God, which dominated Christ in every word, action, and purpose, and indeed made Him what He was, but which did not dominate the Church in its theological evolution. Religion is just as real as the reality of its creative revelation makes it. And in order to acquire a new grasp of religious reality we need a new interpretation of the revelation which creates religion—not a new psychology of our faith, but a new theology of the revelation that makes faith. We need a new interpretation, from the kingdom's point of view, of Bible, Gospel, Church, and Saviour. We need a new construction of evangelical religion, a new insight of what is meant by the grace of a holy God in an historic kingdom of Church and State. We do not duly meet the holiness of God by our idolatry of the saintly. I have spoken of the demonic element now broken out in human affairs. Is that just to be met by what is usually meant as the Holy Ghost? I take pleasure in quoting here a passage from an excellent article in the *Interpreter* for July, 1918, by Rev. W. F. Blount, B.D.

Have we made enough of the element of vehemence, the almost "daemonic" element, in Jesus, which so struck those who saw and heard Him? Mr. G. K. Chesterton found in the Jesus of the New Testament "an extraordinary being, with lips of thunder and acts of lurid decision, flinging down tables, casting out devils, passing with the wild secrecy of the wind from mountain isolation to a sort of dreadful demagogy; a being who often acted like an angry god—and always like a god. . . . The diction used by Christ is quite curiously gigantesque; it is full of camels leaping through needles, and mountains hurled into the sea. Morally it is equally terrific; he called himself a sword of slaughter, and told men to buy swords if they sold their coats for them. That he used other even wilder words on the side of non-resistance greatly increases the mystery; but it also, if anything, rather increases the violence" (*Orthodoxy*, p. 269). This is written about the same Person as the One whom Mr. Wells calls "drooping," "moribund," "a saint of non-resistance," to whom he denies the possession of courage, whom he proposes to "pity." Mr. Chesterton's picture shows immeasurably the subtler understanding of Christ; but have we seen it, or helped others to see Christ's life, as a flaming, furious energy of redemptive love? The Holy Spirit is the Spirit of Jesus. He came at Pentecost as fire and wind, fire the cleansing, wind the bracing, both the great purifiers, but both also the great disturbers. He began His work by "creating a scene," and those who partook of Him were called the men who "turned the world upside down." But is that the Holy Spirit of our Whitsun hymns, of "Our Blest Redeemer," or of "When God of old came down from heaven"? He seems somehow in those hymns to be altogether tamer, and more insinuating.

> "The fires that rushed on Sinai down
> In sudden torrents dread,
> Now gently light, a glorious crown,
> On every sainted head."

It is a picturesque antithesis. But I confess to a very strong doubt whether the attribute of "gentleness" is not the very last that the Christian company at Pentecost would have accepted as descriptive of their experience of the Spirit's descent.

For look at it in this way. When such a war is possible in Christendom, it certainly means the corruption of man's heart. But it means something else. For that evil was taken into account in the Christian revelation; and yet the revelation which was to deal with it has failed to do so. Why this ineffectiveness?

Does it not mean some great perversion imported into God's gospel itself from man's heart? Does it not mean some great error in the apprehension of God's revelation, *i.e.*, in our faith itself, our religion? The patient has infected the doctor. Is there not some corruption in the very cure of corruption? Is there not some unconscious error of the gravest kind in Christianity? I do not mean the error in Rome, as some will promptly think, but something subtler and less canvassed—in the faith which saved from Rome.

We have a parallel complaint from the students of literature. They complain that the brilliant galaxy of genius in the Victorian age has not had a due effect on the nation, and has not been in living *rapport* with it. They say the amazing volume of mental, imaginative, and moral energy has reacted but little on public realities, that it has been the ornament of the nation rather than its organ, that it has been a culture rather than a power, that it conjoined brilliance and inefficiency, and has left us unequal to the total situation of the world, moral and spiritual, "with so much wisdom and so little power of employing it."

It is not my place to answer the literary question. But it might be asked whether much the same might not be said about our religion, with its inner wealth and its outward futility. Does it construe its creed or its society, or even its Saviour from this dynamic centre in the kingdom of God? Does it not far too widely share the Roman idea that the Church is the kingdom of God? Does it not therefore tend to seek the interest of the Church instead of the conversion of the world? Does it seek first the kingdom of God and its righteousness? Does it find its soul by losing its soul's egoism there? Does it not seek a national connexion rather than a national conversion—or, if a conversion, then a conversion to itself, or to some frame of piety, instead of to the kingdom of God? Has it taught the nation that its work was a vital part of its worship, or its commerce a Board of Trade in the kingdom of God?

Have we been taught that the greatest work the soul can do, private or national, is to worship God, to hallow His Name, and to do so not on special occasions only, nor in secluded buildings, nor in the rapt, mystic feeling of individuals, nor in conditions aesthetic, but in the moral trend and conduct of great affairs? Have we been taught, as the apostles of a kingdom of God should teach us, to make worship great action and action great worship—as the two are united in the Cross, which is real revelation only as it sets up the kingdom of God for good and all, both in the soul and in society? That is the type of religion we need to generate. And to that end we must restate, perhaps even recast, much of our theology, especially our amateur and popular theology, which creates the religious type.

And, among other things, must we not enlarge and hallow our Gospel of a kind Fatherhood to Christ's true Gospel of the kingship of a Father whose love is divine only because it is holy? Our start must be the Father's Sovereignty.

Here there are two errors to be undone. First we have to replace the moral holiness into the love of God, lest our new kindness oust the eternal righteousness. And, second, we must lose the idea that God is there chiefly to wait on man's aggrandisement and progress; and we must regain the idea, which gives dignity both to Calvinism and Jesuitism, that man is there to wait on God's kingdom, power, and glory.

First, I say, we must grasp again the holiness of God's love as the divine thing in it and the mighty. There is pedantic talk, which to some seems impressive, of the need "to re-think God." When it comes to thinking God the devilry of culture is much ahead of us. What we need is power to recover in Christ not the thought of God, nor even His love, *per se* (which might be helpless at last), but His holy power to bring His love to pass among the nations. And that will never be done by amateurs of Jesus who joy in girding at theologies of an atoning Christ. The atonement is the power and action of God for the salvation of His own holy name in heaven, and therewith for the establishment of His righteous kingdom on earth. It is the moralizing centre for love's redemption. Holiness is more than saintliness.

And, second, in consequence of the hallowing of God's name we must change our centre of gravity. We must practically own, and it must become the note and type of our religion, that men and nations are not there to give effect to their own genius, but to serve the kingdom of God. They are not there for self-realization, with God as a tutelar in aid, but they are there to realize the kingdom of God and its righteousness, and to sacrifice national life if need be, for that kingdom, as we sacrifice individual life for the nation. We are all there not to exploit God but to glorify Him, as the only final way to enjoy Him for ever.

We need to exalt at Bible sources the idea of Fatherhood, which the poets and romancers have done something to make common and slack. The New Testament keeps uppermost the perennial note of authority in the patriarchal idea. For Christ the Father is the centre of moral authority at least as much as of kind affection. In the Lord's Prayer that is so. It is all in the opening key of a Father in heaven and His hallowed Kingship. It all unfolds the opening petition on the lines of a Kingdom and not a family. The hallowing of love comes before the enjoyment of it, which eludes those that live for nothing else. Love is for Christ a worship before it is a sympathy. He did not Himself ask for love, but faith—sure that living faith in Him must wear the complexion of loving kindness. The love He asked from Peter at the end was not personal affection sublimated, it was the moral love of the much forgiven, it was faith's love. That is the divine kind of love that is the love of the Kingdom. Its foundation is the moral foundation of the forgiveness and the new heart. It does not mean merely love romantic or domestic. The kingliness of the love, the grace of it, the miracle of it (not the instinctive naturalness of it) was the first thing with Christ and the last—even as for Paul, on the forefront of Romans, the gospel was the revelation of the righteousness of God before all else (Rom 1:17). When we say that the one form of love distinctively divine is forgiving love and the love of the forgiven, we are really saying in other words that justification by faith is the article of a standing or falling Church, in proportion as the Church is concerned with moral reality, moral redemption, and the kingdom of God. For the purposes of practical religion justification is forgiveness, and the revelation of it is the revelation of the last reality in an atoning forgiveness. And revelation, in this most pointed and positive sense of it, is the setting up of the kingdom of God; it is not a matter of mere manifestation, nor of mere impression. It is action, it is in the nature of a new creation, a new and final reality, which does not come and go but abides for ever.

Christ's God is the King of the regenerate conscience more than of natural affection transferred. There is indeed no sweeter word than loving kindness; but the loving kindness of Christ is not the kindness of a brother, but of the Holy One of God. The mightiest, and the divinest, and the most miraculous thing in God's love is its holiness, and the atoning way in which His love meets it. And the mightiest thing on earth is the kingdom of this holy God, and His righteousness, which is more than all peoples. The recent war was not only not for the dominance of a nation, nor was it even for the safety of civilization. It is the whole kingdom of God in the history of all the civilizations that has been at stake, through the Teutonic repudiation of a moral control over a Nation and State powerful enough to discard it. And that is the same holy kingship of God as forgives the world and redeems. Compared with that Act all the cosmic majesties and terrors, all historic convulsions, are but the outskirts of His ways (Job 26:14). It is the might and miracle of the Holy One's love of the unholy. It is love at moral issue always with sin. Such is the love at the root of the kingdom of God and its righteousness for the world.

To realize this thoroughly would alter the ruling type of religion, where love means too often an easy impunity and exemption. It would fortify and exalt that type. Our idea of Fatherhood has been too much drawn from the home and too little from the Cross; and therefore it has been softened too far. God has become the kind Providence of the genial life instead of the holy Lord of the righteous Kingdom. We go for our God too little to history and too much to the family. The kind father's little girl (and God never made anything sweeter than a little girl) becomes more of a revelation to him than his Holy Father's unspared Son; and it is held to be almost an outrage when he is told that his Church has claims on him which determine his home, and may not allow him to remove and live a better set. The Christ of the heart becomes the Christ of the story (which is bent to it) instead of the Christ of the story becoming the Christ of the heart (which is reared to it). Hence religion becomes too mobile for affairs, too subjective, unreal, impotent—as in orthodoxy it became too intellectual, too rational. It becomes in both cases dismoralized; so that, while we want reconciliation, we want it detached from its moral foundation in atonement, and reduced to a mere making up. And it becomes too much individualized. It becomes a salvation by private bargain or mystic light, and not by a share in the salvation of a whole world and in the recovery of a moral universe. We are asked to think of the Cross as the classic case of self-sacrifice, and not the crucial offering to a holy God. We think of religion in terms of private rather than public life, though it was upon a national issue that Christ died, and it was a nation's crime that slew Him for a world. Hence our Christianity has been more of a success on the private than on the public scale. It regulates personal conduct and sympathy, but not national. There is much private piety in Germany and no national righteousness. Hence also the moral effect of a great public and ecumenical calamity like the war is disappointing. We fail to respond to it as one of the saving and historic judgments in the dramatic and tragic course of a kingdom of God founded upon a Cross. We dissociate it from the conscience of the world and of eternity. Therefore, also, we lose out of religion the great note of moral sovereignty, of righteousness, of nations in a solemn league and covenant. We can speak of many a great work in religion, but we do not speak of it with the great note. Or when we think of majesty we think of it in the aesthetic way of seemly reverence and not the moral way of searching worship.

But the great note comes from the great belief, as the real hold is our hold on the last moral foundations of things. Is that the power of our creed? Are we as much concerned about its moral reality as about its canonical continuity? How are we to connect the forms of our belief with the last realities of active things? Is it a problem that the individual religionist treats with distain as academic and intellectualist; but it is really the supreme question for a society or a nation. And we are fumbling at social or national religion with a small key that only fits the lock of our private safe. We are interested only in what lends itself to the uses of local pulpits and does not extend to the control of national destiny.

Religion Private and Public

The great beliefs are not intellectualist. They come from the last depths of will, heart, and history. They are the self-exposition exposition of the immanent and royal Redeemer. They are the lineaments of gospel books which enthrone a latent King of history. A Church, like the kingdom it serves, cannot rest on sentiment alone but on certainty. And sentiment is easy and certainty is hard. And so our religion belongs to our weakness, not to our strength, and to our leisure and not our energetic hours, to our preference instead of our obedience. Care less for those things that interest or delight you and cost you nothing; and care more for those things that tax you, but set you on eternal rock.

Private or individual conduct must be largely guided by sentiment, but it is not so with the conduct of societies. It is the nature of our creed that creates the public type of religion; and it is the type of religion that affects society and public life, and does so in a way largely subconscious and even posthumous. By which latter word I mean that it is the creed and type of the religion of a past generation that reforms the ethics of the average mind to-day (though that is, more true of political than of social affairs). It is the nature of Germany's creed and God that has made it the curse of the world. It has sacrificed moral regeneration to godless culture, and the new creation of a world to the grandiose expansion of a race. It needs a great creed to make a nation great.

To maintain the great note is more than to carry on a "great work." It is the poverty, the stridency, or the huskiness of our type of active religion that is the source of the Church's lack of public influence, and therefore of its atonic malaise at the present awful juncture. The gospel has the word for the hour as the Church has not. Our great theology does not come out in our general type of faith, which does not strike the note meet for a great nation or crisis. We talk the language of local congregations, and we do them good. And one would not for a moment discourage the pastor. But where is the apostle, where the prophet, where the word of the Church which is a fear to politicians and a conscience to kings? We have made the Cross a raid shelter instead of a world's crisis, cure, and crown. Our note, with all its greatness, is not the note of a world crisis in the world conscience, as the Cross of our redemption is. It suggests a war shrine, petty and pious. Or it is the note of a process of ordered thought, in which the redemption is but an episode or a tangle in a vast movement of the general reason. It is static not dynamic. It has the note of reflexion but not of tragedy, not of power. It is the work of able thinkers who have never been shaken over the mouth of the pit and scarcely saved. Our note is not deep enough because it is not moral enough. It is donnish and dispassionate. It does not reflect the saving wrath of God. It consoles more than kindles, and interests more than it awes.

Before we can effectually launch out into the deep of new seas and new worlds, the conscience of the race must be readjusted at the Cross to the *summum bonum* of the kingdom of God. We must revise belief and action by penetrating anew Christ's historic revelation, His historic foundation, of the kingdom of God, with its prime and public righteousness dominating all. The Jesus of history is not just a figure into whose outline we may press the most vivid, fine, and homely humanities of modern religion. He is One in whom we discern the gift of God which creates and commands all these pieties and amenities, and forms the crisis of the great moral powers whose action makes history. Those fundamental realities were gathered up, as earth's central fires gather to a volcanic head, into a nation selected by God to be trustee of His Kingdom, the collective prophet of the moral world, and the protagonist of the conscience of the Holy. It was not the cause of the proletariat, that broke Christ's heart, but a nation's treason to a holy God. It was the great refusal of His beloved Israel as the grand falsity of the moral world; where also His own victory was that world's last fidelity and last reality. From that recreant nation these historic realities were gathered up into Christ. And from Christ they were concentrated into His death and resurrection. His resurrection *by the spirit of holiness* (Rom 1:4) meant a new moral world in its wake, and not only a new religion. It was the beginning and source of the world's regeneration. That was the real outpouring of the Spirit, in which the world is not illuminated but born anew (1 Pet 1:3). The exalted Christ takes for Paul the place the kingdom of God took for Jesus. He is the concentrated principle of the kingdom of the world's moral redemption. To return to Him and His moral charge and His moral crisis for it is the only permanent and thorough method for reconstructing either the institutions of society or the institutes of theology. The moral principle of reconstruction is regeneration, not into safety but into the kingdom of God.

I fear that the state of the religious mind, so trivialized and dismoralized, is such that much of what I have said from the heart of God's righteousness in Christ will seem but a preacher's extravagance, or an academic discussion about a moral philosophy of history. Such was Israel's damnatory verdict on Christ, who said that the wickedness of Tyre, Sidon, and Sodom was a venial thing compared with the moral stupidity of the decent religion of Israel in Capernaum and Chorazin.

But let me say again that each single soul is saved only by its response to that same act of holy righteousness which founded the Kingdom, created a Church, exalted the nations, and recovered a world. It is historic faith I have been preaching, and preaching on something else than the conventicle scale or the patriotic. It is not philosophy. It is the soul of the religion of the world's conscience, and the power of the action of the conscience of God. It is powers I am handling, not themes—principalities and power ruling from the heart of all things. I am not lecturing, and not orating, but preaching in print—preaching neither to intellect nor sentiment, but from God's conscience to man's, from man's destiny to his history. It is the word of the evangelical conscience, the conscience not just enlightened but redeemed and morally new made from the throne, that makes everything new. I am preaching the holy conscience of the love in God to the slack conscience of Christian love. I have been trying to penetrate the Cross that with it I might perhaps penetrate the moral soul. It is not easy to harmonize private religion and public, I know, but it must be done at last. And how finely Augustine has done it in words like these:

> Lord, when I look on my own life it seems Thou hast led me so carefully, so tenderly, that Thou canst have attended to no one else. But, when I see how wonderfully Thou hast led the world, and art leading it, I am amazed that Thou hast had time to attend to such as I.

Bibliography

Arnold, Matthew. "Shakespeare." In *Strayed Reveller and Other Poems*. London: B. Fellowes, 1849.

Bosanquet, Bernard. *The Philosophical Theory of the State*. London: Macmillan, 1899.

Brown, Robert McAfee. *PT Forsyth: Prophet for Today*. Philadelphia: Westminster, 1952.

Coleridge, Samuel Taylor. "Kubla Khan." In *Coleridges Ancient Mariner, Kubla Khan And Christable*, edited by Tuley Francis Huntington. London: Macmillan & Co., 1911.

———. *The Rime of the Ancient Mariner*. London: Sampson Low, Son & Co, 1857.

Cowper, William. "Walking with God." In *The Book of Praise: From the Best English Hymn Writers*, edited by Roundell Palmer, 414–15. Cambridge: Sever, Francis & Co., 1870.

Cranshaw, Richard. "Dies Iræ Dies Illa. In Meditation of the Day of Judgment." In *The Works of English Poets: From Chaucer to Cowper*, edited by Samuel Johnson, 596. London, 1810.

Forsyth, Peter Taylor. "The Atonement in Modern Religious Thought." In *The Atonement in Modern Religious Thought: A Theological Symposium*, 3rd ed., 49–78. London: James Clarke & Co., 1907.

———. *The Charter of the Church*. London: Alexander and Shepheard, 1896.

———. "Christ and the Christian Principle." In *London Theological Studies*, 133–66. London: University of London Press, 1911.

———. "Christ's Person and His Cross." *Methodist Review* 66 (Jan. 1917) 3–22.

———. "The Christianity of Christ and Christ our Christianity." *Review and Expositor* 15 (1918) 249–65.

———. *Lectures on the Church and the Sacraments*. London: Longmans, Green, and Co., 1917.

———. "The Conversion of the 'Good'." *The Contemporary Review* 109 (June 1916) 760–71.

———. "The Cross of Christ as the Moral Principle of Society." *Methodist Review* 99 (Jan. 1917) 9–21.

———. *The Cruciality of the Cross*. London: Hodder & Stoughton, 1909.

———. "The Disappointment of the Cross." *The Puritan* 3 (1900) 135–9.

———. "The Evangelical Churches and the Higher Criticism." In *The Gospel and Authority: A P.T. Forsyth Reader*, edited by Marvin W. Anderson, 15–53. 1905. Minneapolis: Augsburg, 1971.

———. "Faith and Mind." *Methodist Review Quarterly* 61 (Oct. 1912) 627–43.

———. "Faith, Metaphysic, and Incarnation." *Methodist Review*, fifth series, 31, no. 5 (Sept. 1915) 696–719.

———. "Forgiveness through Atonement the Essential of Evangelical Christianity." In *Proceedings of the Third International Congregational Council*, edited by J. Brown, 28–53. London: Congregational Union of England, 1908.

———. *God the Holy Father*. London: Hodder and Stoughton, 1897.

———. "Immanence and Incarnation." In *The Old Faith and the New Theology*, edited by C.H. Vine, 47–61. London: Sampson Low, 1907.

———. "The Inner Life of Christ." *The Constructive Quarterly* 7 (1919) 149–62.

———. "Intellectualism and Faith." *The Hibbert Journal* 11, no. 2 (1912–13) 311–28.

———. *The Justification of God: Lectures for War-Time on a Christian Theodicy*. London: Duckworth, 1916.

———. "The Moralization of Religion." *London Quarterly Review* 128 (Oct. 1917) 161–74.

———. *The Person and Place of Jesus Christ*. London: Hodder & Stoughton, 1909.

———. *Positive Preaching and Modern Mind*. London: Independent Press, 1907.

Forsyth, Peter Taylor. *The Principle of Authority in Relation to Certainty, Sanctity and Society: An Essay in the Philosophy of Experimental Religion*. London: Hodder & Stoughton, 1912.

———. "Regeneration, Creation, and Miracle I." *Methodist Review* 63 (Oct. 1914) 627–43.

———. "Regeneration, Creation, and Miracle II." *Methodist Review* 64 (Jan. 1915) 89–103.

———. "Religion Private and Public." *London Quarterly Review* 131 (Jan. 1919) 19–32.

———. "Revelation and the Person of Christ." In *Faith and Criticism: Essays by Congregationalists*, 95–144. London: Sampson Low, 1893.

———. *The Soul of Prayer*. London: Independent Press, 1916.

———. "Unity and Theology, A Liberal Evangelicalism the True Catholicism." In *Towards Reunion*, 51–81. London: Macmillan, 1919.

———. "Veracity, Reality, and Regeneration." *London Quarterly Review* 123 (Apr. 1915) 193–216.

———. "What is Meant by the Blood of Christ?" *The Expositor*, seventh series, 6 (1908) 207–25.

———. *The Work of Christ*. London: Hodder & Stoughton, 1910.

Green, Thomas Hill. *Lectures on the Principles of Political Obligation*. London: Longmans, Green and Co., 1911.

Hartmann, Eduard von. *Die Philosophie des Unbewussten*. Leipzig: Verlag von Wilhelm Friedrich, 1900.

Horace. *The Odes of Horace*. Edited by Theodore Martin. London: John W. Parker & Son, 1860.

Jackson, Henry Ezekiel. *The Meaning of the Cross*. New York: Fleming H. Revell, 1911.

James, William. "Is Life Worth Living?" In *The will to believe: and other essays in popular philosophy*, 32–62. London: Longmans Green and Co, 1903.

Jülicher, Adolf. *Neue Linen in der Kritik der evangelischen Uberliefrung*. Giessen: Alfred Töpelmann, 1906.

Lessing, Gotthold Ephraim. "Über den Beweis des Geistes und der Kraft." In *Werke*, edited by H.G. Göpfert, vol. 8. 1777. Munich: Carl Hanser, 1976.

Macgregor, William Malcolm. *Christian Freedom*. London: Hodder & Stoughton, 1914.

Moser, Paul K. *The God Relationship: The Ethics for Inquiry about the Divine*. Cambridge: Cambridge University Press, 2017.

Newman, John Henry. "The Dream of Gerontius." In *The Dream of Gerontius and Other Poems*, 1–40. London: Oxford, 1914.

Shakespeare, William. *Shakespeare's Comedy of The Tempest*. Edited by William J. Rolfe. New York: Harper & Brothers, 1895.

Sophocles. *Antigone*. Edited by M. A. Bayfield. London: Macmillan, 1901.

Name Index

Abelard, Peter, 191
Angelico, Fra, 79
Anselm of Canterbury, 33, 135, 142, 190, 192
Aristotle, 86, 170
Arnold, Matthew, 223, 307
Athanasius, 327, 355
Augustine, 320, 375

Bacon, Francis, 224
Bergson, Henri, 266, 267
Biedermann, Friedrich Karl, 182, 183
Blount, W. F., 366
Bosanquet, Bernard, 294
Bousset, Wilhelm, 173
Browning, Robert, 333
Burroughs, E. A., 234
Butler, Joseph, 232

Caesar, 215, 296
Caiaphas, 113
Caird, Edward, 225
Carlyle, Thomas, 133, 320, 321
Chesterton, Gilbert Keith, 367
Coleridge, Samuel Taylor, 301, 311
Cowper, William, 48
Cranshaw, Richard, 298
Croce, Benedetto, 352
Cyrus the Great, 284

Dale, Robert William, 69, 75
Dalman, Gustaf Hermann, 173
Dante Alighieri, 303
Darwin, Charles Robert, 224

Descartes, René, 133

Erasmus of Rotterdam, 225, 320
Eucken, Rudolf Christoph, 266, 271

Ferrier, John Todd, 166
Foxe, John, 63
Francis of Assisi, 79

Gordon, Charles George, 158
Gore, Charles, 255
Green, Thomas Hill, 225, 226, 294
Grotius, Hugo, 193, 194

von Harnack, Adolf, 61, 147
von Hartmann, Karl Robert Eduard, 164, 332
Hazlitt, William, 321
Hegel, Georg Wilhelm Friedrich, 110, 143, 163, 168, 169, 186, 225, 226
Heine, Christian Johann Heinrich, 137
von Helmholtz, Hermann, 43
Herod, 215, 277
Herrmann, Johann Georg Wilhelm, 53–5, 120, 331
Hoffmann, Georg, 226
Horace, 356
Hunziger, A. W., 55

Ibsen, Henrik Johan, 308
Irenaeus, 145
Isaiah, 319

Jackson, Henry Ezekiel, 202

Name Index

James, 65, 113
James, William, 225, 249, 266, 294
John, 64, 113, 174, 209, 217, 275–7, 307
John the Baptist, 59
Johnson, Samuel, 318
Josephus, 211
Judas, 87, 113
Jülicher, Adolf, 307

Kant, Immanuel, 103, 167, 170, 226, 311, 321

Lawrence, John, 158
Lessing, Gotthold Ephraim, 165–8, 182, 192
Loane, Martha J., 62
Loisy, Alfred Firmin, 95
Luke, 209
Luther, Martin, 129, 146, 265, 277, 296

MacDonald, George, 333
Macgregor, William Malcolm, 164
Machiavelli, Niccolò, 335
Mary Magdalen, 87, 281
Melanchthon, Philip, 146
Meredith, George, 320
Mill, Harriet Taylor, 321
Milton, John, 43, 143
Muhammad, 355

Nelson, Horatio, 229
Newman, John Henry, 104
Nietzsche, Friedrich Wilhelm, 162, 309, 332

Ostwald, Friedrich Wilhelm, 269

Pascal, Blaise, 319
Paul, 32, 62–6, 129, 130, 132, 134, 143, 173, 174, 181, 209, 219, 220, 271, 287, 307, 309, 319, 320, 325, 374
Pelagius, 62
Peter, 87, 113, 215, 281, 307

Philo, 211
Pilate, 113, 215, 246, 276, 319
Plato, 104

Ritschl, Albrecht, 191, 193, 194, 226
Rothe, Richard, 183, 225

Schleiermacher, Friedrich Daniel Ernst, 189, 191, 193, 202, 203, 224–6, 228, 231, 302
Schmiedel, Paul Wilhelm, 51
Scott, Walter, 320, 322
Shakespeare, William, 99, 212, 303, 319, 321, 322
Shamil, Imam, 39
Shaw, George Bernard, 308, 318
Socrates, 211, 319
Sophocles, 229
Sozzini, Fausto Paolo, 33, 38, 86
Spinoza, 42
Strauss, David Friedrich, 186, 295, 332
Syrophoenician woman, 319

Tennyson, Alfred, 333
Tertullian, 320
Titus Flavius Caesar Vespasianus Augustus, 284
de Torquemada, Tomás, 337
Traherne, Thomas, 184
Troeltsch, Ernst Peter Wilhelm, 168, 268, 271
Tyndall, John, 43

Washington, George, 296
Wells, Herbert George, 367
Wendland, Paul, 268
Wernle, Paul, 288
Whittier, John Greenleaf, 333
Wilhelm II, 262, 284, 286
Windelband, Wilhelm, 266
Wundt, Wilhelm, 104, 268, 271

Zaccheus, 87
Zwingli, Ulrich, 320

Subject Index

aesthetic, 44, 50, 52, 57, 63, 68, 78, 122, 123, 167, 169, 195, 196, 198, 205, 225, 226, 250, 251, 257, 260, 261, 292, 295, 296, 328, 329, 331, 333, 335, 340, 349, 352, 360
agnosticism, 98, 103, 104, 106, 188, 242
anthropocentric, 172
anthropology, 29
anthropomorphism, 79, 237
antichrist, 286, 288, 335
apologetics, 249, 311
apostles, 50, 51, 57, 63, 65, 94–6, 198, 213, 220, 263, 327, 334, 337, 350, 369, 373
Arianism, 79
ascension, 171, 252
atheism, 121, 242
atonement, 28, 29, 31–4, 36–8, 45, 50, 56–9, 61–6, 69, 71, 73, 74, 76, 78, 82, 83, 85–91, 93–5, 145–7, 171, 176, 184, 193, 194, 203, 207, 221, 231, 262, 283, 289, 290, 297, 298, 325, 352–4, 360, 369, 372
authority, 32, 51, 62, 65, 79, 94, 95, 100, 102, 126, 127, 144, 147, 148, 162, 183, 192, 199, 226, 227, 260, 273, 280, 290–2, 299, 305, 334, 336, 339, 342, 347, 348, 351, 353, 357, 360, 362, 370

baptism, 64
baptismal regeneration, 225, 231, 246, 360
belief, 49, 51, 52, 67, 68, 71, 93, 102, 104, 107–9, 113, 115, 117, 118, 121, 143, 145, 166, 167, 173, 198, 256, 257, 259, 260, 262, 273, 277, 278, 281, 304–6, 330, 333, 334, 337, 346, 355, 364, 366, 372
Bible, 31, 32, 64, 81, 85, 101, 125, 126, 129, 145, 147, 217, 226, 227, 244, 259, 278, 287, 304, 320, 350, 359, 361, 366, 370
Buddhism, 143, 175, 304

Calvinism, 369
Catholic, 50, 62, 93–5, 98, 125, 128, 147, 189, 199, 200, 206, 225, 226, 261, 289, 305, 312, 341, 350, 356, 362
certainty, 47, 57, 58, 68, 70, 76, 100, 110, 119–24, 127–30, 132, 133, 135–7, 146, 150, 163, 165, 168, 177, 183, 186, 188, 197, 207, 219, 265, 316, 328, 348, 357, 373
chaos, 234, 242, 272
Christendom, 120, 144, 205, 312, 340, 354, 365, 368

Subject Index

Christology, 67, 98, 117, 173, 184, 187, 302, 309
civilization, 100, 128, 134, 157, 232, 264, 313, 344, 354, 371
collective or corporate, 29, 71, 105, 108, 109, 171, 176, 180, 198, 201, 206, 231–3, 252, 253, 275–7, 284, 290, 293, 305, 314, 332, 345, 355, 361, 366, 374
Confessionalism, 125
Congregationalism, 63
conscience, 32, 34, 35, 37, 38, 47, 51, 57, 60, 63, 67, 69, 71, 73, 74, 76–8, 84, 85, 88–92, 94, 97, 104, 106, 122, 124, 126, 127, 134, 147, 148, 153, 155, 156, 159, 164, 167, 169, 174, 176, 178, 179, 181, 184, 188, 191–4, 196, 203, 226, 228–32, 243, 247, 248, 251, 254–6, 259, 260, 262, 265, 266, 270, 273, 278, 283, 289–92, 295–301, 311, 316, 322, 325, 326, 330, 332, 334, 337, 338, 340–2, 344, 346, 350, 351, 355–8, 360–3, 365, 371–5
consubstantiality, 147
cosmos, 46, 121, 170, 177, 188, 243, 249, 250, 267, 268, 314, 324
creed, 42, 94, 101, 109, 125, 126, 137, 146, 162, 164, 181, 203, 226, 256, 260, 277, 305, 308–10, 312, 313, 333, 334, 347, 352, 354, 355, 358, 360, 363, 368, 372, 373
    Athanasian, 103, 310, 312, 327
crucifixion, 33, 64, 67, 83, 93, 151, 201, 207, 223, 265, 290, 348, 349
crusades, 354

damnation, 45, 72, 90, 104, 149, 265, 287, 375
deism, 41, 42, 191, 241, 242
determinism, 43, 174

devil or demon, 97, 143, 151, 158, 159, 197, 198, 204, 205, 275, 284, 335, 364, 366, 367, 369
divinity, 68, 69, 83, 123, 187, 197, 230, 232, 325, 359
docetism, 113
dogma, 94, 107, 117, 170, 176, 187, 226, 310
dogmatism and dogmatics, 33, 63, 64, 88, 138, 167, 184, 219, 256, 258, 327, 332, 339, 357

England, 69, 98, 255, 262, 293, 358
eudaemonism, 273
Europe, 100, 134, 262, 289, 354, 355
evangelical, 41, 45, 47, 53, 62, 63, 65, 67, 68, 79, 81, 85, 86, 88, 95, 97, 100, 102, 109, 148, 167, 181, 199, 225, 248, 260, 271, 289, 307, 333–5, 342, 350, 356, 358–62, 366, 375
evil, 34, 45, 80, 91, 174, 206, 207, 214, 229, 230, 235, 264, 265, 267, 271, 273, 275, 278, 283, 286, 287, 292, 314, 355, 360, 364, 368
evolution, 42, 43, 61, 62, 82, 161, 162, 170, 172, 174, 178, 185, 186, 232, 233, 242, 244, 247, 248, 263–5, 267–9, 271, 308, 332, 366
expiation, 28, 31–5, 37, 38, 61, 148, 149, 298

fall, 29, 175, 192, 245
fate, 59, 83, 84, 139, 163, 164, 174, 179, 202, 224, 229, 330, 331
fides implicita, 144
filial principle, 122, 138
finality, 43, 61, 81, 89, 97, 100, 106, 128, 129, 161, 170, 187, 188, 299, 300, 309, 313, 334
forgiveness, 28–37, 39, 44, 47, 54, 63, 67, 68, 71, 77, 83, 88,

90–2, 94, 97, 118, 122, 127, 134, 137, 142–4, 146–8, 175, 178, 202, 204, 214, 218–20, 222, 246, 273, 274, 280, 281, 300, 314–7, 326, 349, 350, 365, 370, 371

Germany, 41, 53, 115, 203, 266, 275, 277, 284, 286, 288, 292, 293, 302, 335, 343, 372, 373
gnosticism, 46, 103, 172–4
God-consciousness, 129, 138, 164, 189
grace, 29, 33, 35, 37, 39, 42, 44, 45, 50, 61, 63, 65, 69, 70, 72, 73, 76, 78–80, 85, 86, 90–3, 95, 101, 102, 105, 109, 112, 133, 140, 141, 149, 155, 164, 174, 175, 193–5, 197, 199, 201, 202, 204, 205, 207, 209, 225, 227, 228, 230, 248, 250, 252–4, 258–60, 263–6, 272–4, 276, 278–84, 288, 300, 302, 306, 308, 310, 314–7, 337, 342, 349, 350, 352, 354, 356, 357, 360, 361, 366, 370
guilt, 28–30, 34–8, 42, 43, 45, 66, 87, 96, 122, 124, 149, 164, 175, 177, 191, 201, 228, 230–2, 248, 264, 273, 274, 276, 289, 290, 298, 308, 313, 315, 317, 326

heart, 29, 36, 39, 43, 45, 47, 69, 76, 80, 92, 95, 101, 103, 108, 109, 117, 119, 122, 126, 133, 139, 142, 154–7, 159, 169, 180, 181, 188, 192, 193, 196, 197, 199, 202, 215, 220, 225, 229, 230, 246, 247, 259, 265, 273, 277, 278, 281, 287, 291, 297, 300–2, 309, 315, 319, 320, 322, 325, 326, 329, 330, 333, 336, 343, 345, 351, 354, 358, 360, 364, 365, 368, 370–5

heresy, 93, 166, 259, 310
heterodoxy, 127, 182, 303, 316, 331
historicism, 99, 112, 331
history, 32, 49, 50, 52, 53, 55–8, 61, 63–5, 68, 73, 74, 77, 79, 81, 82, 86, 89, 93, 96, 101, 103, 104, 107, 112, 113, 121, 122, 126, 128, 129, 133, 134, 136, 137, 142, 148, 157, 161–3, 165–8, 170–3, 175, 177, 182–7, 189, 190, 192, 193, 199, 202, 207, 210, 211, 213, 219, 223, 224, 226–9, 231–4, 245, 250, 251, 253, 257, 260, 263, 264, 267, 271, 283, 284, 289–91, 293–5, 304, 306–11, 313, 314, 317, 318, 323, 326, 329, 330, 336, 340, 341, 346–8, 351, 358, 361, 364, 366, 371, 373–5
holy love, 30, 34, 73, 80, 95, 102, 108, 112, 114, 149, 187, 193, 237, 238, 242, 278, 283, 298, 334, 337, 338, 342–4, 349
Holy Spirit, 33, 52, 66, 93, 113, 116, 117, 125, 129, 130, 134, 150, 155, 171, 187, 193, 196, 198, 217, 219, 220, 227, 247, 253, 256, 269, 271, 281, 285, 286, 310, 313, 314, 330, 349, 351, 354, 357, 367, 368, 374

idealism, 58, 103, 104, 123, 126, 169, 170, 177, 185, 260, 265, 295, 299, 314, 336
immanence, 41–5, 85, 173, 176, 179, 180, 183, 191, 238, 240–2, 244, 247, 251, 264, 270, 308, 373
incarnation, 41, 42, 44, 61, 79, 82, 94, 104, 110, 117–9, 125, 141, 144–7, 150, 159, 171, 176, 177, 179–84, 221, 225, 227, 231, 264, 295, 297, 312, 316, 352, 358

Subject Index

individualism, 32, 102, 108, 126, 253, 292, 305, 361
inner life of Christ, 52, 53, 55–9, 119, 138, 142, 143, 307, 331
inner light, 250, 254, 267
intellectualism, 50, 103, 166, 170, 301, 306, 308–10, 312, 316, 318, 322, 323, 325, 326, 328, 329, 331, 348, 372, 373
international, 335, 338, 340, 358
Islam, 157, 331
Israel, 64–6, 96, 137, 152, 156, 157, 170, 206, 214, 215, 227, 228, 244, 275, 276, 278–84, 288, 319, 331, 359, 374, 375

Jerusalem, 59, 82, 152, 173, 275, 282, 283, 307, 320
Jesuitism, 369
Judaism, 48, 63–5, 77, 173, 281, 304
justice, 31, 58, 61, 62, 72, 86, 146, 155, 158, 191–4, 207, 221, 223, 248, 265, 289, 316, 355, 356
justification, 28, 32, 70, 92, 117, 145, 288, 348–50, 370, 371

kenoticism, 83, 114, 116, 118, 180
Kingdom of God, 53, 54, 57, 71–3, 79–81, 84, 91, 96, 107, 125, 130, 133, 137, 142, 150, 151, 153, 157, 158, 168, 174, 199, 205, 211, 212, 215–7, 220, 221, 235, 267, 277, 278, 280, 281, 283, 285, 288–91, 293, 294, 299, 300, 304, 311, 314, 315, 330, 334–8, 340–4, 349, 352, 355–9, 363, 365, 366, 368–75

liberalism, 32, 53, 82, 101, 104, 194, 200, 240, 260, 265, 305, 358, 361
  evangelical, 361
Logos, 117, 196, 220, 352, 354, 359

martyr, 59, 63, 65, 68, 74, 83, 84, 140, 183, 202, 210, 329, 330, 335, 337, 338
materialism, 106
mercy, 30, 31, 77, 86, 90, 97, 145, 149, 154, 159, 160, 175, 192, 201, 203, 204, 211, 273, 274, 283, 284, 287, 300, 357
messiah, 83, 84, 130, 151, 152, 173, 205, 212, 214, 215, 218, 276, 282, 283, 315, 343, 358
metaphysics, 67, 68, 76, 89, 98–101, 103–8, 110, 117–9, 124, 137, 138, 148, 163, 185, 187, 199, 200, 219, 225–7, 230–2, 251, 253, 266–8, 308, 310, 313, 327
miracle, 31, 42, 44, 45, 56, 67, 82, 84, 85, 112, 117, 119, 144, 145, 149, 150, 202, 211, 224, 227, 235, 236, 238, 247–9, 261, 264, 265, 267, 270, 273, 282, 297, 313, 332, 350, 354, 357, 360, 361, 370, 371
monism, 41, 42, 80, 100, 103, 107, 163, 171, 179, 181, 186, 240, 253, 272
monotheism, 173, 218, 219, 361
mysticism, 34, 42, 53, 55, 78, 83, 103, 104, 122, 123, 126, 139, 148, 165, 167, 175, 181, 184, 189, 190, 196, 198–201, 203, 209, 227, 228, 235, 246, 251, 260, 261, 265, 289–91, 301, 303, 333, 341, 352, 358, 366, 369, 372
myth, 50, 79, 163, 172

nation, 53, 58, 59, 66, 73, 100, 101, 201, 206, 227, 229, 262, 275–86, 288, 289, 292–6, 298, 323, 335, 340, 346, 358, 363, 365, 366, 368–74
neoplatonism, 352

new creation, 53, 54, 69, 82, 92, 95, 118, 119, 188, 223, 224, 227, 228, 230, 231, 234, 236, 242–4, 247, 249, 250, 254, 264–6, 268, 269, 271, 273, 314, 330, 350, 357, 359, 360, 364, 365, 371, 373

New Testament, 30, 34, 60–3, 65, 86, 90, 93, 102, 106, 107, 118, 126, 131, 132, 141, 164, 172, 204, 205, 207, 209, 216, 218, 220, 225, 251, 257, 284, 289, 290, 306, 308, 319, 328, 331, 359, 367, 370

Old Testament, 50, 60, 217, 219, 220, 244, 278, 361

one thing needful, 77, 182, 287, 348

orthodoxy, 32, 49, 51, 69, 70, 101, 104, 123, 127, 142, 145, 166, 167, 175, 182, 189, 191, 194, 224, 226, 228, 257, 259, 262, 279, 303, 307, 316, 326, 328, 329, 331, 334, 342, 348, 350, 360, 372

pantheism, 42, 122, 175, 176, 240, 242

parables, 50, 55, 65, 216
    prodigal son, 31, 50, 75, 314, 315

paradox, 111, 225, 234, 272, 311, 318, 319, 321, 325

patristic, 99, 225, 279

Pentecost, 349, 367, 368

Pharisee, 206, 275, 277–88, 315, 331, 341

physics, 46

pietism, 75, 99, 125, 167, 200, 259, 272, 290, 303, 308, 324, 341, 362

piety, 42, 44, 53, 54, 58, 72, 75, 76, 122, 155, 156, 160, 184, 190, 203, 222, 225, 258, 260, 277, 279–81, 284, 287, 290, 318, 320, 336, 341, 345–9, 353, 356, 369, 372

Pope, 88, 94, 95, 277, 305

pre-existence, 107, 113, 115, 116, 124, 173, 207

priest, 58, 59, 144, 151, 159, 216, 350, 358

prolegomena, 184, 243

prophet, 37, 48, 58, 59, 63, 67–9, 81, 84, 93, 95, 96, 112–4, 122, 125, 133, 142, 157, 162, 170, 172, 181, 182, 197, 212, 261, 263, 271, 276, 277, 279, 286, 288, 291, 308, 317, 319, 320, 323, 326–8, 331, 339, 349, 350, 352, 359, 373, 374

Protestant, 42, 50, 62, 86, 120, 121, 126, 128, 191, 200, 255, 265

Protestant Reformation, 42, 46, 88, 95, 102, 143, 172, 192, 310, 334, 354, 362

psychologism, 99

psychology, 29, 49, 51–3, 57, 60, 79, 87, 89, 104, 111, 113, 117, 118, 165, 166, 169, 170, 174, 192, 195, 231, 243, 245, 271, 292, 298, 302, 307, 312, 330, 333, 348, 361, 366

Puritan, 98, 292

quietism, 81, 125

rationalism, 46, 48, 49, 52, 75, 86, 102, 106, 127, 166, 171, 181, 200, 217, 224, 226, 253, 290, 303, 312, 329, 331, 333

reconciliation, 29, 38, 39, 42, 61–3, 66, 68, 73, 77, 82, 85, 91, 93, 106, 119, 122, 128, 133, 135, 137, 146, 178, 184, 193, 196, 207, 220, 221, 225, 232, 233, 267, 269, 272, 296, 297, 301, 312, 314, 326, 331, 354, 356, 359–61, 372

Subject Index

regeneration, 50, 52, 54, 56, 58, 63, 73, 77, 82, 90, 171, 175, 176, 190, 192, 198, 200, 213, 220, 223, 225, 227, 228, 244–6, 248, 259, 261, 262, 268, 269, 271, 273, 278, 279, 282, 313, 314, 330, 331, 350, 352, 357, 365, 366, 371, 373, 374
resurrection, 36, 56, 57, 63, 66, 67, 88, 104, 142, 146, 165, 171, 190, 202, 213, 221, 235, 252, 254, 261, 271, 281, 328, 374
   historicity of, 145
Rome, 32, 54, 62, 94, 120, 126, 152, 174, 200, 206, 215, 265, 282, 288, 305, 336, 368

sacrament, 52, 55, 62, 74, 104, 112, 166, 174, 188, 195, 199–201, 227, 248, 289, 290, 305, 315, 316, 329, 330, 333, 349–51, 357–9
Sadducee, 206, 260, 331
salvation, 37, 43, 45, 50, 58, 66–9, 76, 78–80, 82, 87, 89, 91, 93, 95, 97, 102, 106, 108, 109, 114, 118, 121, 128, 135, 140–2, 144, 159, 180, 185, 188, 190, 192, 200, 204, 212, 216, 219, 227, 228, 230, 248, 249, 259, 260, 264, 265, 281, 284, 300, 317, 326–9, 335, 338, 362, 366, 369, 372
Salvation Army, 334
sanctification, 29, 144, 247, 269
scholasticism, 49, 50, 86, 144, 227
Scripturalism, 125
scripture, 32, 66, 86, 126, 138, 145, 147, 150, 226, 246, 278, 283, 301, 361

second Adam, 37, 38
sect, 120, 259, 275, 305, 306, 340
Sermon on the Mount, 31, 215, 216, 279, 327
sermons, 156, 255
sin as *felix culpa*, 45
socialism, 73, 141, 277, 333
socinianism, 33, 38, 86, 141, 143
soteriology, 67, 184
State, 107, 159, 192, 196, 203, 279, 288–90, 292–4, 300, 335, 344, 346, 366, 371
succession
   apostolic, 145, 291, 350
   episcopal, 94, 145, 148, 360
   evangelical, 79, 350, 360
   spiritual, 278

theism, 42, 124, 176, 242
theodicy, 228, 273
theology, primary and secondary, 301, 303, 322, 352
transcendence, 114–6, 173, 177, 180, 201, 238, 239, 241, 242, 247, 264, 270, 271, 360
transubstantiation, 63
Trinity, 43, 76, 101, 108–10, 147, 187, 201, 219, 220, 293, 302, 304, 311, 355

unitarianism, 41, 42, 85, 131, 142

virgin birth, 56, 117, 150

war, 63, 83, 88, 102, 198, 207, 229, 262, 283, 284, 286, 288, 311, 318, 325, 335, 336, 339, 343, 344, 355, 364, 365, 368, 371–3
wisdom, 136, 173, 213, 302, 319, 325, 368
wrath, 31, 37, 148, 320, 374

www.ingramcontent.com/pod-product-compliance
Lightning Source LLC
Chambersburg PA
CBHW071231290426
44108CB00013B/1373